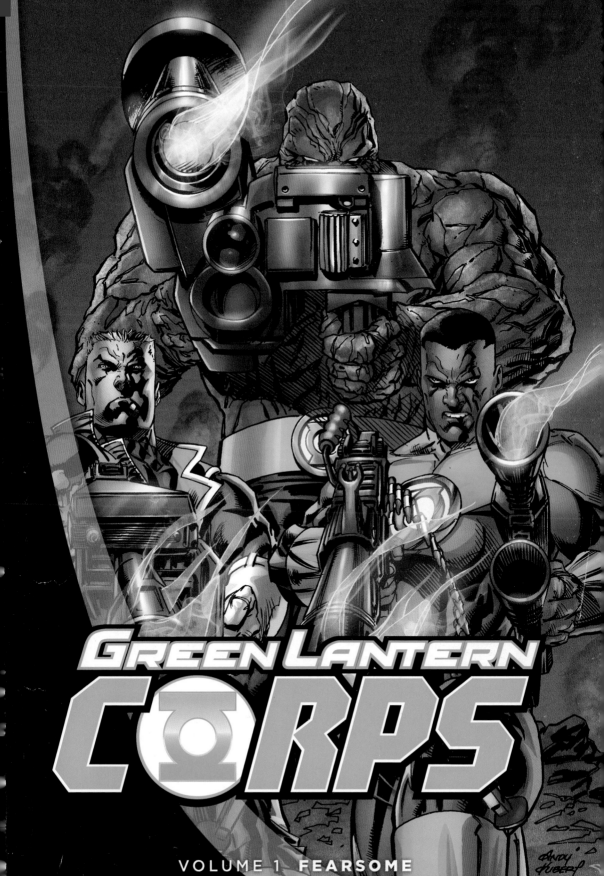

GREEN LANTERN
CORPS

VOLUME 1 FEARSOME

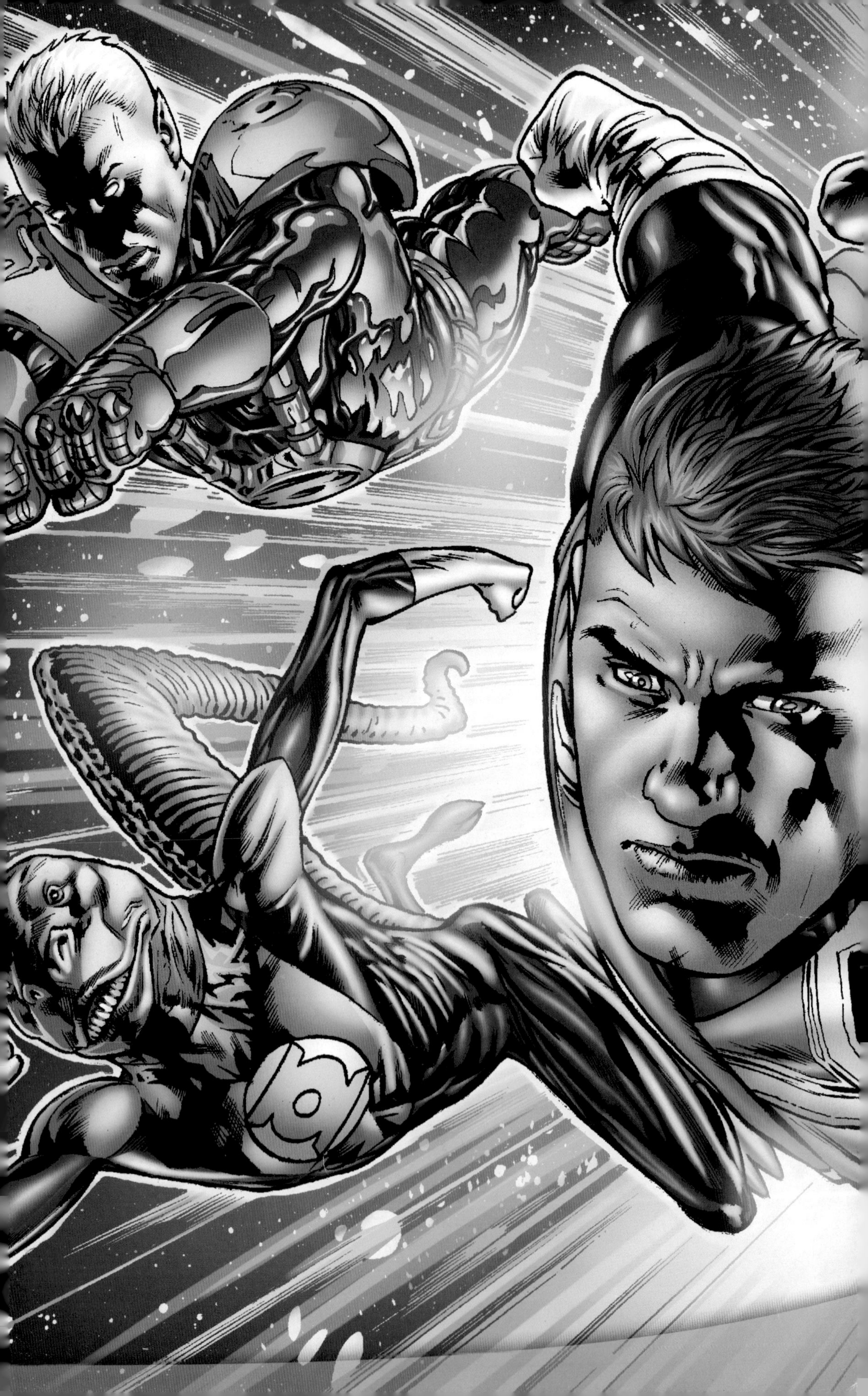

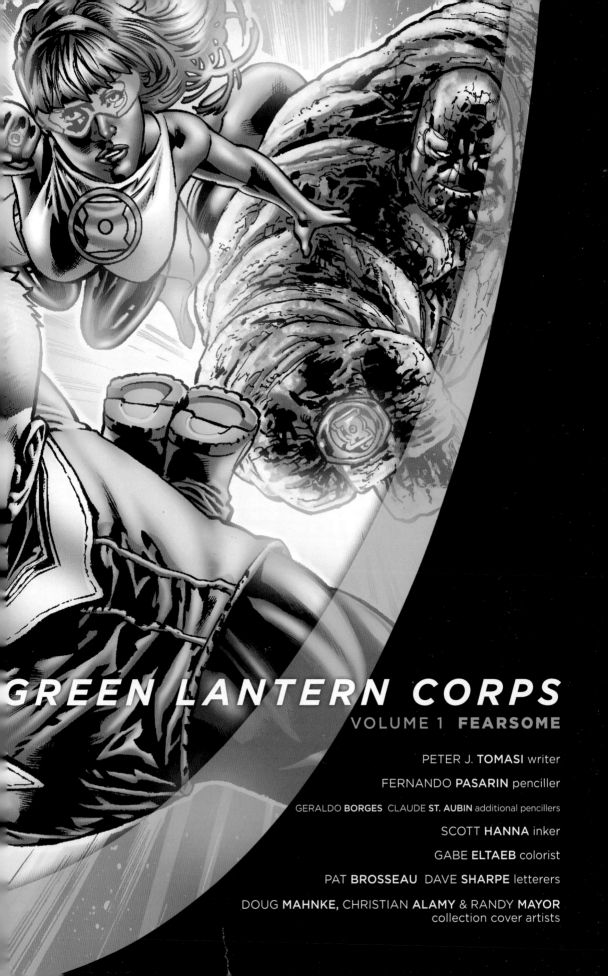

GREEN LANTERN CORPS

VOLUME 1 FEARSOME

PETER J. **TOMASI** writer

FERNANDO **PASARIN** penciller

GERALDO **BORGES** CLAUDE **ST. AUBIN** additional pencillers

SCOTT **HANNA** inker

GABE **ELTAEB** colorist

PAT **BROSSEAU** DAVE **SHARPE** letterers

DOUG **MAHNKE,** CHRISTIAN **ALAMY** & RANDY **MAYOR**
collection cover artists

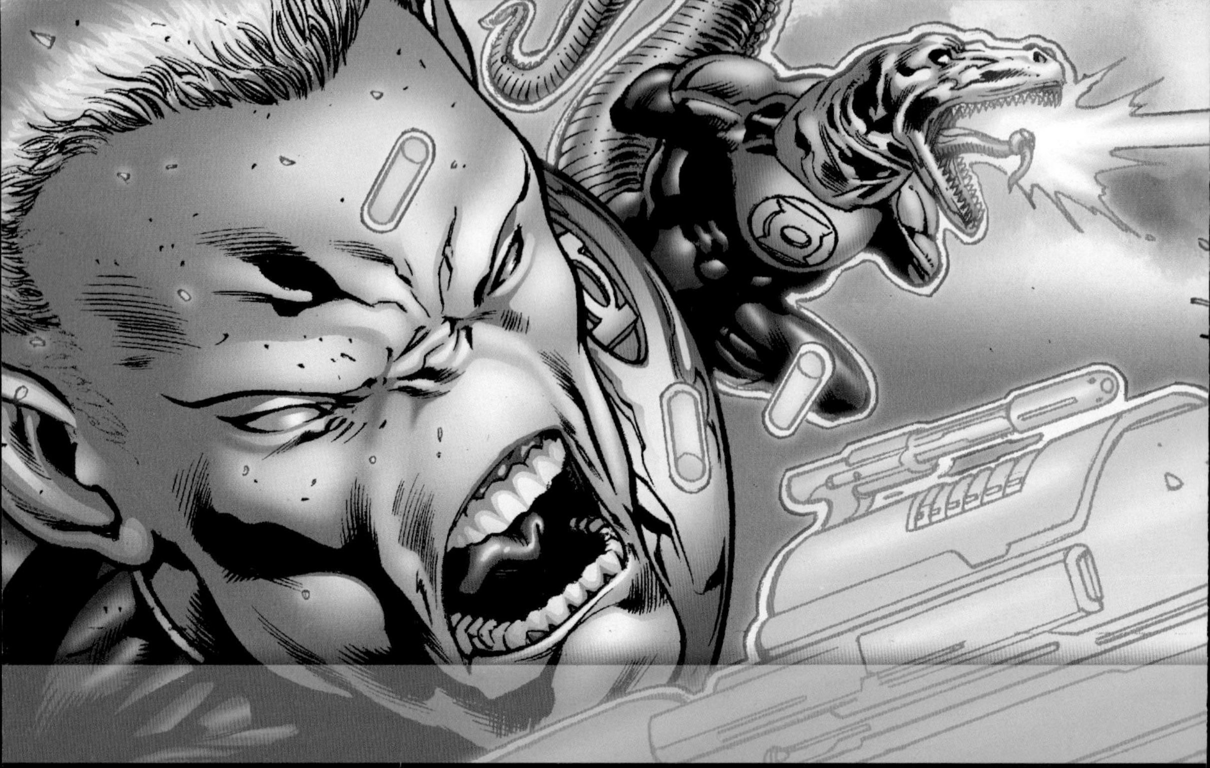

BRIAN CUNNINGHAM Editor - Original Series DARREN SHAN Assistant Editor - Original Series
PETER HAMBOUSSI Editor ROBBIN BROSTERMAN Design Director - Books
ROBBIE BIEDERMAN Publication Design

BOB HARRAS VP - Editor-in-Chief

DIANE NELSON President DAN DIDIO and JIM LEE Co-Publishers
GEOFF JOHNS Chief Creative Officer
JOHN ROOD Executive VP - Sales, Marketing and Business Development
AMY GENKINS Senior VP - Business and Legal Affairs NAIRI GARDINER Senior VP - Finance
JEFF BOISON VP - Publishing Operations MARK CHIARELLO VP - Art Direction and Design
JOHN CUNNINGHAM VP - Marketing TERRI CUNNINGHAM VP - Talent Relations and Services
ALISON GILL Senior VP - Manufacturing and Operations HANK KANALZ Senior VP - Digital
JAY KOGAN VP - Business and Legal Affairs, Publishing JACK MAHAN VP - Business Affairs, Talent
NICK NAPOLITANO VP - Manufacturing Administration SUE POHJA VP - Book Sales
COURTNEY SIMMONS Senior VP - Publicity BOB WAYNE Senior VP - Sales

GREEN LANTERN CORPS VOLUME 1: FEARSOME
Published by DC Comics.

DC Comics, 1700 Broadway, New York, NY 10019
A Warner Bros. Entertainment Company
Printed by RR Donnelley, Salem, VA, USA. 8/17/12. First Printing.
HC ISBN: 978-1-4012-3701-1
SC ISBN: 978-1-4012-3702-8

SUSTAINABLE FORESTRY INITIATIVE
Certified Chain of Custody
At Least 25% Certified Forest Content
www.sfiprogram.org
SFI-01042
APPLIES TO TEXT STOCK ONLY

Library of Congress Cataloging-in-Publication Data

Tomasi, Peter.
Green Lantern Corps. Volume 1, Fearsome / Peter J. Tomasi.
p. cm.
ISBN 978-1-4012-3701-1
1. Graphic novels. I. Pasarin, Fernando. II. Hanna, Scott. III.
Title. IV. Title: Fearsome.
PN6728.G742T6 2012
741.5'973—dc23

2012018769

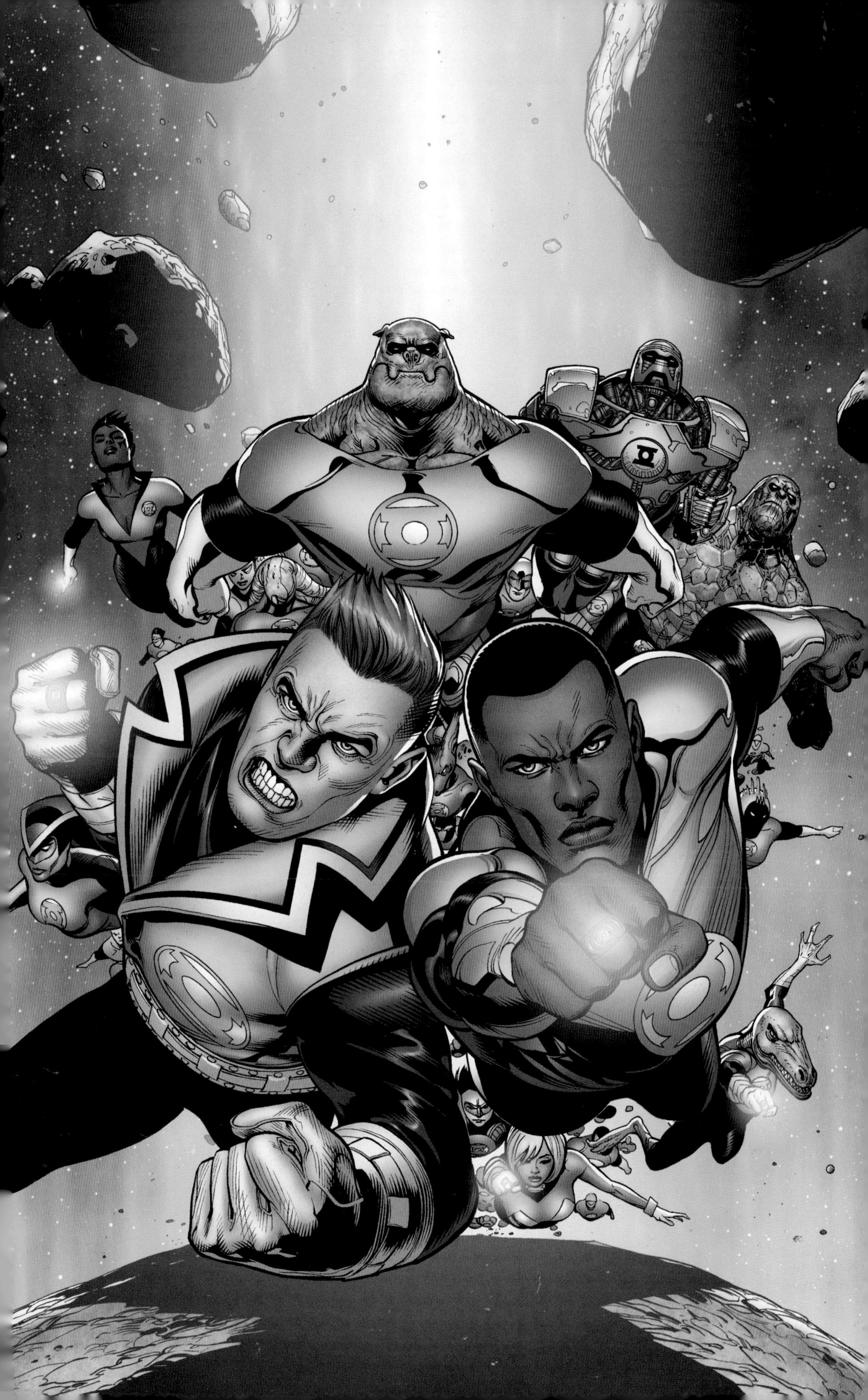

TRIUMPH OF THE WILL

PETER J. TOMASI writer **FERNANDO PASARIN** penciller **SCOTT HANNA** inker cover by **DOUG MAHNKE & CHRISTIAN ALAMY** with **RANDY MAYOR**

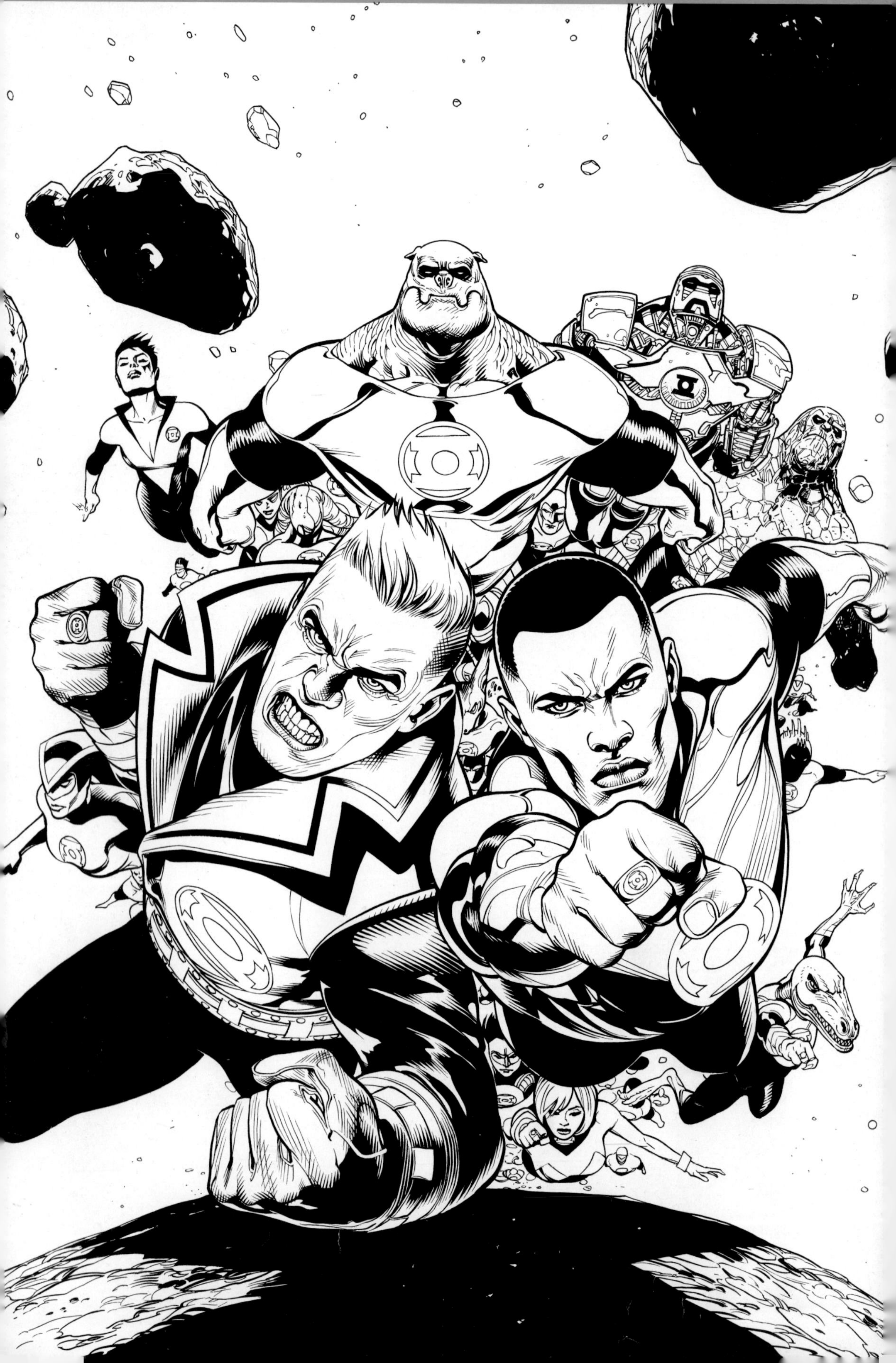

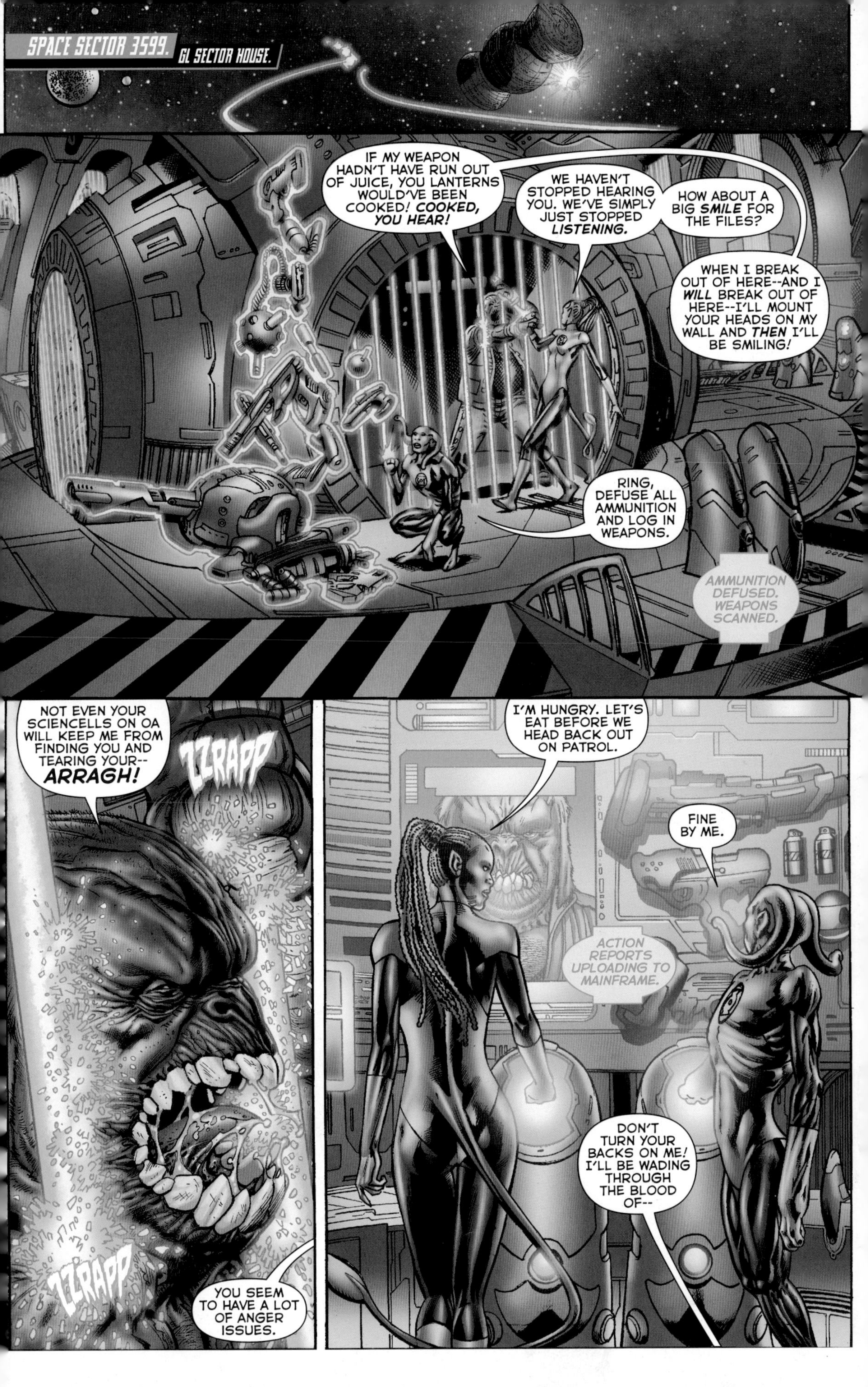
SPACE SECTOR 3599.
GL SECTOR HOUSE.
IF MY WEAPON HADN'T HAVE RUN OUT OF JUICE, YOU LANTERNS WOULD'VE BEEN COOKED! COOKED, YOU HEAR!
WE HAVEN'T STOPPED HEARING YOU. WE'VE SIMPLY JUST STOPPED LISTENING.
HOW ABOUT A BIG SMILE FOR THE FILES?
WHEN I BREAK OUT OF HERE--AND I WILL BREAK OUT OF HERE--I'LL MOUNT YOUR HEADS ON MY WALL AND THEN I'LL BE SMILING!
RING, DEFUSE ALL AMMUNITION AND LOG IN WEAPONS.
AMMUNITION DEFUSED. WEAPONS SCANNED.
NOT EVEN YOUR SCIENCELLS ON OA WILL KEEP ME FROM FINDING YOU AND TEARING YOUR-- ARRAGH!
ZZRAPP
ZZRAPP
YOU SEEM TO HAVE A LOT OF ANGER ISSUES.
I'M HUNGRY. LET'S EAT BEFORE WE HEAD BACK OUT ON PATROL.
FINE BY ME.
ACTION REPORTS UPLOADING TO MAINFRAME.
DON'T TURN YOUR BACKS ON ME! I'LL BE WADING THROUGH THE BLOOD OF--

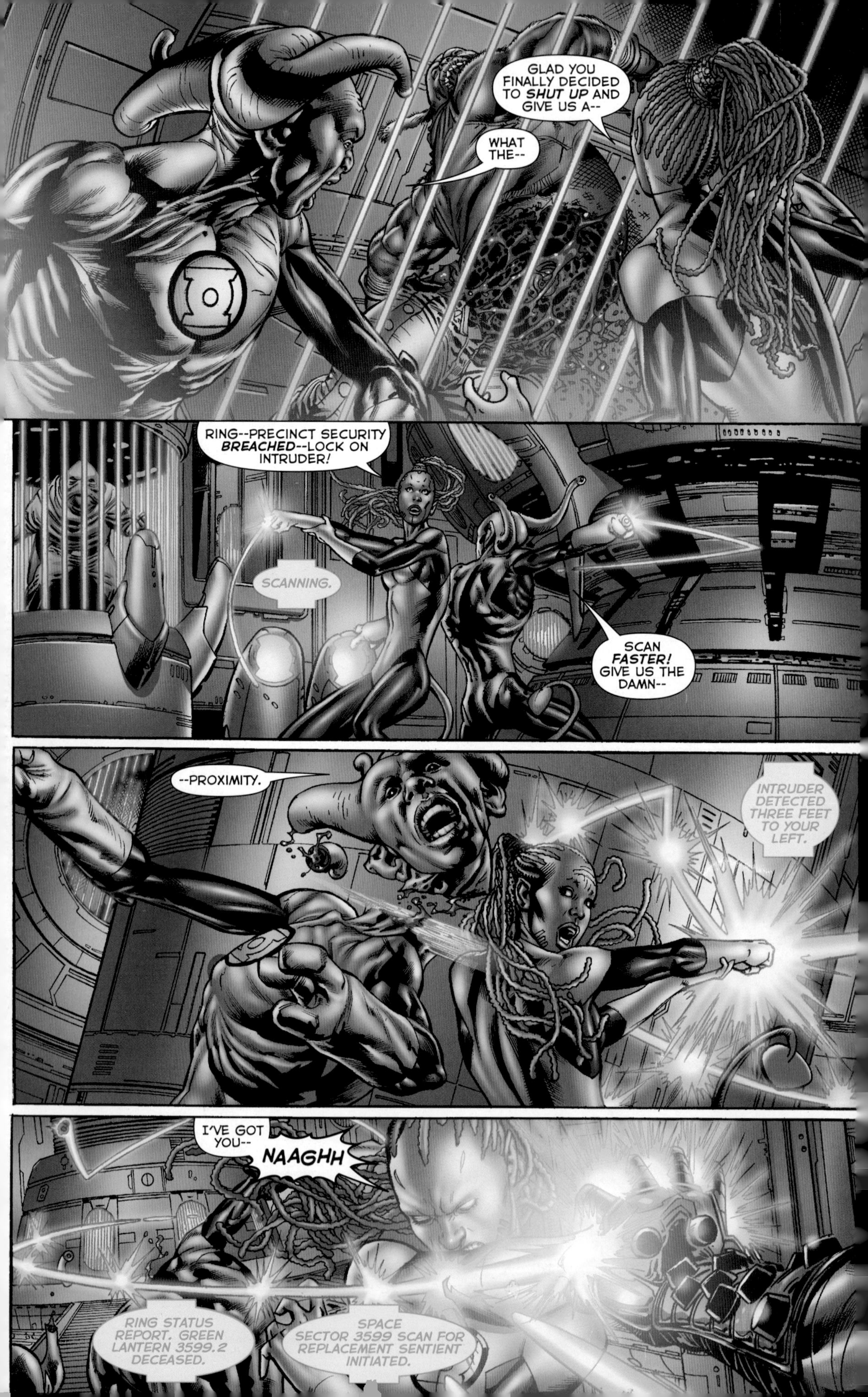

GLAD YOU FINALLY DECIDED TO **SHUT UP** AND GIVE US A--
WHAT THE--
RING--PRECINCT SECURITY **BREACHED**--LOCK ON INTRUDER!
SCANNING.
SCAN **FASTER!** GIVE US THE DAMN--
--PROXIMITY.
INTRUDER DETECTED THREE FEET TO YOUR LEFT.
I'VE GOT YOU--
NAAGHH
RING STATUS REPORT. GREEN LANTERN 3599.2 DECEASED.
SPACE SECTOR 3599 SCAN FOR REPLACEMENT SENTIENT INITIATED.

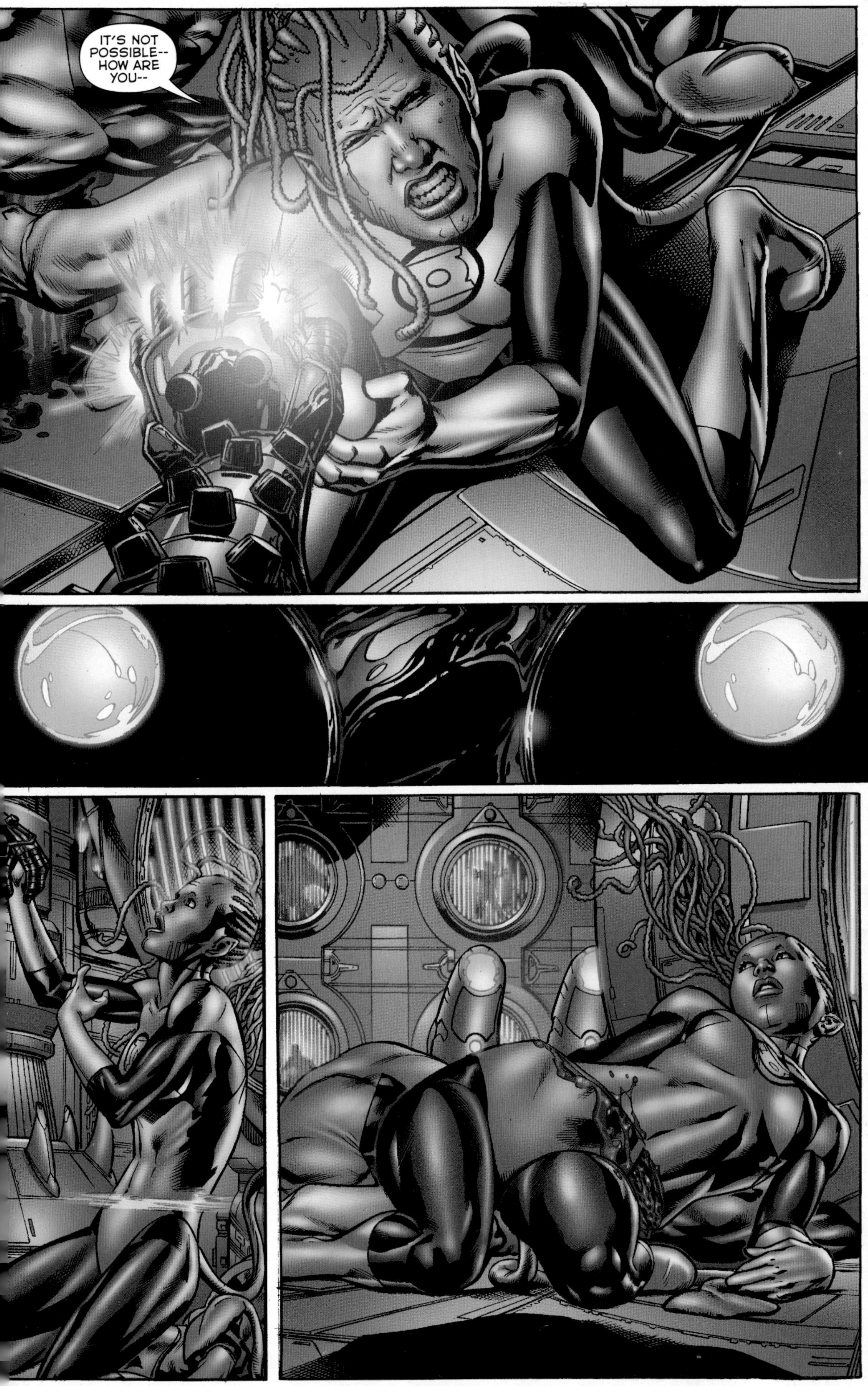
IT'S NOT POSSIBLE-- HOW ARE YOU--

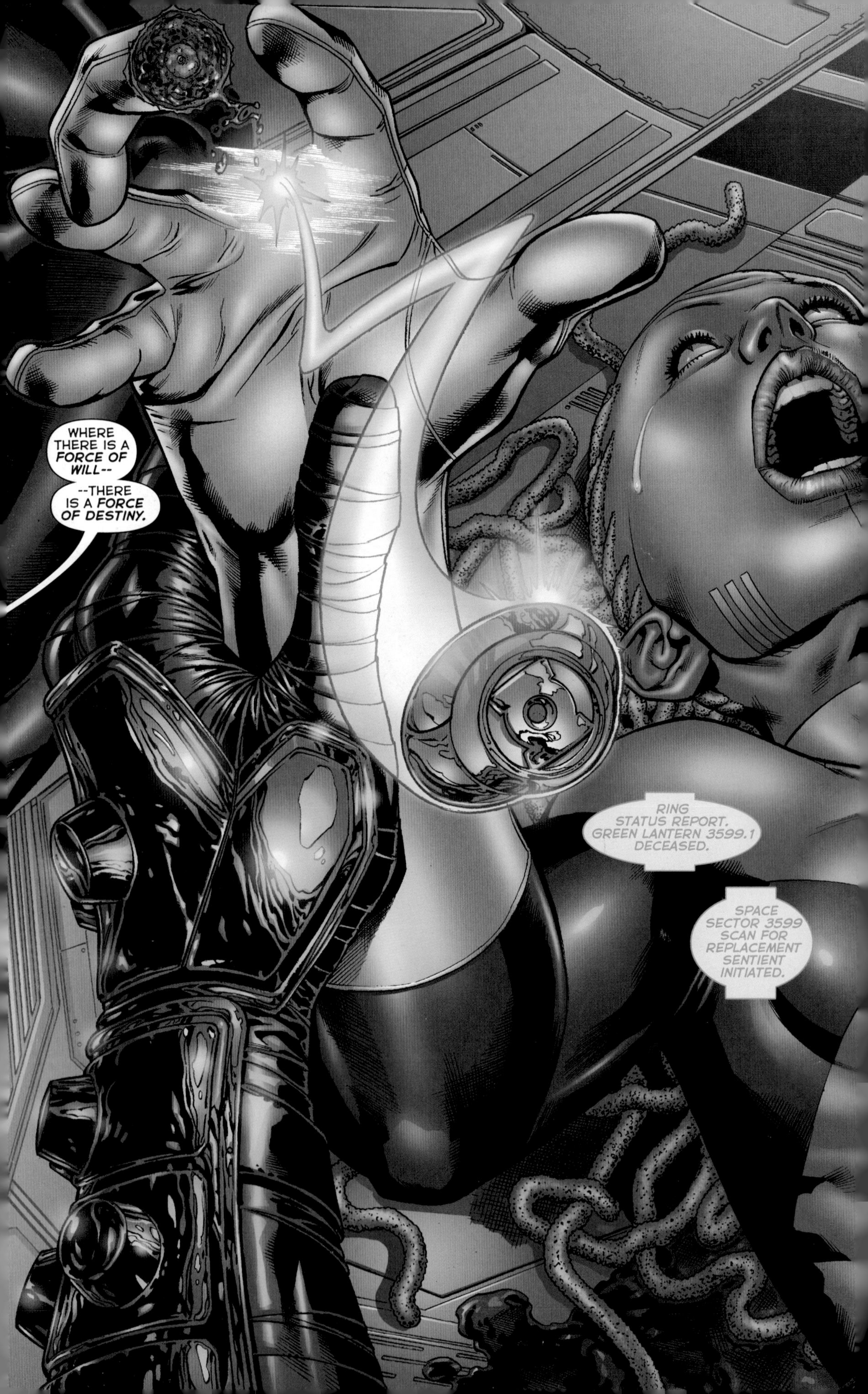

WHERE THERE IS A FORCE OF WILL--
--THERE IS A FORCE OF DESTINY.
RING STATUS REPORT. GREEN LANTERN 3599.1 DECEASED.
SPACE SECTOR 3599 SCAN FOR REPLACEMENT SENTIENT INITIATED.

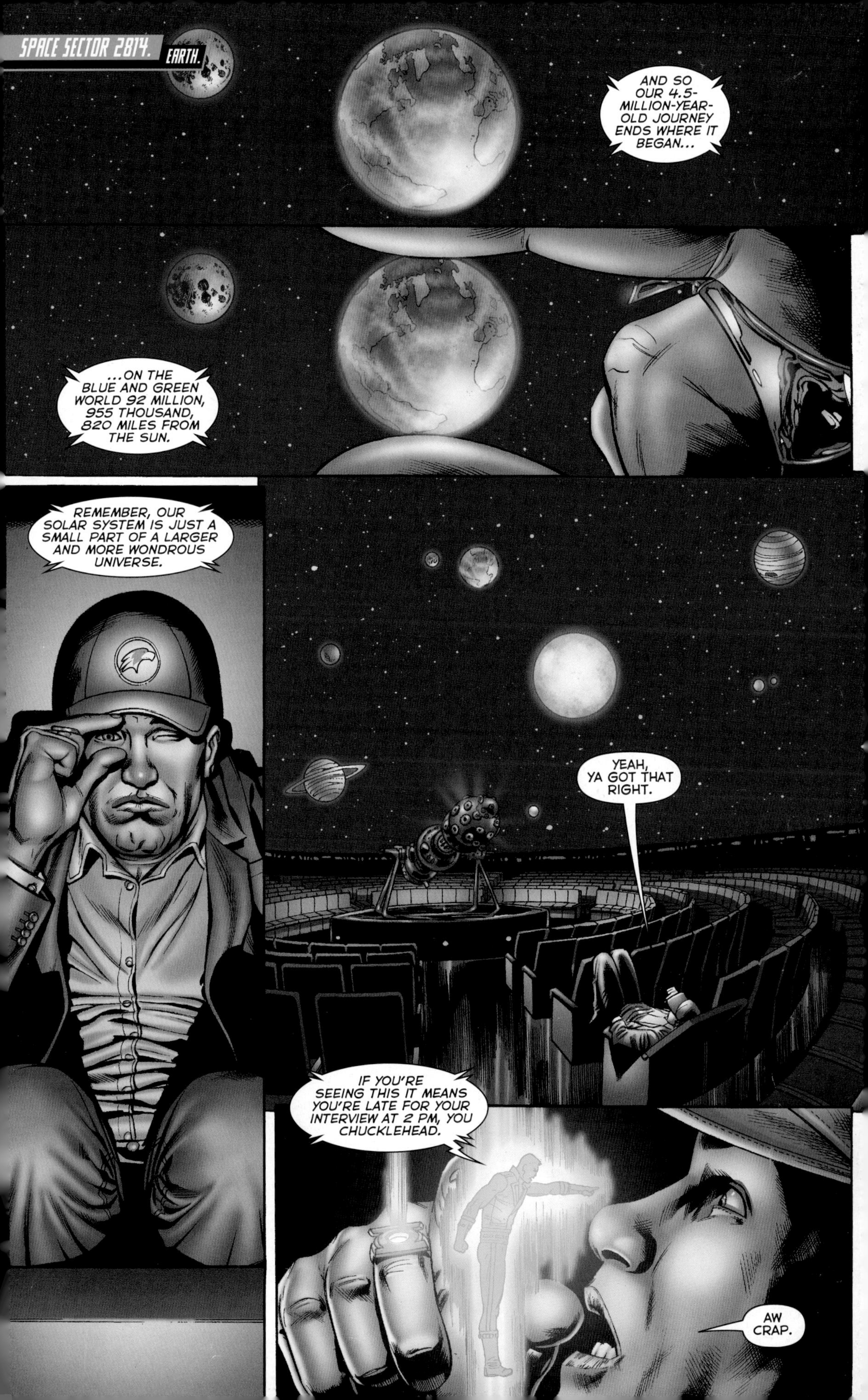
SPACE SECTOR 2814.
EARTH.
AND SO OUR 4.5-MILLION-YEAR-OLD JOURNEY ENDS WHERE IT BEGAN...
...ON THE BLUE AND GREEN WORLD 92 MILLION, 955 THOUSAND, 820 MILES FROM THE SUN.
REMEMBER, OUR SOLAR SYSTEM IS JUST A SMALL PART OF A LARGER AND MORE WONDROUS UNIVERSE.
YEAH, YA GOT THAT RIGHT.
IF YOU'RE SEEING THIS IT MEANS YOU'RE LATE FOR YOUR INTERVIEW AT 2 PM, YOU CHUCKLEHEAD.
AW CRAP.

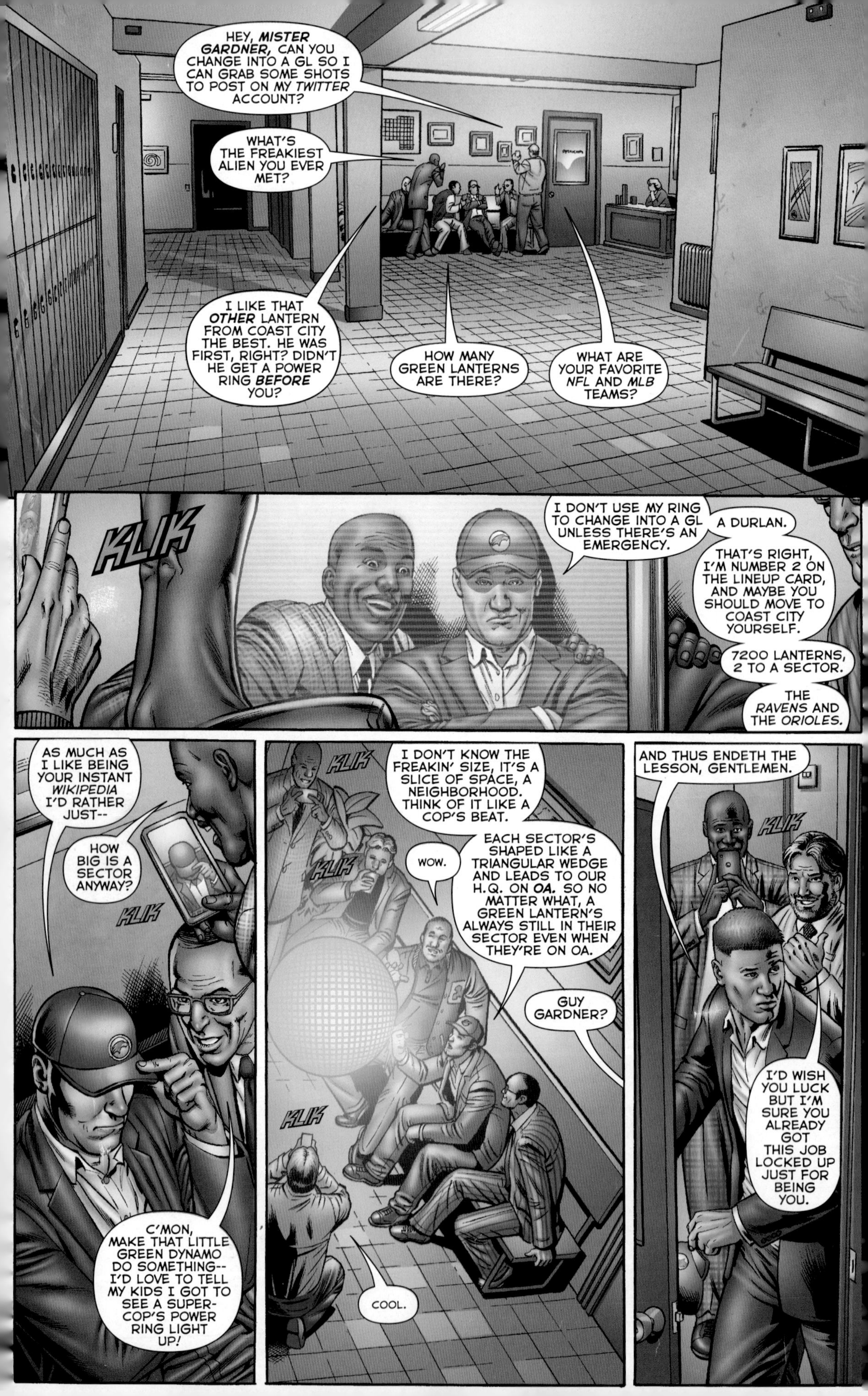

HEY, MISTER GARDNER, CAN YOU CHANGE INTO A GL SO I CAN GRAB SOME SHOTS TO POST ON MY TWITTER ACCOUNT?
WHAT'S THE FREAKIEST ALIEN YOU EVER MET?
I LIKE THAT OTHER LANTERN FROM COAST CITY THE BEST. HE WAS FIRST, RIGHT? DIDN'T HE GET A POWER RING BEFORE YOU?
HOW MANY GREEN LANTERNS ARE THERE?
WHAT ARE YOUR FAVORITE NFL AND MLB TEAMS?
KLIK
I DON'T USE MY RING TO CHANGE INTO A GL UNLESS THERE'S AN EMERGENCY.
A DURLAN.
THAT'S RIGHT, I'M NUMBER 2 ON THE LINEUP CARD, AND MAYBE YOU SHOULD MOVE TO COAST CITY YOURSELF.
7200 LANTERNS, 2 TO A SECTOR.
THE RAVENS AND THE ORIOLES.
AS MUCH AS I LIKE BEING YOUR INSTANT WIKIPEDIA I'D RATHER JUST--
HOW BIG IS A SECTOR ANYWAY?
KLIK
C'MON, MAKE THAT LITTLE GREEN DYNAMO DO SOMETHING-- I'D LOVE TO TELL MY KIDS I GOT TO SEE A SUPER-COP'S POWER RING LIGHT UP!
KLIK
I DON'T KNOW THE FREAKIN' SIZE, IT'S A SLICE OF SPACE, A NEIGHBORHOOD. THINK OF IT LIKE A COP'S BEAT.
KLIK
WOW.
EACH SECTOR'S SHAPED LIKE A TRIANGULAR WEDGE AND LEADS TO OUR H.Q. ON OA. SO NO MATTER WHAT, A GREEN LANTERN'S ALWAYS STILL IN THEIR SECTOR EVEN WHEN THEY'RE ON OA.
GUY GARDNER?
KLIK
COOL.
AND THUS ENDETH THE LESSON, GENTLEMEN.
KLIK
I'D WISH YOU LUCK BUT I'M SURE YOU ALREADY GOT THIS JOB LOCKED UP JUST FOR BEING YOU.

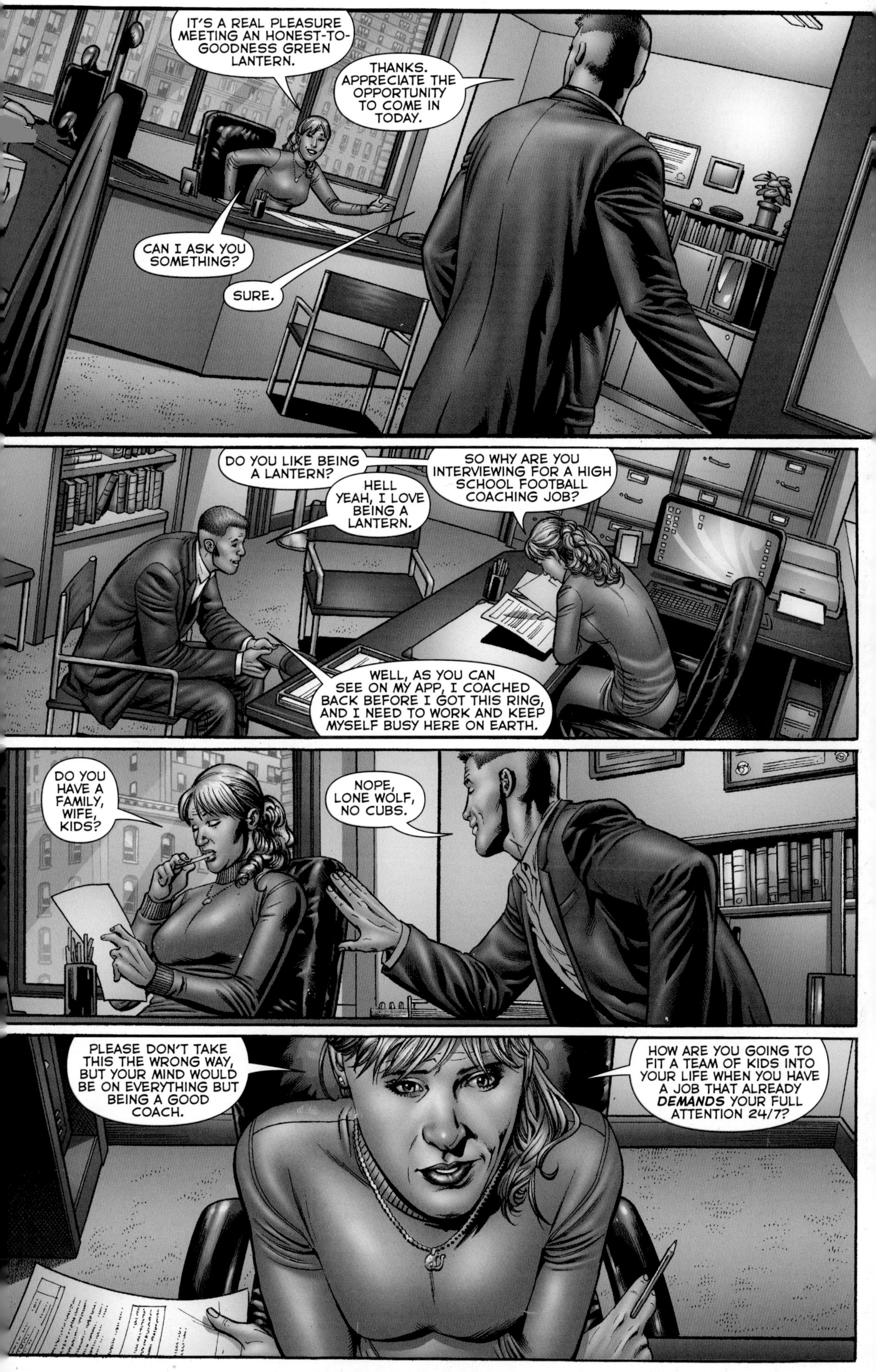
IT'S A REAL PLEASURE MEETING AN HONEST-TO-GOODNESS GREEN LANTERN.
THANKS. APPRECIATE THE OPPORTUNITY TO COME IN TODAY.
CAN I ASK YOU SOMETHING?
SURE.
DO YOU LIKE BEING A LANTERN?
HELL YEAH, I LOVE BEING A LANTERN.
SO WHY ARE YOU INTERVIEWING FOR A HIGH SCHOOL FOOTBALL COACHING JOB?
WELL, AS YOU CAN SEE ON MY APP, I COACHED BACK BEFORE I GOT THIS RING, AND I NEED TO WORK AND KEEP MYSELF BUSY HERE ON EARTH.
DO YOU HAVE A FAMILY, WIFE, KIDS?
NOPE, LONE WOLF, NO CUBS.
PLEASE DON'T TAKE THIS THE WRONG WAY, BUT YOUR MIND WOULD BE ON EVERYTHING BUT BEING A GOOD COACH.
HOW ARE YOU GOING TO FIT A TEAM OF KIDS INTO YOUR LIFE WHEN YOU HAVE A JOB THAT ALREADY **DEMANDS** YOUR FULL ATTENTION 24/7?

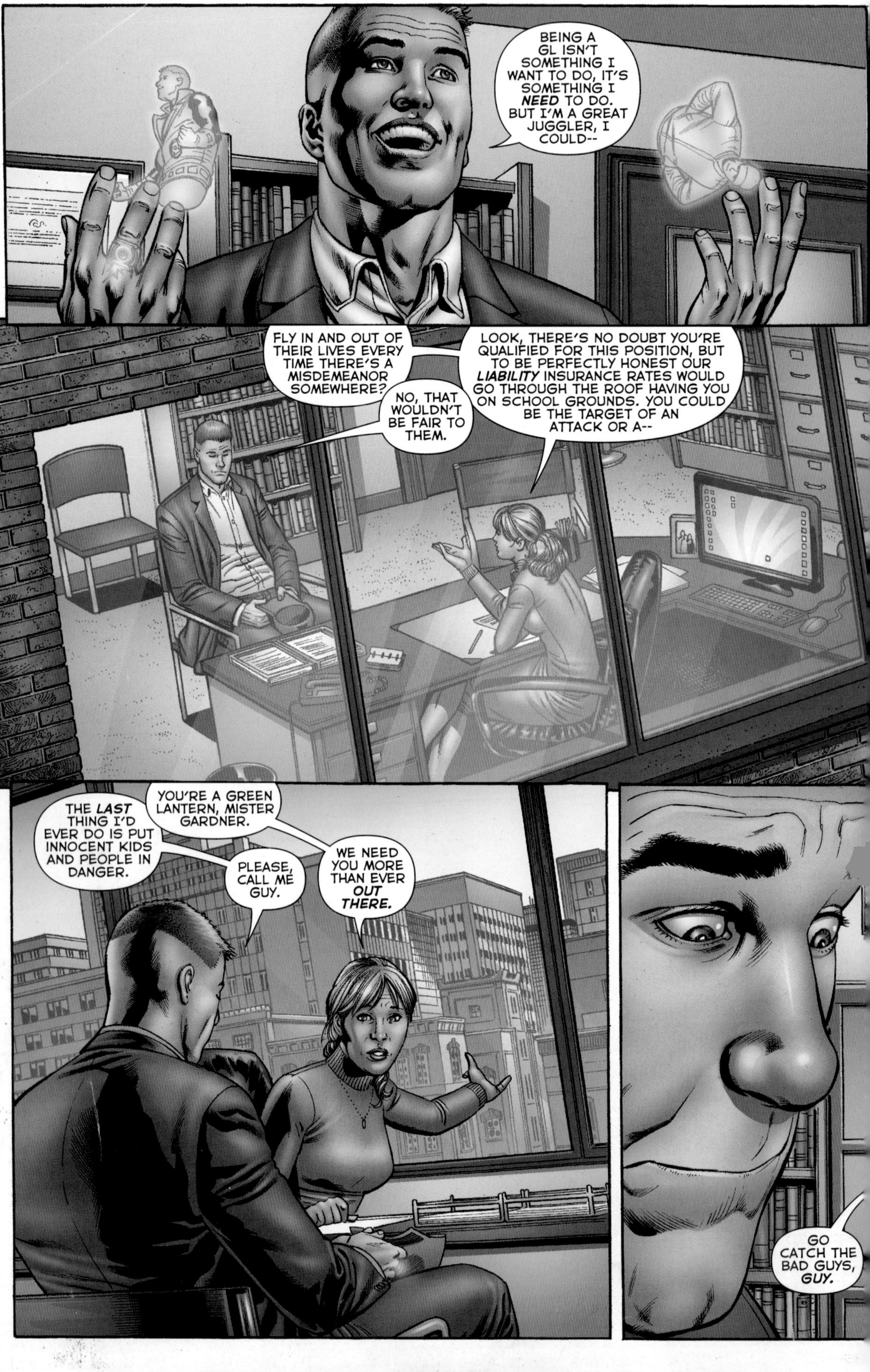
BEING A GL ISN'T SOMETHING I WANT TO DO, IT'S SOMETHING I *NEED* TO DO. BUT I'M A GREAT JUGGLER, I COULD--
FLY IN AND OUT OF THEIR LIVES EVERY TIME THERE'S A MISDEMEANOR SOMEWHERE?
NO, THAT WOULDN'T BE FAIR TO THEM.
LOOK, THERE'S NO DOUBT YOU'RE QUALIFIED FOR THIS POSITION, BUT TO BE PERFECTLY HONEST OUR *LIABILITY* INSURANCE RATES WOULD GO THROUGH THE ROOF HAVING YOU ON SCHOOL GROUNDS. YOU COULD BE THE TARGET OF AN ATTACK OR A--
THE *LAST* THING I'D EVER DO IS PUT INNOCENT KIDS AND PEOPLE IN DANGER.
YOU'RE A GREEN LANTERN, MISTER GARDNER.
PLEASE, CALL ME GUY.
WE NEED YOU MORE THAN EVER ***OUT THERE.***
GO CATCH THE BAD GUYS, ***GUY.***

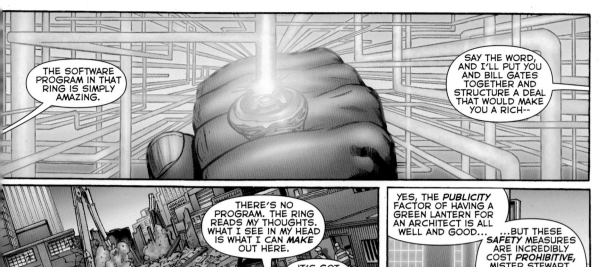

THE SOFTWARE PROGRAM IN THAT RING IS SIMPLY AMAZING.

SAY THE WORD, AND I'LL PUT YOU AND BILL GATES TOGETHER AND STRUCTURE A DEAL THAT WOULD MAKE YOU A RICH--

THERE'S NO PROGRAM. THE RING READS MY THOUGHTS. WHAT I SEE IN MY HEAD IS WHAT I CAN *MAKE* OUT HERE.

IT'S GOT WEIGHT AND EDGES.

HARD LIGHT, SOFT LIGHT, ONE OUNCE, ONE TON, ALL I NEED TO DO IS THINK IT AND THE RING INSTANTLY PROJECTS IT.

YES, THE *PUBLICITY* FACTOR OF HAVING A GREEN LANTERN FOR AN ARCHITECT IS ALL WELL AND GOOD...

...BUT THESE *SAFETY* MEASURES ARE INCREDIBLY COST *PROHIBITIVE*, MISTER STEWART. YOU'RE ASKING US TO GO ABOVE *AND* BEYOND WHAT EVERY OTHER BUILDING OWNER IS DOING IN THE CITY.

BECAUSE IT'S THE *RIGHT* THING TO DO, AND *I'M* NOT TAKING SHORTCUTS.

C'MON, AS LONG AS WE'RE UP TO *CODE* WHY DO YOU INSIST ON--

IT'S ABOUT HAVING A *CODE OF HONOR*, NOT A CODE OF WEALTH.

WE'RE ALL FAMILIAR *AND* APPRECIATIVE OF YOUR *MARINE CORPS* SERVICE, MISTER STEWART, BUT IT DOESN'T MEAN WE HAVE TO HAVE YOUR *MOTTOS* THROWN OUR WAY.

MOTHERS, FATHERS, SONS, AND DAUGHTERS SPEND A BIG PART OF THEIR LIVES INSIDE THE STEEL AND GLASS WE BUILD AROUND THEM TO BRING HOME A PAYCHECK. THE LEAST WE CAN DO IS MAKE SURE THEY'RE SAFE DOING IT.

AND THESE *S.P.I.R.* NOTATIONS--EXPLAIN TO ME HOW I CONVINCE MY BOARD TO APPROVE SUCH A PRODIGIOUS OUTLAY OF FUNDS FOR SOMETHING WE'RE NOT EVEN *LEGALLY* OBLIGATED TO DO, HMM?

SURE, LET ME TAKE A CRACK AT IT.

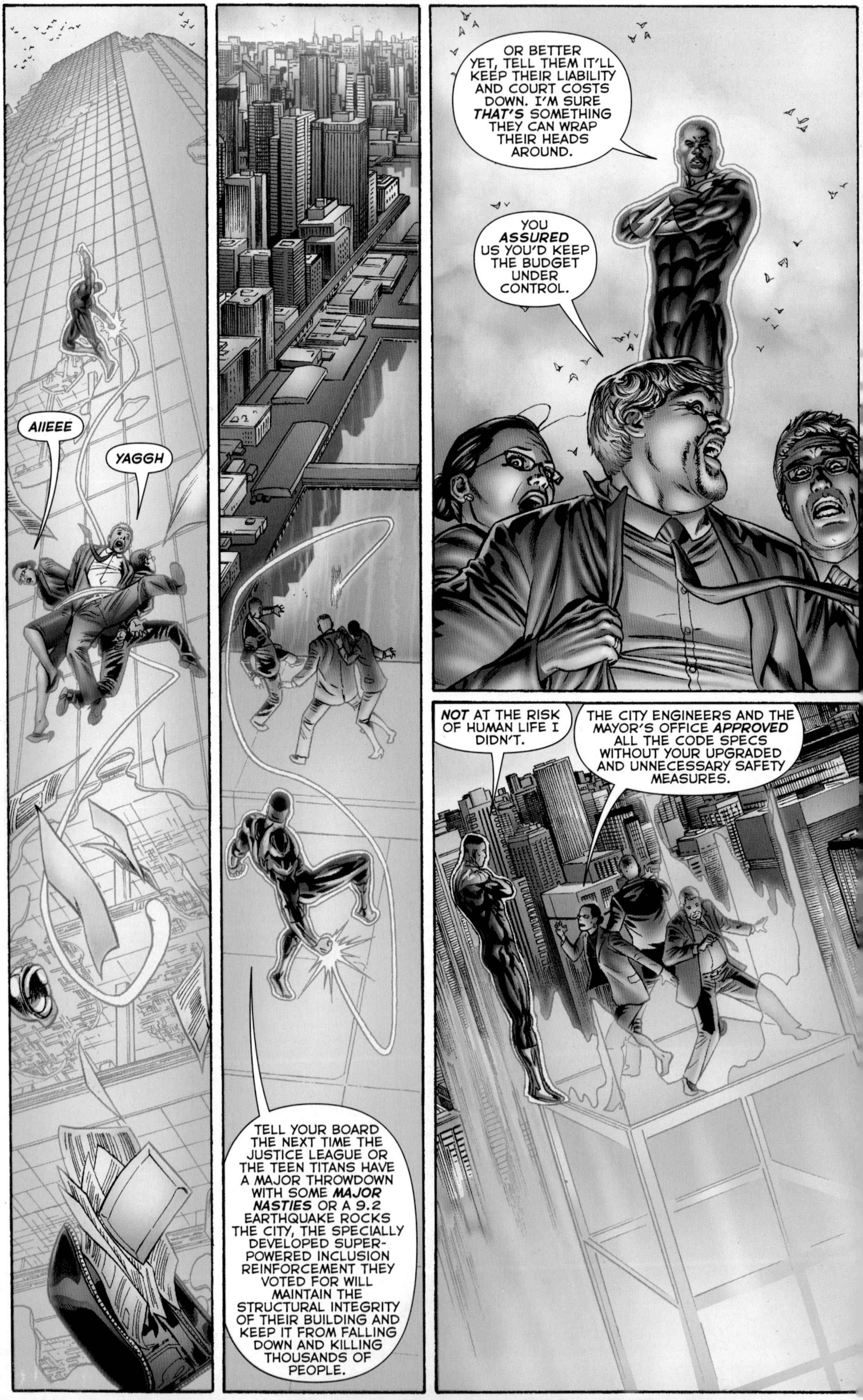
AIIEEE
YAGGH
TELL YOUR BOARD THE NEXT TIME THE JUSTICE LEAGUE OR THE TEEN TITANS HAVE A MAJOR THROWDOWN WITH SOME MAJOR NASTIES OR A 9.2 EARTHQUAKE ROCKS THE CITY, THE SPECIALLY DEVELOPED SUPER-POWERED INCLUSION REINFORCEMENT THEY VOTED FOR WILL MAINTAIN THE STRUCTURAL INTEGRITY OF THEIR BUILDING AND KEEP IT FROM FALLING DOWN AND KILLING THOUSANDS OF PEOPLE.
OR BETTER YET, TELL THEM IT'LL KEEP THEIR LIABILITY AND COURT COSTS DOWN. I'M SURE THAT'S SOMETHING THEY CAN WRAP THEIR HEADS AROUND.
YOU ASSURED US YOU'D KEEP THE BUDGET UNDER CONTROL.
NOT AT THE RISK OF HUMAN LIFE I DIDN'T.
THE CITY ENGINEERS AND THE MAYOR'S OFFICE APPROVED ALL THE CODE SPECS WITHOUT YOUR UPGRADED AND UNNECESSARY SAFETY MEASURES.

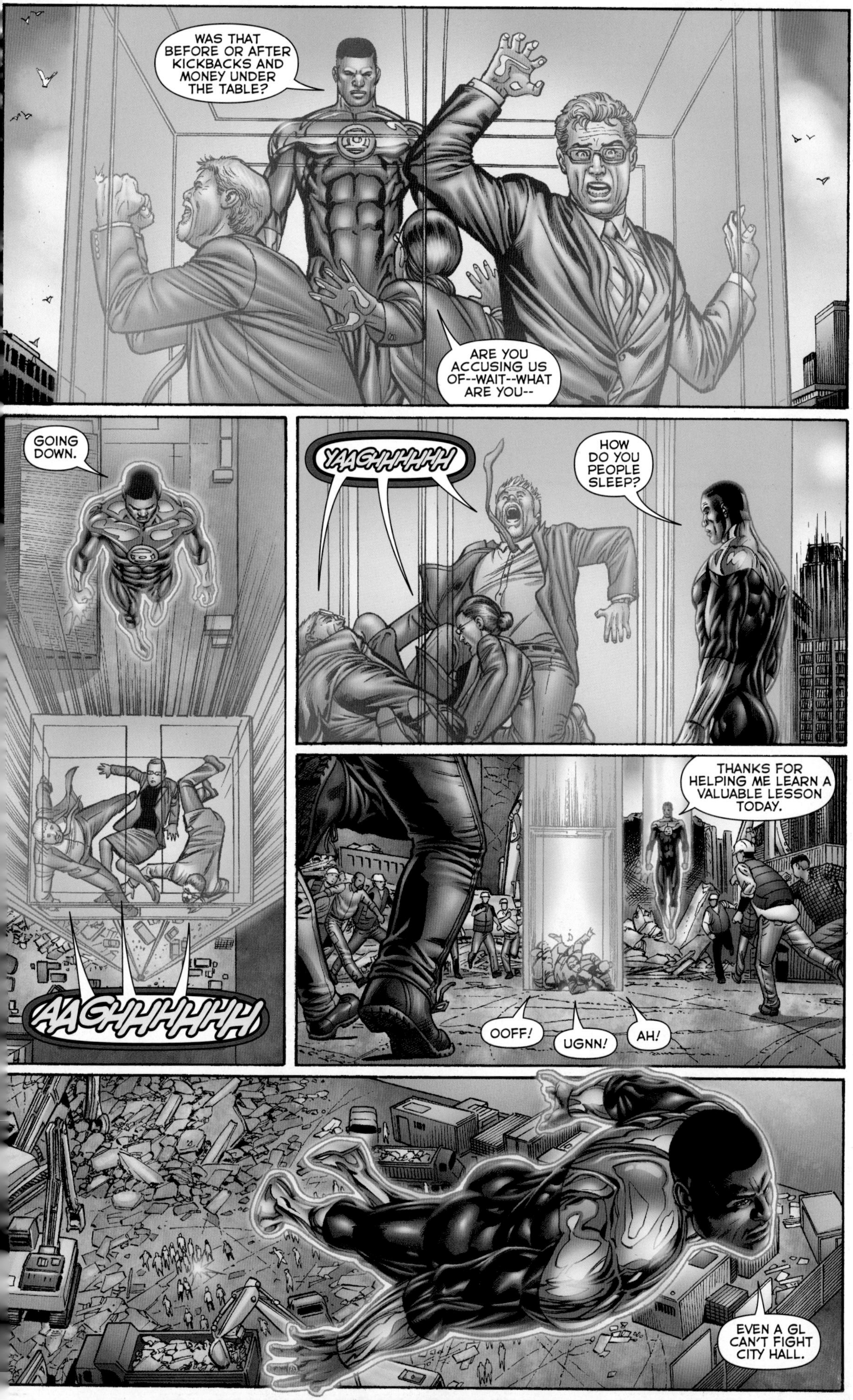

WAS THAT BEFORE OR AFTER KICKBACKS AND MONEY UNDER THE TABLE?
ARE YOU ACCUSING US OF--WAIT--WHAT ARE YOU--
GOING DOWN.
AAGHHHHHH
YAAGHHHHHH
HOW DO YOU PEOPLE SLEEP?
THANKS FOR HELPING ME LEARN A VALUABLE LESSON TODAY.
OOFF!
UGNN!
AH!
EVEN A GL CAN'T FIGHT CITY HALL.

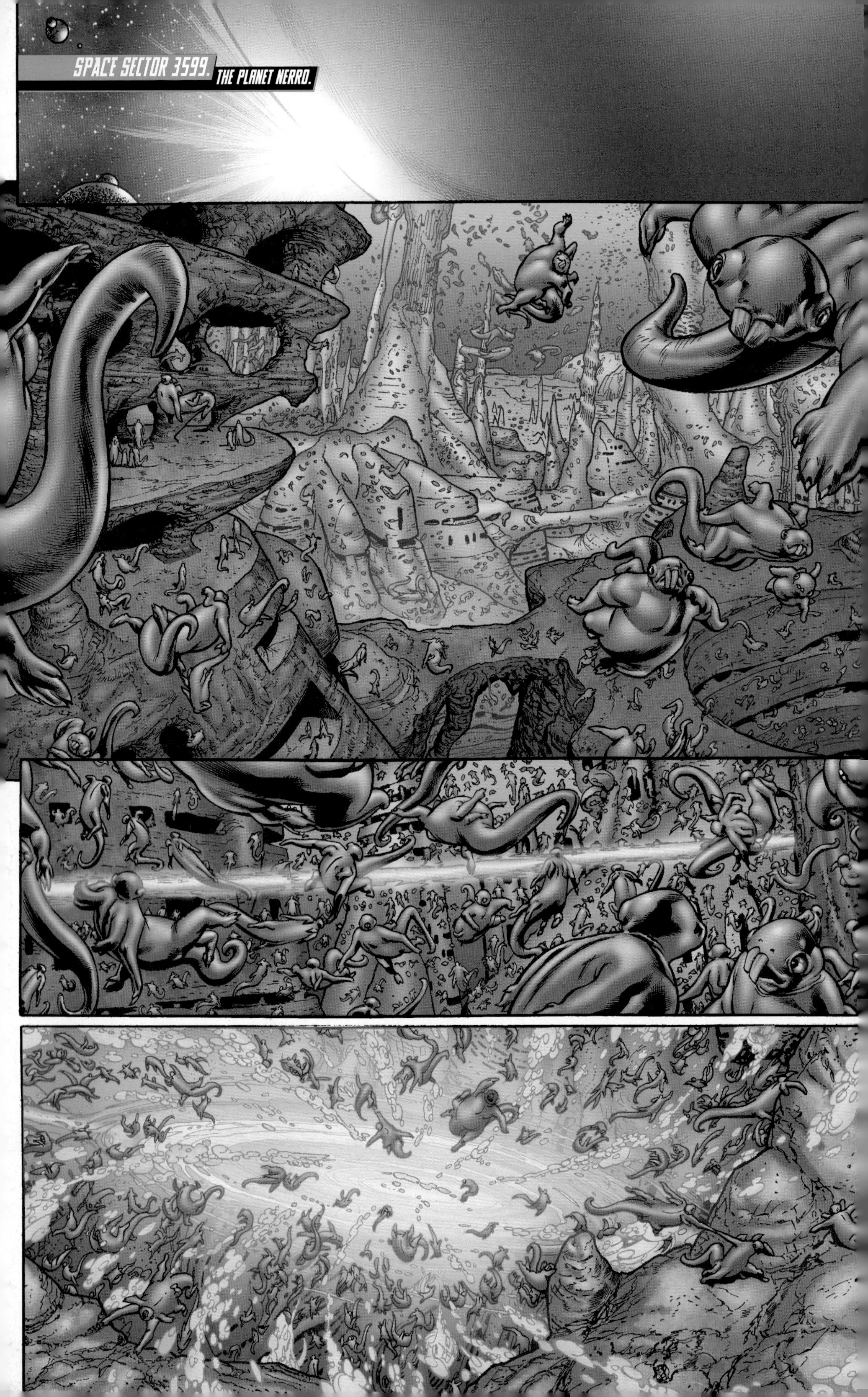
SPACE SECTOR 3599.
THE PLANET NERRO.

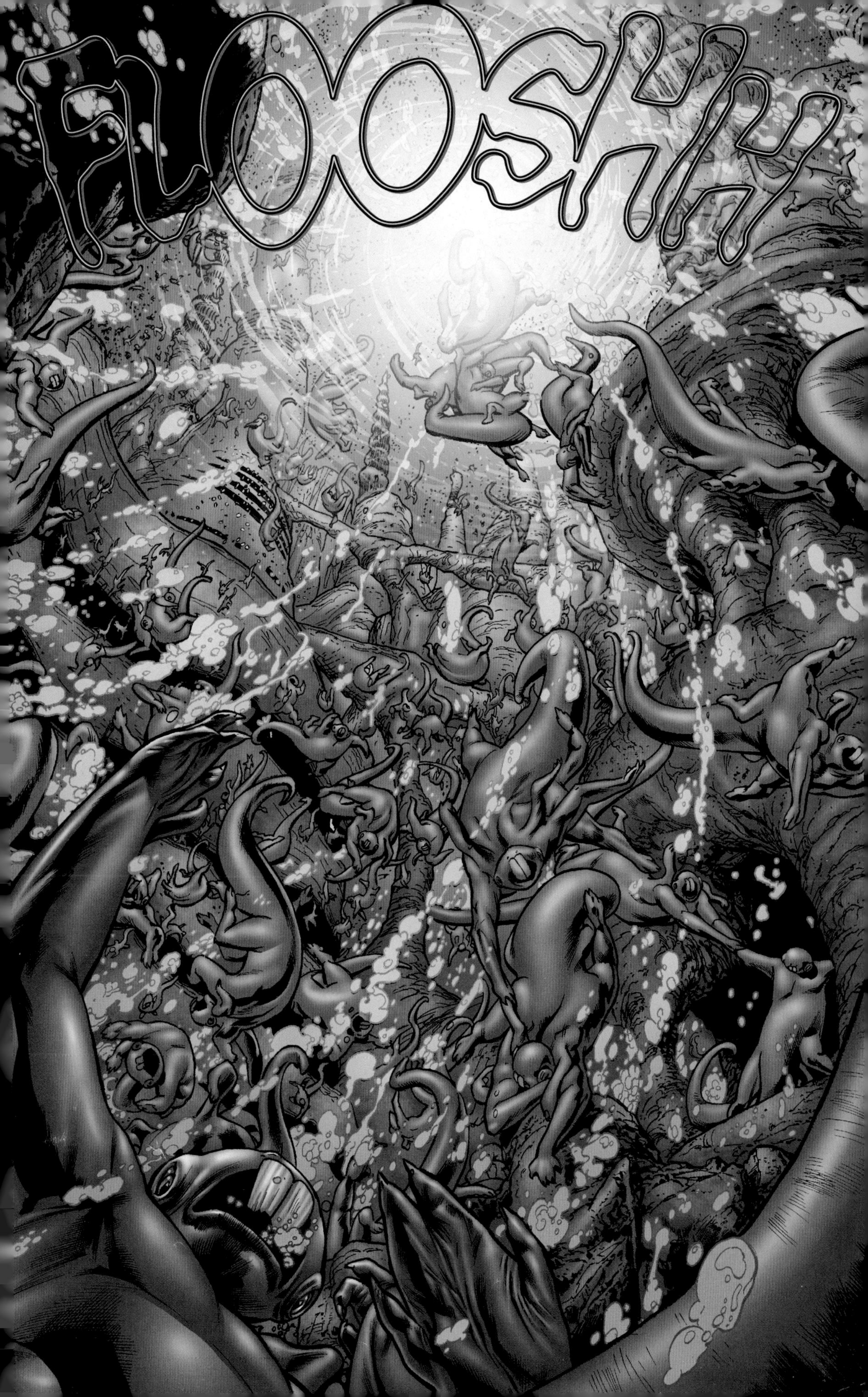
FLOOSHHH

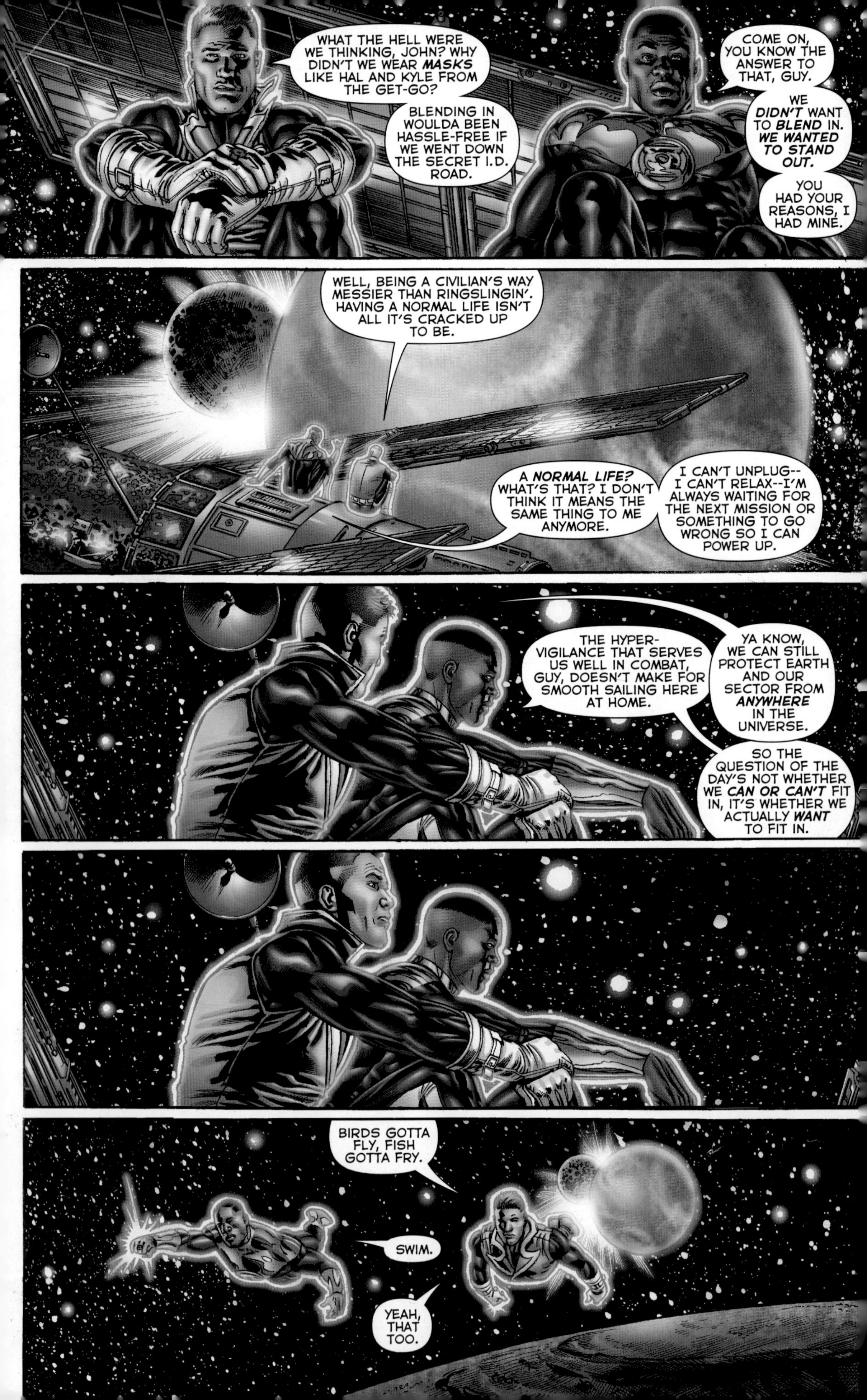
WHAT THE HELL WERE WE THINKING, JOHN? WHY DIDN'T WE WEAR MASKS LIKE HAL AND KYLE FROM THE GET-GO?
BLENDING IN WOULDA BEEN HASSLE-FREE IF WE WENT DOWN THE SECRET I.D. ROAD.
COME ON, YOU KNOW THE ANSWER TO THAT, GUY.
WE DIDN'T WANT TO BLEND IN. WE WANTED TO STAND OUT.
YOU HAD YOUR REASONS, I HAD MINE.
WELL, BEING A CIVILIAN'S WAY MESSIER THAN RINGSLINGIN'. HAVING A NORMAL LIFE ISN'T ALL IT'S CRACKED UP TO BE.
A NORMAL LIFE? WHAT'S THAT? I DON'T THINK IT MEANS THE SAME THING TO ME ANYMORE.
I CAN'T UNPLUG-- I CAN'T RELAX--I'M ALWAYS WAITING FOR THE NEXT MISSION OR SOMETHING TO GO WRONG SO I CAN POWER UP.
THE HYPER-VIGILANCE THAT SERVES US WELL IN COMBAT, GUY, DOESN'T MAKE FOR SMOOTH SAILING HERE AT HOME.
YA KNOW, WE CAN STILL PROTECT EARTH AND OUR SECTOR FROM ANYWHERE IN THE UNIVERSE.
SO THE QUESTION OF THE DAY'S NOT WHETHER WE CAN OR CAN'T FIT IN, IT'S WHETHER WE ACTUALLY WANT TO FIT IN.
BIRDS GOTTA FLY, FISH GOTTA FRY.
SWIM.
YEAH, THAT TOO.

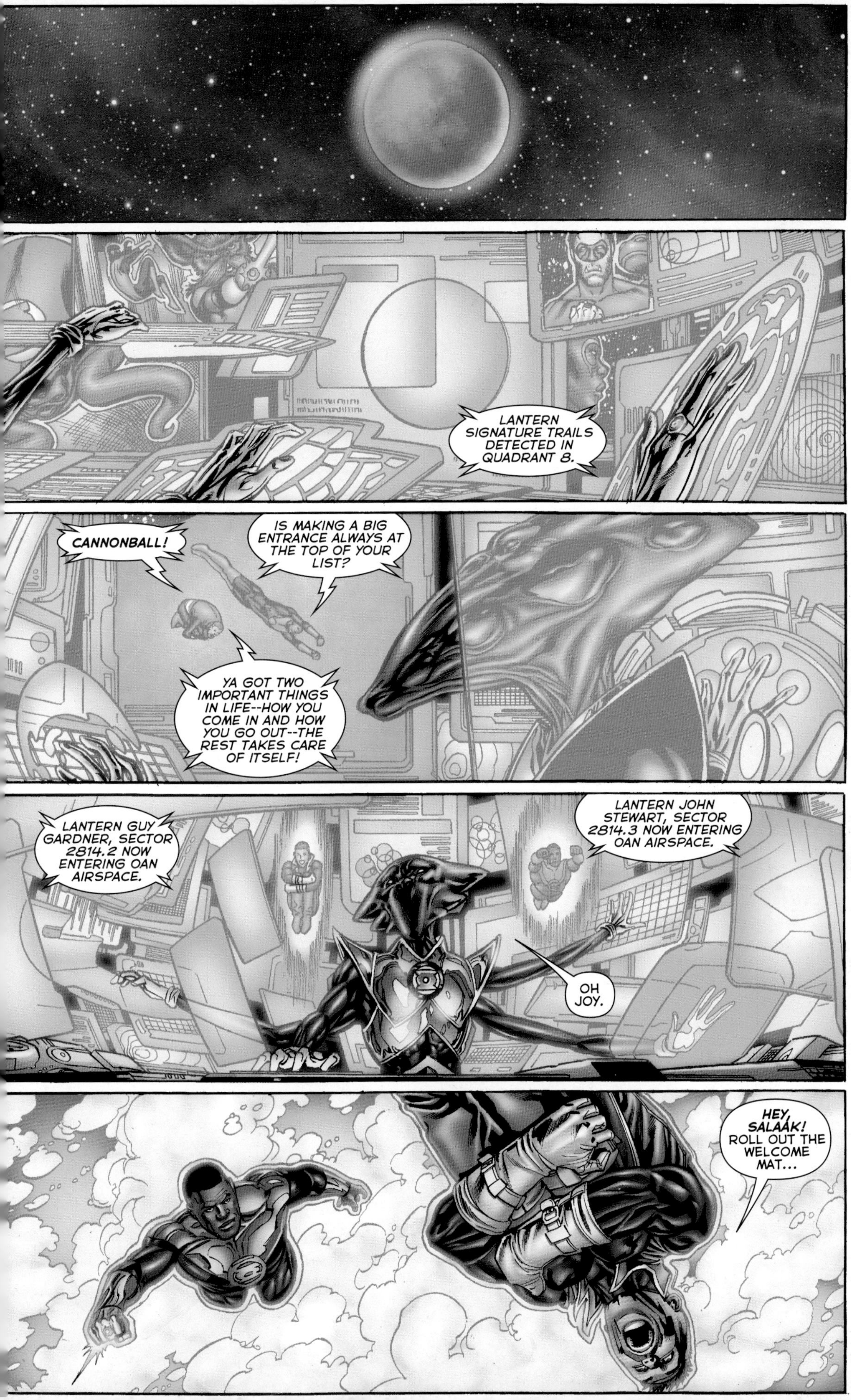
LANTERN SIGNATURE TRAILS DETECTED IN QUADRANT 8.
CANNONBALL!
IS MAKING A BIG ENTRANCE ALWAYS AT THE TOP OF YOUR LIST?
YA GOT TWO IMPORTANT THINGS IN LIFE--HOW YOU COME IN AND HOW YOU GO OUT--THE REST TAKES CARE OF ITSELF!
LANTERN GUY GARDNER, SECTOR 2814.2 NOW ENTERING OAN AIRSPACE.
LANTERN JOHN STEWART, SECTOR 2814.3 NOW ENTERING OAN AIRSPACE.
OH JOY.
HEY, SALAAK! ROLL OUT THE WELCOME MAT...

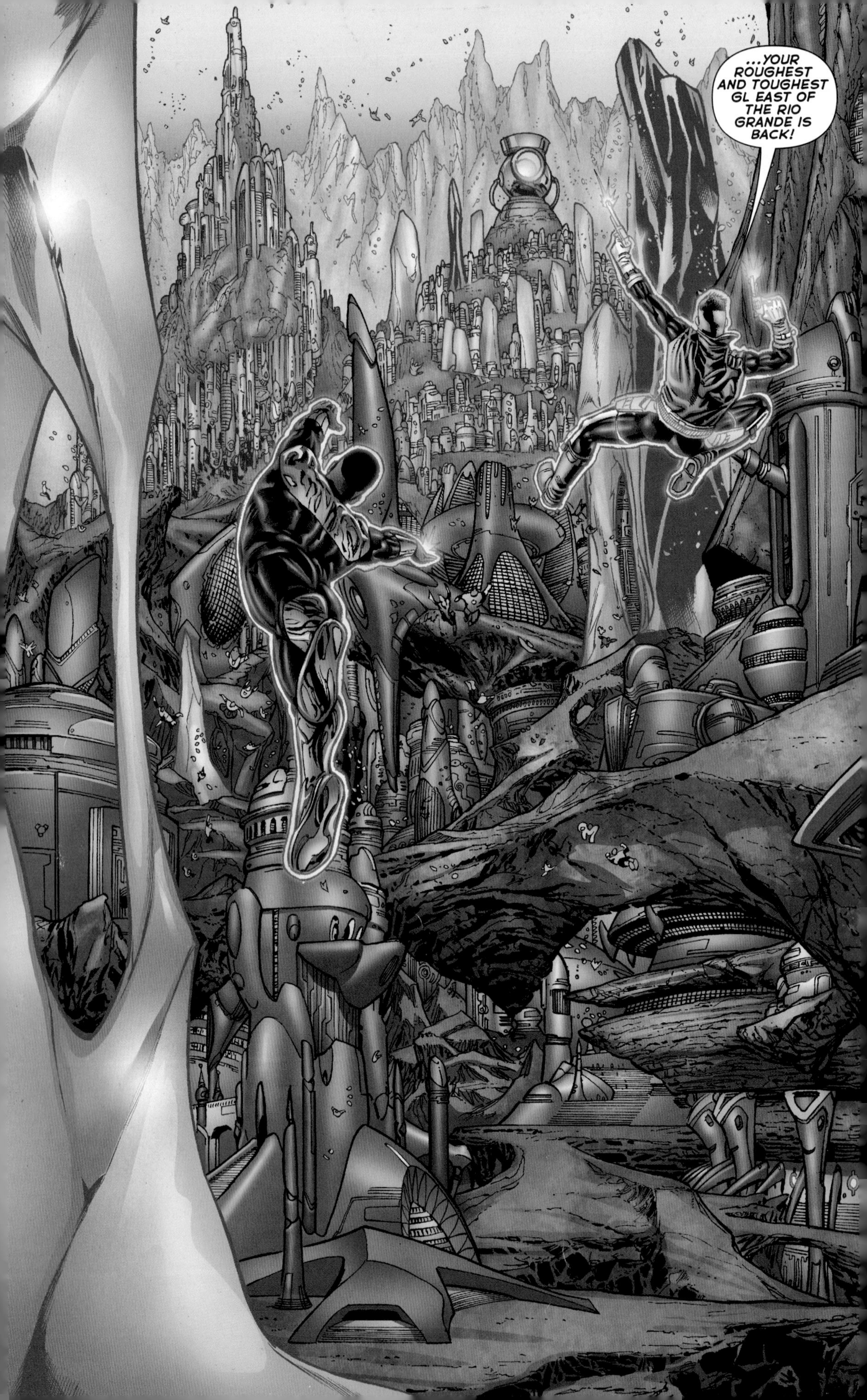
...YOUR ROUGHEST AND TOUGHEST GL EAST OF THE RIO GRANDE IS BACK!

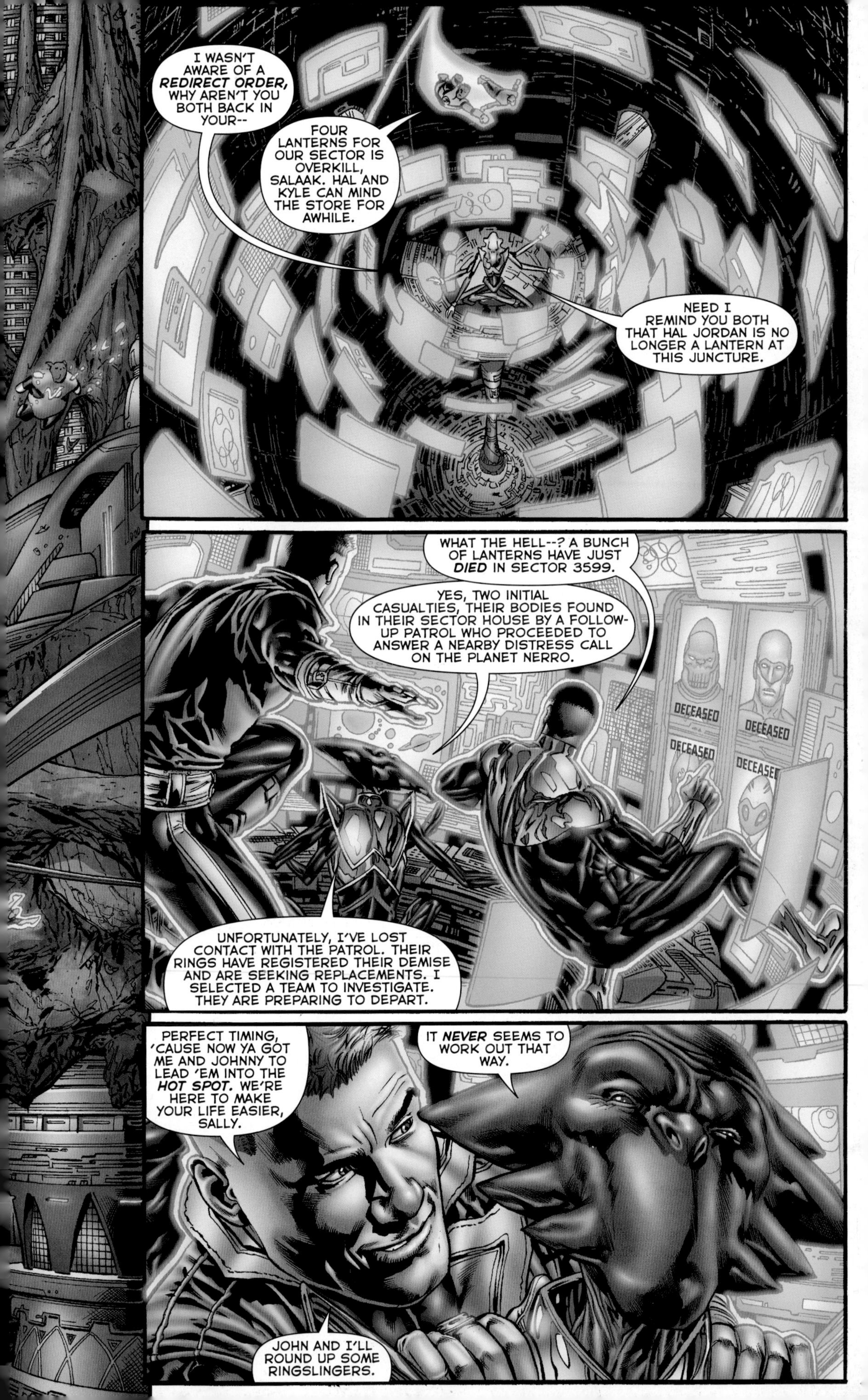
I WASN'T AWARE OF A ***REDIRECT ORDER,*** WHY AREN'T YOU BOTH BACK IN YOUR--
FOUR LANTERNS FOR OUR SECTOR IS OVERKILL, SALAAK. HAL AND KYLE CAN MIND THE STORE FOR AWHILE.
NEED I REMIND YOU BOTH THAT HAL JORDAN IS NO LONGER A LANTERN AT THIS JUNCTURE.
WHAT THE HELL--? A BUNCH OF LANTERNS HAVE JUST ***DIED*** IN SECTOR 3599.
YES, TWO INITIAL CASUALTIES, THEIR BODIES FOUND IN THEIR SECTOR HOUSE BY A FOLLOW-UP PATROL WHO PROCEEDED TO ANSWER A NEARBY DISTRESS CALL ON THE PLANET NERRO.
DECEASED
DECEASED
DECEASED
UNFORTUNATELY, I'VE LOST CONTACT WITH THE PATROL. THEIR RINGS HAVE REGISTERED THEIR DEMISE AND ARE SEEKING REPLACEMENTS. I SELECTED A TEAM TO INVESTIGATE. THEY ARE PREPARING TO DEPART.
PERFECT TIMING, 'CAUSE NOW YA GOT ME AND JOHNNY TO LEAD 'EM INTO THE ***HOT SPOT.*** WE'RE HERE TO MAKE YOUR LIFE EASIER, SALLY.
IT ***NEVER*** SEEMS TO WORK OUT THAT WAY.
JOHN AND I'LL ROUND UP SOME RINGSLINGERS.

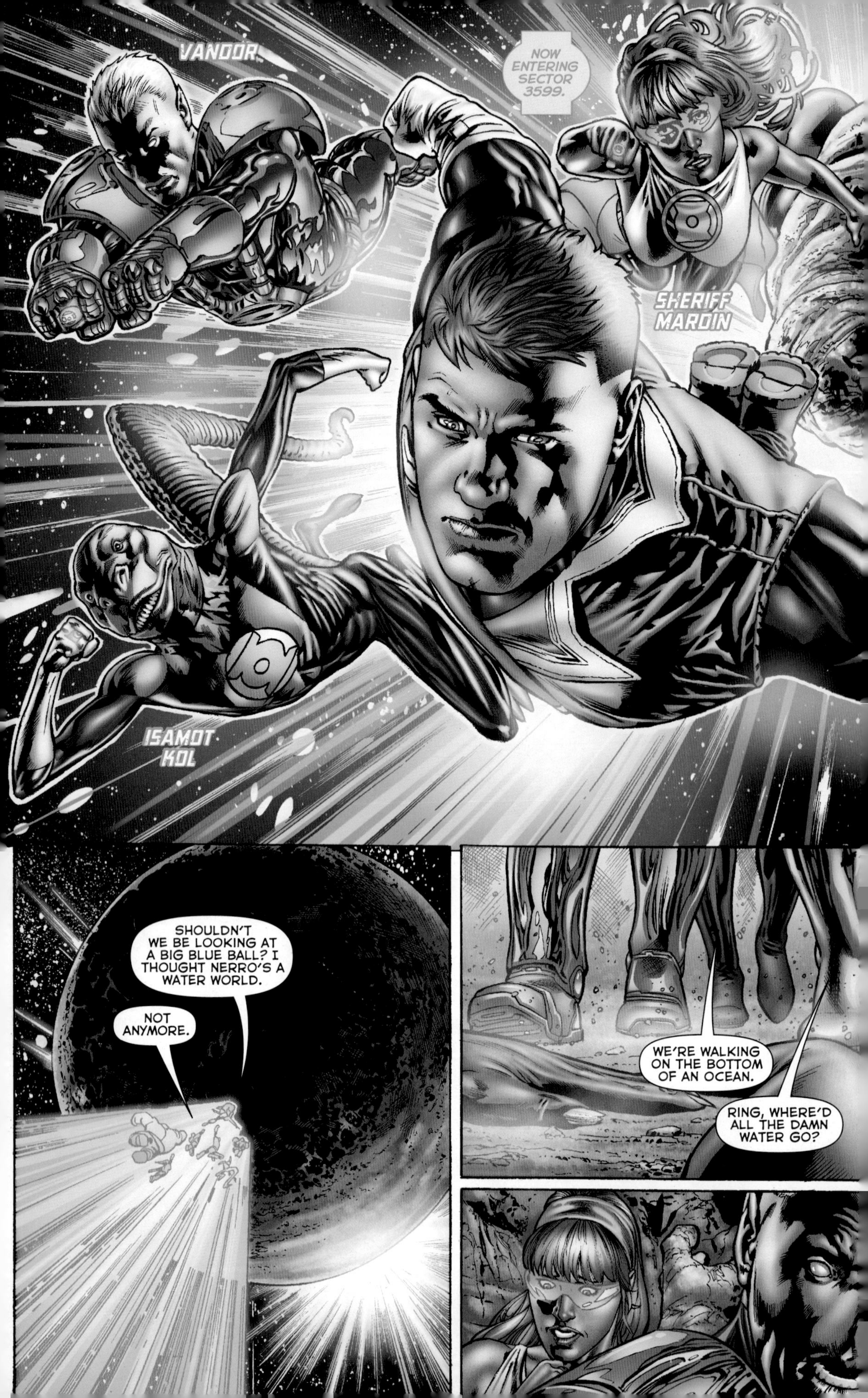
VANDOR
NOW ENTERING SECTOR 3599.
SHERIFF MARDIN
ISAMOT KOL
SHOULDN'T WE BE LOOKING AT A BIG BLUE BALL? I THOUGHT NERRO'S A WATER WORLD.
NOT ANYMORE.
WE'RE WALKING ON THE BOTTOM OF AN OCEAN.
RING, WHERE'D ALL THE DAMN WATER GO?

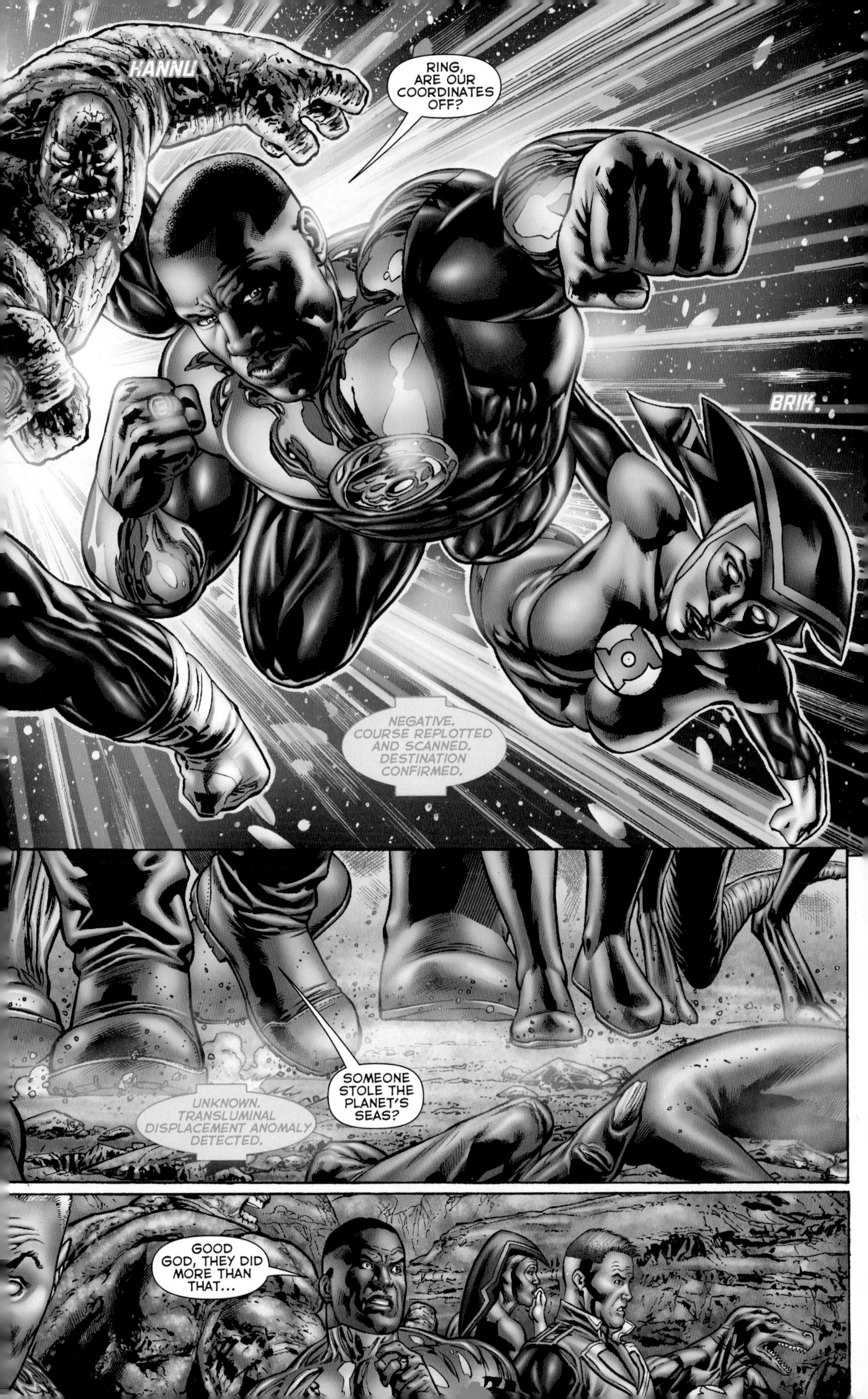

HANNU
RING, ARE OUR COORDINATES OFF?
BRIK.
NEGATIVE. COURSE REPLOTTED AND SCANNED. DESTINATION CONFIRMED.
SOMEONE STOLE THE PLANET'S SEAS?
UNKNOWN. TRANSLUMINAL DISPLACEMENT ANOMALY DETECTED.
GOOD GOD, THEY DID MORE THAN THAT...

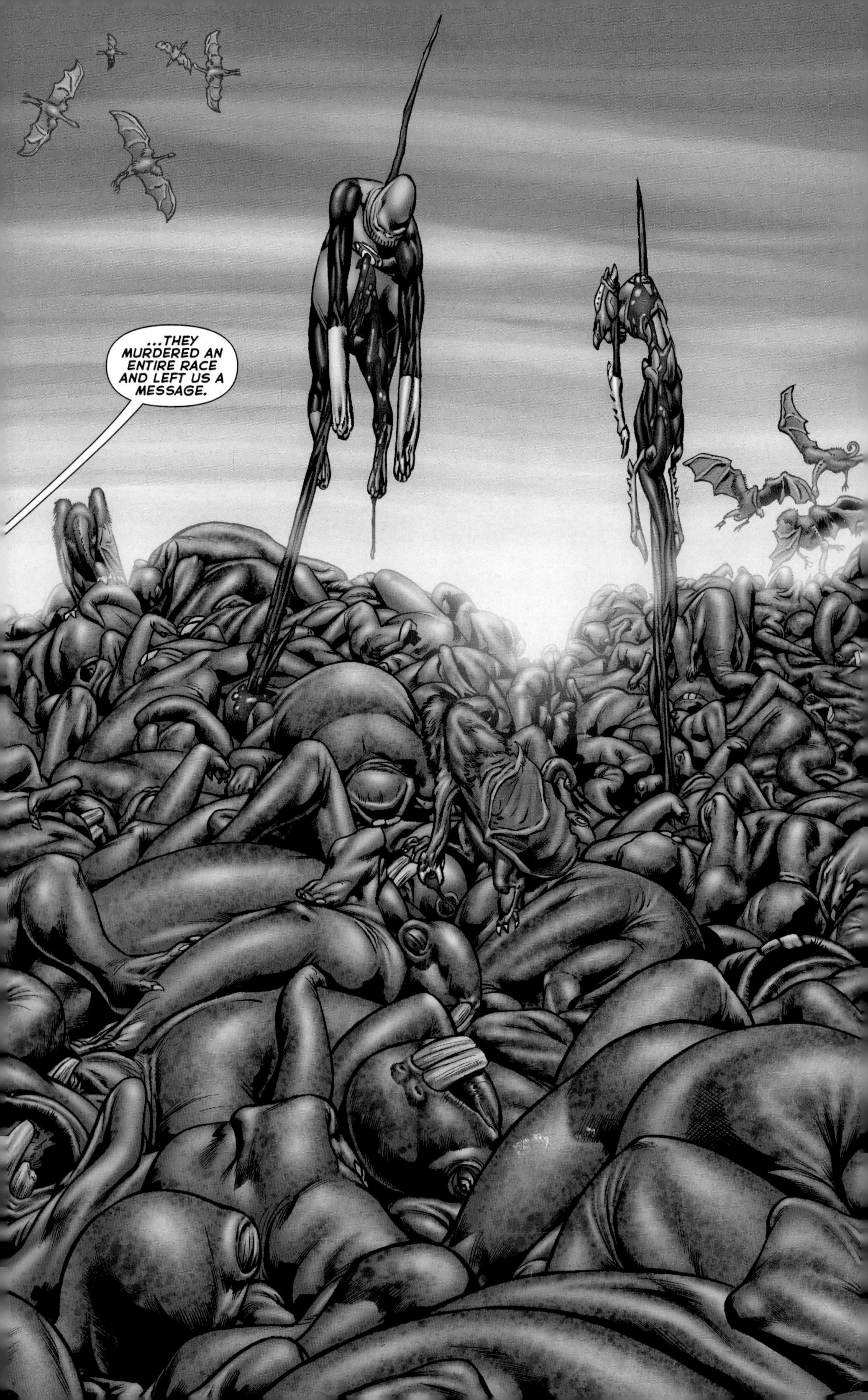
...THEY MURDERED AN ENTIRE RACE AND LEFT US A MESSAGE.

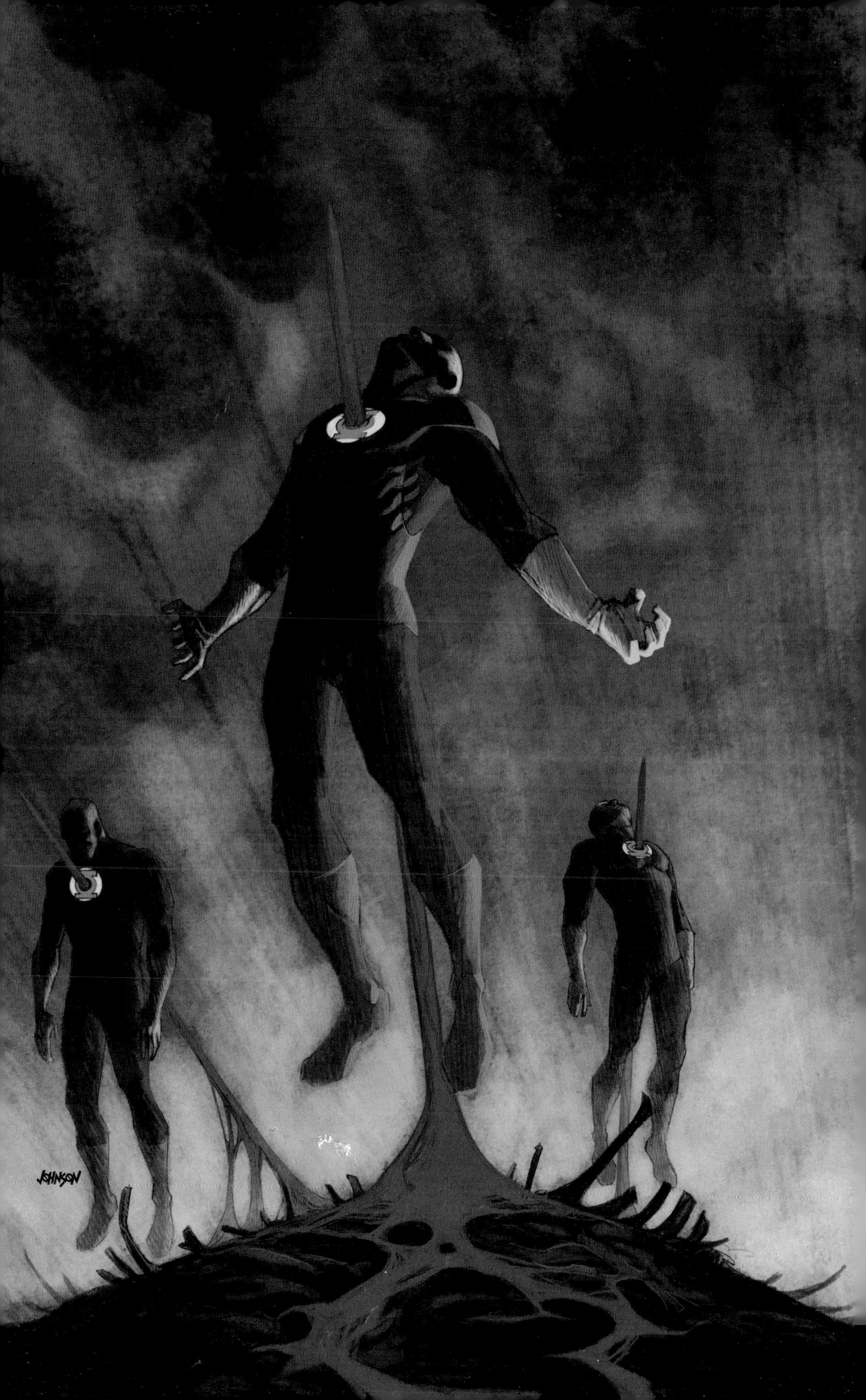
JOHNSON

WILLFUL

PETER J. TOMASI writer **FERNANDO PASARIN** penciller **SCOTT HANNA** inker cover by **DAVE JOHNSON**

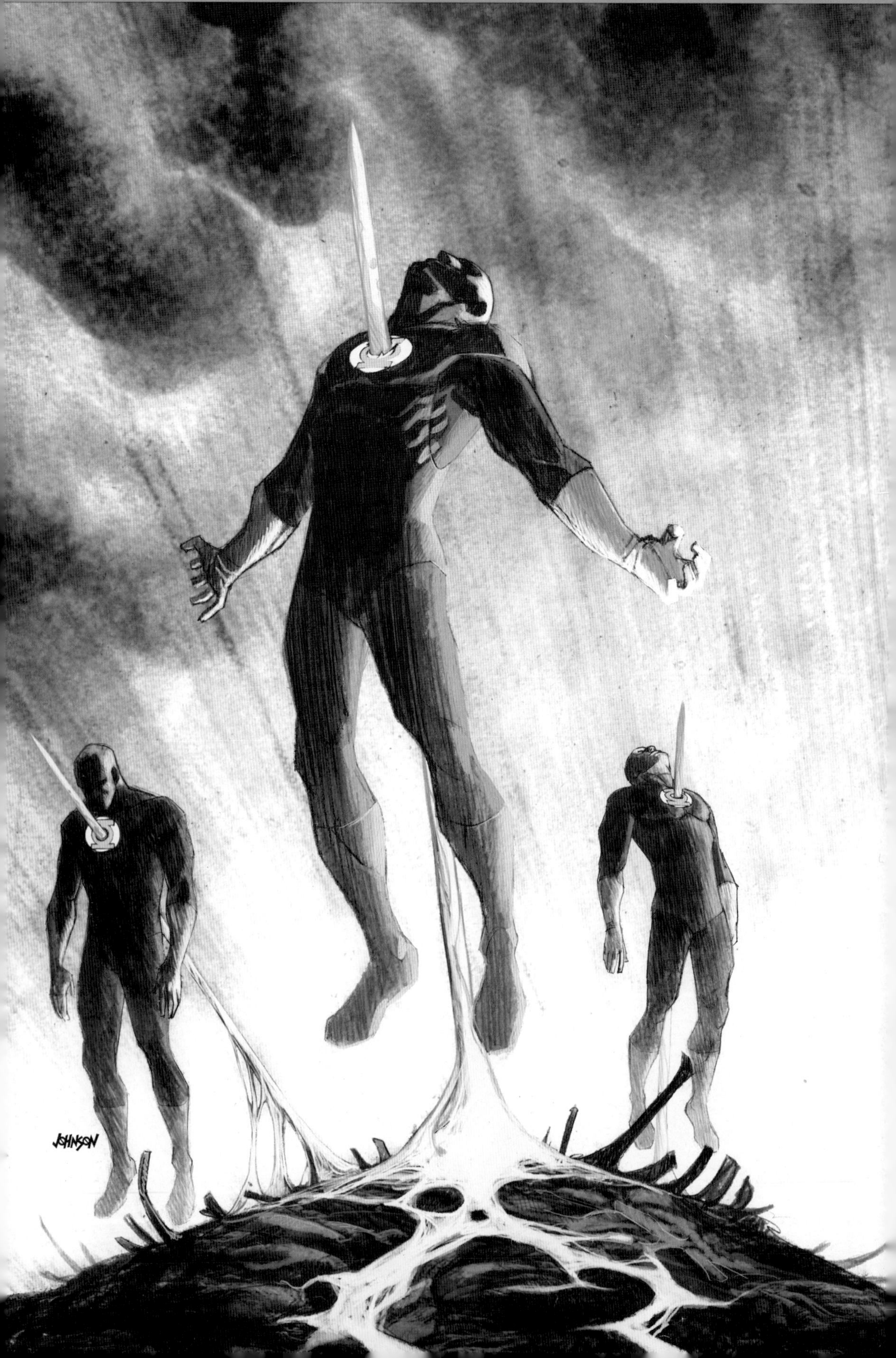
JOHNSON

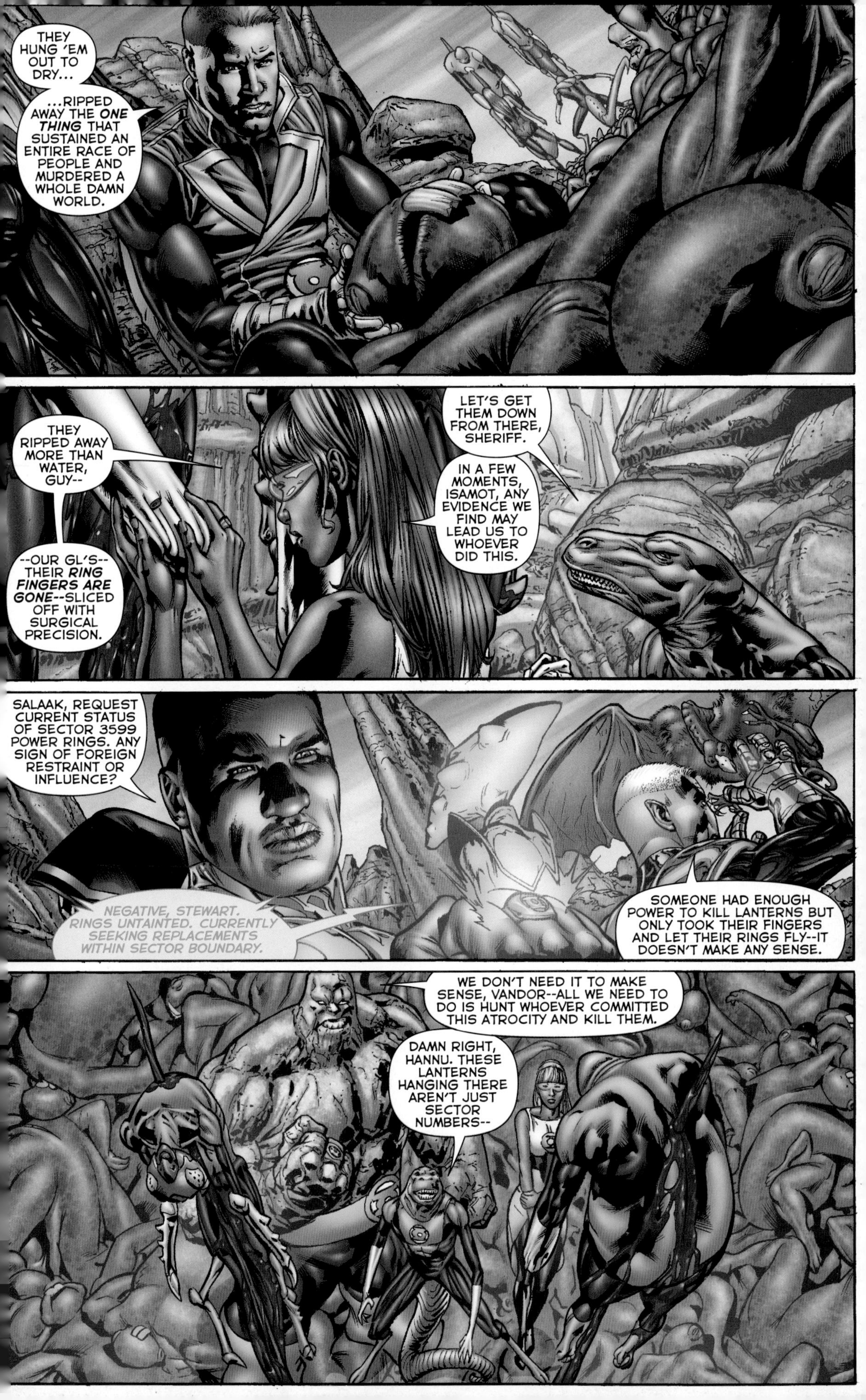
THEY HUNG 'EM OUT TO DRY...
...RIPPED AWAY THE ONE THING THAT SUSTAINED AN ENTIRE RACE OF PEOPLE AND MURDERED A WHOLE DAMN WORLD.
THEY RIPPED AWAY MORE THAN WATER, GUY--
--OUR GL'S--THEIR RING FINGERS ARE GONE--SLICED OFF WITH SURGICAL PRECISION.
LET'S GET THEM DOWN FROM THERE, SHERIFF.
IN A FEW MOMENTS, ISAMOT, ANY EVIDENCE WE FIND MAY LEAD US TO WHOEVER DID THIS.
SALAAK, REQUEST CURRENT STATUS OF SECTOR 3599 POWER RINGS. ANY SIGN OF FOREIGN RESTRAINT OR INFLUENCE?
NEGATIVE, STEWART. RINGS UNTAINTED. CURRENTLY SEEKING REPLACEMENTS WITHIN SECTOR BOUNDARY.
SOMEONE HAD ENOUGH POWER TO KILL LANTERNS BUT ONLY TOOK THEIR FINGERS AND LET THEIR RINGS FLY--IT DOESN'T MAKE ANY SENSE.
WE DON'T NEED IT TO MAKE SENSE, VANDOR--ALL WE NEED TO DO IS HUNT WHOEVER COMMITTED THIS ATROCITY AND KILL THEM.
DAMN RIGHT, HANNU. THESE LANTERNS HANGING THERE AREN'T JUST SECTOR NUMBERS--

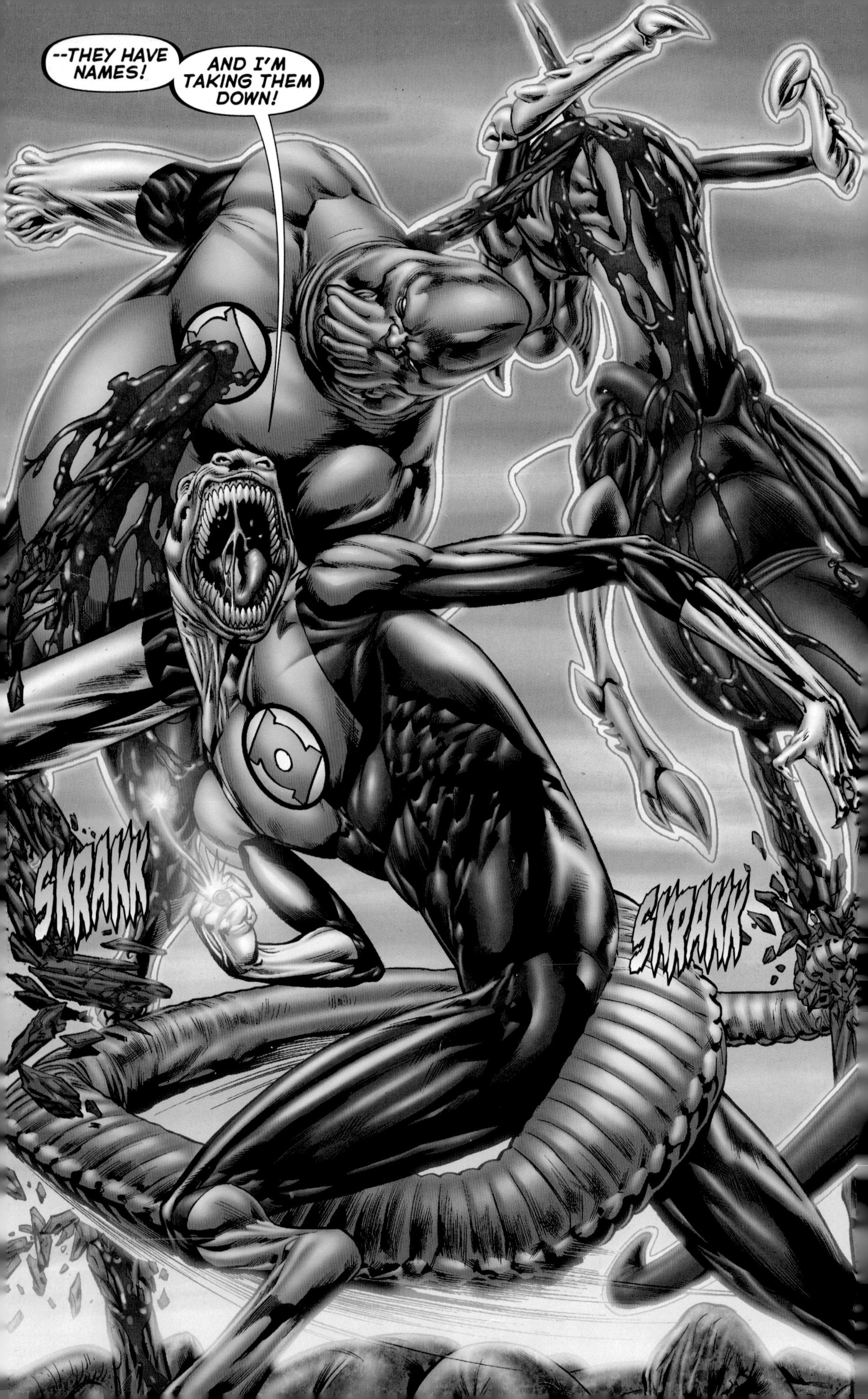
--THEY HAVE NAMES!
AND I'M TAKING THEM DOWN!
SKRAKK
SKRAKK

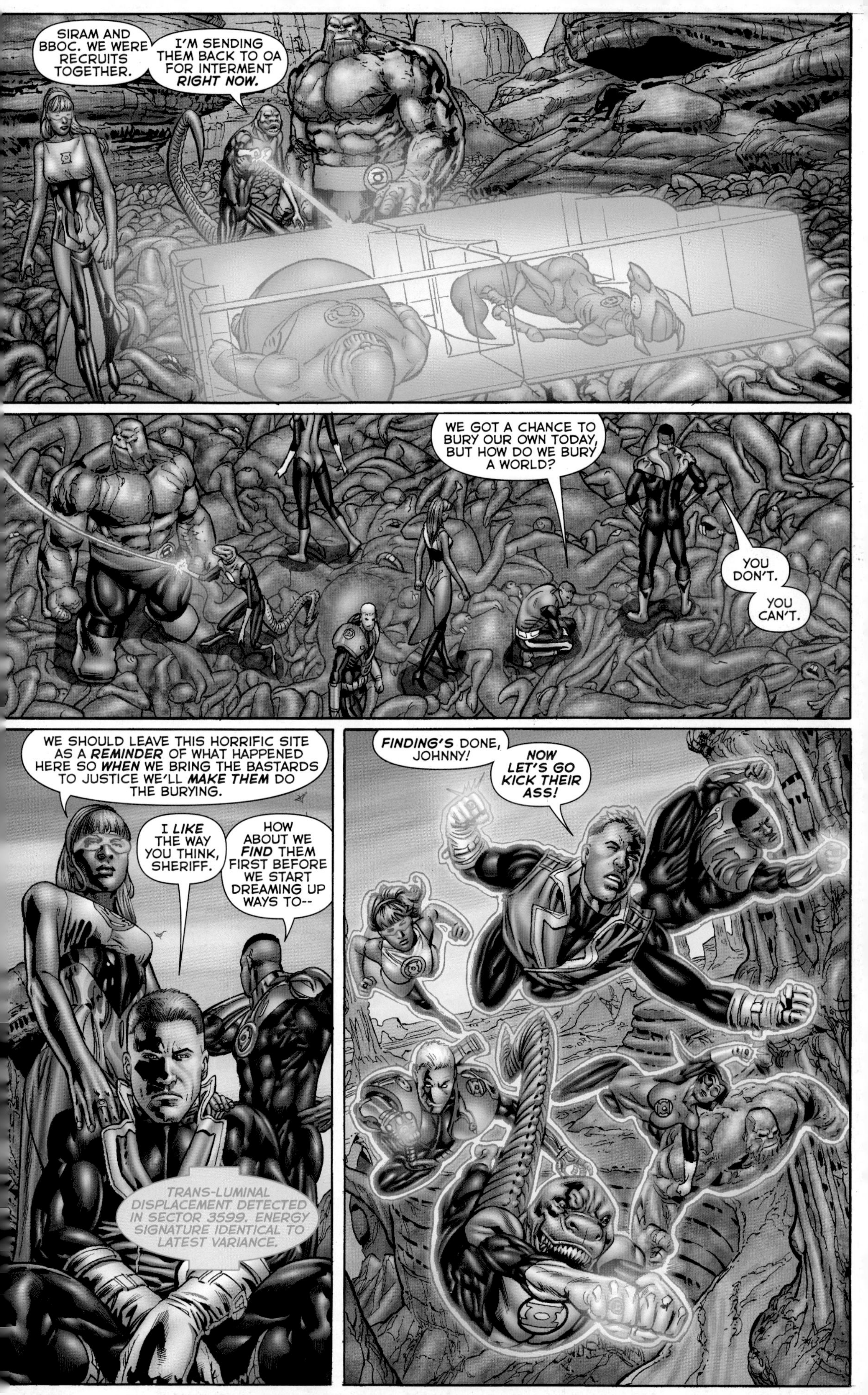
SIRAM AND BBOC. WE WERE RECRUITS TOGETHER.
I'M SENDING THEM BACK TO OA FOR INTERMENT *RIGHT NOW.*
WE GOT A CHANCE TO BURY OUR OWN TODAY, BUT HOW DO WE BURY A WORLD?
YOU DON'T.
YOU CAN'T.
WE SHOULD LEAVE THIS HORRIFIC SITE AS A *REMINDER* OF WHAT HAPPENED HERE SO *WHEN* WE BRING THE BASTARDS TO JUSTICE WE'LL *MAKE THEM* DO THE BURYING.
I *LIKE* THE WAY YOU THINK, SHERIFF.
HOW ABOUT WE *FIND* THEM FIRST BEFORE WE START DREAMING UP WAYS TO--
TRANS-LUMINAL DISPLACEMENT DETECTED IN SECTOR 3599. ENERGY SIGNATURE IDENTICAL TO LATEST VARIANCE.
FINDING'S DONE, JOHNNY!
NOW LET'S GO KICK THEIR ASS!

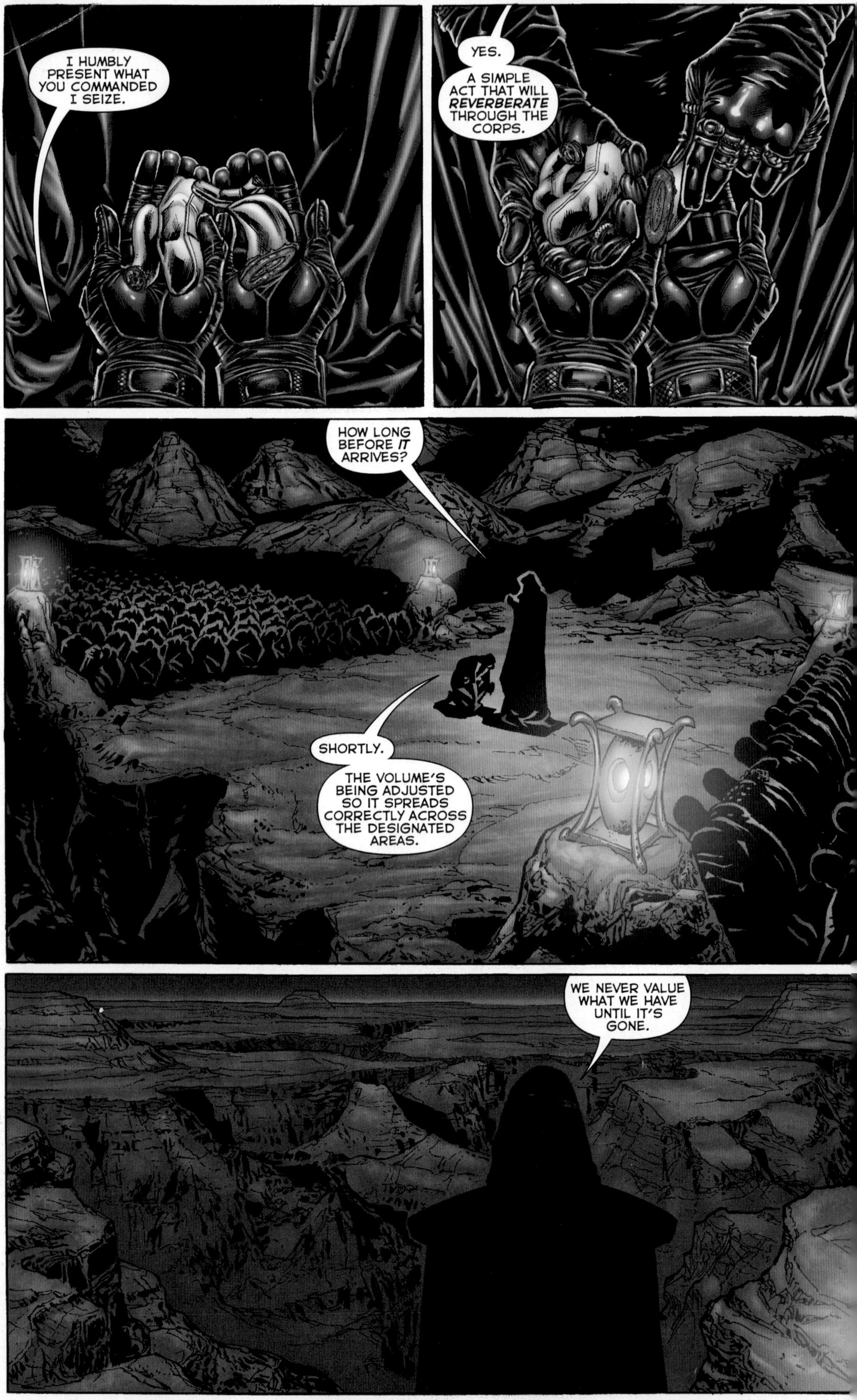
I HUMBLY PRESENT WHAT YOU COMMANDED I SEIZE.
YES.
A SIMPLE ACT THAT WILL *REVERBERATE* THROUGH THE CORPS.
HOW LONG BEFORE *IT* ARRIVES?
SHORTLY.
THE VOLUME'S BEING ADJUSTED SO IT SPREADS CORRECTLY ACROSS THE DESIGNATED AREAS.
WE NEVER VALUE WHAT WE HAVE UNTIL IT'S GONE.

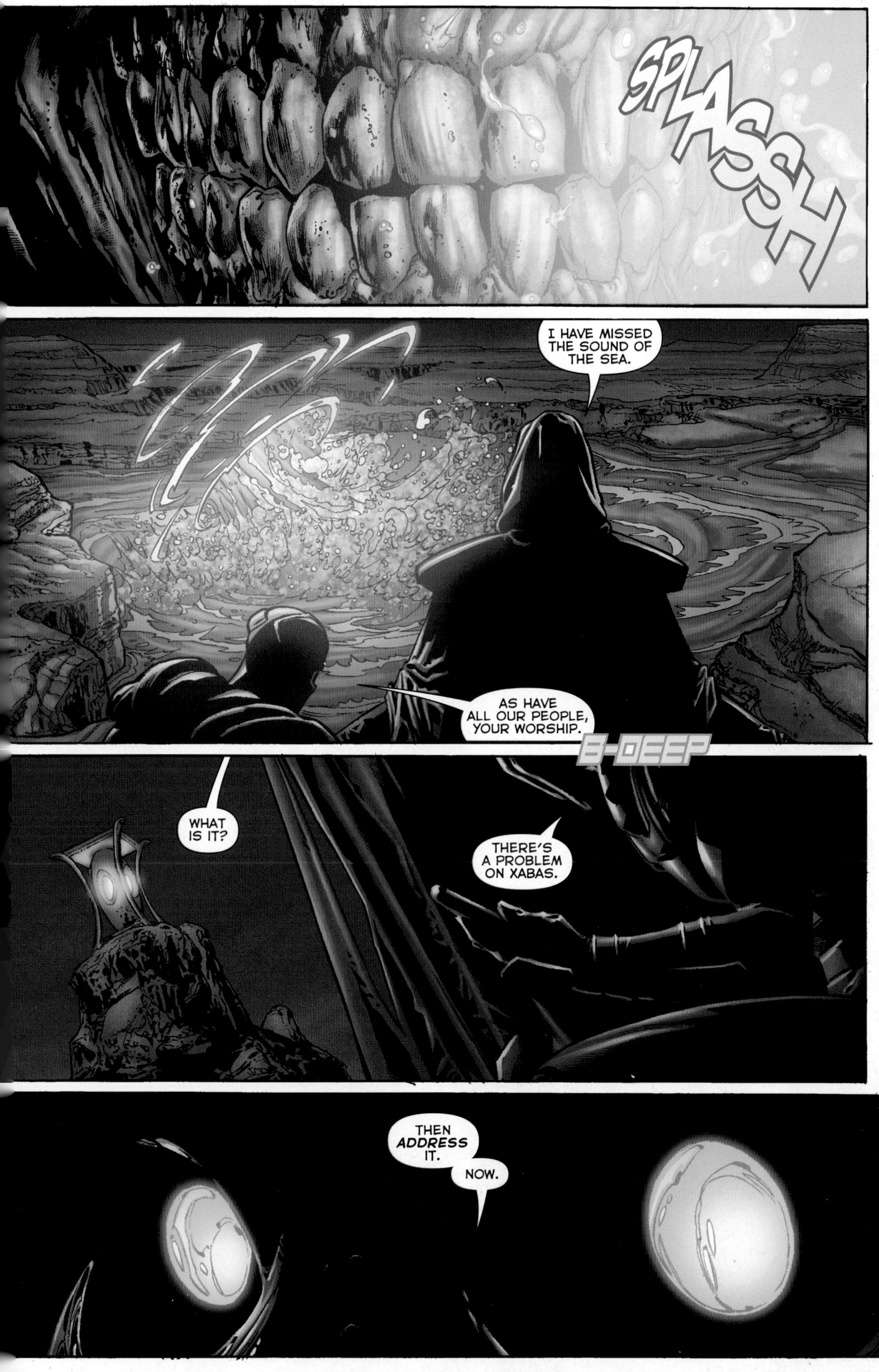
SPLASSH
I HAVE MISSED THE SOUND OF THE SEA.
AS HAVE ALL OUR PEOPLE, YOUR WORSHIP.
B-DEEP
WHAT IS IT?
THERE'S A PROBLEM ON XABAS.
THEN ADDRESS IT.
NOW.

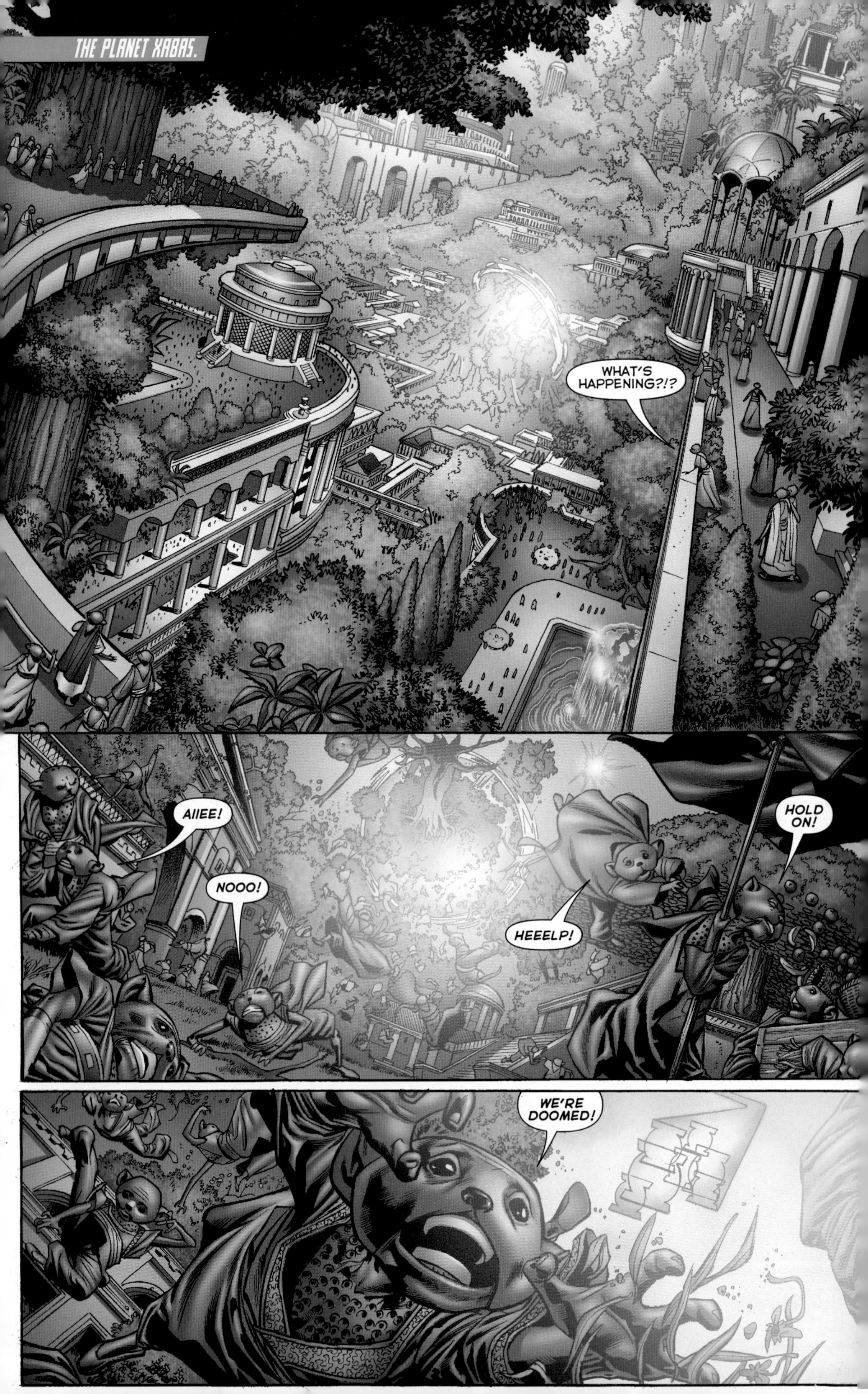
THE PLANET XABAS.
WHAT'S HAPPENING?!?
AIIEE!
NOOO!
HEEELP!
HOLD ON!
WE'RE DOOMED!

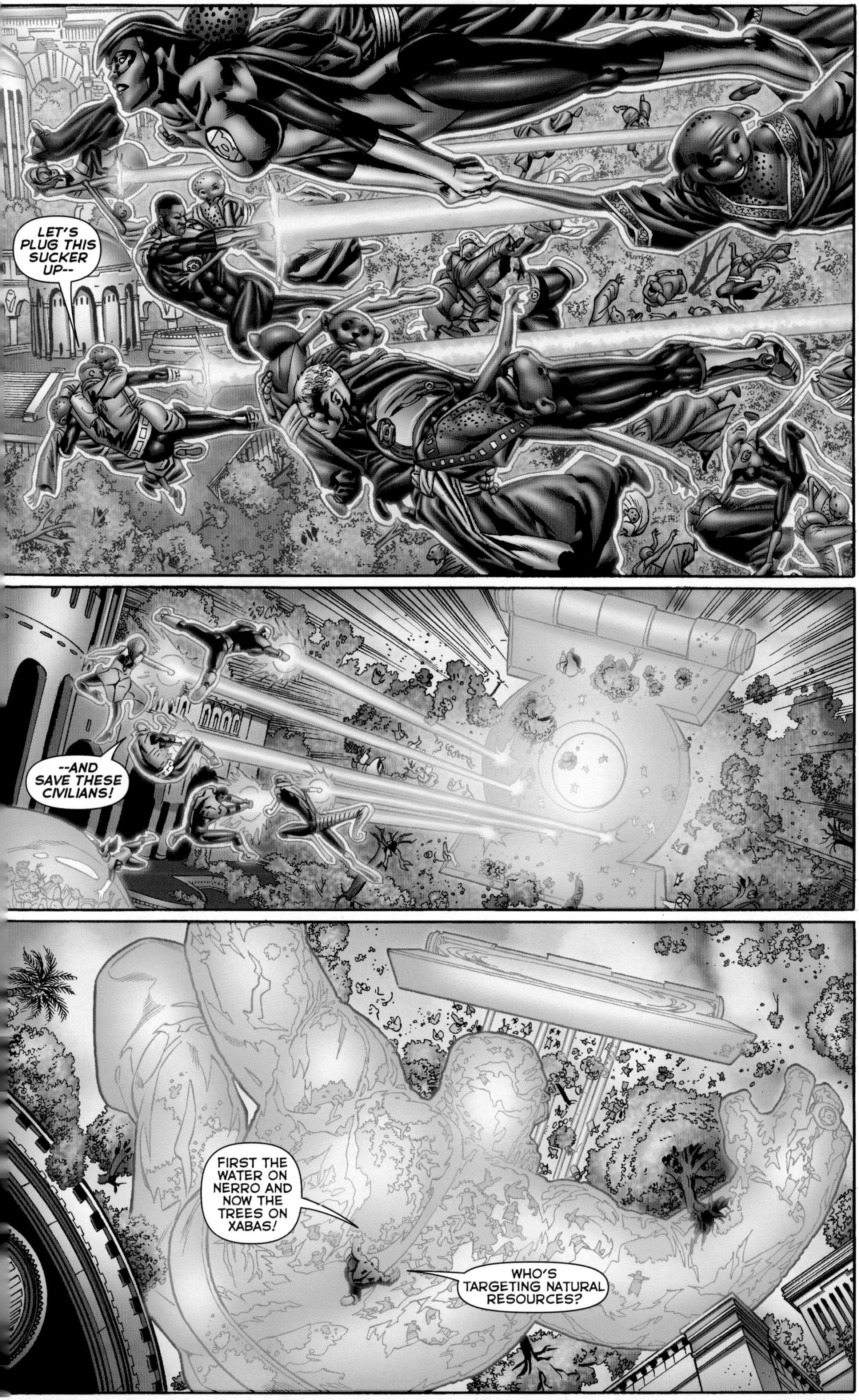
LET'S PLUG THIS SUCKER UP--
--AND SAVE THESE CIVILIANS!
FIRST THE WATER ON NERRO AND NOW THE TREES ON XABAS!
WHO'S TARGETING NATURAL RESOURCES?

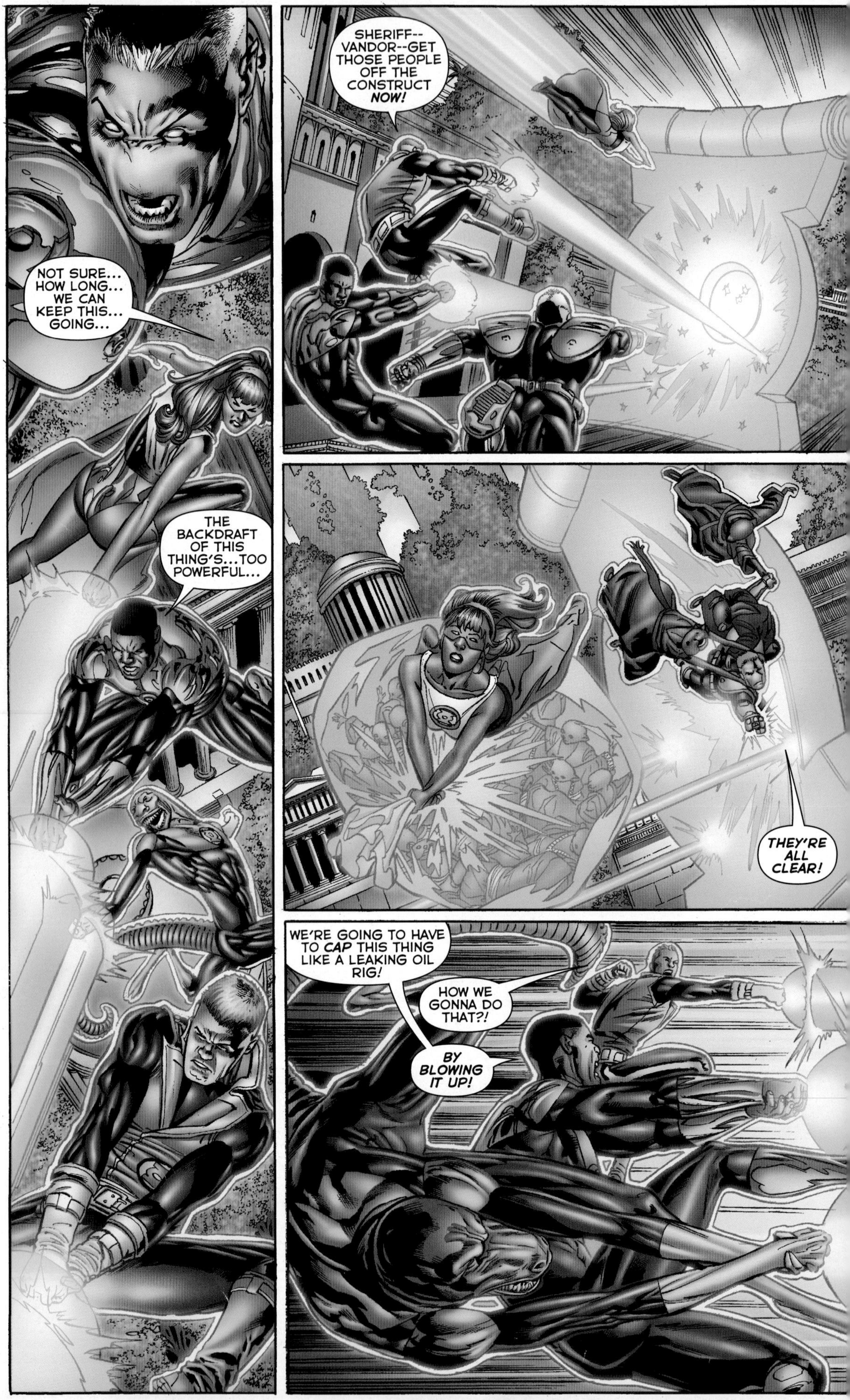
SHERIFF--VANDOR--GET THOSE PEOPLE OFF THE CONSTRUCT NOW!
NOT SURE... HOW LONG... WE CAN KEEP THIS... GOING...
THE BACKDRAFT OF THIS THING'S...TOO POWERFUL...
THEY'RE ALL CLEAR!
WE'RE GOING TO HAVE TO CAP THIS THING LIKE A LEAKING OIL RIG!
HOW WE GONNA DO THAT?!
BY BLOWING IT UP!

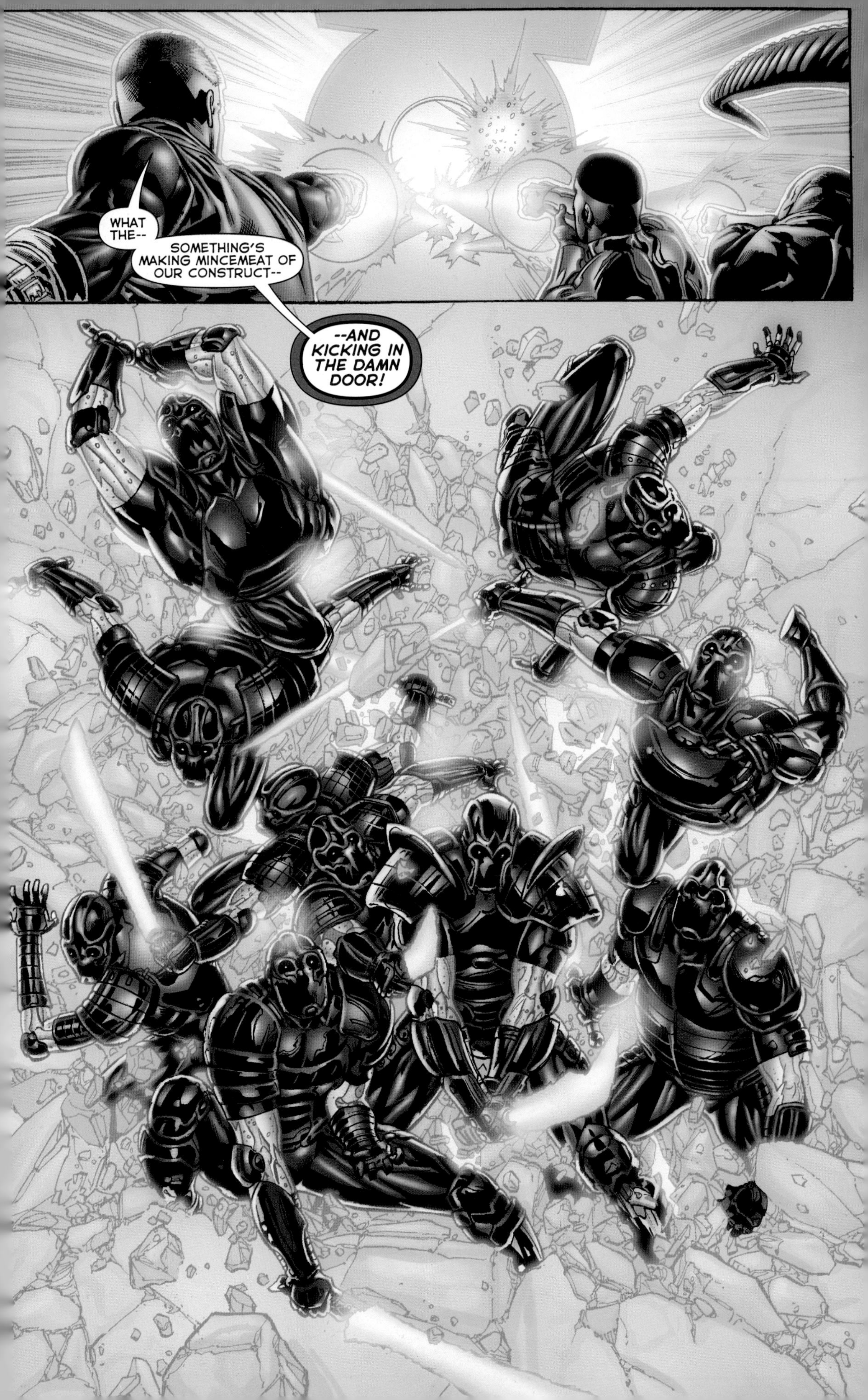
WHAT THE--
SOMETHING'S MAKING MINCEMEAT OF OUR CONSTRUCT--
--AND KICKING IN THE DAMN DOOR!

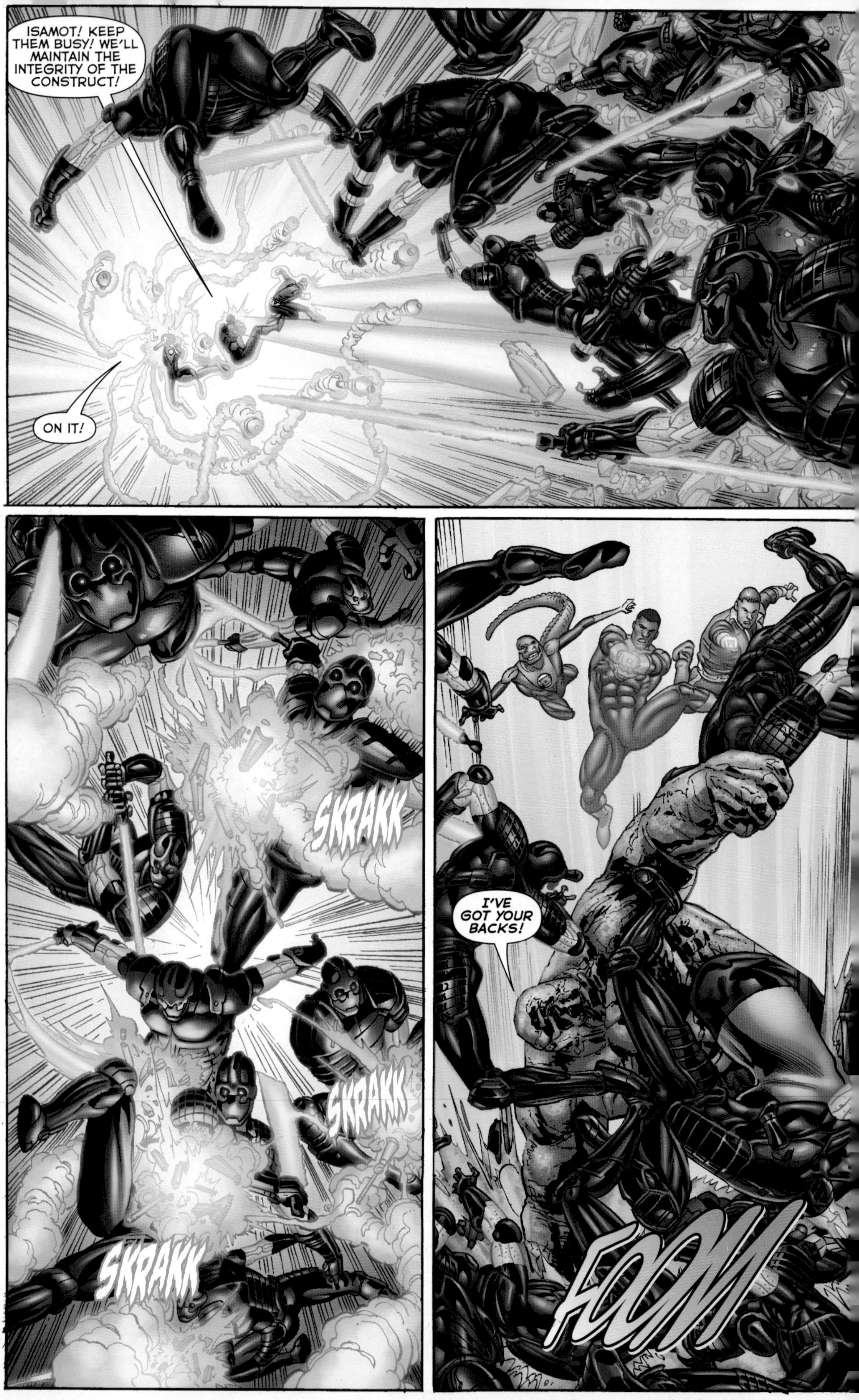
ISAMOT! KEEP THEM BUSY! WE'LL MAINTAIN THE INTEGRITY OF THE CONSTRUCT!
ON IT!
SKRAKK
SKRAKK
SKRAKK
I'VE GOT YOUR BACKS!
FOOM

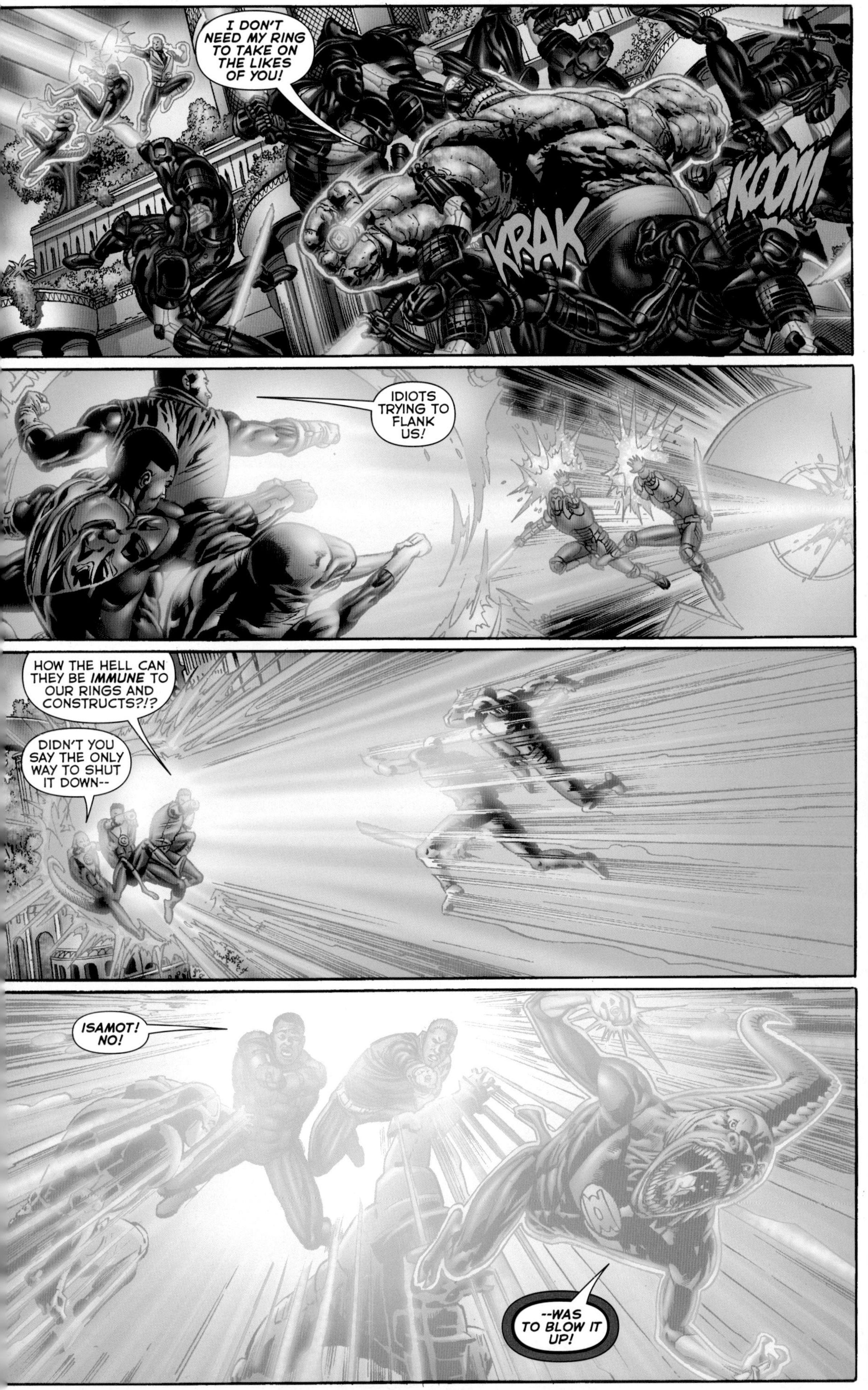

I DON'T NEED MY RING TO TAKE ON THE LIKES OF YOU!
KRAK
KOOM
IDIOTS TRYING TO FLANK US!
HOW THE HELL CAN THEY BE *IMMUNE* TO OUR RINGS AND CONSTRUCTS?!?
DIDN'T YOU SAY THE ONLY WAY TO SHUT IT DOWN--
ISAMOT! NO!
--WAS TO BLOW IT UP!

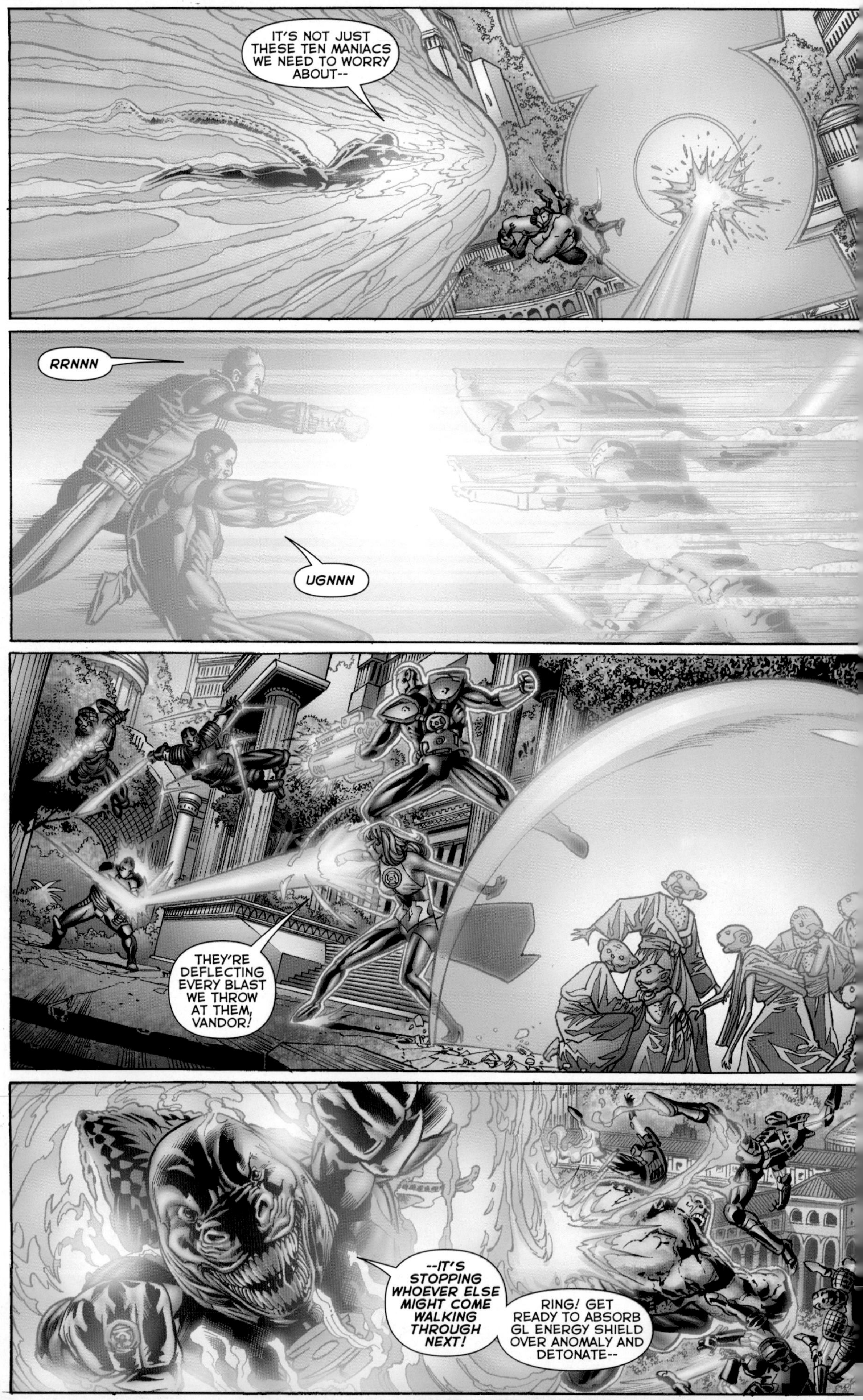
IT'S NOT JUST THESE TEN MANIACS WE NEED TO WORRY ABOUT--
RRNNN
UGNNN
THEY'RE DEFLECTING EVERY BLAST WE THROW AT THEM, VANDOR!
--IT'S STOPPING WHOEVER ELSE MIGHT COME WALKING THROUGH NEXT!
RING! GET READY TO ABSORB GL ENERGY SHIELD OVER ANOMALY AND DETONATE--

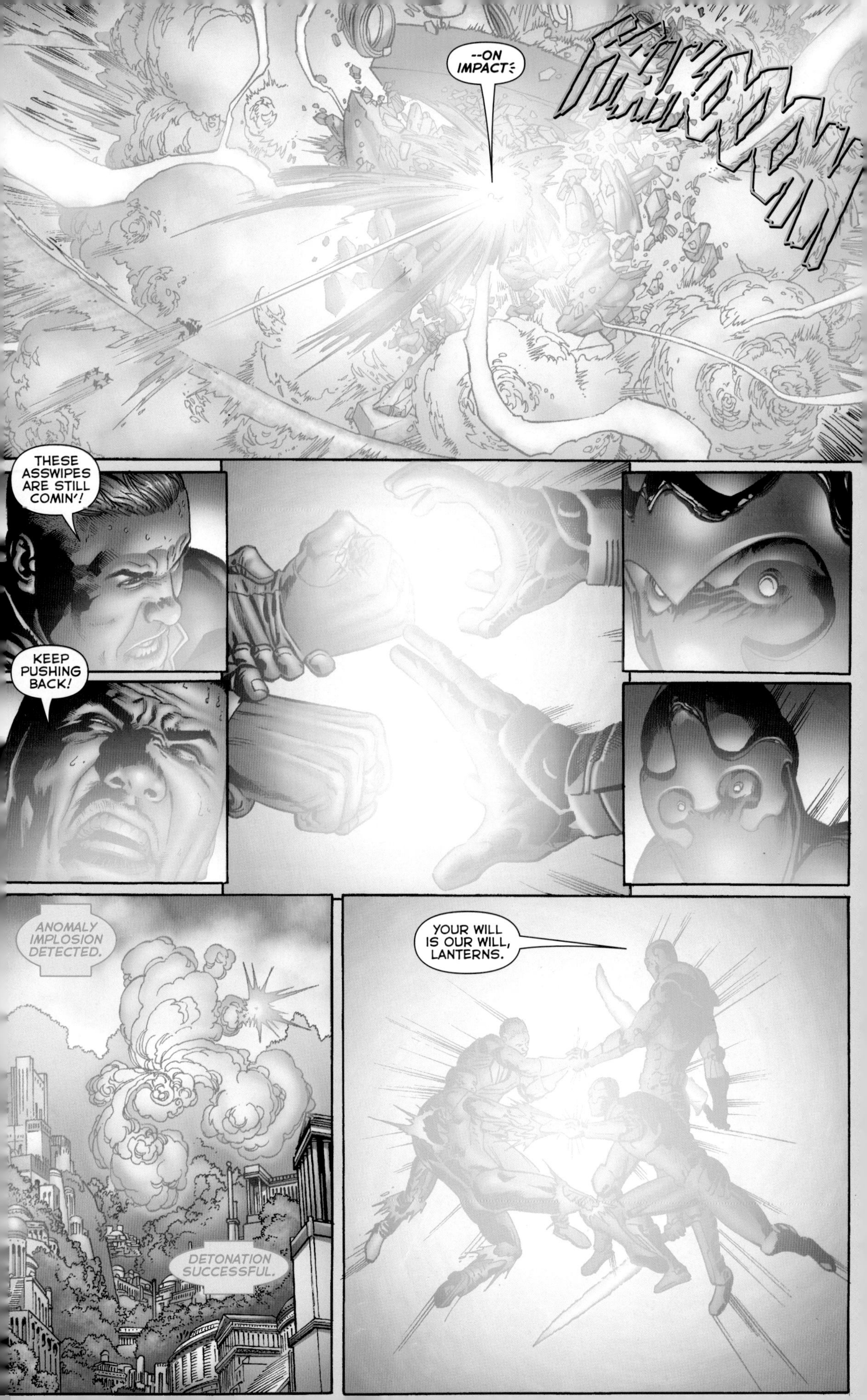
--ON IMPACT--
FRAKOOOM
THESE ASSWIPES ARE STILL COMIN'!
KEEP PUSHING BACK!
ANOMALY IMPLOSION DETECTED.
DETONATION SUCCESSFUL.
YOUR WILL IS OUR WILL, LANTERNS.

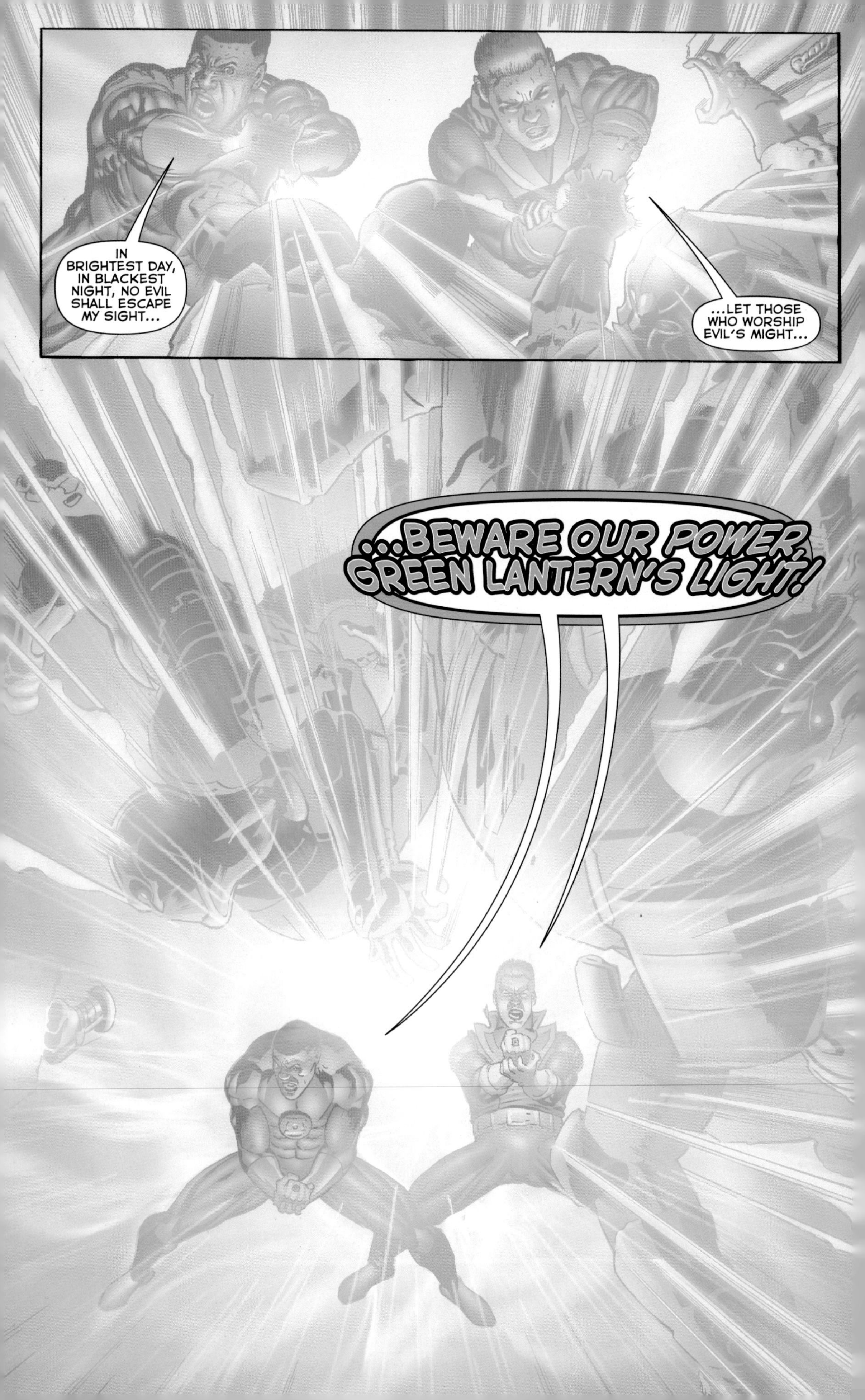
IN BRIGHTEST DAY, IN BLACKEST NIGHT, NO EVIL SHALL ESCAPE MY SIGHT...
...LET THOSE WHO WORSHIP EVIL'S MIGHT...
...BEWARE OUR POWER, GREEN LANTERN'S LIGHT!

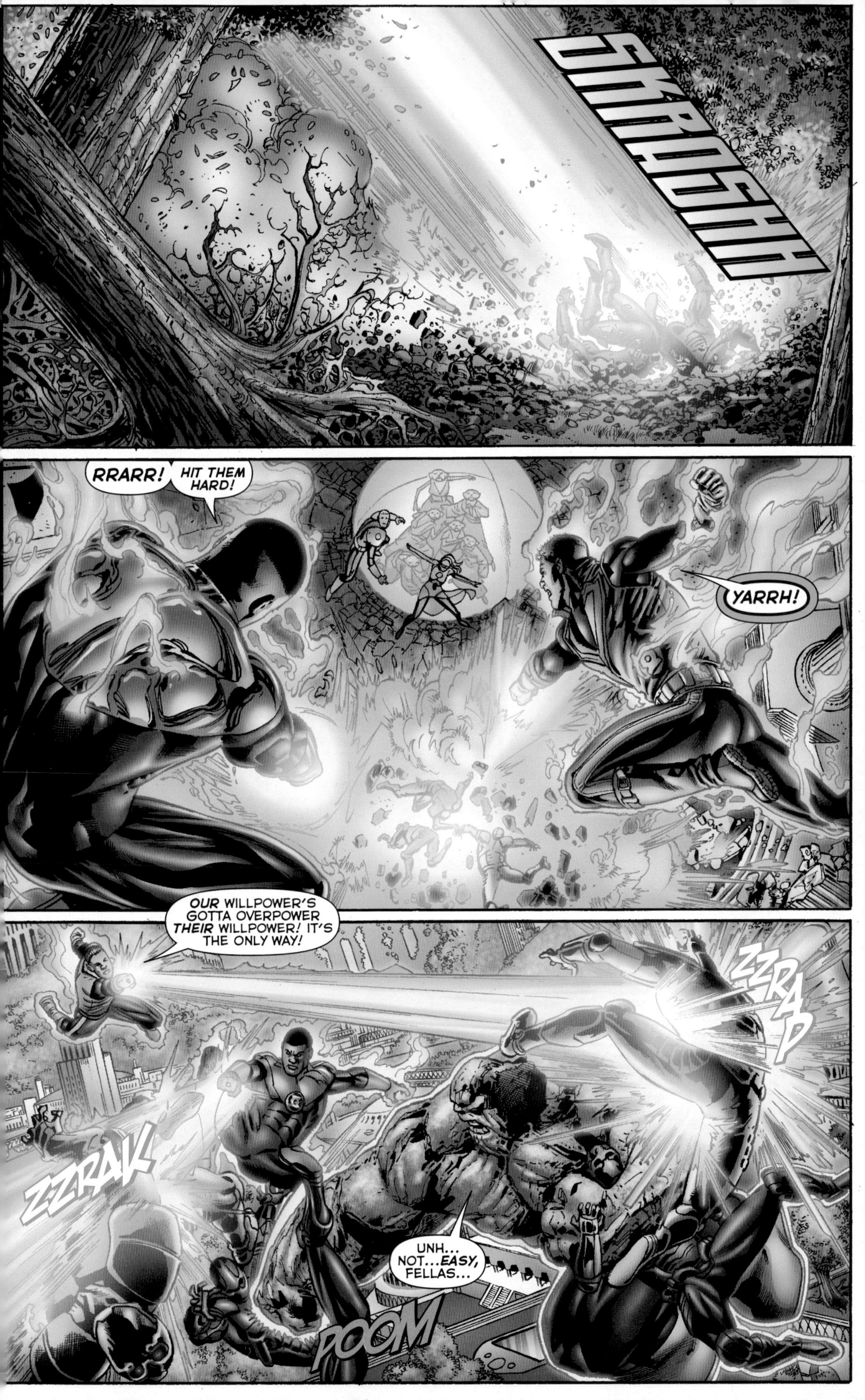
SKRASHH
RRARR!
HIT THEM HARD!
YARRH!
OUR WILLPOWER'S GOTTA OVERPOWER THEIR WILLPOWER! IT'S THE ONLY WAY!
ZZRAP
ZZRAK
UNH... NOT...EASY, FELLAS...
POOM

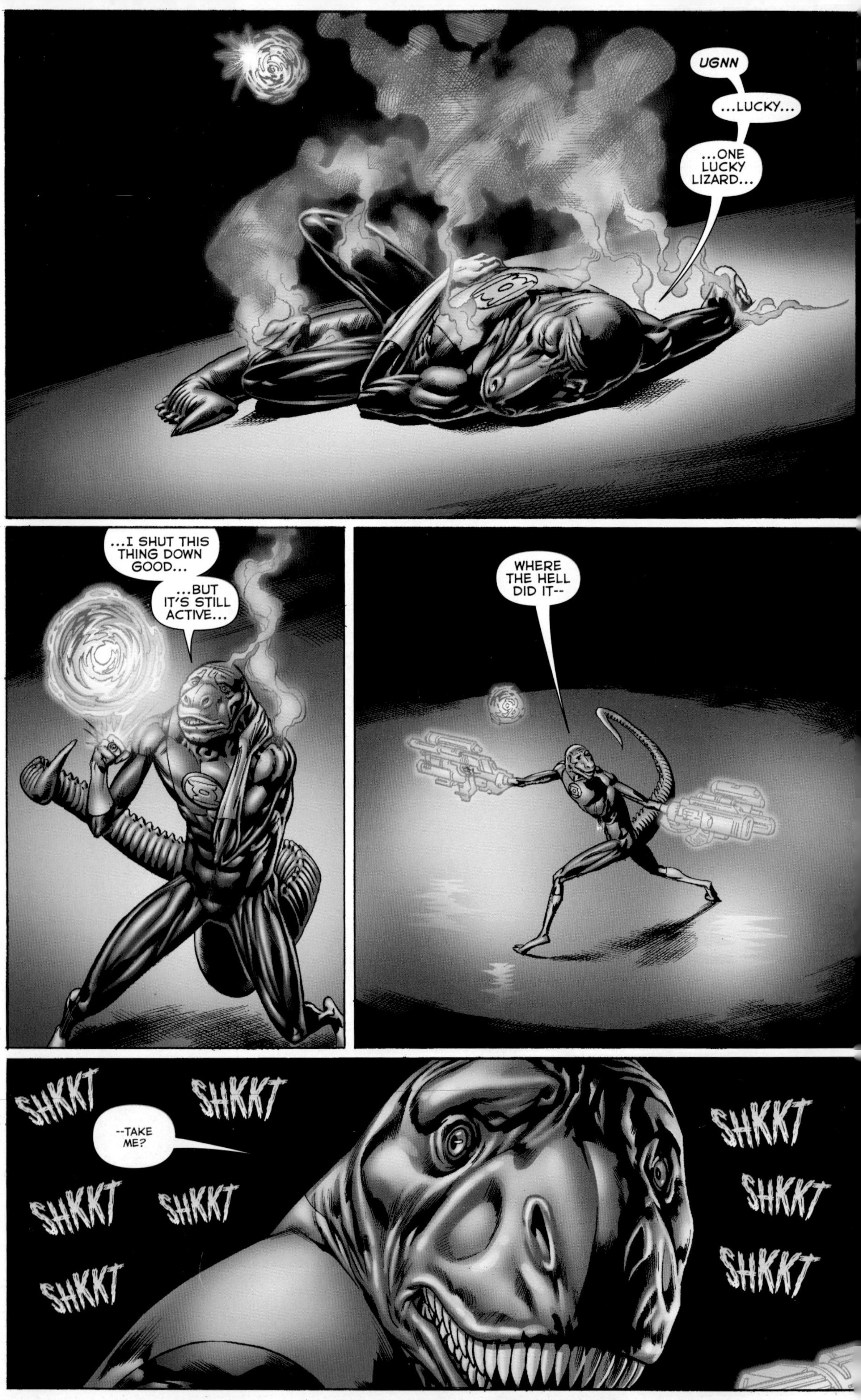
UGNN
...LUCKY...
...ONE LUCKY LIZARD...
...I SHUT THIS THING DOWN GOOD...
...BUT IT'S STILL ACTIVE...
WHERE THE HELL DID IT--
SHKKT
SHKKT
--TAKE ME?
SHKKT
SHKKT
SHKKT
SHKKT
SHKKT
SHKKT

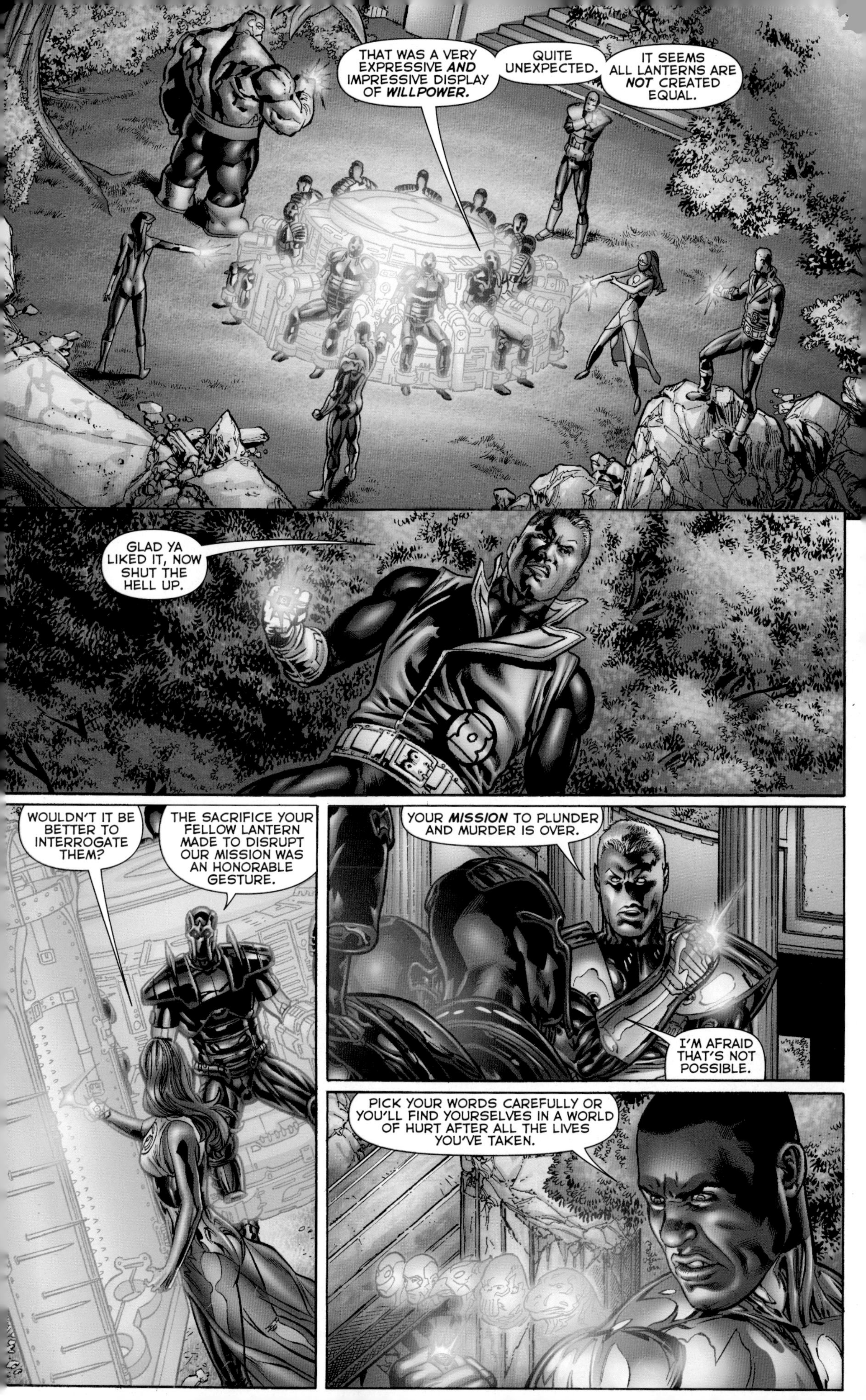

THAT WAS A VERY EXPRESSIVE AND IMPRESSIVE DISPLAY OF WILLPOWER.
QUITE UNEXPECTED.
IT SEEMS ALL LANTERNS ARE NOT CREATED EQUAL.
GLAD YA LIKED IT, NOW SHUT THE HELL UP.
WOULDN'T IT BE BETTER TO INTERROGATE THEM?
THE SACRIFICE YOUR FELLOW LANTERN MADE TO DISRUPT OUR MISSION WAS AN HONORABLE GESTURE.
YOUR MISSION TO PLUNDER AND MURDER IS OVER.
I'M AFRAID THAT'S NOT POSSIBLE.
PICK YOUR WORDS CAREFULLY OR YOU'LL FIND YOURSELVES IN A WORLD OF HURT AFTER ALL THE LIVES YOU'VE TAKEN.

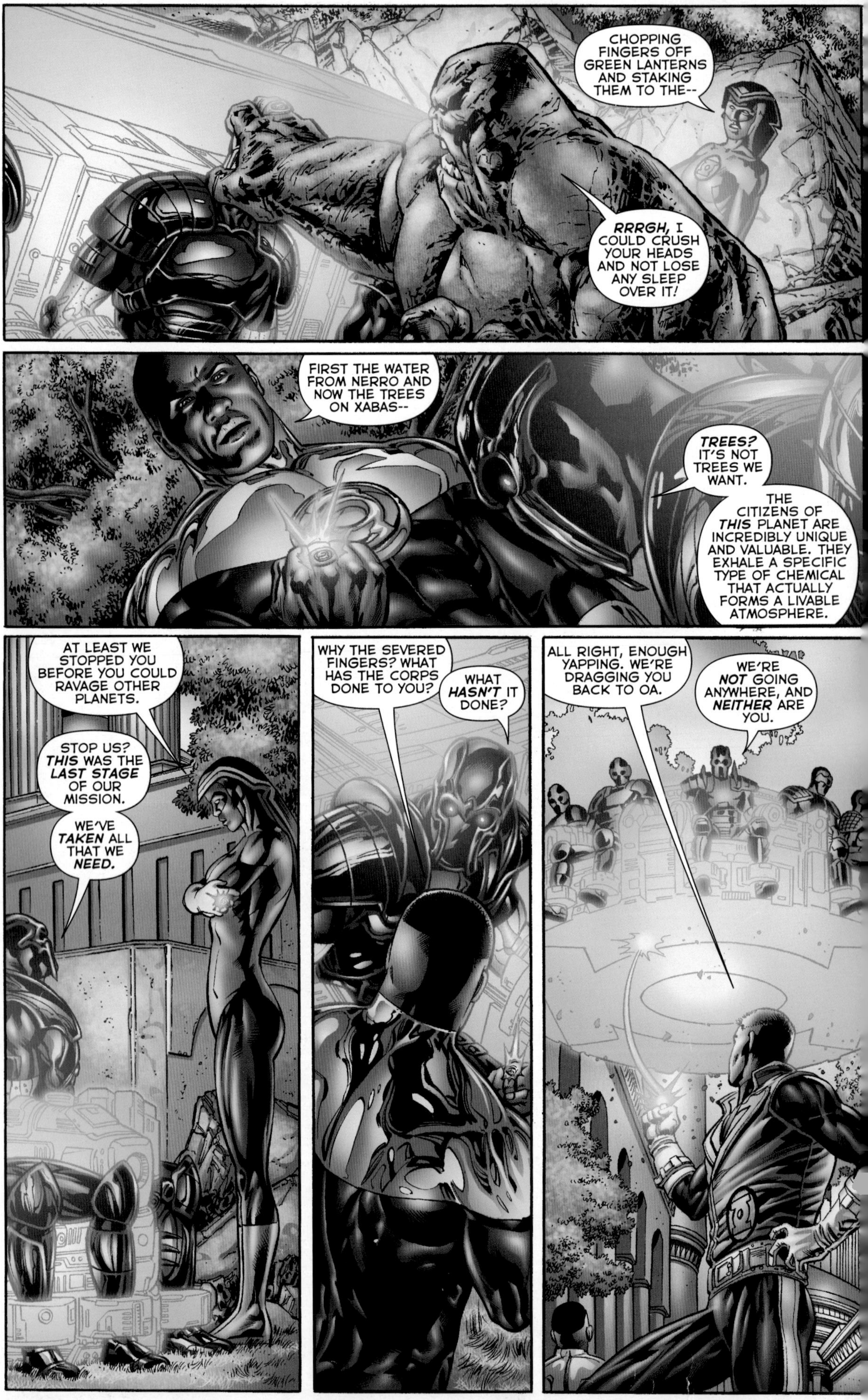
CHOPPING FINGERS OFF GREEN LANTERNS AND STAKING THEM TO THE--
RRRGH, I COULD CRUSH YOUR HEADS AND NOT LOSE ANY SLEEP OVER IT!
FIRST THE WATER FROM NERRO AND NOW THE TREES ON XABAS--
TREES? IT'S NOT TREES WE WANT.
THE CITIZENS OF THIS PLANET ARE INCREDIBLY UNIQUE AND VALUABLE. THEY EXHALE A SPECIFIC TYPE OF CHEMICAL THAT ACTUALLY FORMS A LIVABLE ATMOSPHERE.
AT LEAST WE STOPPED YOU BEFORE YOU COULD RAVAGE OTHER PLANETS.
STOP US? THIS WAS THE LAST STAGE OF OUR MISSION.
WE'VE TAKEN ALL THAT WE NEED.
WHY THE SEVERED FINGERS? WHAT HAS THE CORPS DONE TO YOU?
WHAT HASN'T IT DONE?
ALL RIGHT, ENOUGH YAPPING. WE'RE DRAGGING YOU BACK TO OA.
WE'RE NOT GOING ANYWHERE, AND NEITHER ARE YOU.

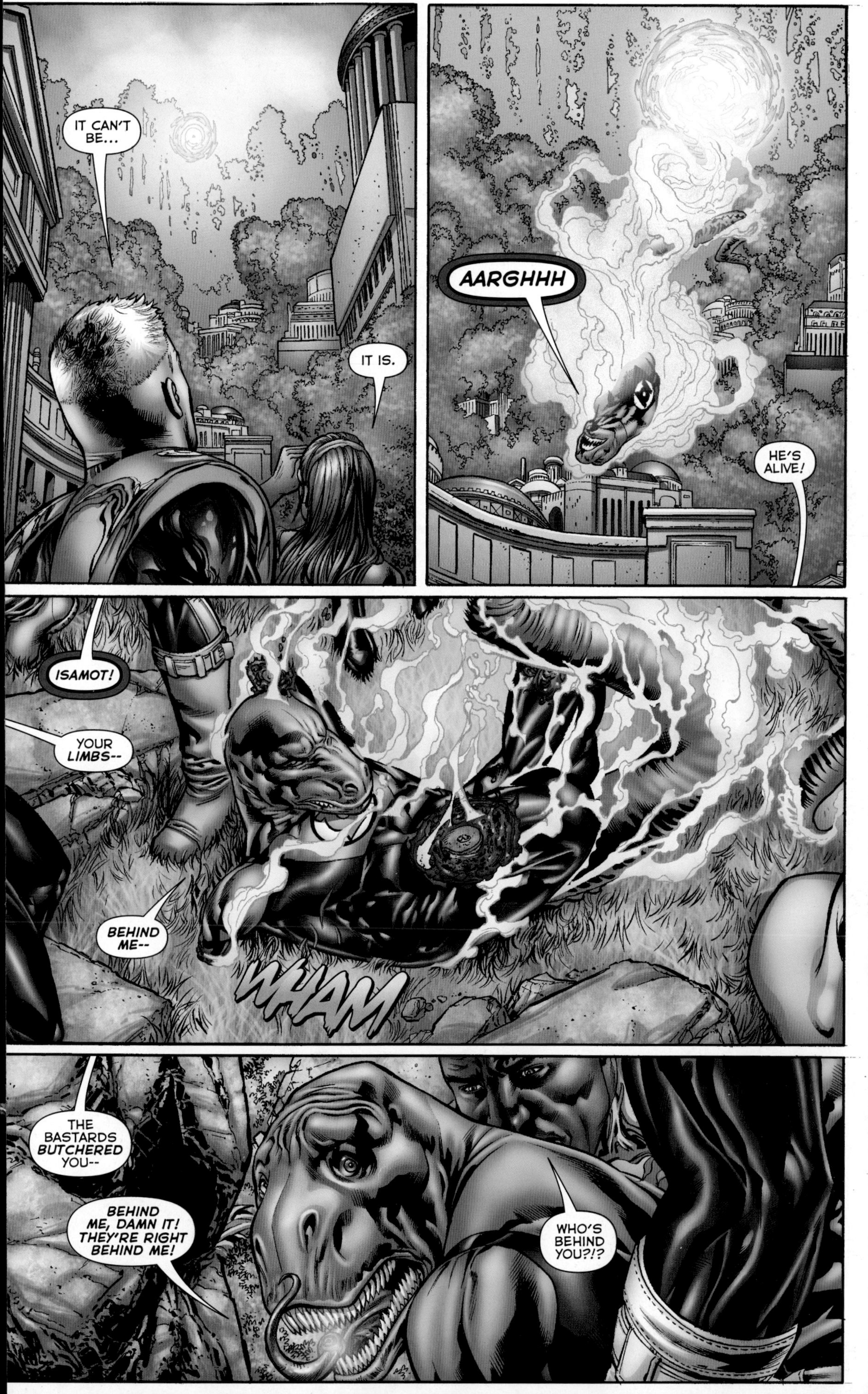
IT CAN'T BE...
IT IS.
AARGHHH
HE'S ALIVE!
ISAMOT!
YOUR LIMBS--
BEHIND ME--
WHAM
THE BASTARDS BUTCHERED YOU--
BEHIND ME, DAMN IT! THEY'RE RIGHT BEHIND ME!
WHO'S BEHIND YOU?!?

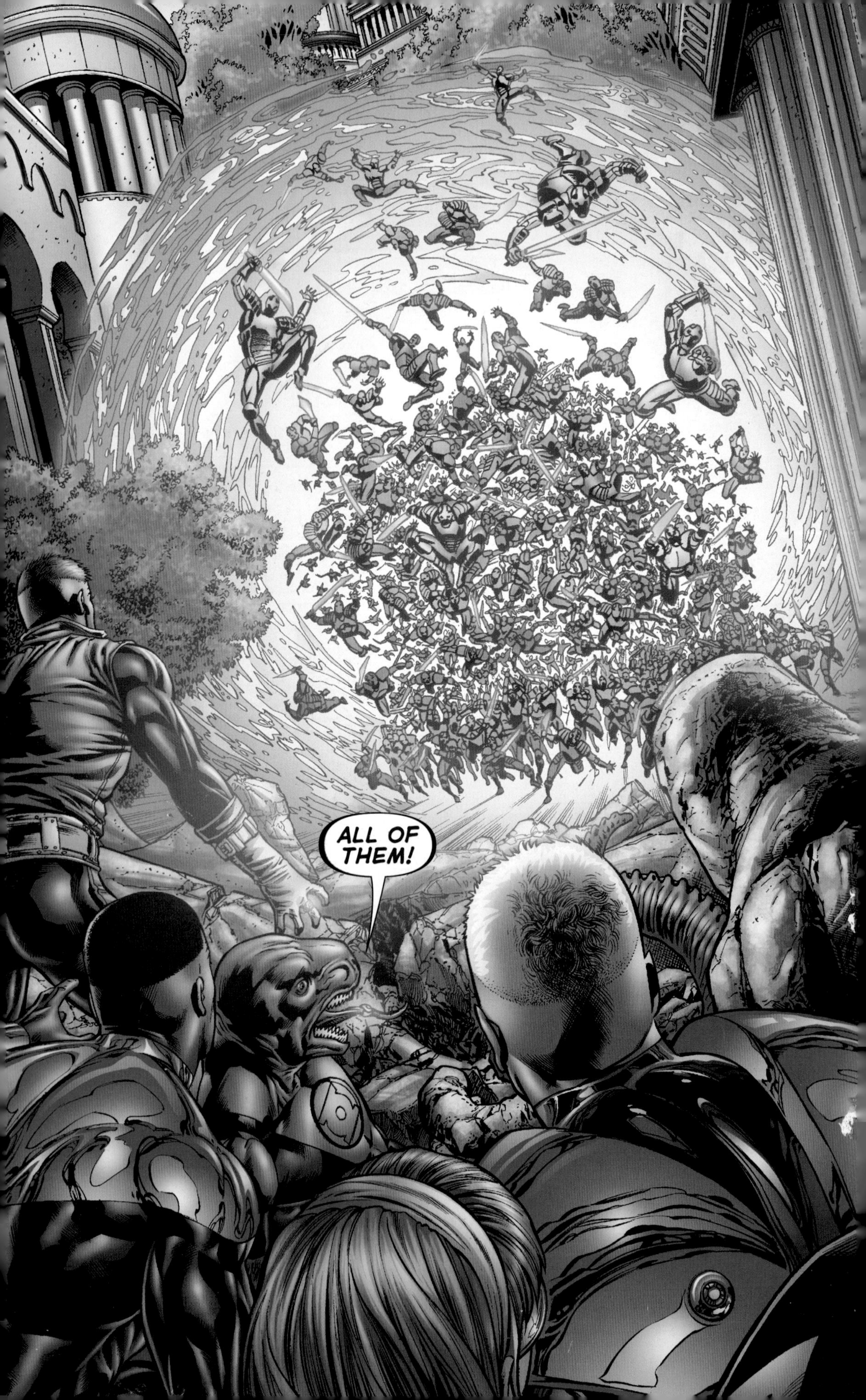
ALL OF THEM!

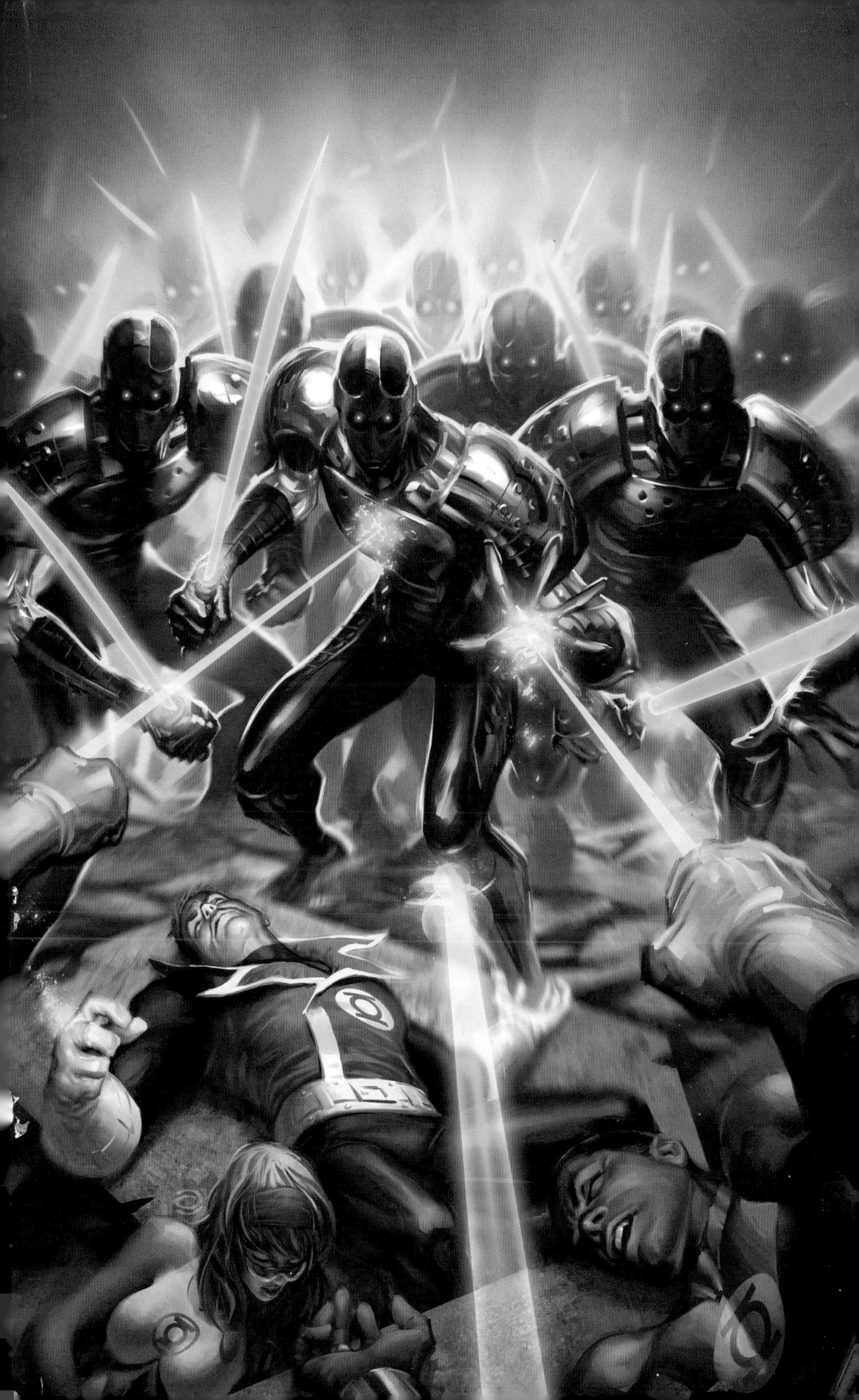

FORCE OF WILL

PETER J. TOMASI writer **GERALDO BORGES** penciller **SCOTT HANNA** inker cover by **ALEX GARNER**

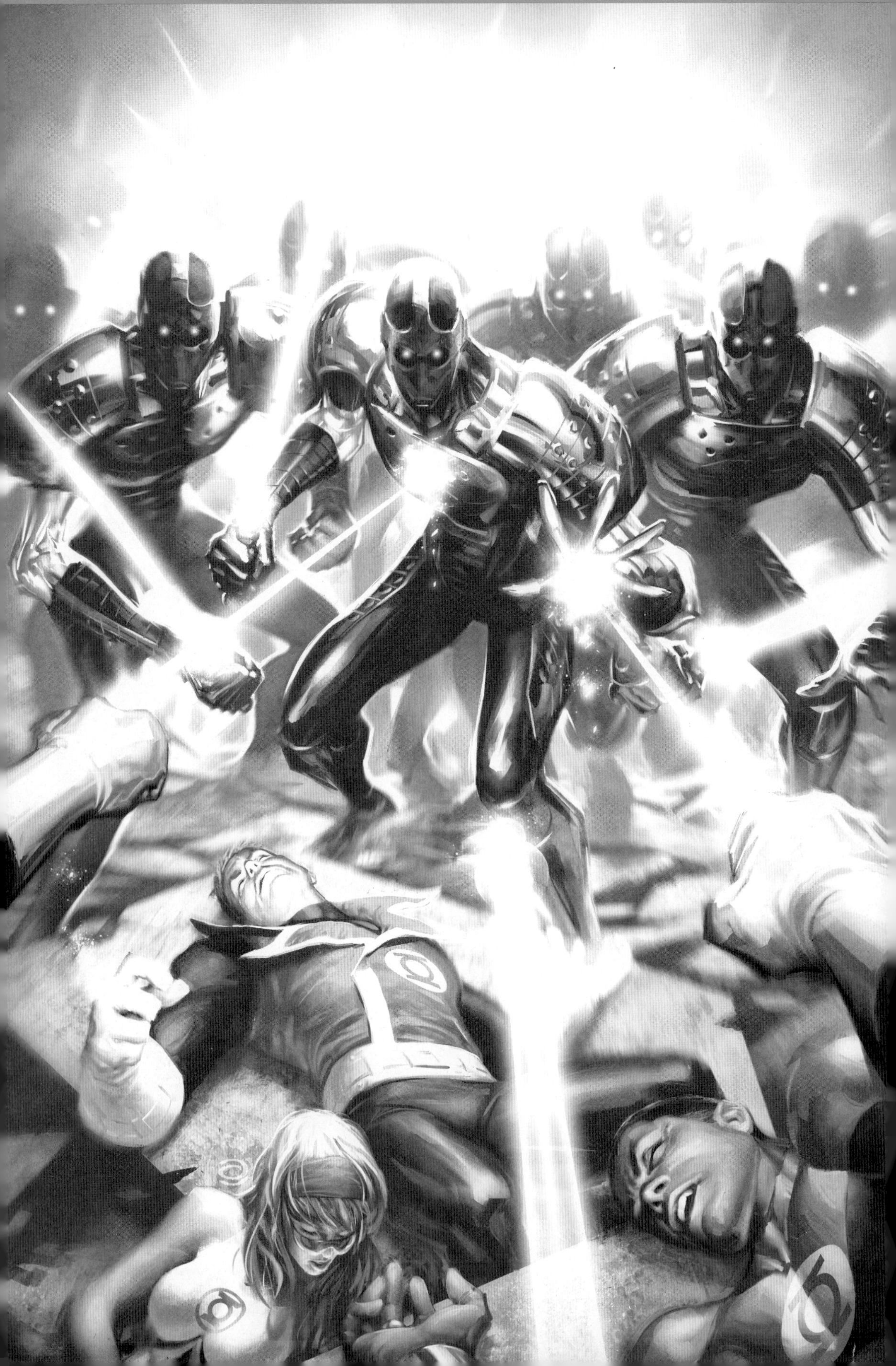

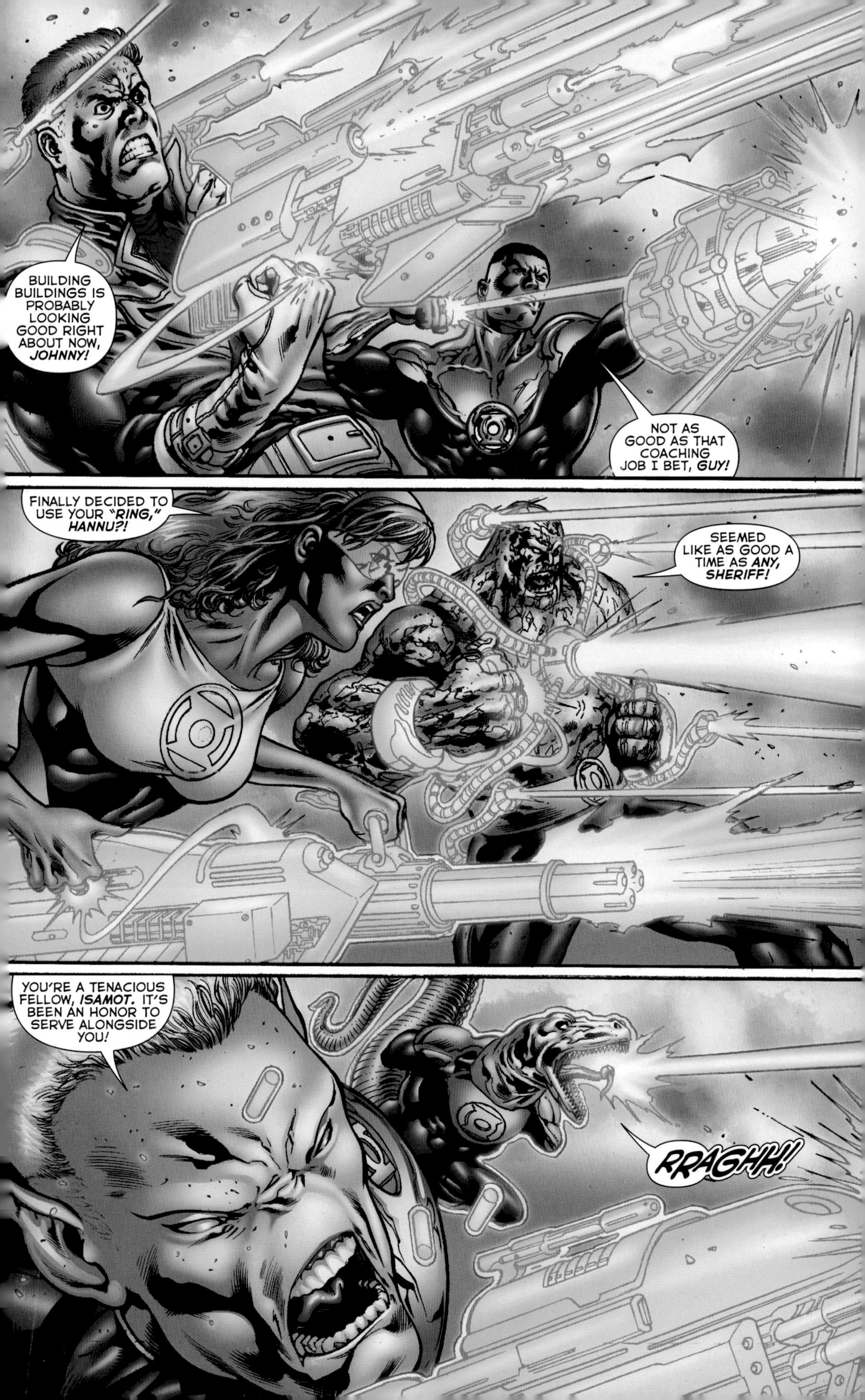
BUILDING BUILDINGS IS PROBABLY LOOKING GOOD RIGHT ABOUT NOW, JOHNNY!
NOT AS GOOD AS THAT COACHING JOB I BET, GUY!
FINALLY DECIDED TO USE YOUR "RING," HANNU?!
SEEMED LIKE AS GOOD A TIME AS ANY, SHERIFF!
YOU'RE A TENACIOUS FELLOW, ISAMOT. IT'S BEEN AN HONOR TO SERVE ALONGSIDE YOU!
RRAGHH!

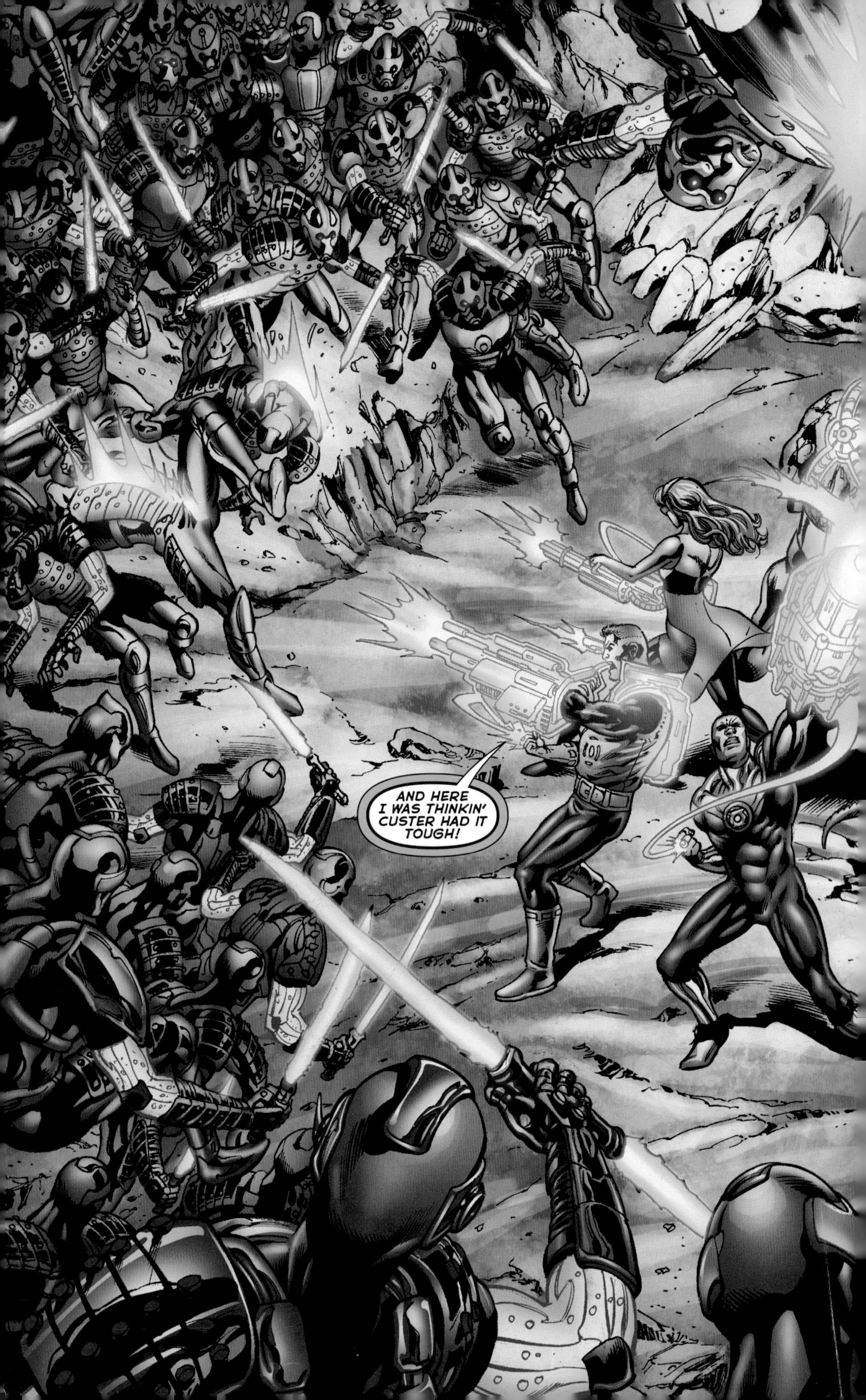
AND HERE I WAS THINKIN' CUSTER HAD IT TOUGH!

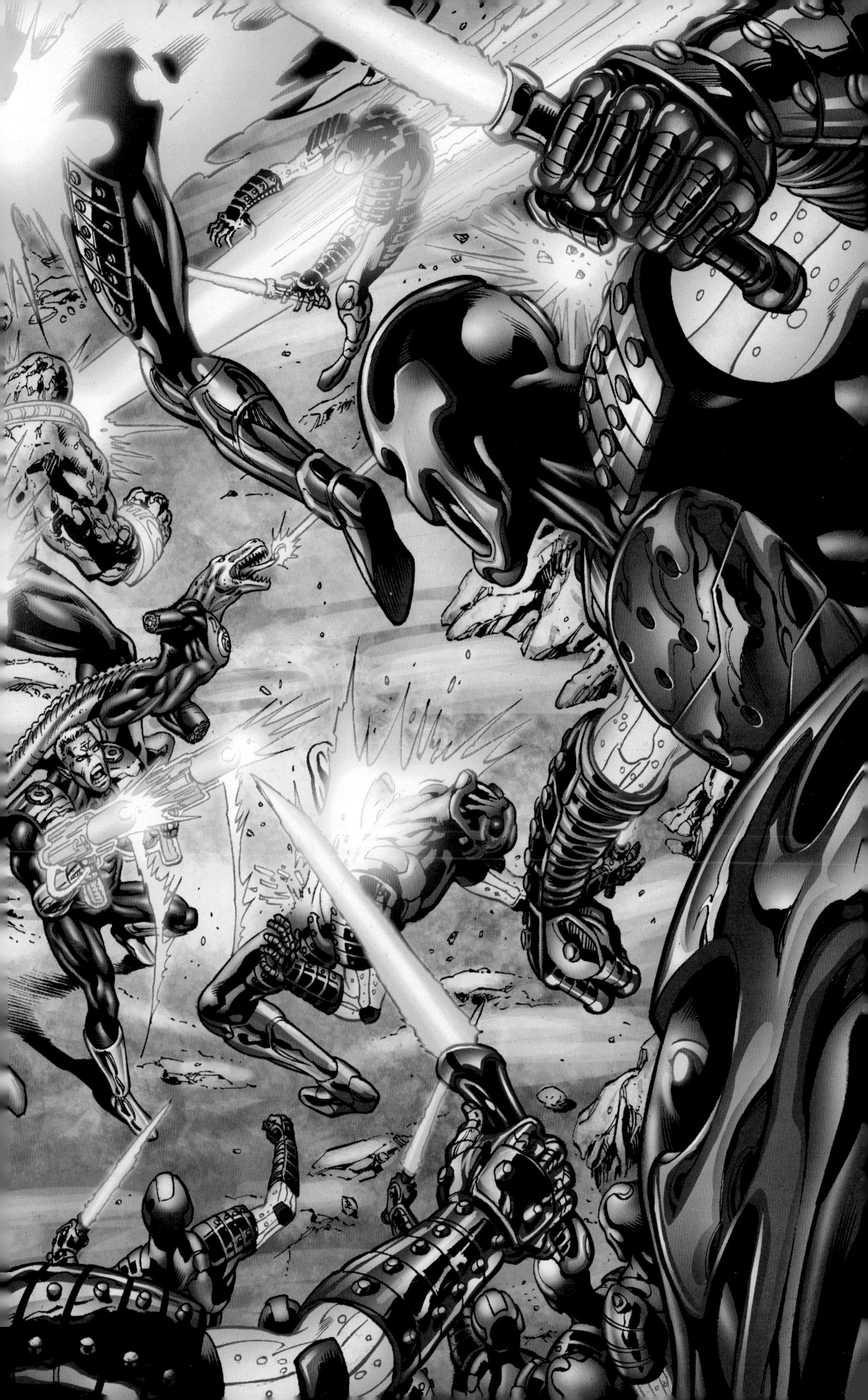

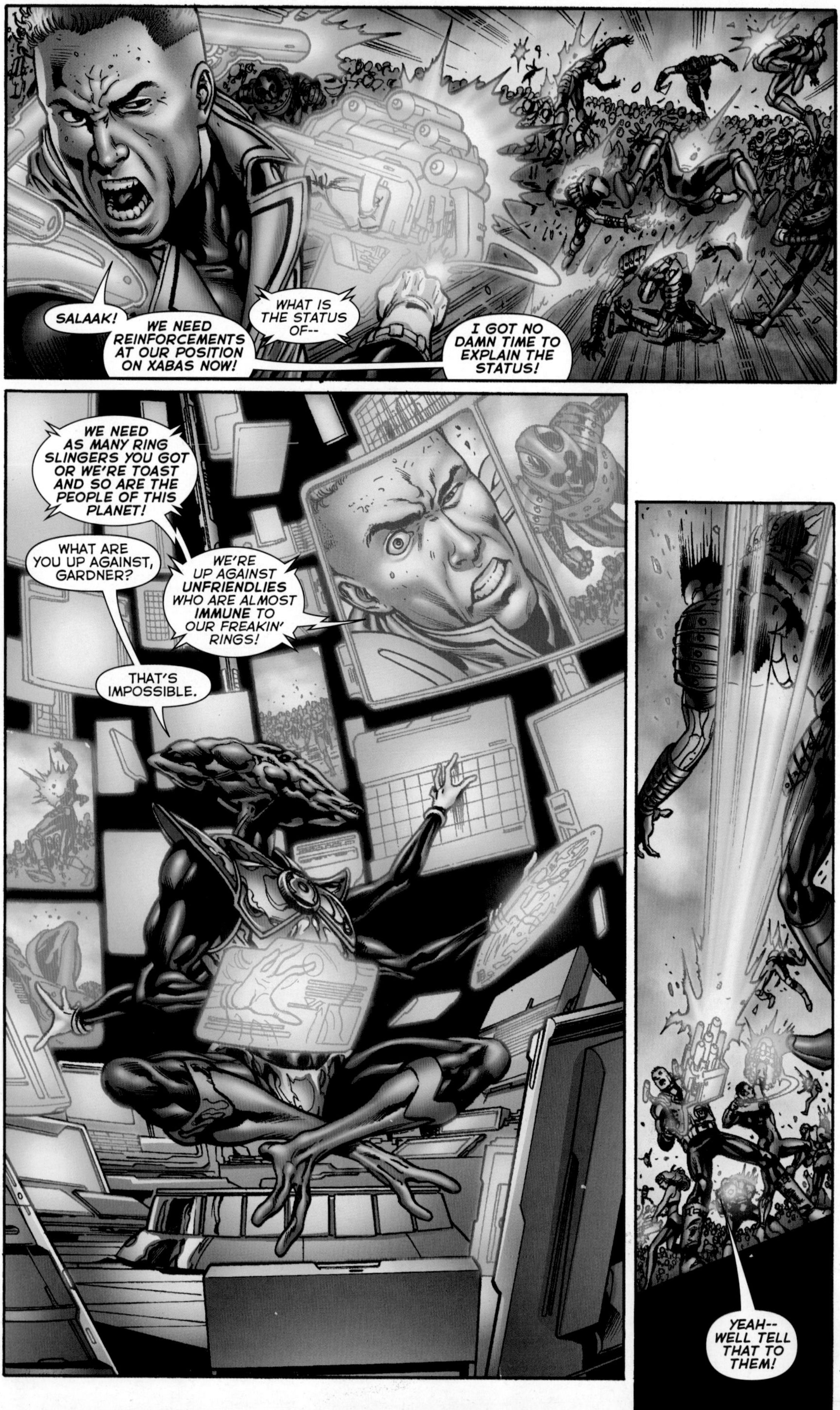
SALAAK!
WE NEED REINFORCEMENTS AT OUR POSITION ON XABAS NOW!
WHAT IS THE STATUS OF--
I GOT NO DAMN TIME TO EXPLAIN THE STATUS!
WE NEED AS MANY RING SLINGERS YOU GOT OR WE'RE TOAST AND SO ARE THE PEOPLE OF THIS PLANET!
WHAT ARE YOU UP AGAINST, GARDNER?
WE'RE UP AGAINST UNFRIENDLIES WHO ARE ALMOST IMMUNE TO OUR FREAKIN' RINGS!
THAT'S IMPOSSIBLE.
YEAH-- WELL TELL THAT TO THEM!

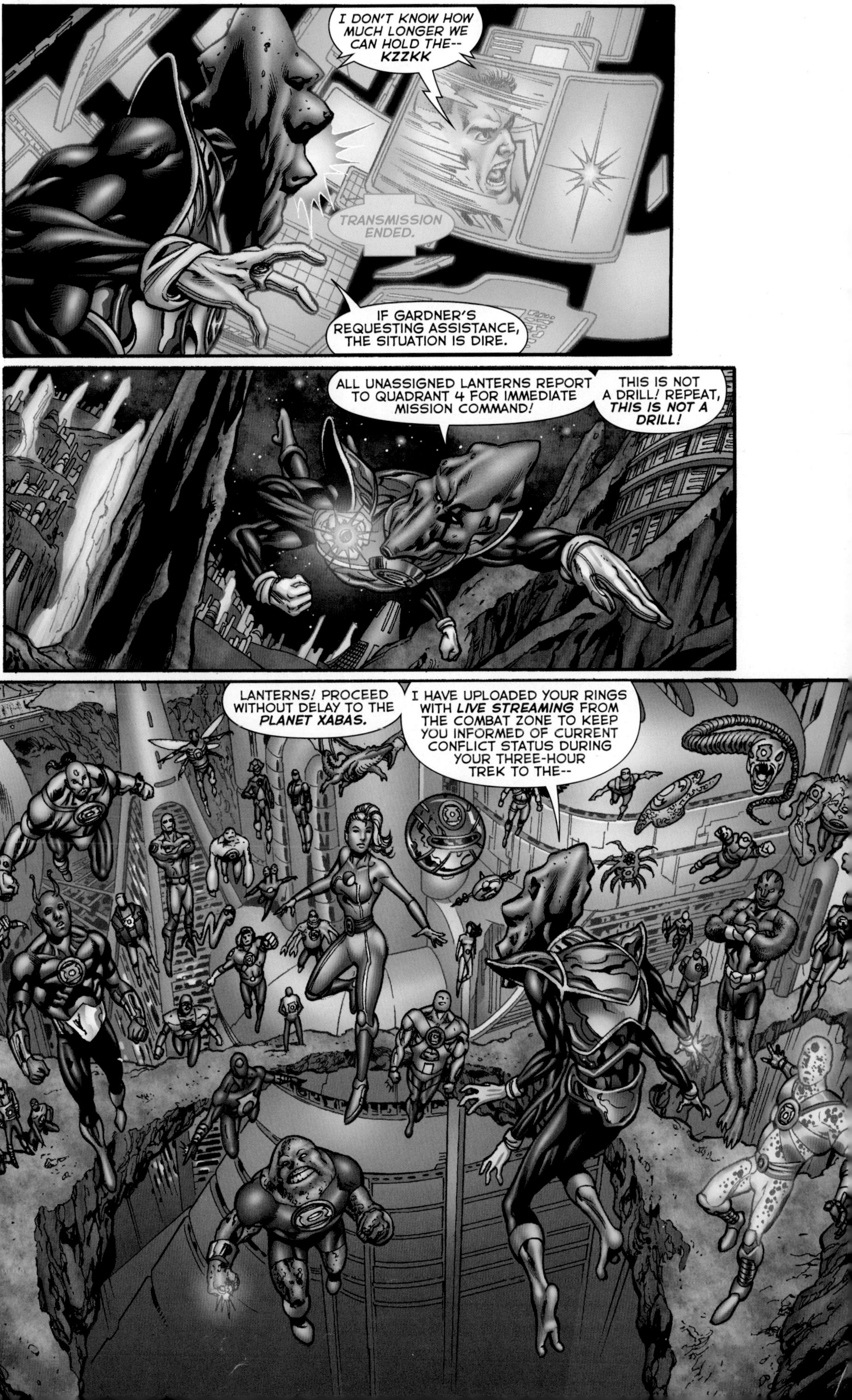
I DON'T KNOW HOW MUCH LONGER WE CAN HOLD THE-- KZZKK
TRANSMISSION ENDED.
IF GARDNER'S REQUESTING ASSISTANCE, THE SITUATION IS DIRE.
ALL UNASSIGNED LANTERNS REPORT TO QUADRANT 4 FOR IMMEDIATE MISSION COMMAND!
THIS IS NOT A DRILL! REPEAT, THIS IS NOT A DRILL!
LANTERNS! PROCEED WITHOUT DELAY TO THE PLANET XABAS.
I HAVE UPLOADED YOUR RINGS WITH LIVE STREAMING FROM THE COMBAT ZONE TO KEEP YOU INFORMED OF CURRENT CONFLICT STATUS DURING YOUR THREE-HOUR TREK TO THE--

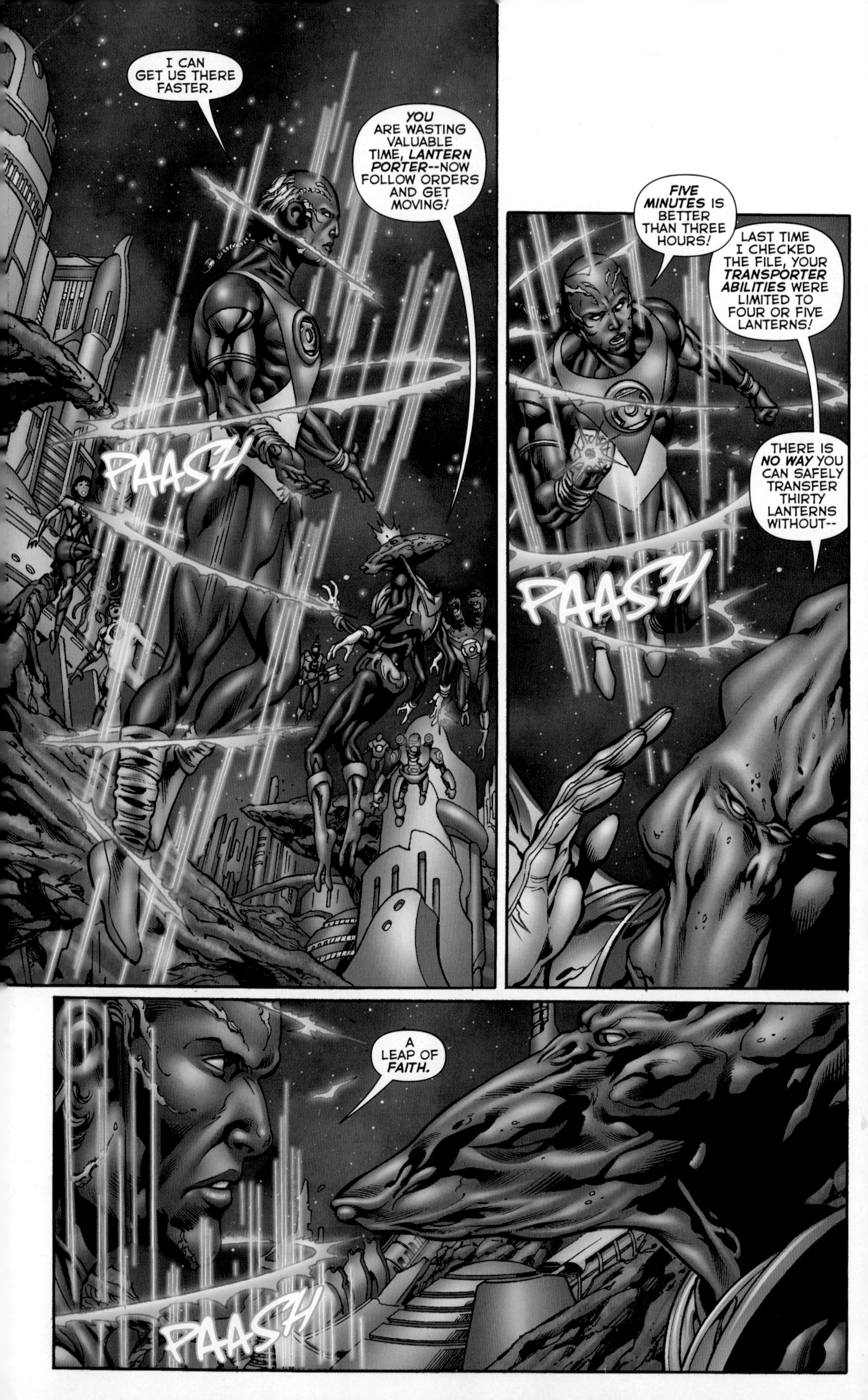
I CAN GET US THERE FASTER.
YOU ARE WASTING VALUABLE TIME, LANTERN PORTER--NOW FOLLOW ORDERS AND GET MOVING!
PAASH
FIVE MINUTES IS BETTER THAN THREE HOURS!
LAST TIME I CHECKED THE FILE, YOUR TRANSPORTER ABILITIES WERE LIMITED TO FOUR OR FIVE LANTERNS!
THERE IS NO WAY YOU CAN SAFELY TRANSFER THIRTY LANTERNS WITHOUT--
PAASH
A LEAP OF FAITH.
PAASH

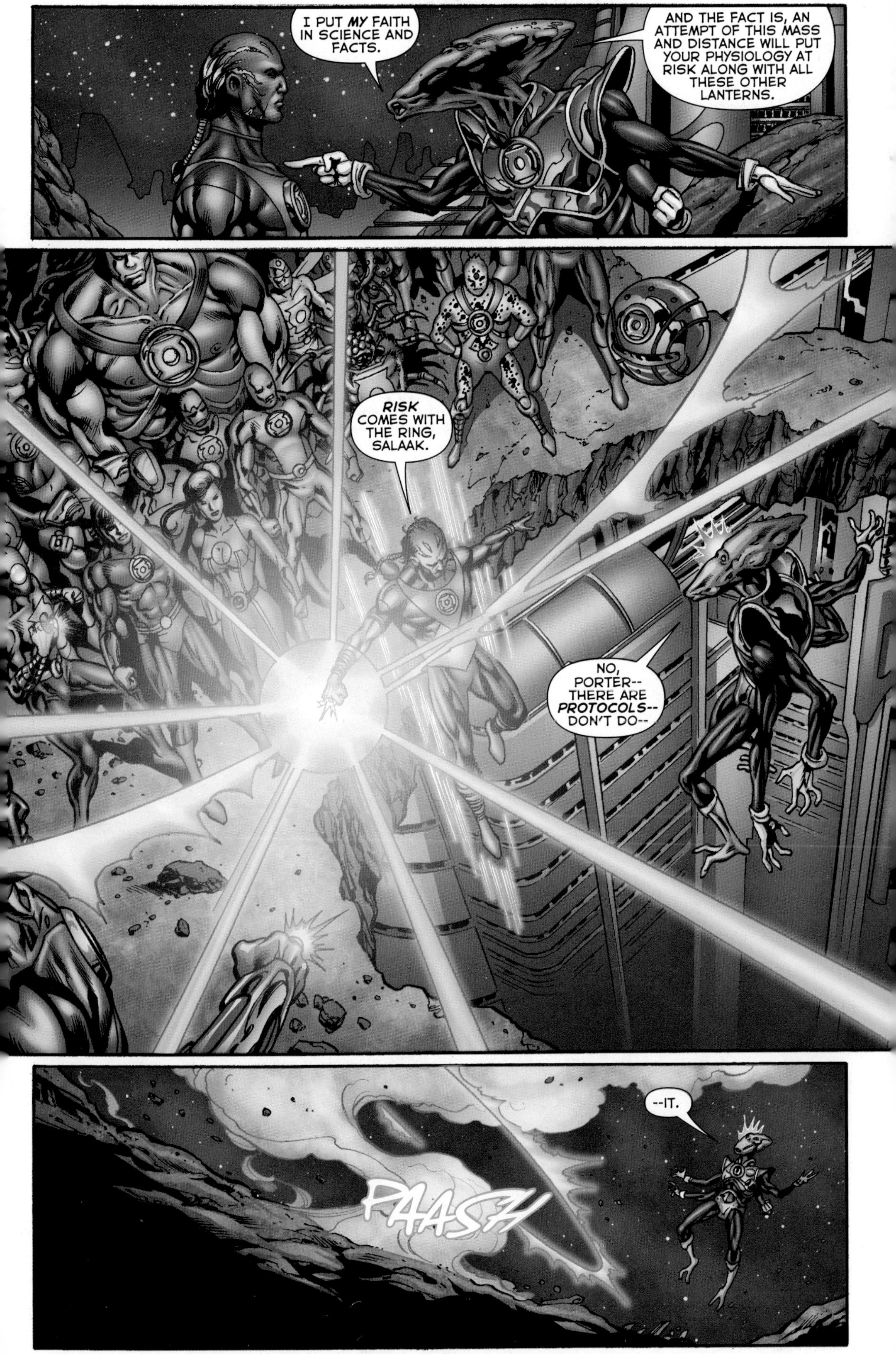
I PUT MY FAITH IN SCIENCE AND FACTS.
AND THE FACT IS, AN ATTEMPT OF THIS MASS AND DISTANCE WILL PUT YOUR PHYSIOLOGY AT RISK ALONG WITH ALL THESE OTHER LANTERNS.
RISK COMES WITH THE RING, SALAAK.
NO, PORTER-- THERE ARE PROTOCOLS-- DON'T DO--
--IT.
PAASH

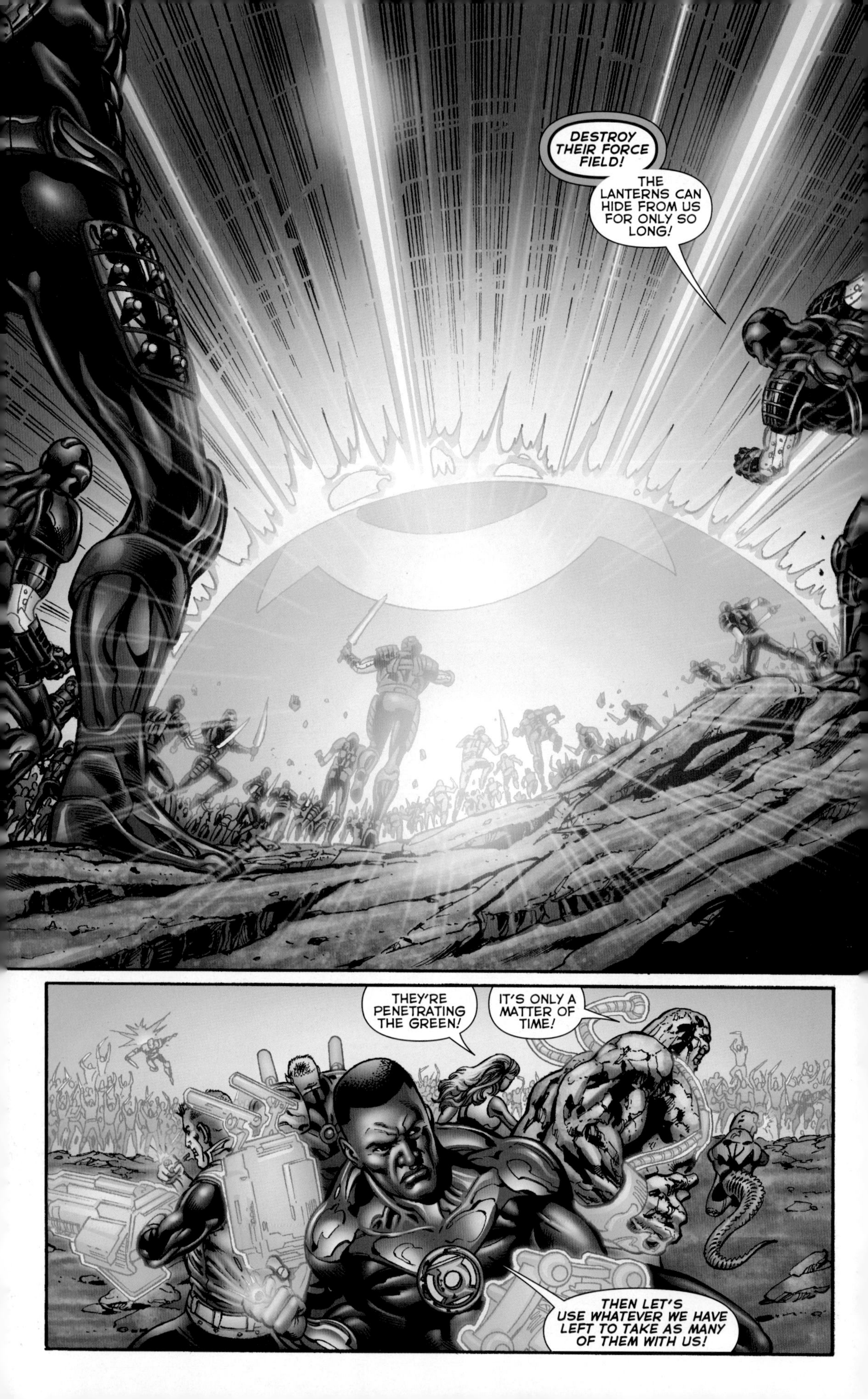
DESTROY THEIR FORCE FIELD!
THE LANTERNS CAN HIDE FROM US FOR ONLY SO LONG!
THEY'RE PENETRATING THE GREEN!
IT'S ONLY A MATTER OF TIME!
THEN LET'S USE WHATEVER WE HAVE LEFT TO TAKE AS MANY OF THEM WITH US!

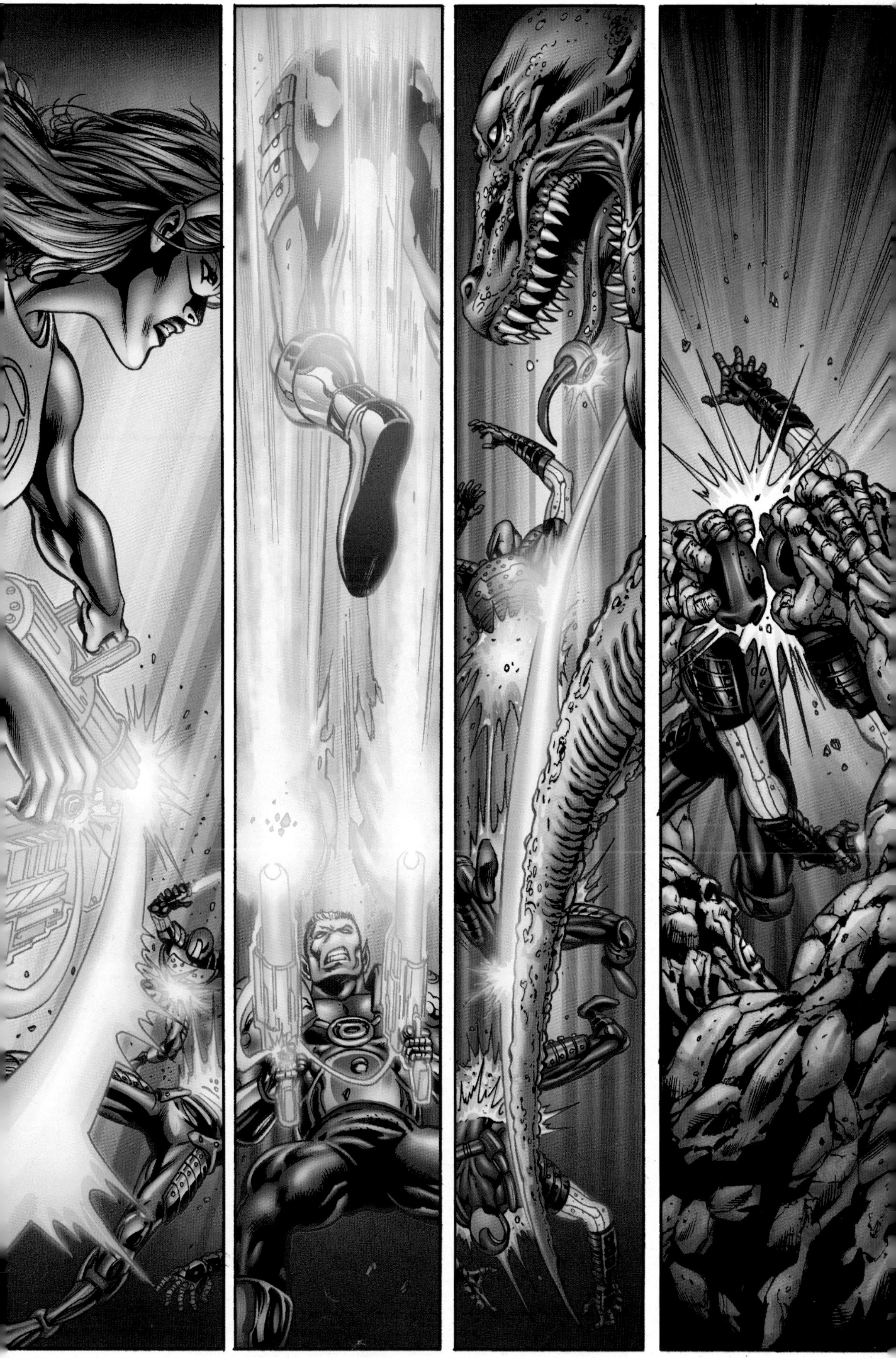

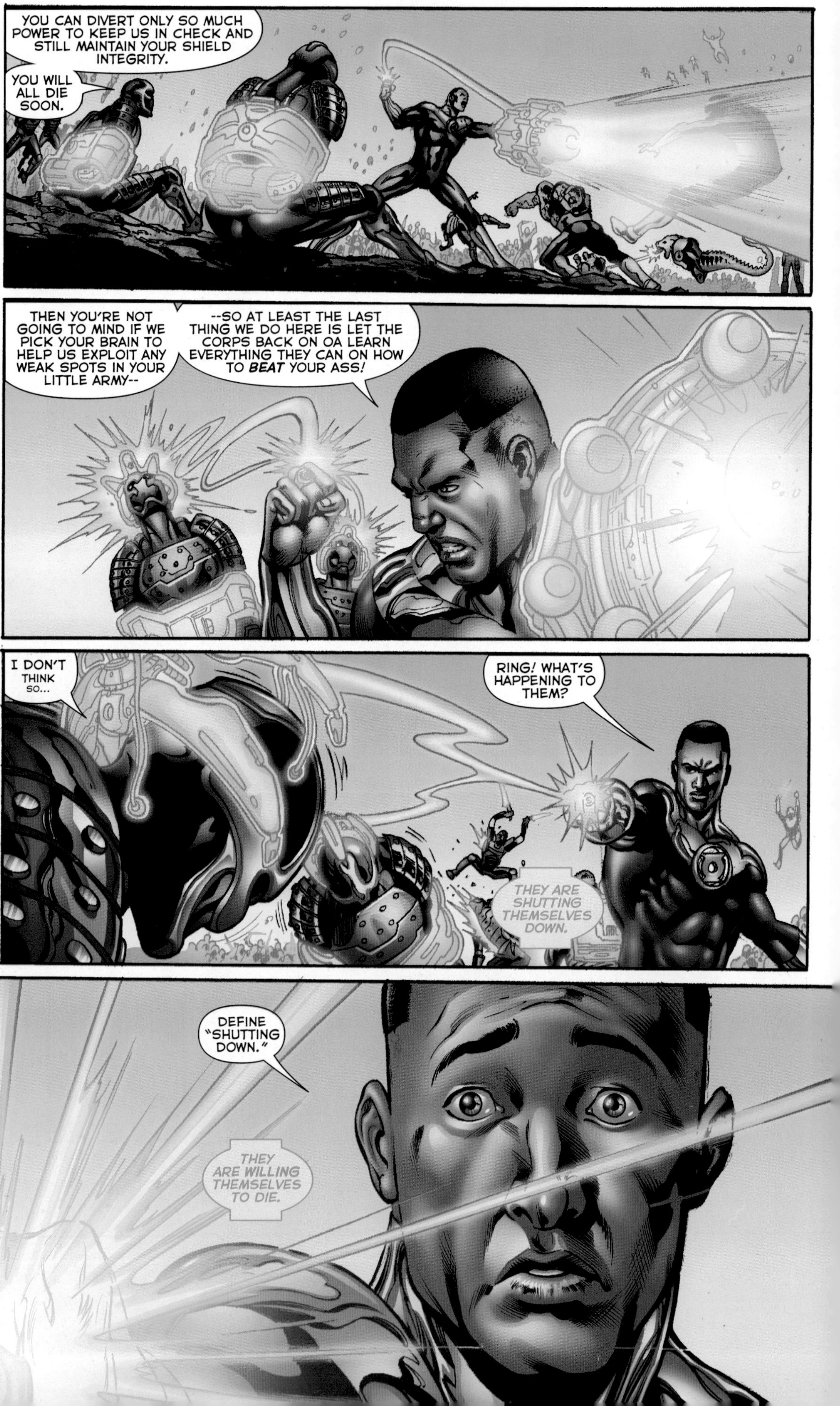
YOU CAN DIVERT ONLY SO MUCH POWER TO KEEP US IN CHECK AND STILL MAINTAIN YOUR SHIELD INTEGRITY.
YOU WILL ALL DIE SOON.
THEN YOU'RE NOT GOING TO MIND IF WE PICK YOUR BRAIN TO HELP US EXPLOIT ANY WEAK SPOTS IN YOUR LITTLE ARMY--
--SO AT LEAST THE LAST THING WE DO HERE IS LET THE CORPS BACK ON OA LEARN EVERYTHING THEY CAN ON HOW TO BEAT YOUR ASS!
I DON'T THINK SO...
RING! WHAT'S HAPPENING TO THEM?
THEY ARE SHUTTING THEMSELVES DOWN.
DEFINE "SHUTTING DOWN."
THEY ARE WILLING THEMSELVES TO DIE.

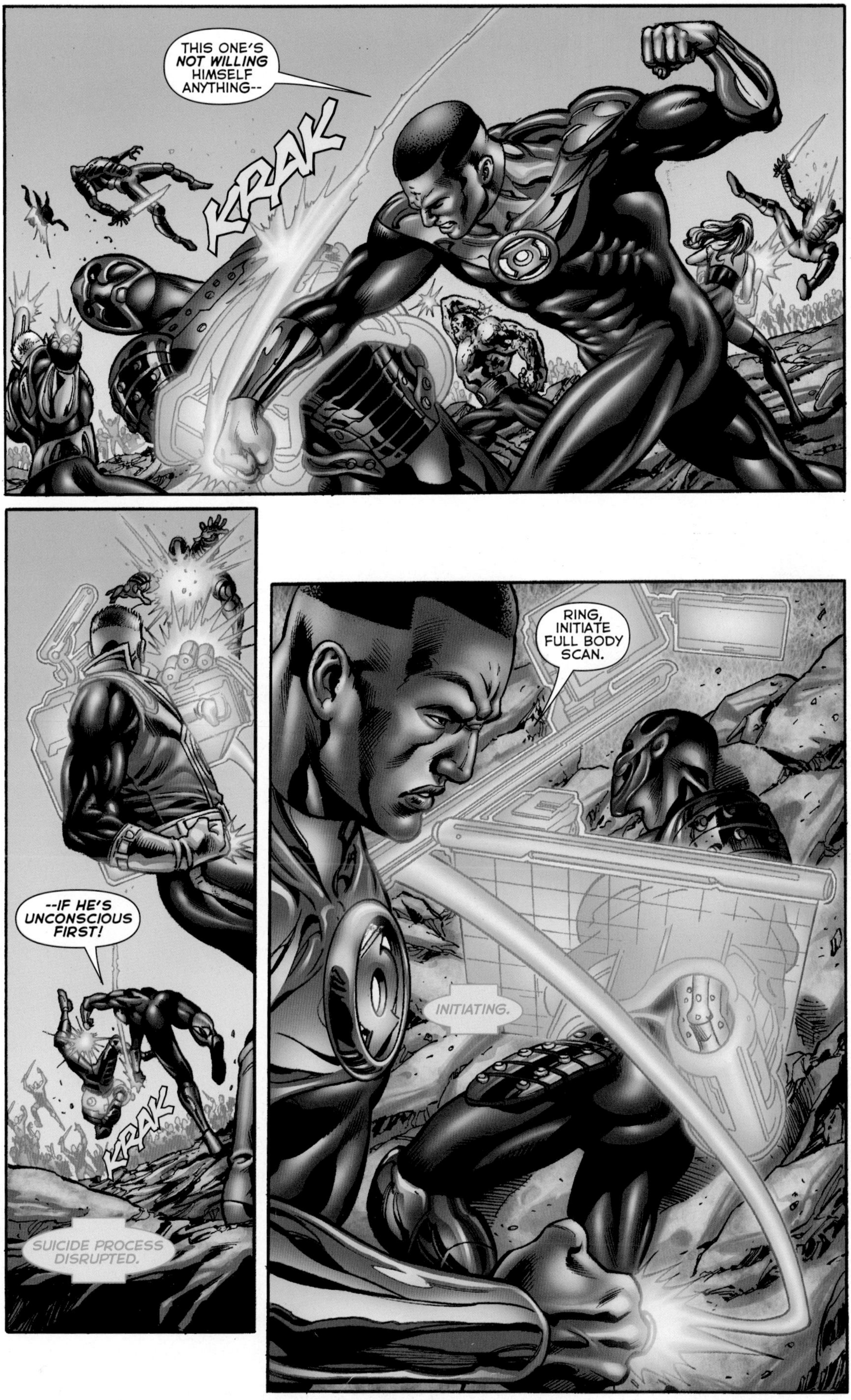
THIS ONE'S *NOT WILLING* HIMSELF ANYTHING--
KRAK
--IF HE'S UNCONSCIOUS *FIRST!*
KRAK
SUICIDE PROCESS DISRUPTED.
RING, INITIATE FULL BODY SCAN.
INITIATING.

BODY SCAN COMPLETE.

SPECIES UNRECOGNIZED. NOT ON FILE.

UNRECOGNIZED? WHAT ELSE?

THESE BEINGS POSSESS AN INNATE RESERVE OF WILLPOWER THAT IS OVERWHELMING AND NOT IN PROPORTION TO THEIR RELATIVELY COMMON FORMS.

DID YOU HEAR THAT? THAT'S WHY THEY'VE BEEN ABLE TO TAKE OUR BLASTS.

THAT CONFIRMS IT, GUY--WE'RE FIGHTING WILLPOWER WITH WILLPOWER!

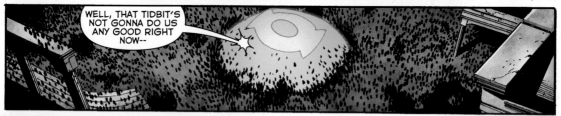

WELL, THAT TIDBIT'S NOT GONNA DO US ANY GOOD RIGHT NOW--

--'CAUSE I THINK IT'S DO OR DIE TIME, JOHNNY--

PAASH

DO OR--

SALAAK, YOU BEAUTIFUL UGLY BASTARD --

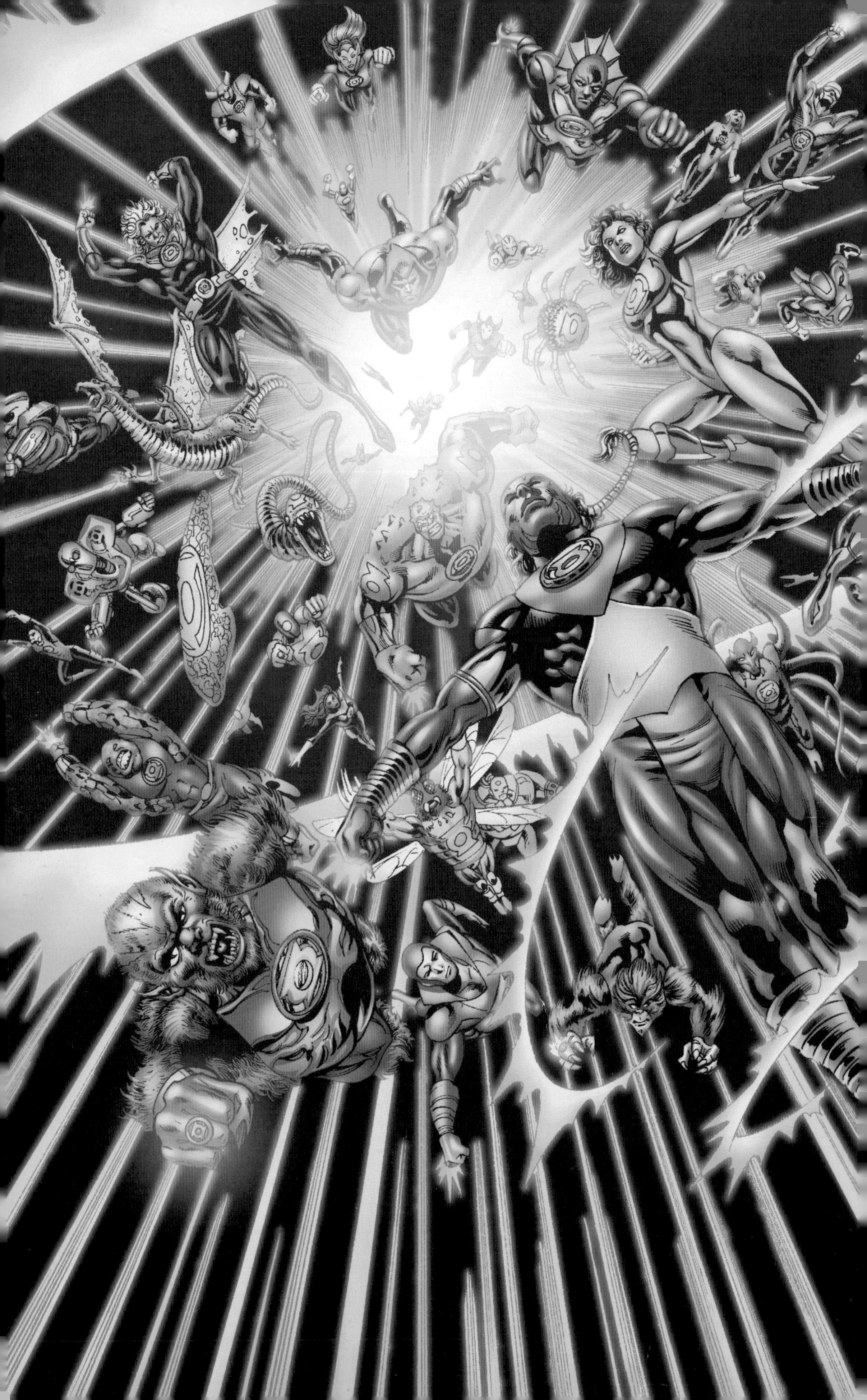

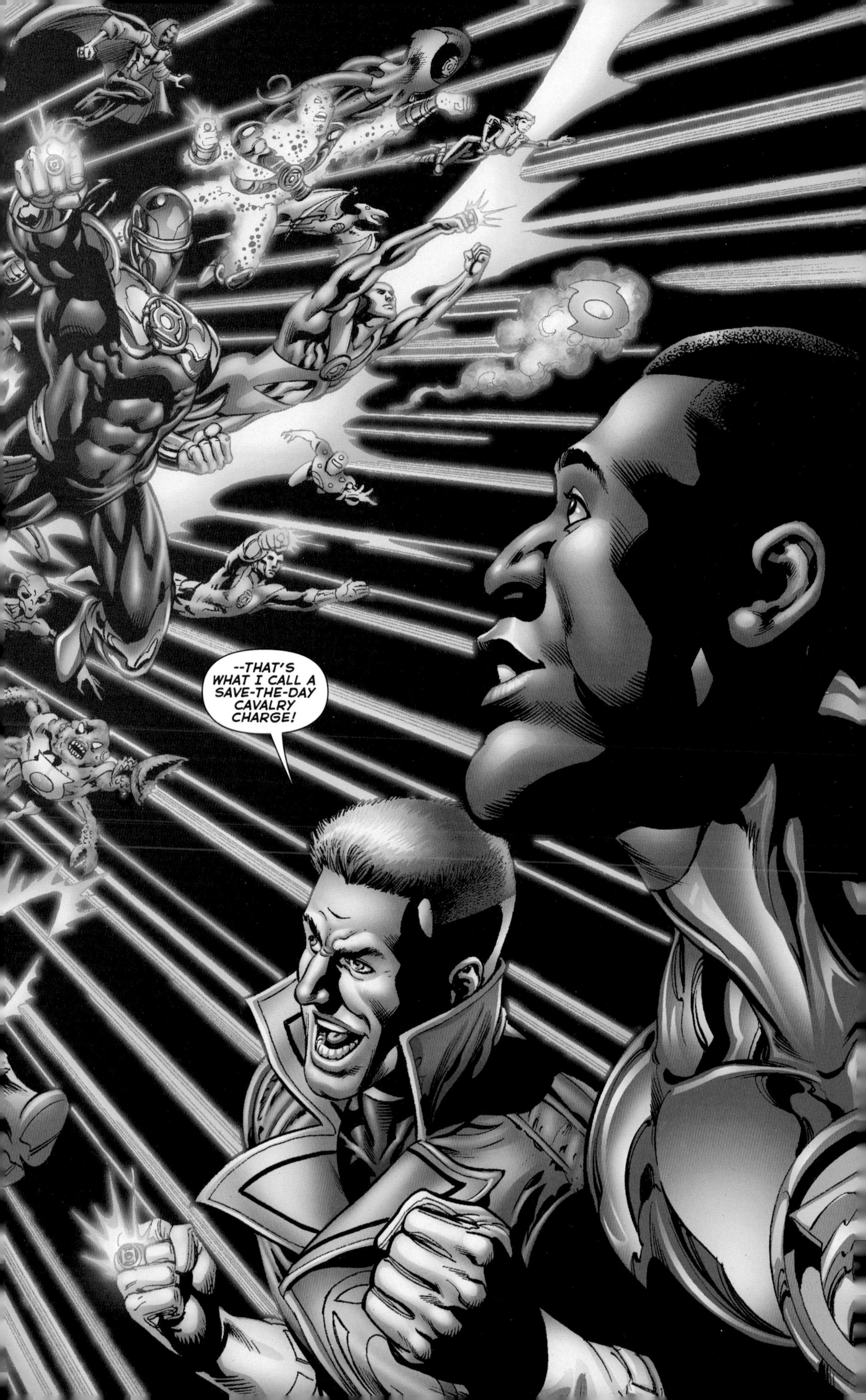
--THAT'S WHAT I CALL A SAVE-THE-DAY CAVALRY CHARGE!

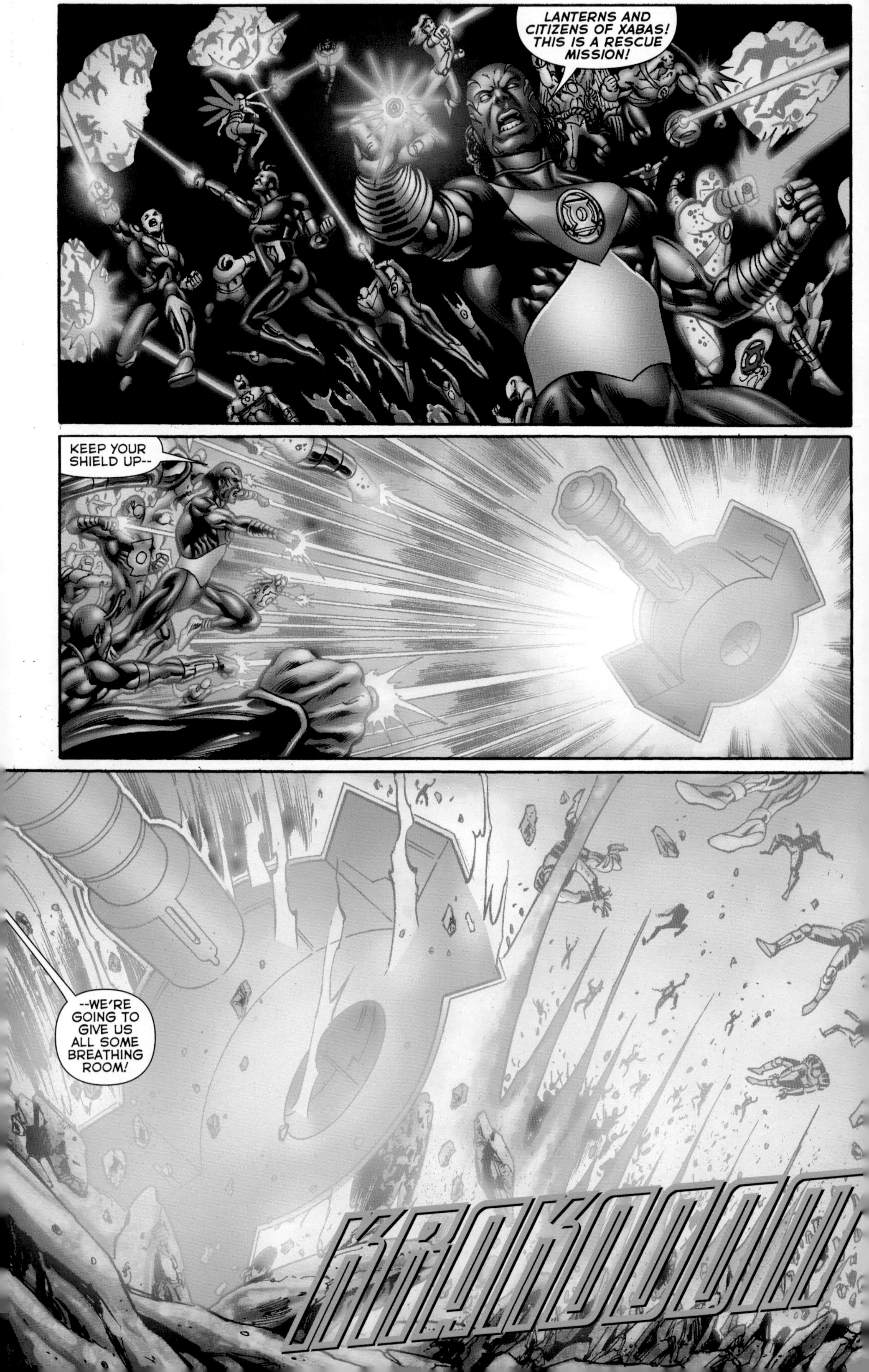
LANTERNS AND CITIZENS OF XABAS! THIS IS A RESCUE MISSION!
KEEP YOUR SHIELD UP--
--WE'RE GOING TO GIVE US ALL SOME BREATHING ROOM!
KRAKOOOM

RING, TRANSLATE: EVERYONE STAY CALM AND REMAIN CLOSE.

ᓇᒫᒪᒧᔭᒧ ᒫᓇᒧ ᒉᐊᓯ ᐊᓇᔭ ᓂᔭᒐᓯ ᒉᔭᓯᒧ.

DON'T KNOW HOW YOU PULLED ALL THOSE GL'S HERE WITHOUT BLOWING A GASKET, BUT I HOPE YOU BOOKED A RETURN TICKET FOR ALL OF US.

SURE DID... BUT WE DON'T HAVE MUCH TIME, WHOEVER THEY ARE...THEY'RE MASSING AGAIN FOR ANOTHER ATTACK.

THE LANTERNS THAT CAME WITH ME WILL FORM A DEFENSE RING...

...SO WE CAN GET YOU AND THESE REMAINING PEOPLE OUT OF HERE...

YOUR EYES ARE BLEEDING--OR MAYBE WE CAN BUY YOU SOME RECOVERY TIME BEFORE YOU TRY TELEPORTING AGAIN.

I'M FINE... JUST NEED TO FOCUS...

HERE COMES THE SECOND WAVE!

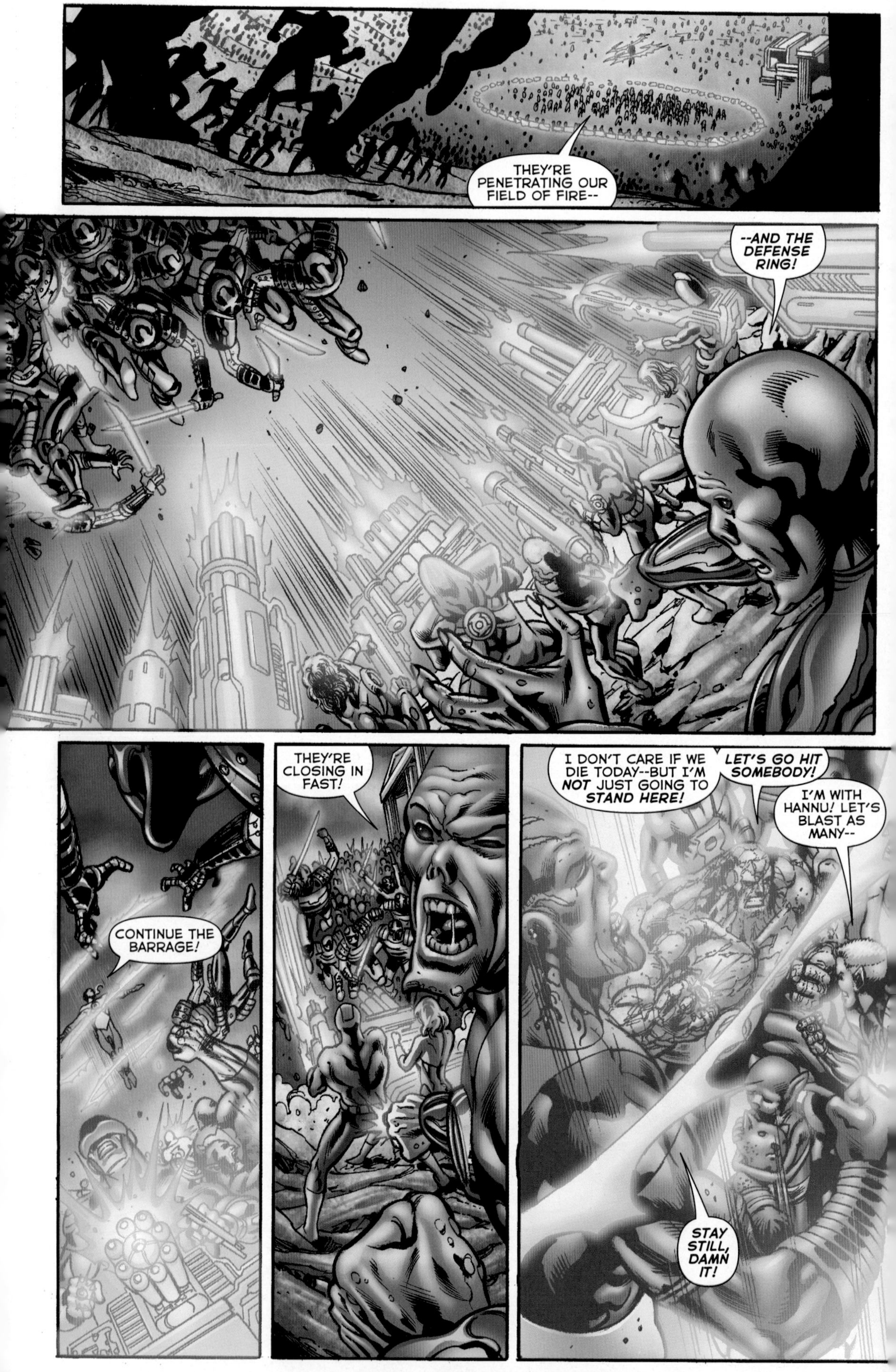
THEY'RE PENETRATING OUR FIELD OF FIRE--
--AND THE DEFENSE RING!
CONTINUE THE BARRAGE!
THEY'RE CLOSING IN FAST!
I DON'T CARE IF WE DIE TODAY--BUT I'M NOT JUST GOING TO STAND HERE!
LET'S GO HIT SOMEBODY!
I'M WITH HANNU! LET'S BLAST AS MANY--
STAY STILL, DAMN IT!

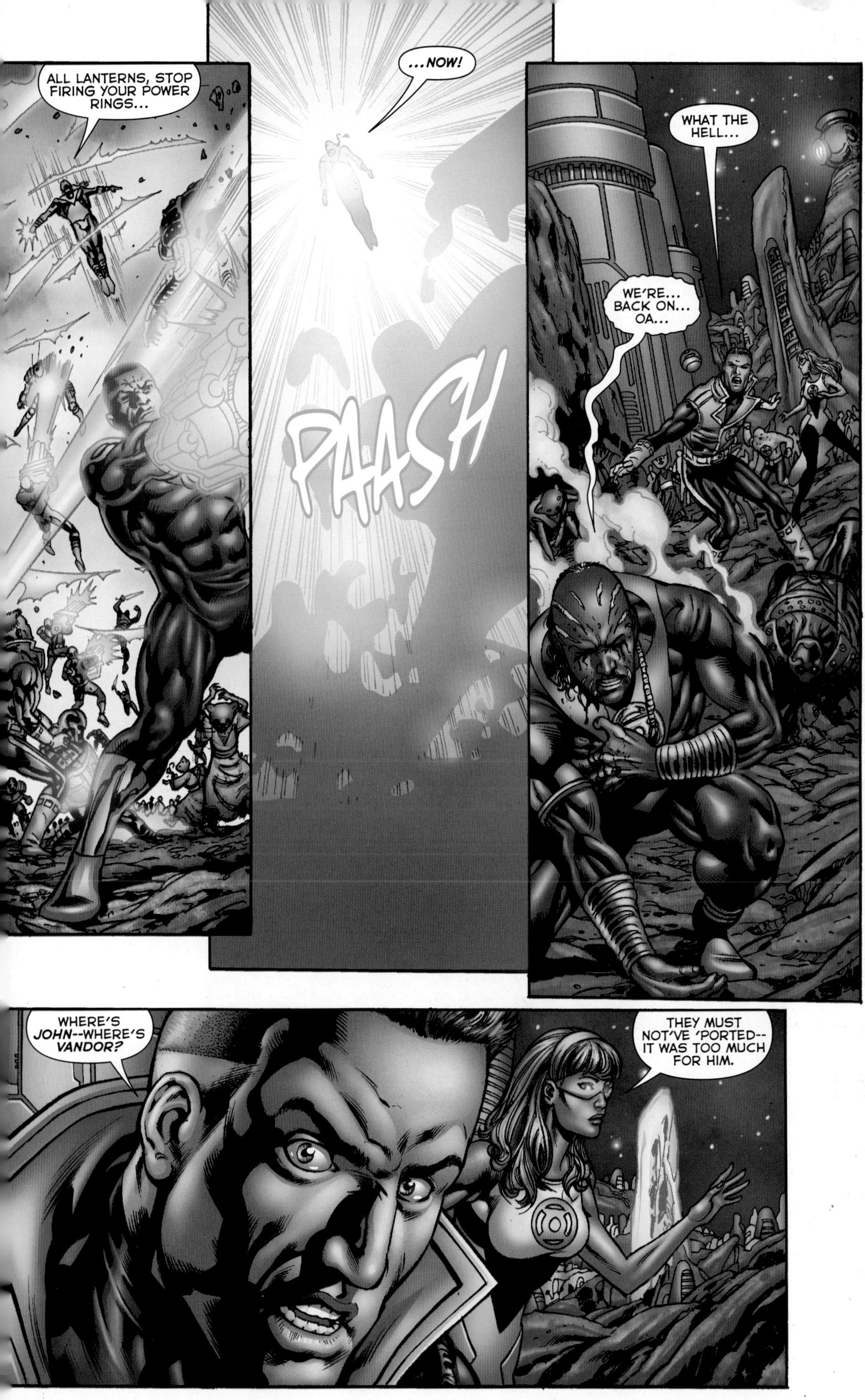
ALL LANTERNS, STOP FIRING YOUR POWER RINGS...
...NOW!
PAASH
WHAT THE HELL...
WE'RE... BACK ON... OA...
WHERE'S JOHN--WHERE'S VANDOR?
THEY MUST NOT'VE 'PORTED-- IT WAS TOO MUCH FOR HIM.

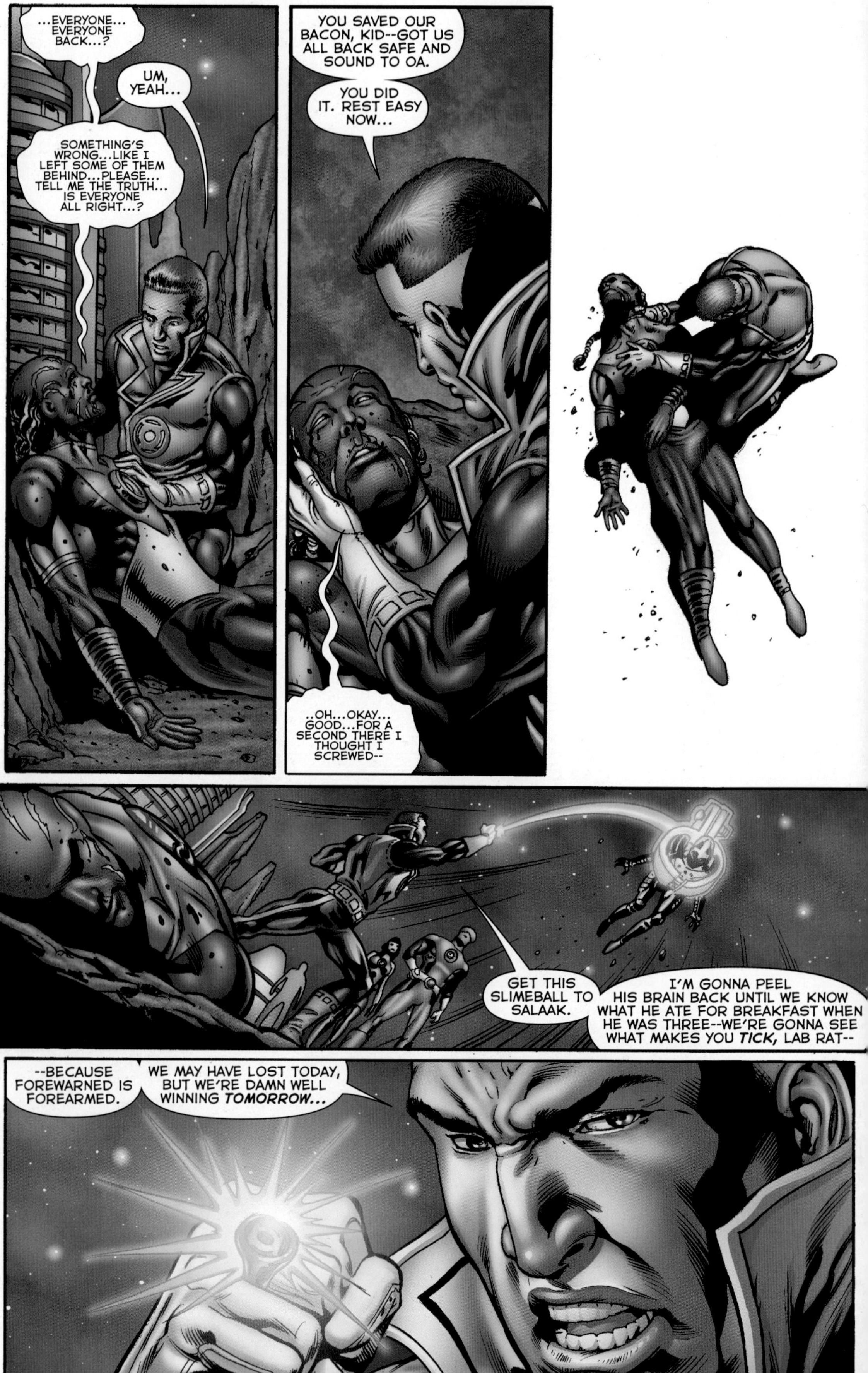
...EVERYONE... EVERYONE BACK...?
UM, YEAH...
SOMETHING'S WRONG...LIKE I LEFT SOME OF THEM BEHIND...PLEASE... TELL ME THE TRUTH... IS EVERYONE ALL RIGHT...?
YOU SAVED OUR BACON, KID--GOT US ALL BACK SAFE AND SOUND TO OA.
YOU DID IT. REST EASY NOW...
..OH...OKAY... GOOD...FOR A SECOND THERE I THOUGHT I SCREWED--
GET THIS SLIMEBALL TO SALAAK.
I'M GONNA PEEL HIS BRAIN BACK UNTIL WE KNOW WHAT HE ATE FOR BREAKFAST WHEN HE WAS THREE--WE'RE GONNA SEE WHAT MAKES YOU *TICK,* LAB RAT--
--BECAUSE FOREWARNED IS FOREARMED.
WE MAY HAVE LOST TODAY, BUT WE'RE DAMN WELL WINNING *TOMORROW...*

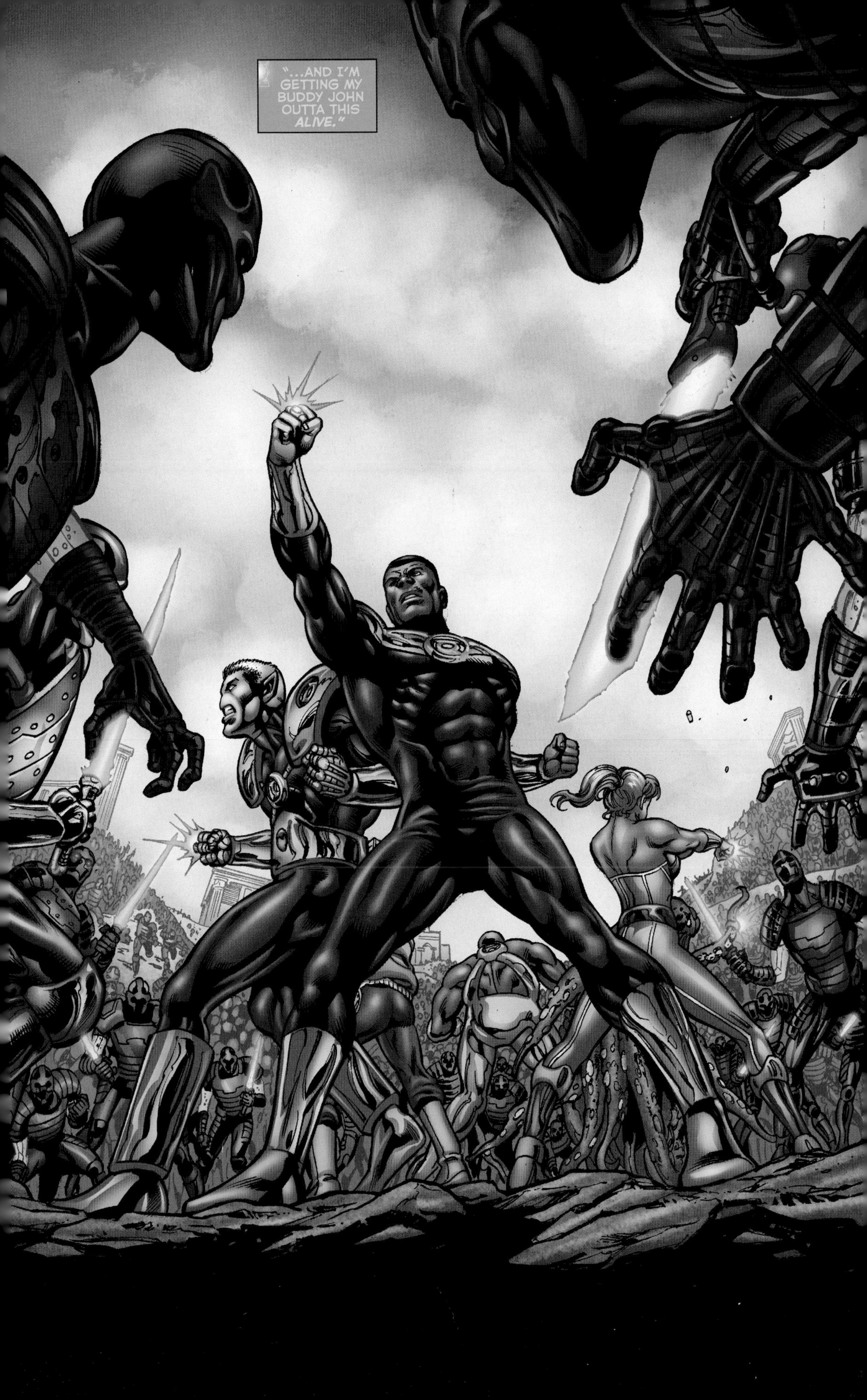
"...AND I'M GETTING MY BUDDY JOHN OUTTA THIS *ALIVE*."

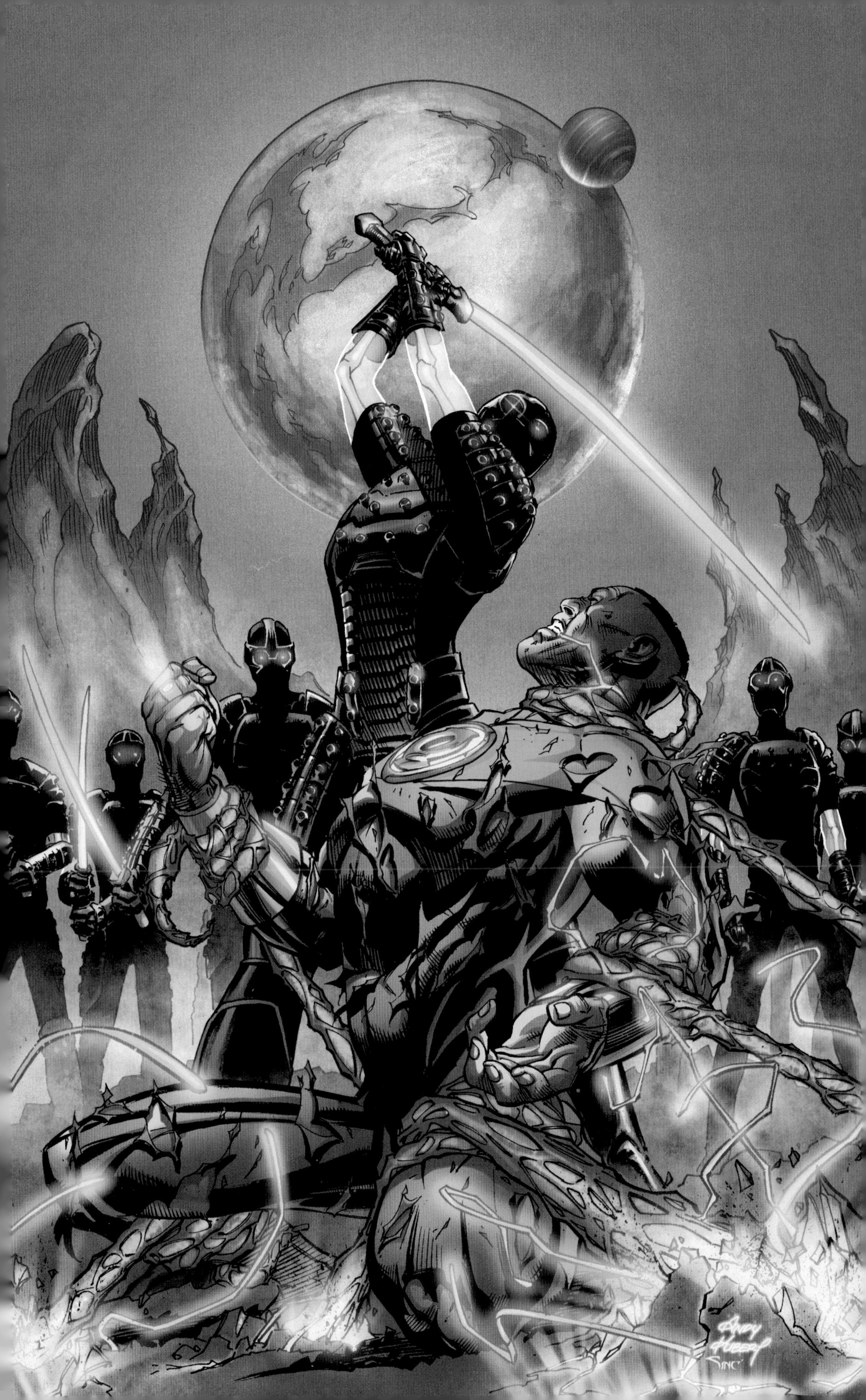

PRISONERS OF WAR

PETER J. TOMASI writer FERNANDO PASARIN penciller SCOTT HANNA inker cover by ANDY KUBERT with ALEX SINCLAIR

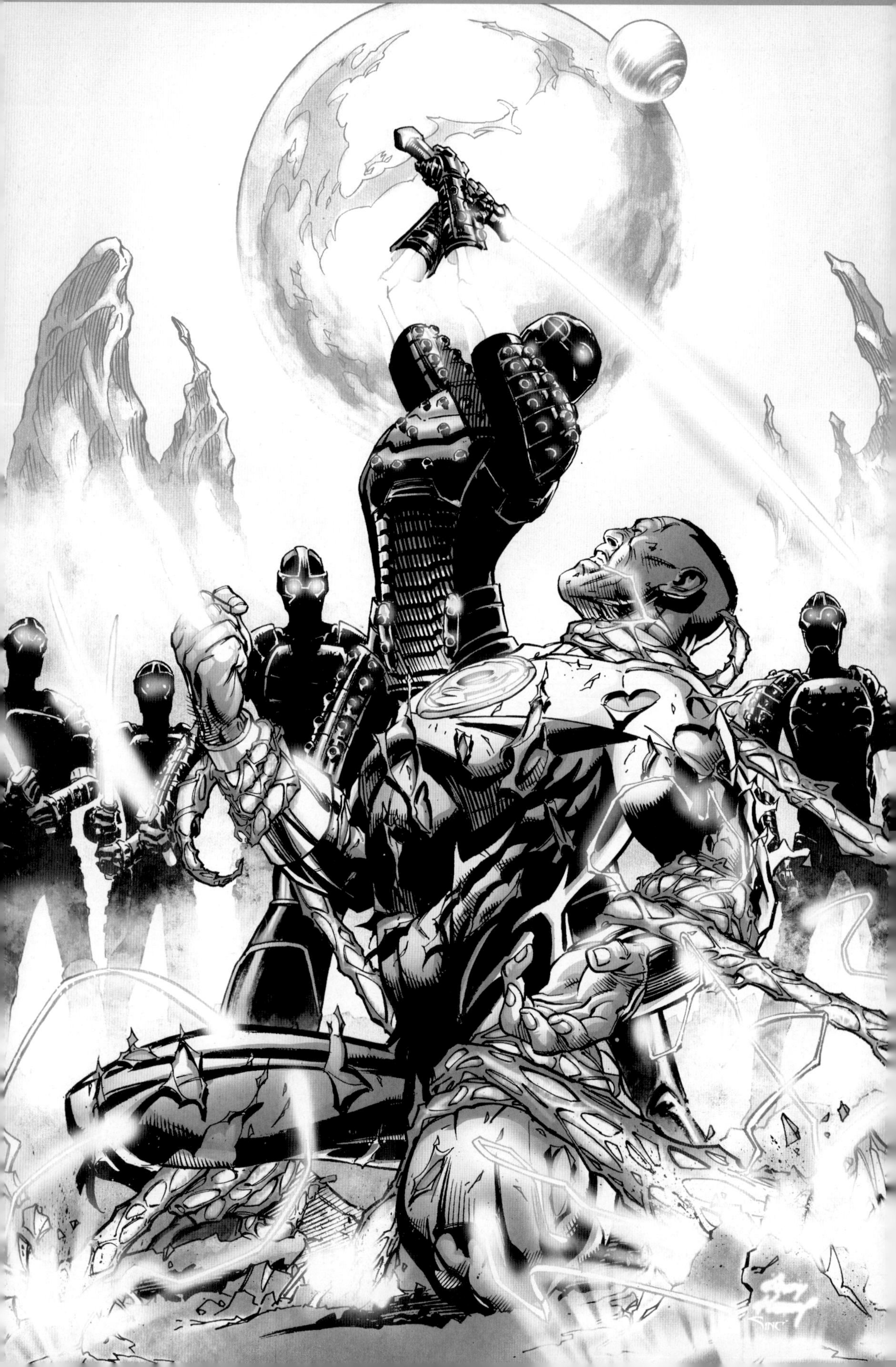

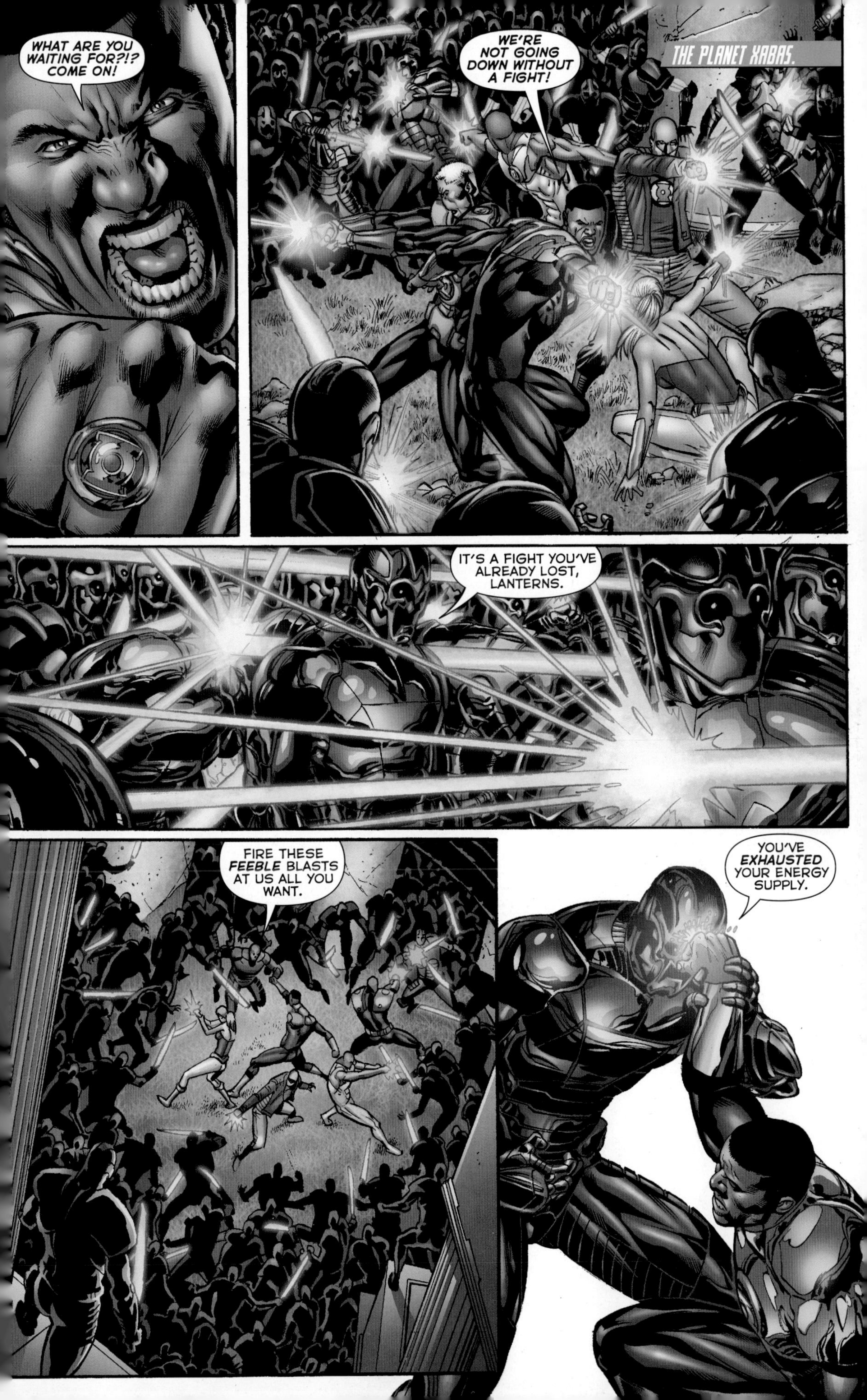

WHAT ARE YOU WAITING FOR?!? COME ON!
THE PLANET XABAS.
WE'RE NOT GOING DOWN WITHOUT A FIGHT!
IT'S A FIGHT YOU'VE ALREADY LOST, LANTERNS.
FIRE THESE FEEBLE BLASTS AT US ALL YOU WANT.
YOU'VE EXHAUSTED YOUR ENERGY SUPPLY.

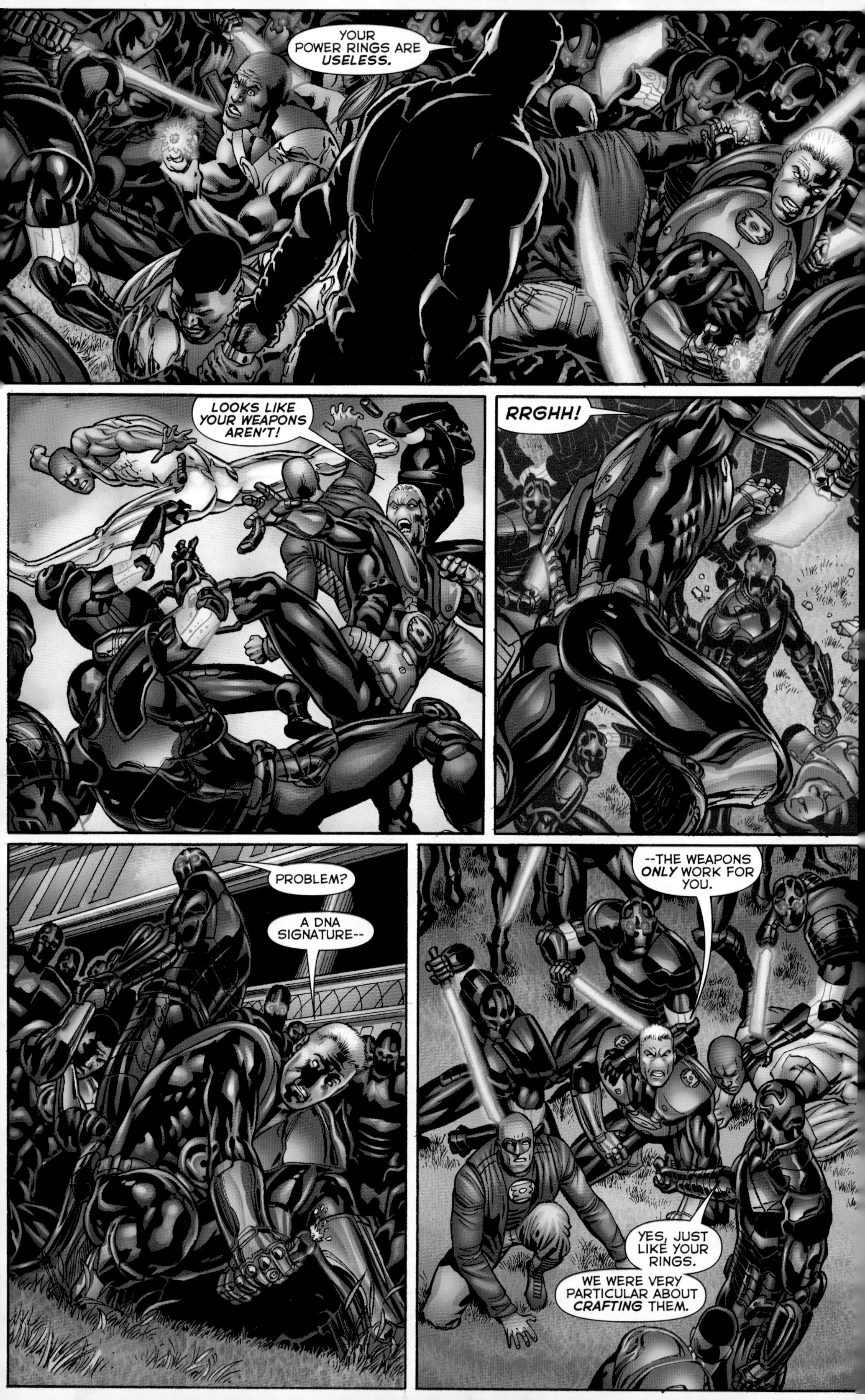
YOUR POWER RINGS ARE USELESS.
LOOKS LIKE YOUR WEAPONS AREN'T!
RRGHH!
PROBLEM?
A DNA SIGNATURE--
--THE WEAPONS ONLY WORK FOR YOU.
YES, JUST LIKE YOUR RINGS.
WE WERE VERY PARTICULAR ABOUT CRAFTING THEM.

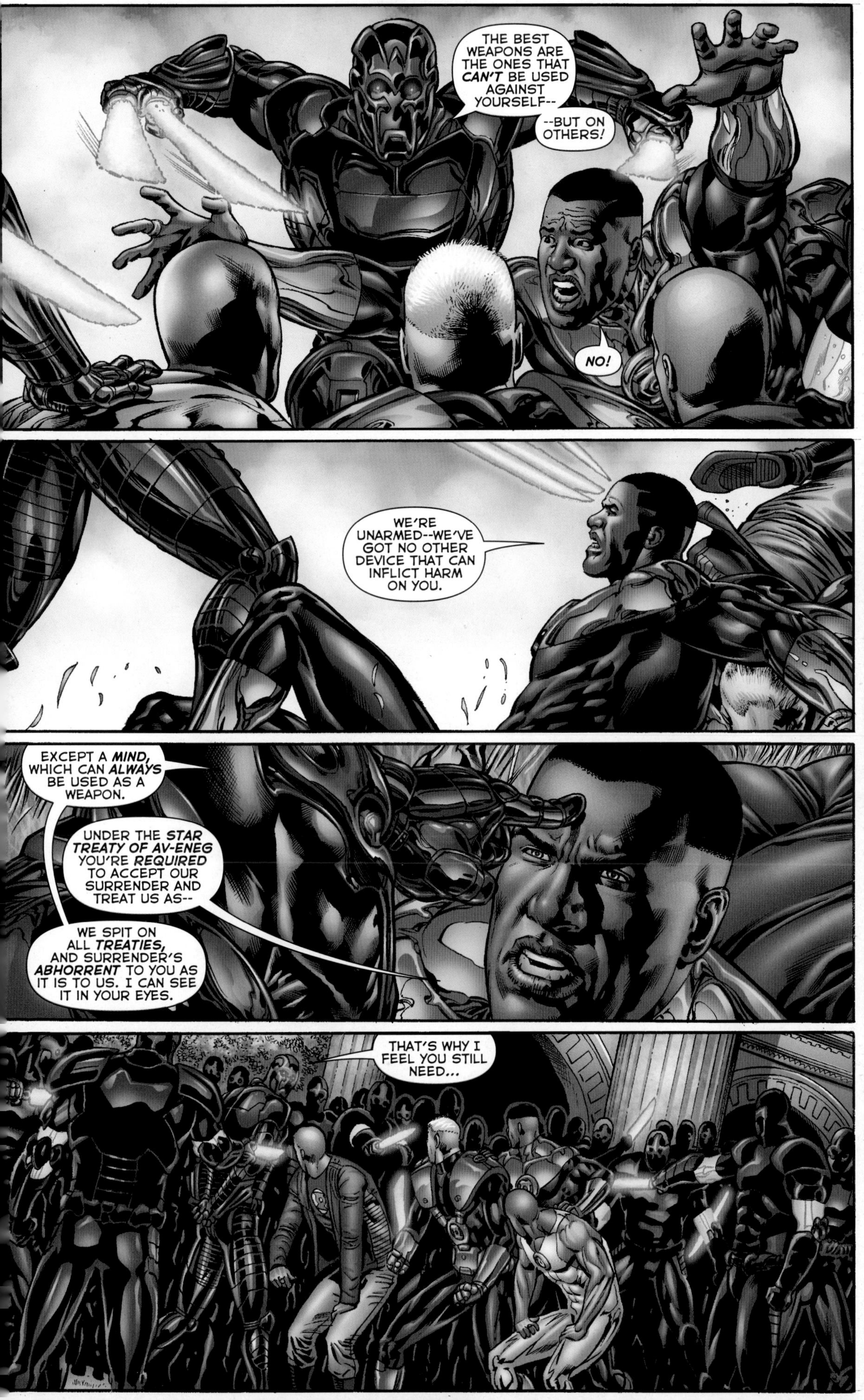
THE BEST WEAPONS ARE THE ONES THAT *CAN'T* BE USED AGAINST YOURSELF--
--BUT ON OTHERS!
NO!
WE'RE UNARMED--WE'VE GOT NO OTHER DEVICE THAT CAN INFLICT HARM ON YOU.
EXCEPT A *MIND,* WHICH CAN *ALWAYS* BE USED AS A WEAPON.
UNDER THE *STAR TREATY OF AV-ENEG* YOU'RE *REQUIRED* TO ACCEPT OUR SURRENDER AND TREAT US AS--
WE SPIT ON ALL *TREATIES,* AND SURRENDER'S *ABHORRENT* TO YOU AS IT IS TO US. I CAN SEE IT IN YOUR EYES.
THAT'S WHY I FEEL YOU STILL NEED...

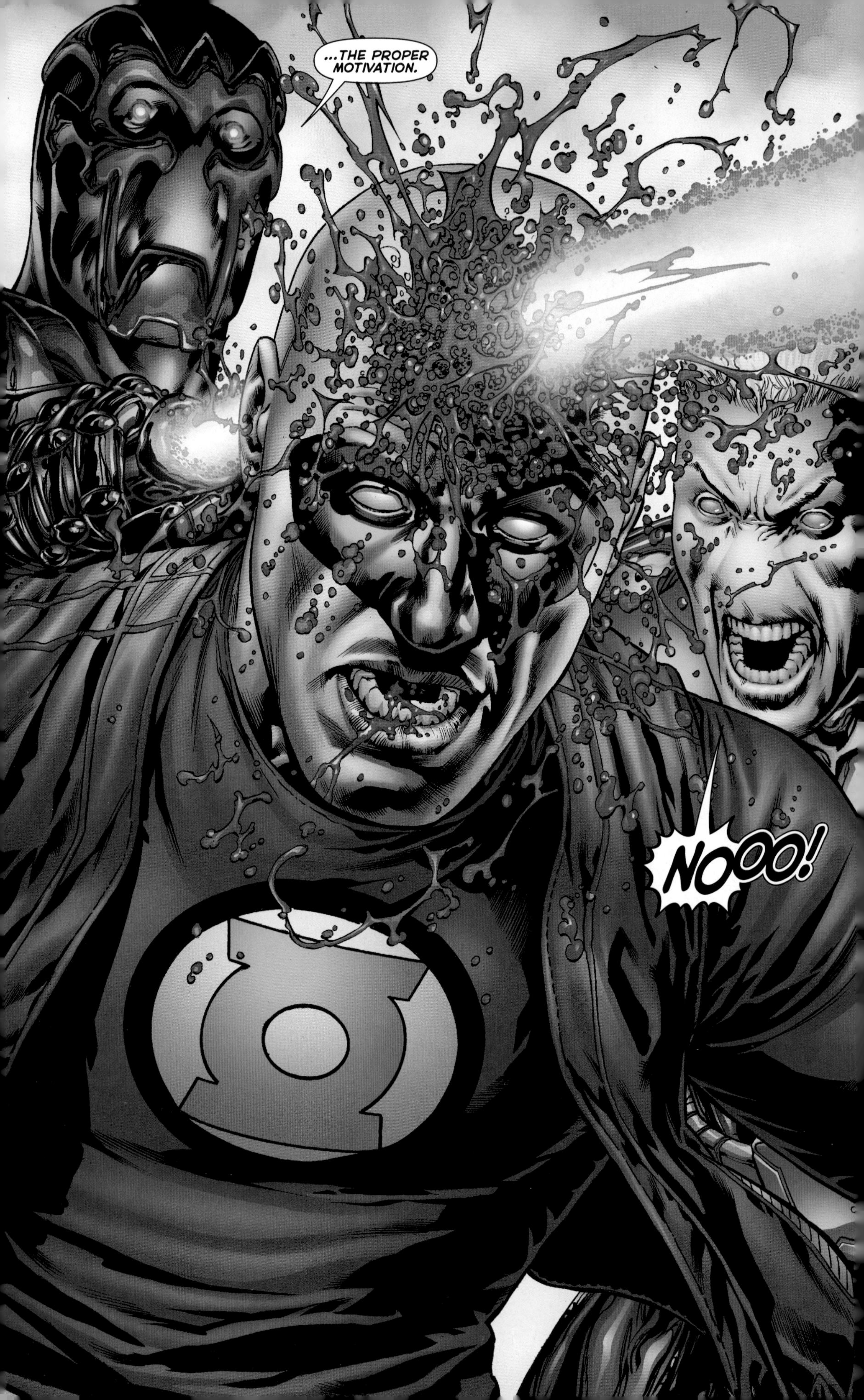
...THE PROPER MOTIVATION.
NOOO!

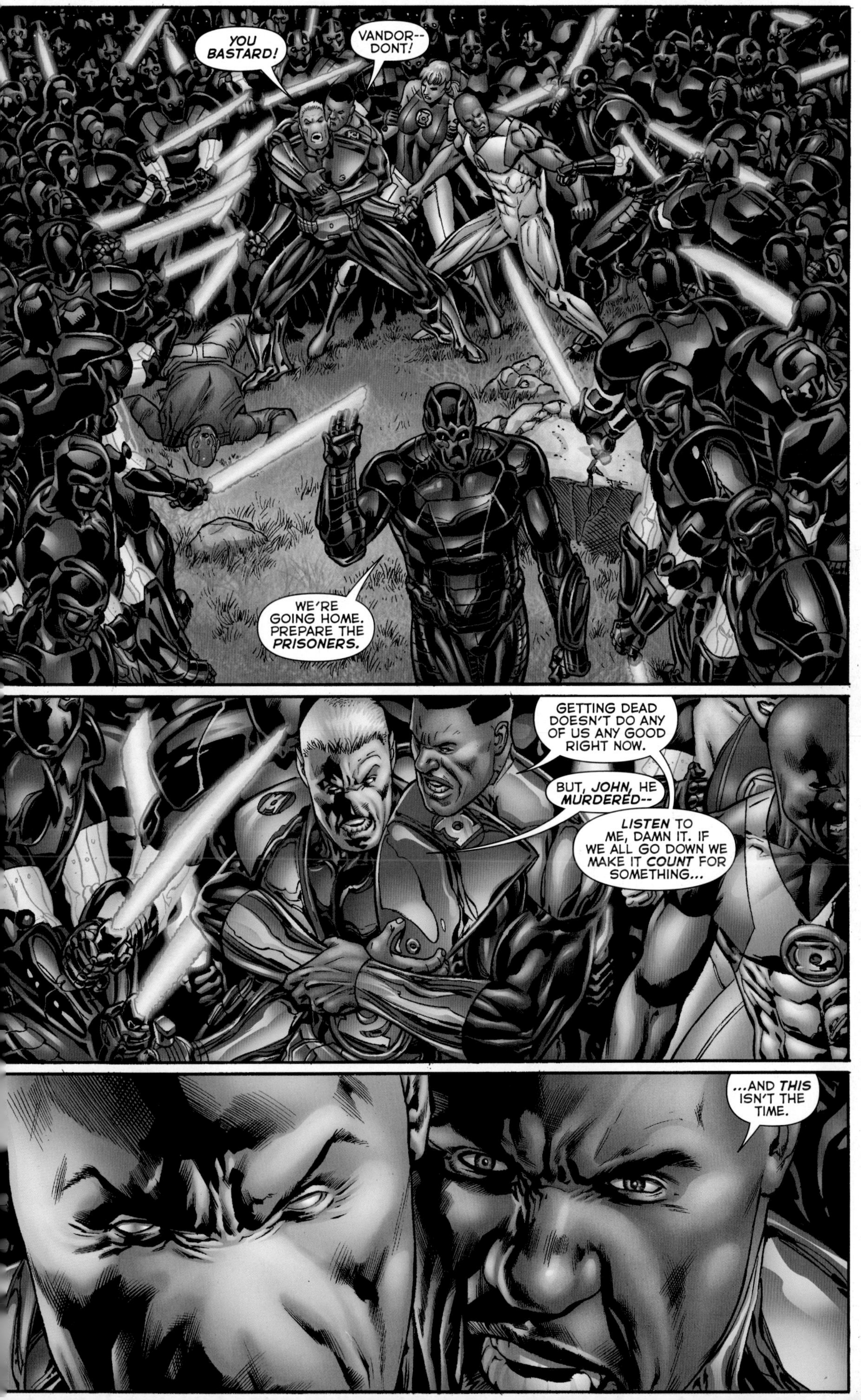
YOU BASTARD!
VANDOR-- DONT!
WE'RE GOING HOME. PREPARE THE PRISONERS.
GETTING DEAD DOESN'T DO ANY OF US ANY GOOD RIGHT NOW.
BUT, JOHN, HE MURDERED--
LISTEN TO ME, DAMN IT. IF WE ALL GO DOWN WE MAKE IT COUNT FOR SOMETHING...
...AND THIS ISN'T THE TIME.

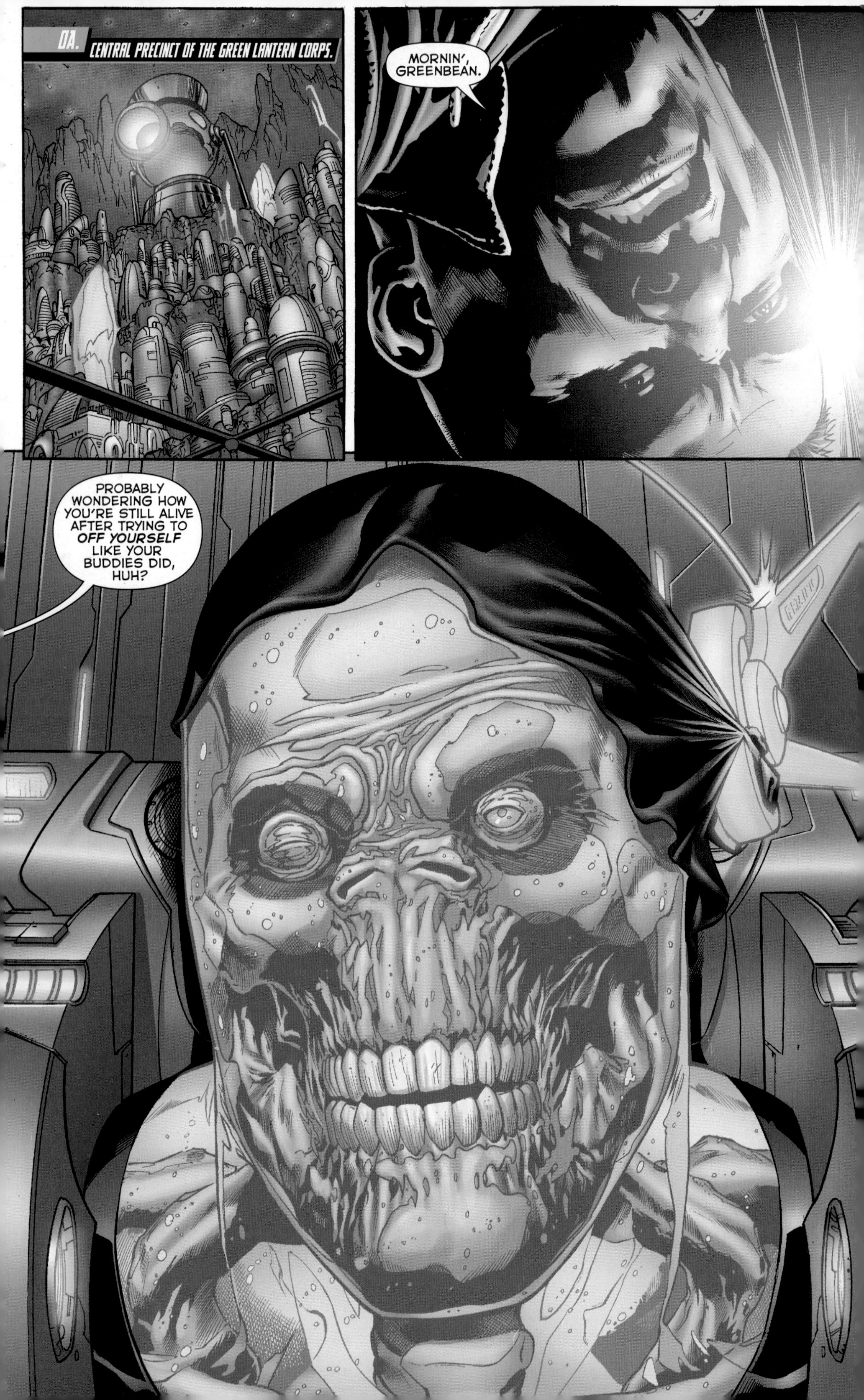
OA. CENTRAL PRECINCT OF THE GREEN LANTERN CORPS.
MORNIN', GREENBEAN.
PROBABLY WONDERING HOW YOU'RE STILL ALIVE AFTER TRYING TO ***OFF YOURSELF*** LIKE YOUR BUDDIES DID, HUH?

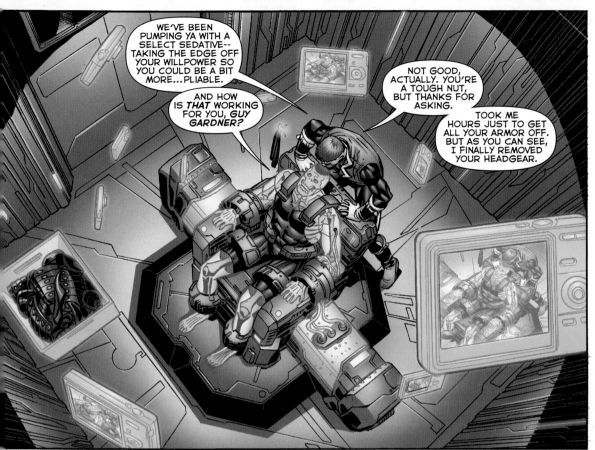

WE'VE BEEN PUMPING YA WITH A SELECT SEDATIVE-- TAKING THE EDGE OFF YOUR WILLPOWER SO YOU COULD BE A BIT MORE...PLIABLE.

AND HOW IS *THAT* WORKING FOR YOU, *GUY GARDNER?*

NOT GOOD, ACTUALLY. YOU'RE A TOUGH NUT, BUT THANKS FOR ASKING.

TOOK ME HOURS JUST TO GET ALL YOUR ARMOR OFF. BUT AS YOU CAN SEE, I FINALLY REMOVED YOUR HEADGEAR.

WITH A FACE LIKE YOURS, I SEE WHY YA WENT WITH A MASK.

AT LEAST NOW YOU'RE READY--

--FOR YOUR CLOSE-UP!

OOPS, MY BAD--A LITTLE *TOO* CLOSE, HUH?

SKRAK

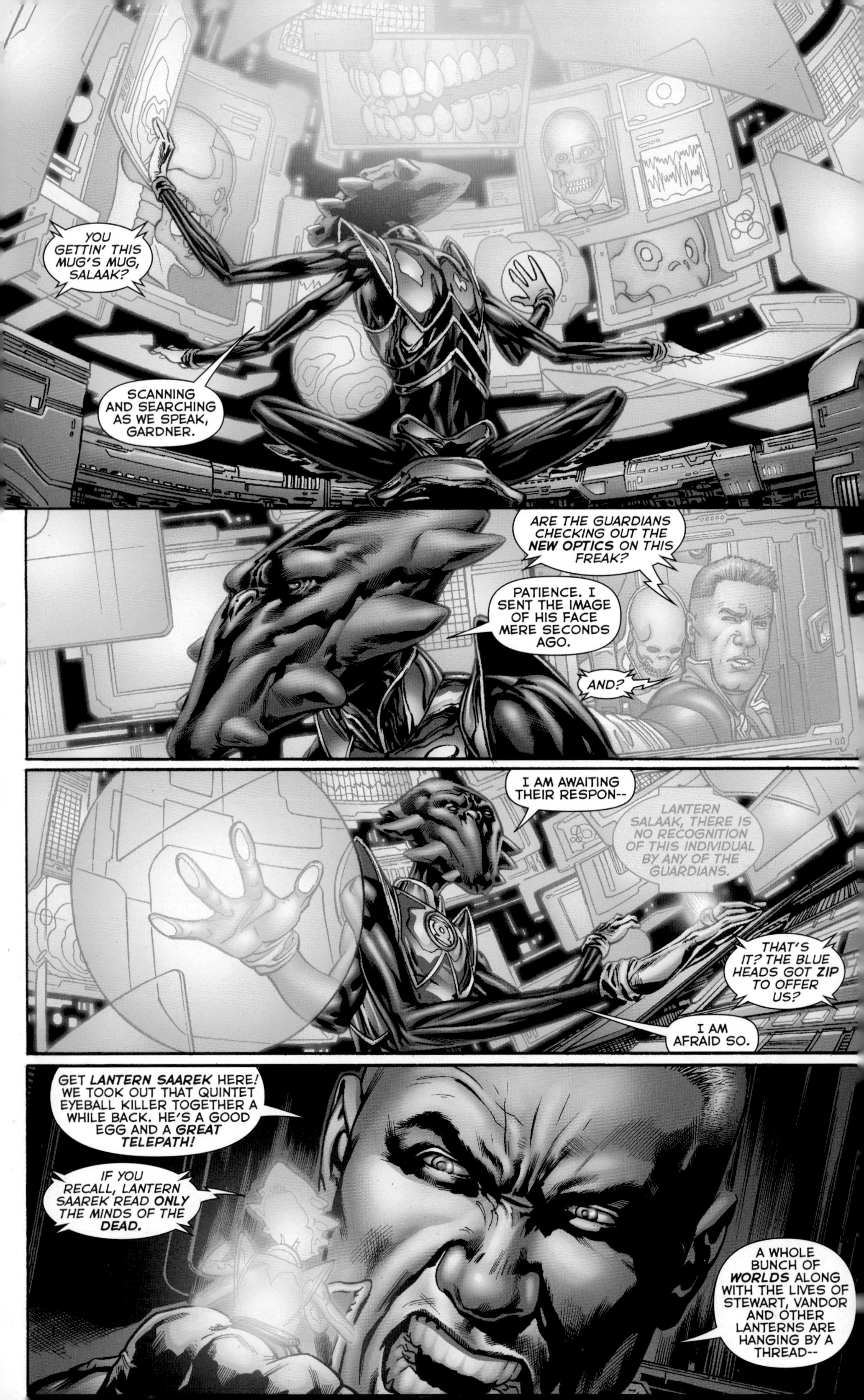
YOU GETTIN' THIS MUG'S MUG, SALAAK?
SCANNING AND SEARCHING AS WE SPEAK, GARDNER.
ARE THE GUARDIANS CHECKING OUT THE NEW OPTICS ON THIS FREAK?
PATIENCE. I SENT THE IMAGE OF HIS FACE MERE SECONDS AGO.
AND?
I AM AWAITING THEIR RESPON--
LANTERN SALAAK, THERE IS NO RECOGNITION OF THIS INDIVIDUAL BY ANY OF THE GUARDIANS.
THAT'S IT? THE BLUE HEADS GOT ZIP TO OFFER US?
I AM AFRAID SO.
GET LANTERN SAAREK HERE! WE TOOK OUT THAT QUINTET EYEBALL KILLER TOGETHER A WHILE BACK. HE'S A GOOD EGG AND A GREAT TELEPATH!
IF YOU RECALL, LANTERN SAAREK READ ONLY THE MINDS OF THE DEAD.
A WHOLE BUNCH OF WORLDS ALONG WITH THE LIVES OF STEWART, VANDOR AND OTHER LANTERNS ARE HANGING BY A THREAD--

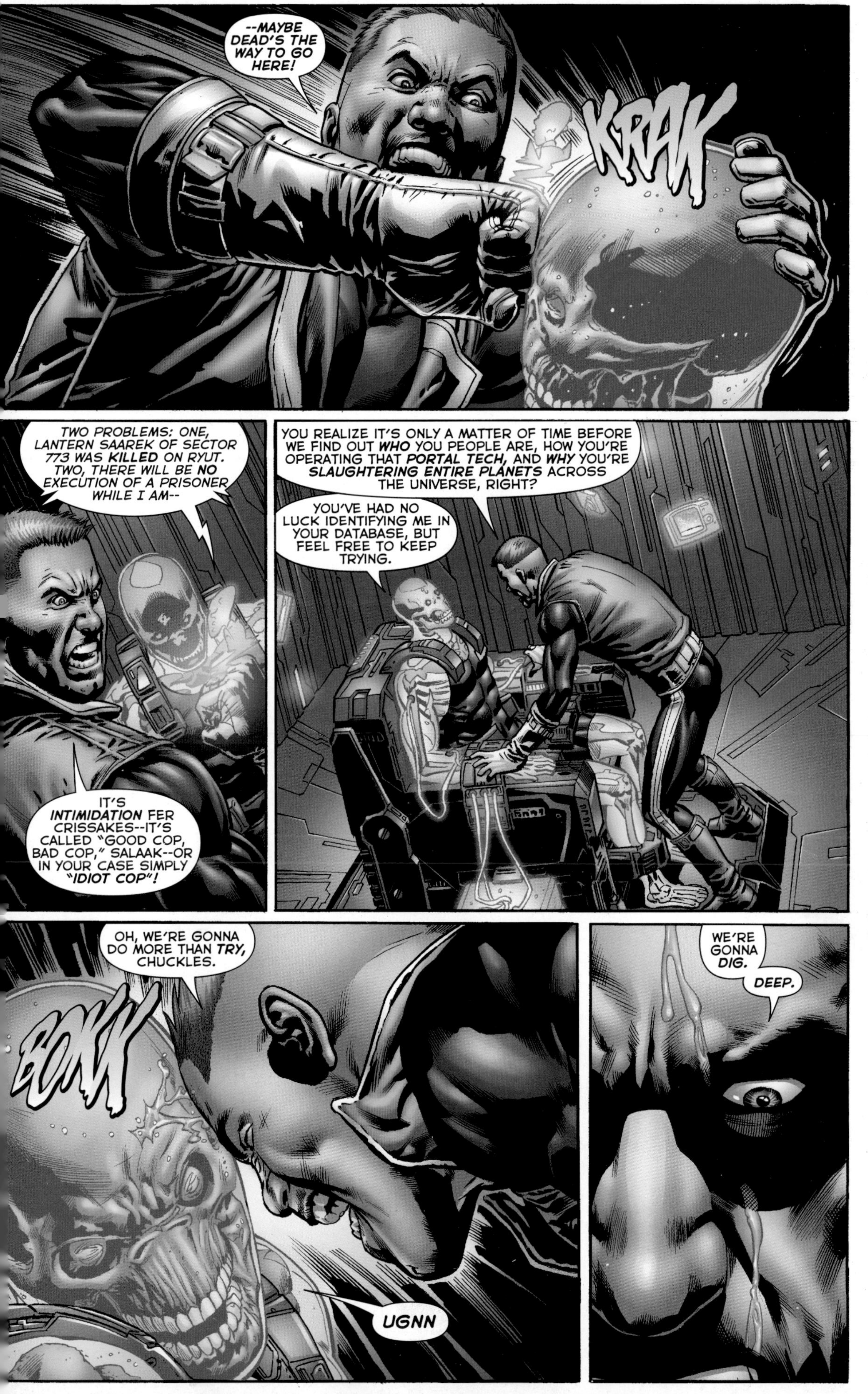
--MAYBE DEAD'S THE WAY TO GO HERE!
KRAK
TWO PROBLEMS: ONE, LANTERN SAAREK OF SECTOR 773 WAS KILLED ON RYUT. TWO, THERE WILL BE NO EXECUTION OF A PRISONER WHILE I AM--
IT'S INTIMIDATION FER CRISSAKES--IT'S CALLED "GOOD COP, BAD COP," SALAAK--OR IN YOUR CASE SIMPLY "IDIOT COP"!
YOU REALIZE IT'S ONLY A MATTER OF TIME BEFORE WE FIND OUT WHO YOU PEOPLE ARE, HOW YOU'RE OPERATING THAT PORTAL TECH, AND WHY YOU'RE SLAUGHTERING ENTIRE PLANETS ACROSS THE UNIVERSE, RIGHT?
YOU'VE HAD NO LUCK IDENTIFYING ME IN YOUR DATABASE, BUT FEEL FREE TO KEEP TRYING.
OH, WE'RE GONNA DO MORE THAN TRY, CHUCKLES.
BONK
UGNN
WE'RE GONNA DIG.
DEEP.

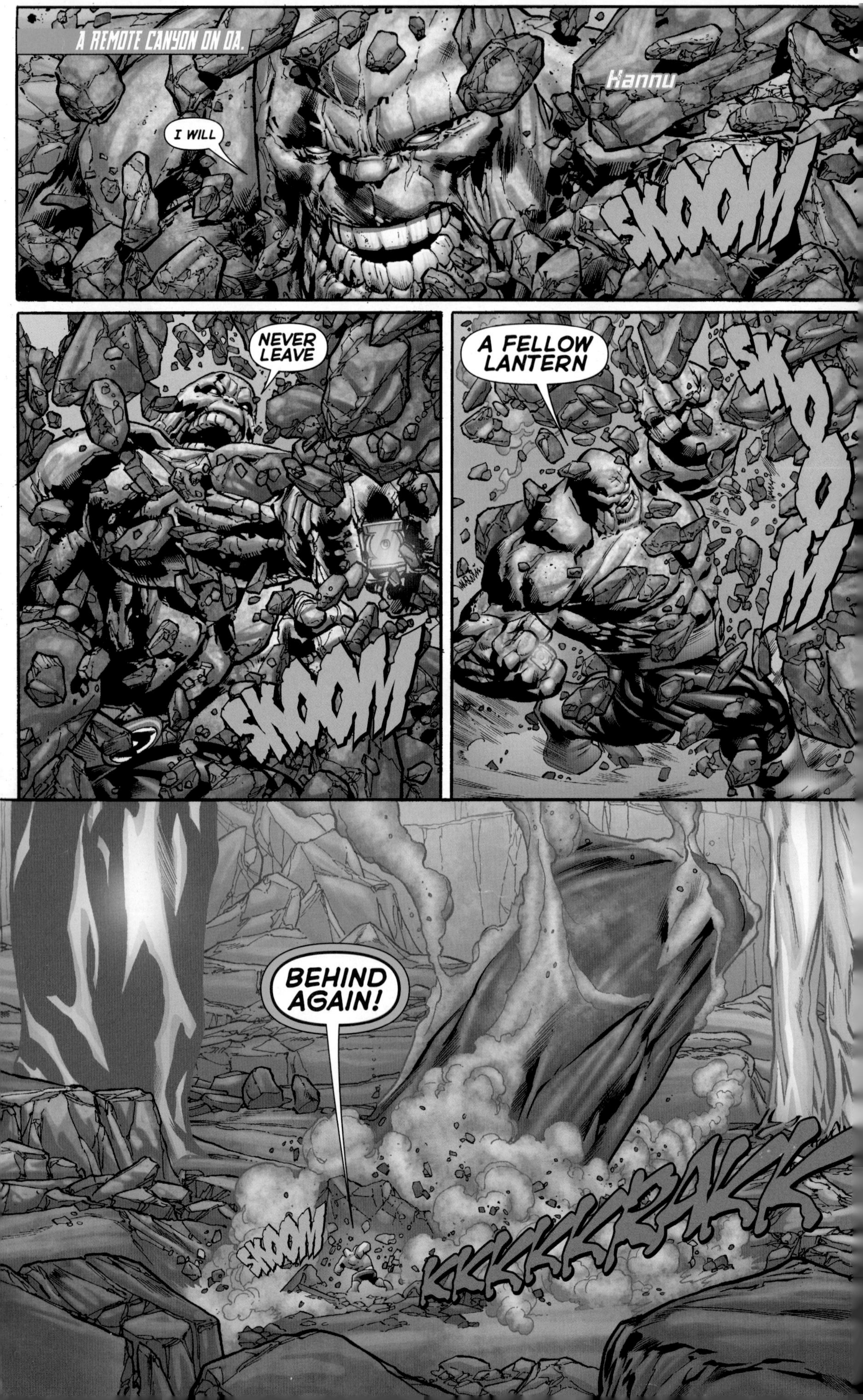
A REMOTE CANYON ON OA.
Kannu
I WILL
SKOOM
NEVER LEAVE
SKOOM
A FELLOW LANTERN
SKOOM
BEHIND AGAIN!
SKOOM
KKKKKRAKK

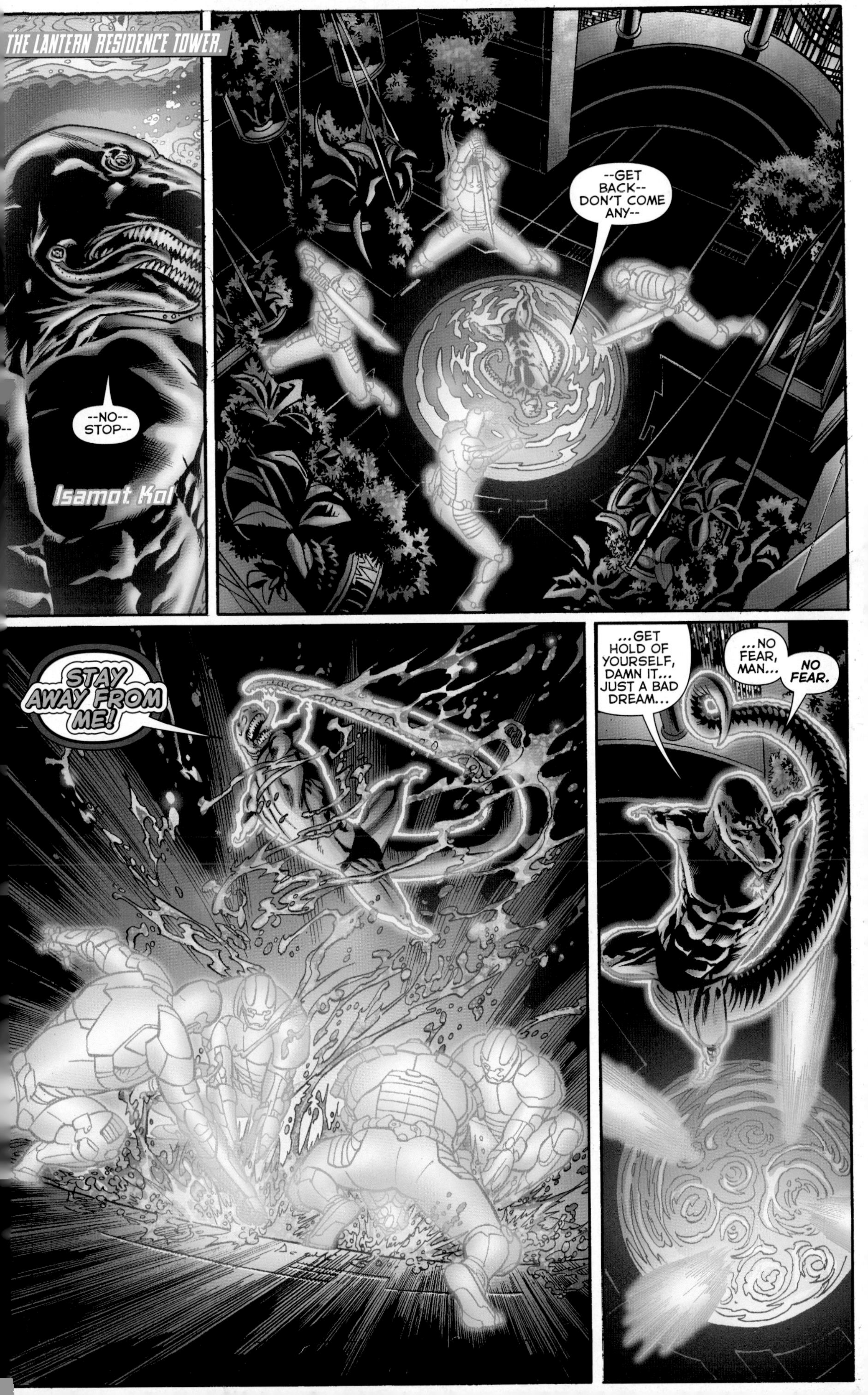
THE LANTERN RESIDENCE TOWER.
--NO-- STOP--
Isamot Kol
--GET BACK-- DON'T COME ANY--
STAY AWAY FROM ME!
...GET HOLD OF YOURSELF, DAMN IT... JUST A BAD DREAM...
...NO FEAR, MAN...
NO FEAR.

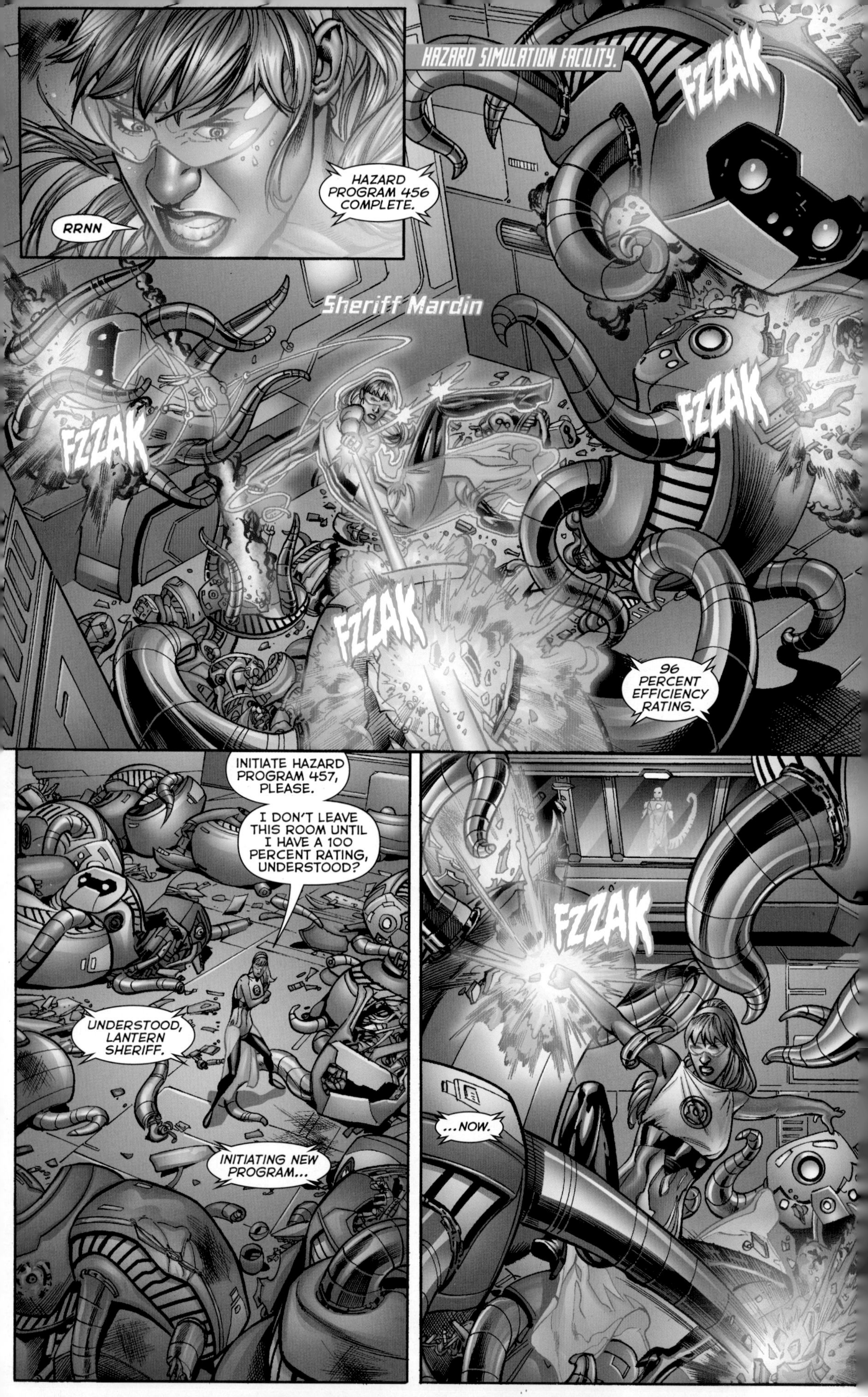
HAZARD SIMULATION FACILITY.
FZZAK
HAZARD PROGRAM 456 COMPLETE.
RRNN
Sheriff Mardin
FZZAK
FZZAK
FZZAK
96 PERCENT EFFICIENCY RATING.
INITIATE HAZARD PROGRAM 457, PLEASE.
I DON'T LEAVE THIS ROOM UNTIL I HAVE A 100 PERCENT RATING, UNDERSTOOD?
UNDERSTOOD, LANTERN SHERIFF.
INITIATING NEW PROGRAM...
FZZAK
...NOW.

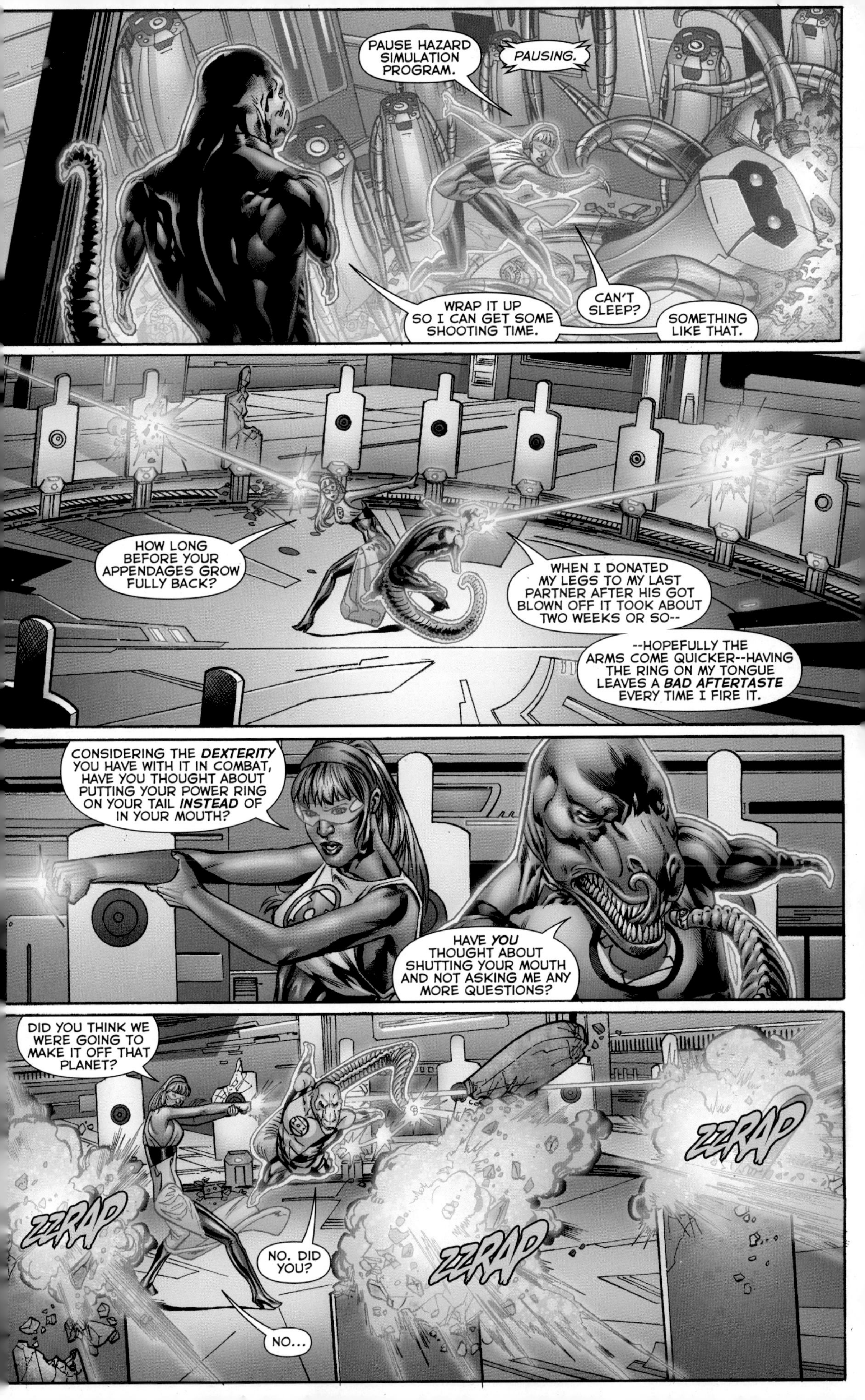
PAUSE HAZARD SIMULATION PROGRAM.
PAUSING.
WRAP IT UP SO I CAN GET SOME SHOOTING TIME.
CAN'T SLEEP?
SOMETHING LIKE THAT.
HOW LONG BEFORE YOUR APPENDAGES GROW FULLY BACK?
WHEN I DONATED MY LEGS TO MY LAST PARTNER AFTER HIS GOT BLOWN OFF IT TOOK ABOUT TWO WEEKS OR SO--
--HOPEFULLY THE ARMS COME QUICKER--HAVING THE RING ON MY TONGUE LEAVES A *BAD AFTERTASTE* EVERY TIME I FIRE IT.
CONSIDERING THE *DEXTERITY* YOU HAVE WITH IT IN COMBAT, HAVE YOU THOUGHT ABOUT PUTTING YOUR POWER RING ON YOUR TAIL *INSTEAD* OF IN YOUR MOUTH?
HAVE *YOU* THOUGHT ABOUT SHUTTING YOUR MOUTH AND NOT ASKING ME ANY MORE QUESTIONS?
DID YOU THINK WE WERE GOING TO MAKE IT OFF THAT PLANET?
ZZRAP
NO. DID YOU?
ZZRAP
ZZRAP
NO...

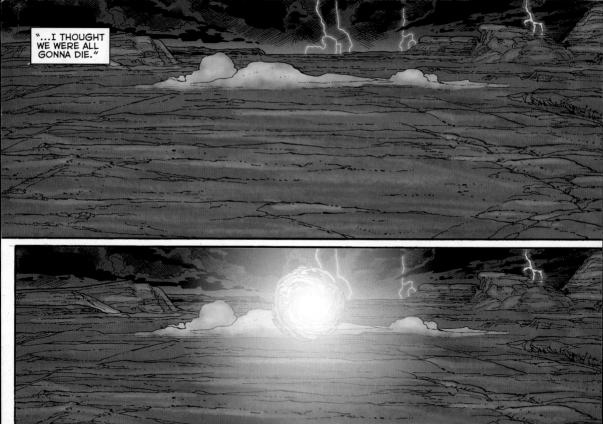

"...I THOUGHT WE WERE ALL GONNA DIE."

WHAT THE HELL--

BE PREPARED TO LOSE YOUR WILL AND MAYBE YOUR LIVES...

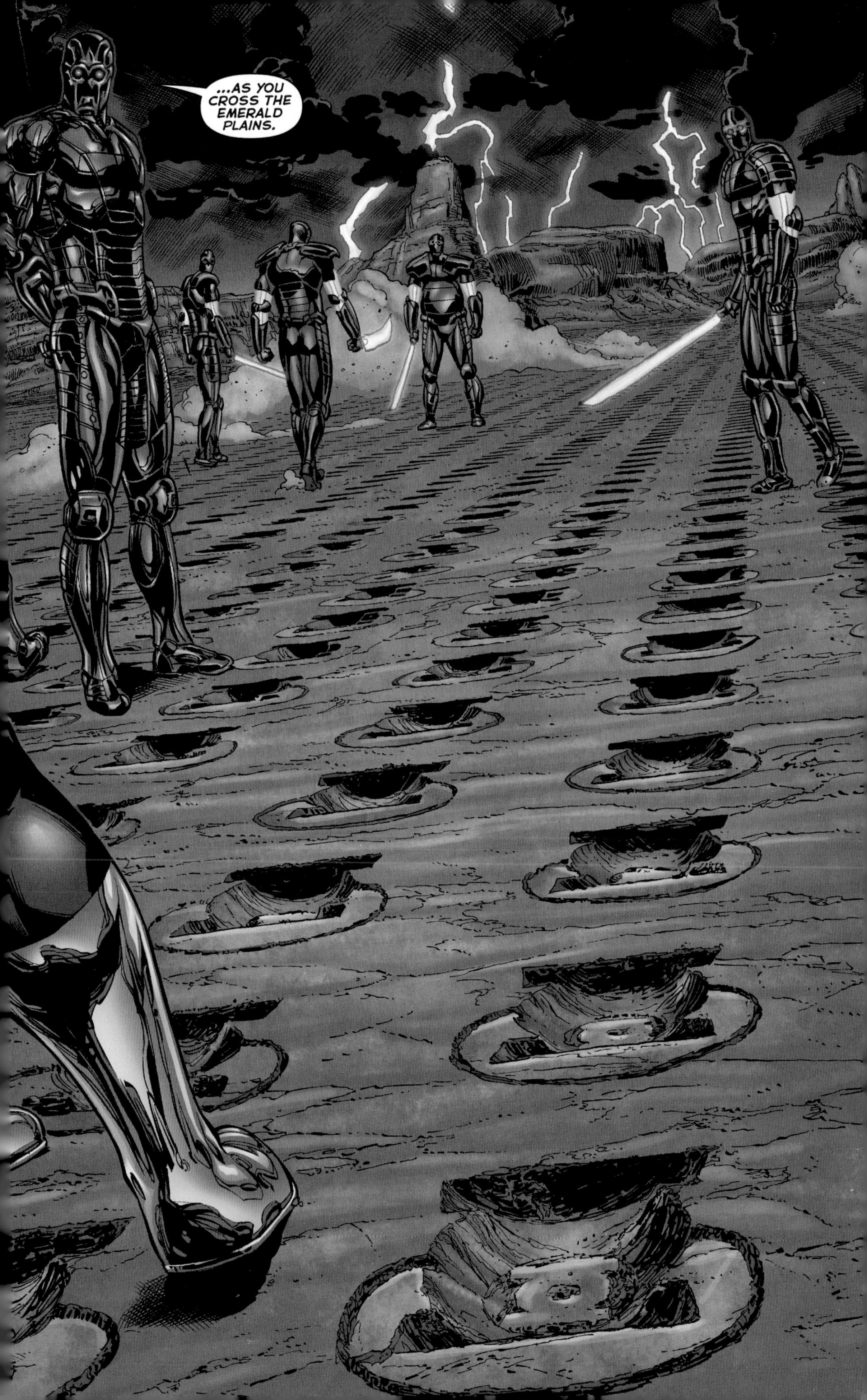
...AS YOU CROSS THE EMERALD PLAINS.

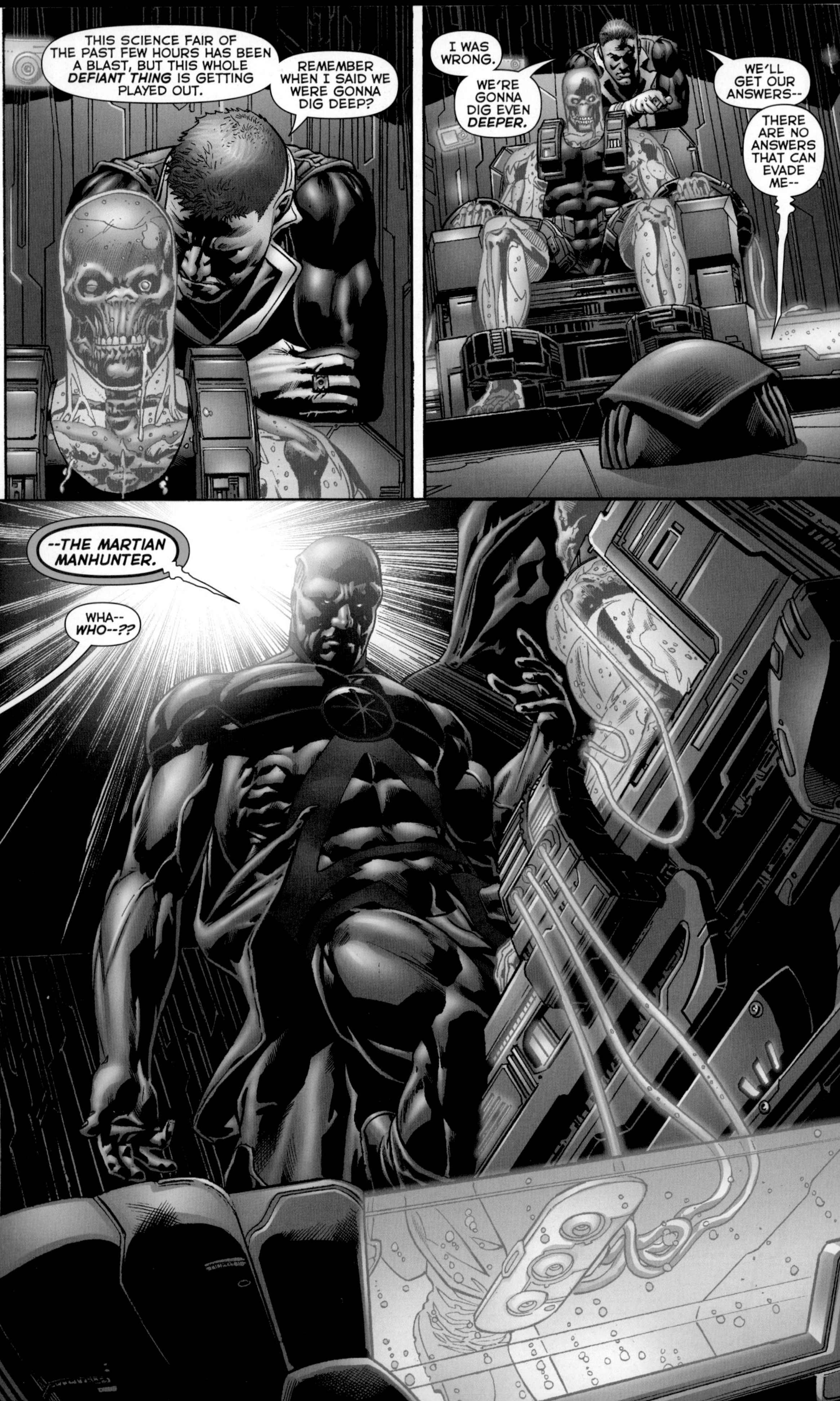
THIS SCIENCE FAIR OF THE PAST FEW HOURS HAS BEEN A BLAST, BUT THIS WHOLE *DEFIANT THING* IS GETTING PLAYED OUT.
REMEMBER WHEN I SAID WE WERE GONNA DIG DEEP?
I WAS WRONG.
WE'RE GONNA DIG EVEN *DEEPER.*
WE'LL GET OUR ANSWERS--
THERE ARE NO ANSWERS THAT CAN EVADE ME--
--THE MARTIAN MANHUNTER.
WHA-- *WHO--??*

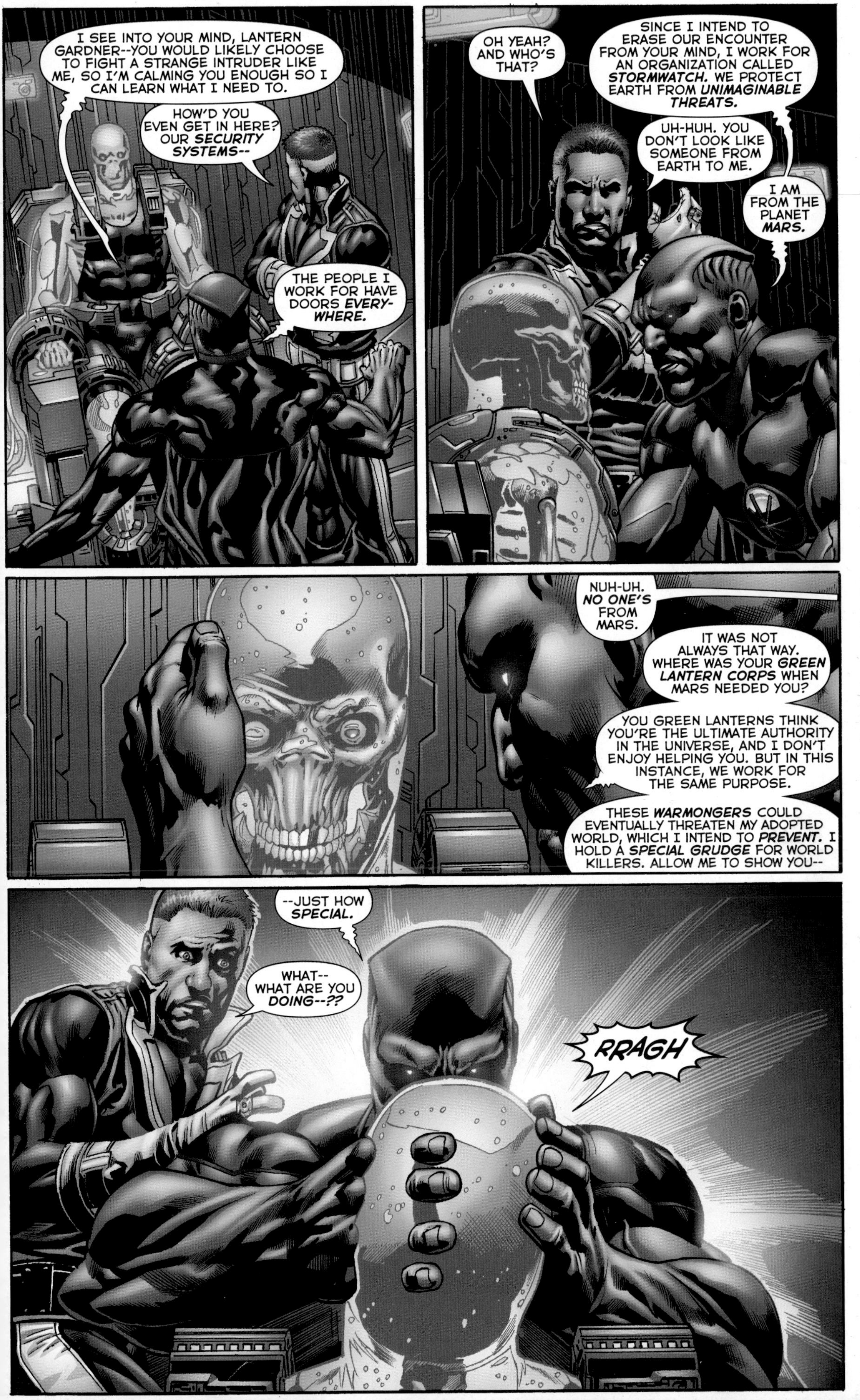
I SEE INTO YOUR MIND, LANTERN GARDNER--YOU WOULD LIKELY CHOOSE TO FIGHT A STRANGE INTRUDER LIKE ME, SO I'M CALMING YOU ENOUGH SO I CAN LEARN WHAT I NEED TO.
HOW'D YOU EVEN GET IN HERE? OUR SECURITY SYSTEMS--
THE PEOPLE I WORK FOR HAVE DOORS EVERY-WHERE.
OH YEAH? AND WHO'S THAT?
SINCE I INTEND TO ERASE OUR ENCOUNTER FROM YOUR MIND, I WORK FOR AN ORGANIZATION CALLED STORMWATCH. WE PROTECT EARTH FROM UNIMAGINABLE THREATS.
UH-HUH. YOU DON'T LOOK LIKE SOMEONE FROM EARTH TO ME.
I AM FROM THE PLANET MARS.
NUH-UH. NO ONE'S FROM MARS.
IT WAS NOT ALWAYS THAT WAY. WHERE WAS YOUR GREEN LANTERN CORPS WHEN MARS NEEDED YOU?
YOU GREEN LANTERNS THINK YOU'RE THE ULTIMATE AUTHORITY IN THE UNIVERSE, AND I DON'T ENJOY HELPING YOU. BUT IN THIS INSTANCE, WE WORK FOR THE SAME PURPOSE.
THESE WARMONGERS COULD EVENTUALLY THREATEN MY ADOPTED WORLD, WHICH I INTEND TO PREVENT. I HOLD A SPECIAL GRUDGE FOR WORLD KILLERS. ALLOW ME TO SHOW YOU--
--JUST HOW SPECIAL.
WHAT-- WHAT ARE YOU DOING--??
RRAGH

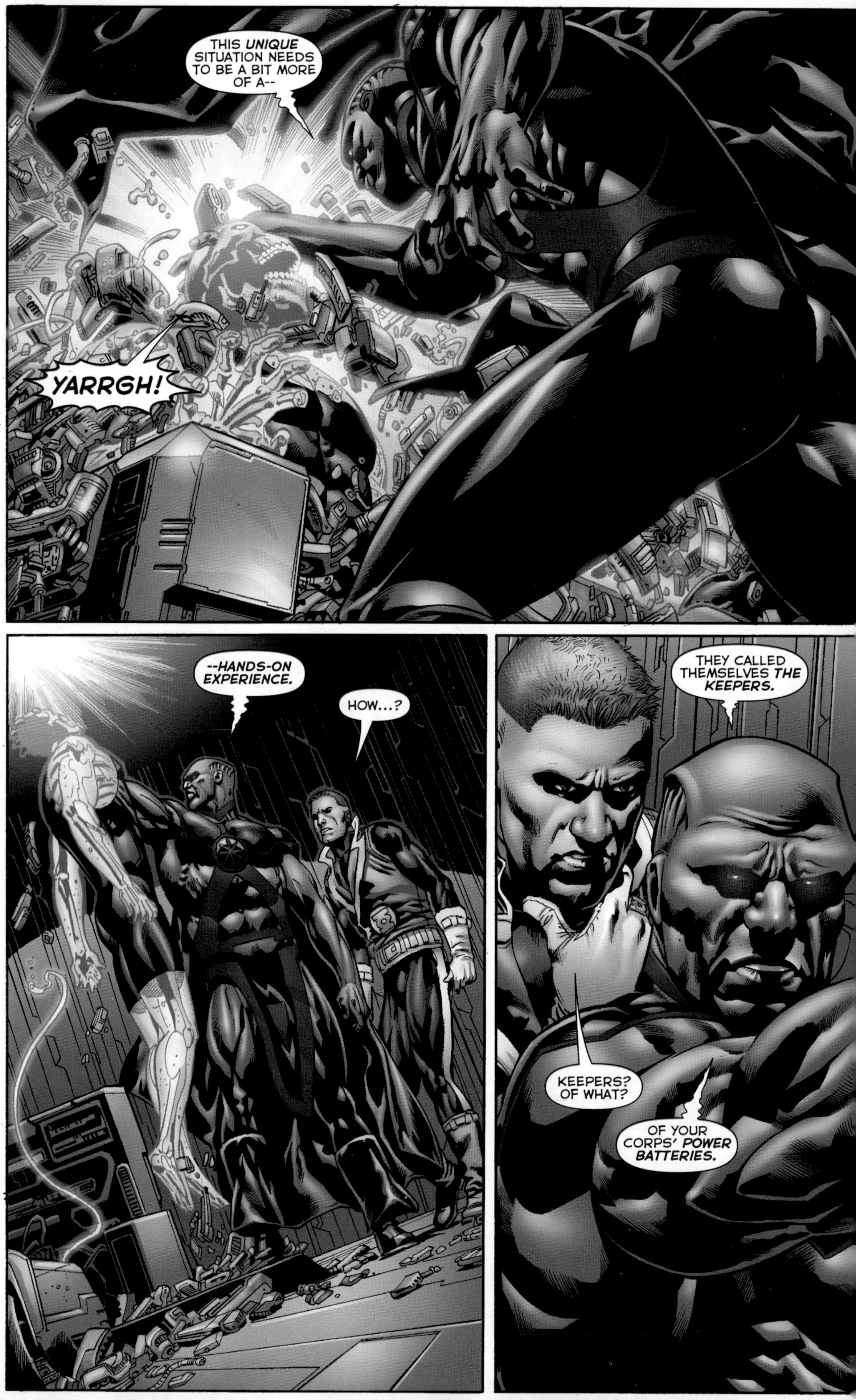
THIS UNIQUE SITUATION NEEDS TO BE A BIT MORE OF A--
YARRGH!
--HANDS-ON EXPERIENCE.
HOW...?
THEY CALLED THEMSELVES THE KEEPERS.
KEEPERS? OF WHAT?
OF YOUR CORPS' POWER BATTERIES.

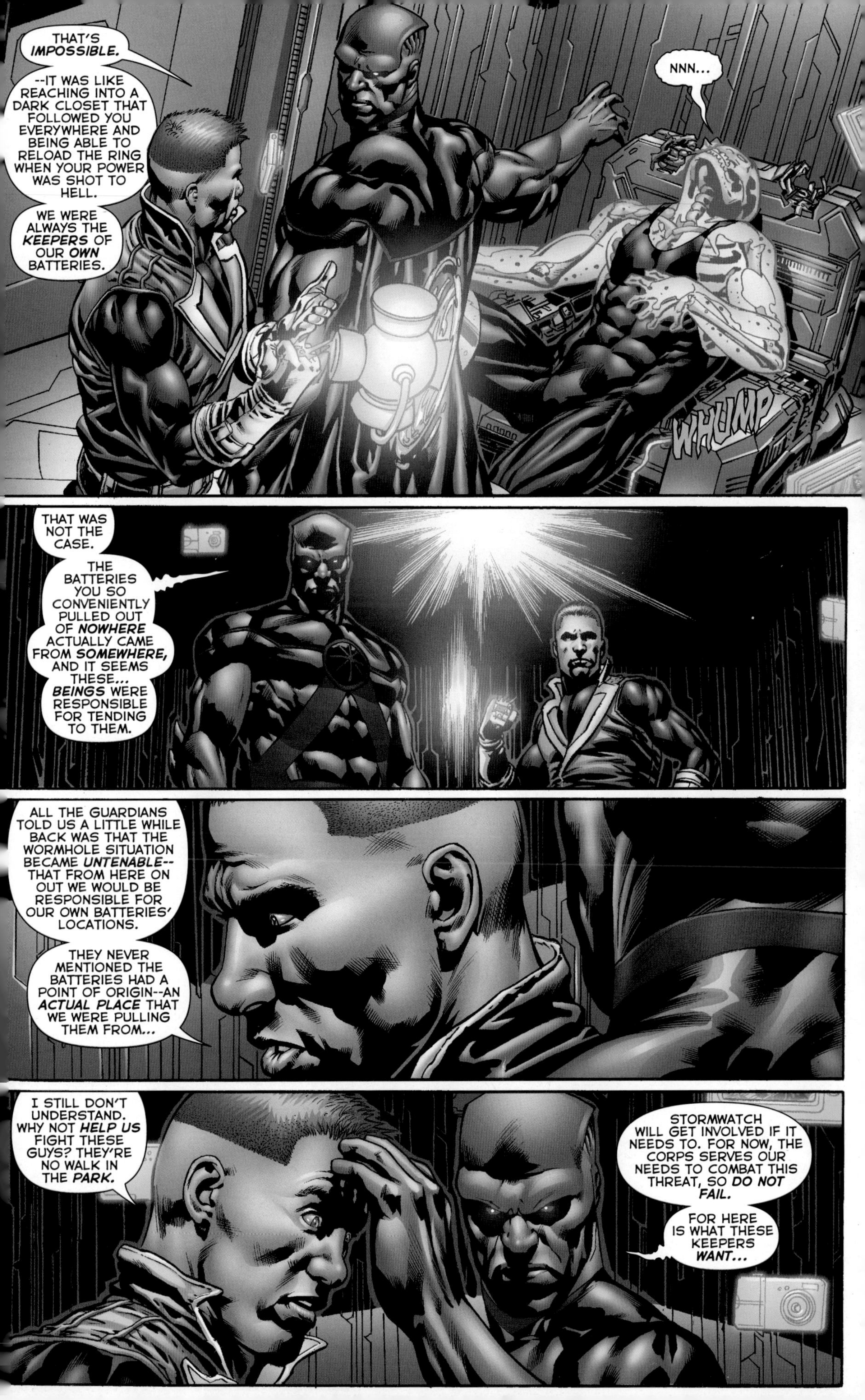
THAT'S *IMPOSSIBLE.*
--IT WAS LIKE REACHING INTO A DARK CLOSET THAT FOLLOWED YOU EVERYWHERE AND BEING ABLE TO RELOAD THE RING WHEN YOUR POWER WAS SHOT TO HELL.
WE WERE ALWAYS THE *KEEPERS* OF OUR *OWN* BATTERIES.
NNN...
WHUMP
THAT WAS NOT THE CASE.
THE BATTERIES YOU SO CONVENIENTLY PULLED OUT OF *NOWHERE* ACTUALLY CAME FROM *SOMEWHERE,* AND IT SEEMS THESE... *BEINGS* WERE RESPONSIBLE FOR TENDING TO THEM.
ALL THE GUARDIANS TOLD US A LITTLE WHILE BACK WAS THAT THE WORMHOLE SITUATION BECAME *UNTENABLE*-- THAT FROM HERE ON OUT WE WOULD BE RESPONSIBLE FOR OUR OWN BATTERIES' LOCATIONS.
THEY NEVER MENTIONED THE BATTERIES HAD A POINT OF ORIGIN--AN *ACTUAL PLACE* THAT WE WERE PULLING THEM FROM...
I STILL DON'T UNDERSTAND. WHY NOT *HELP US* FIGHT THESE GUYS? THEY'RE NO WALK IN THE *PARK.*
STORMWATCH WILL GET INVOLVED IF IT NEEDS TO. FOR NOW, THE CORPS SERVES OUR NEEDS TO COMBAT THIS THREAT, SO *DO NOT FAIL.*
FOR HERE IS WHAT THESE KEEPERS *WANT...*

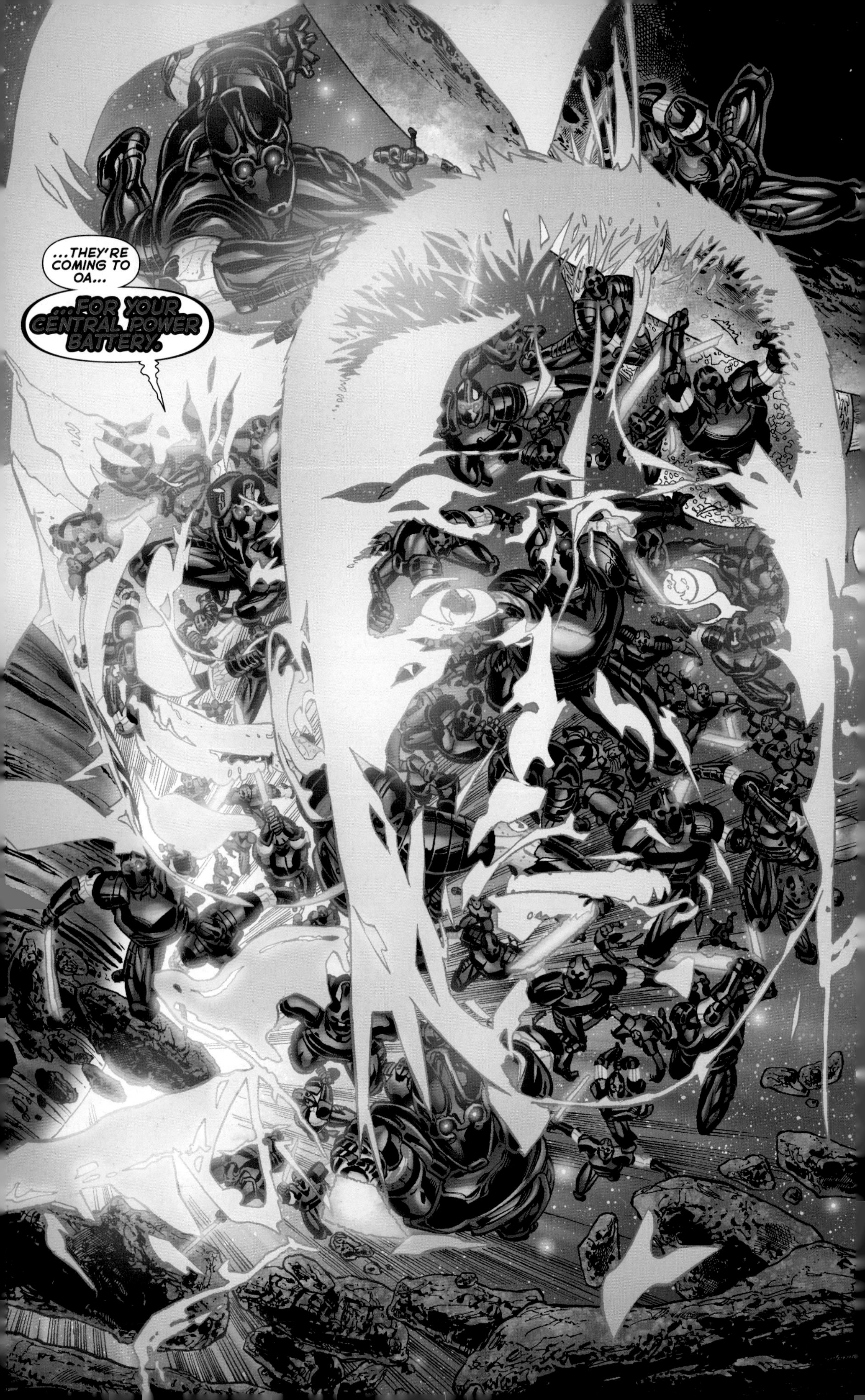
...THEY'RE COMING TO OA...
...FOR YOUR CENTRAL POWER BATTERY.

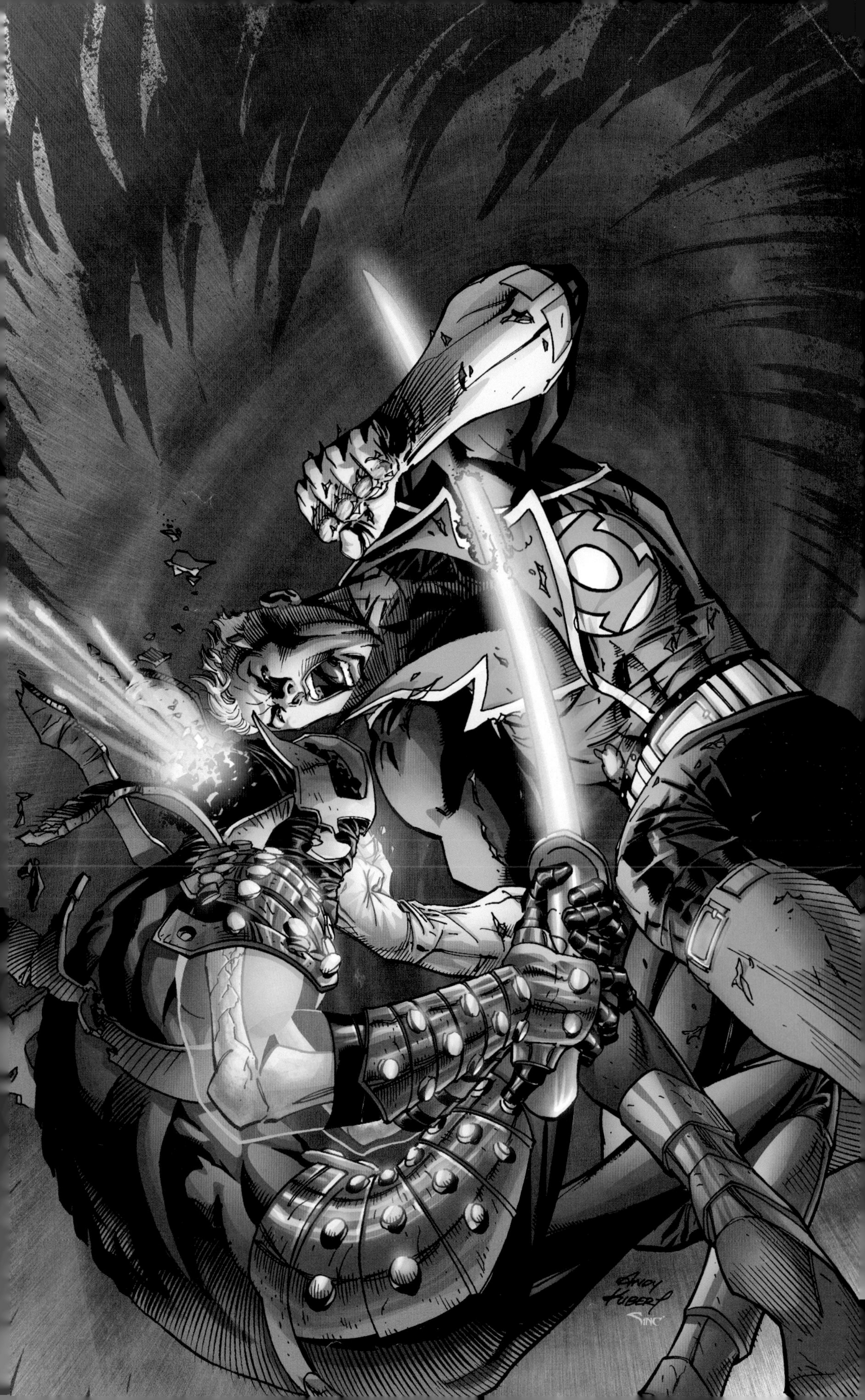
ANDY
KUBERT
SINC

MEAN MACHINE

PETER J. TOMASI writer **FERNANDO PASARIN** penciller **SCOTT HANNA** inker cover by **ANDY KUBERT** with **ALEX SINCLAIR**

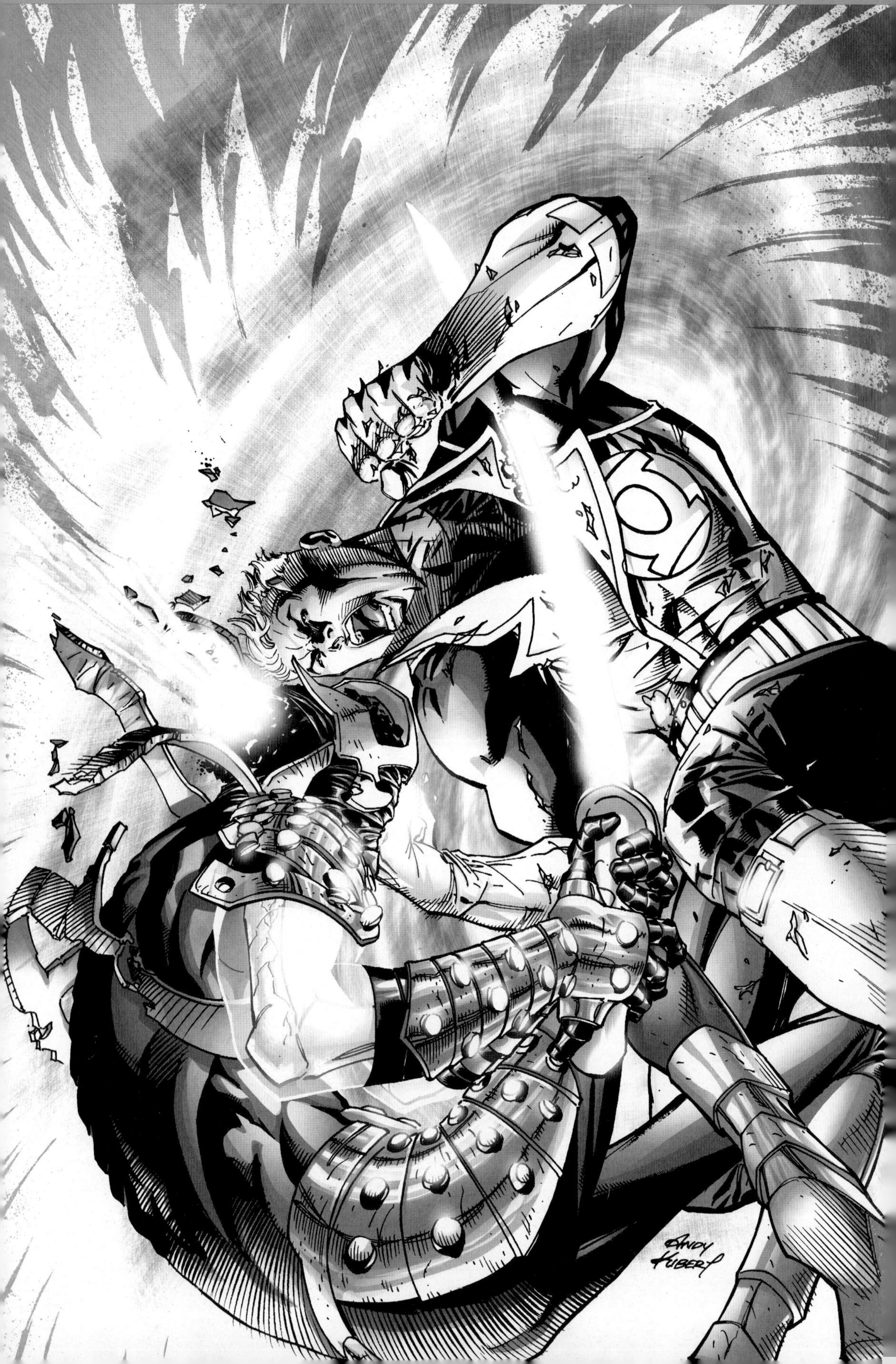
ANDY KUBERT

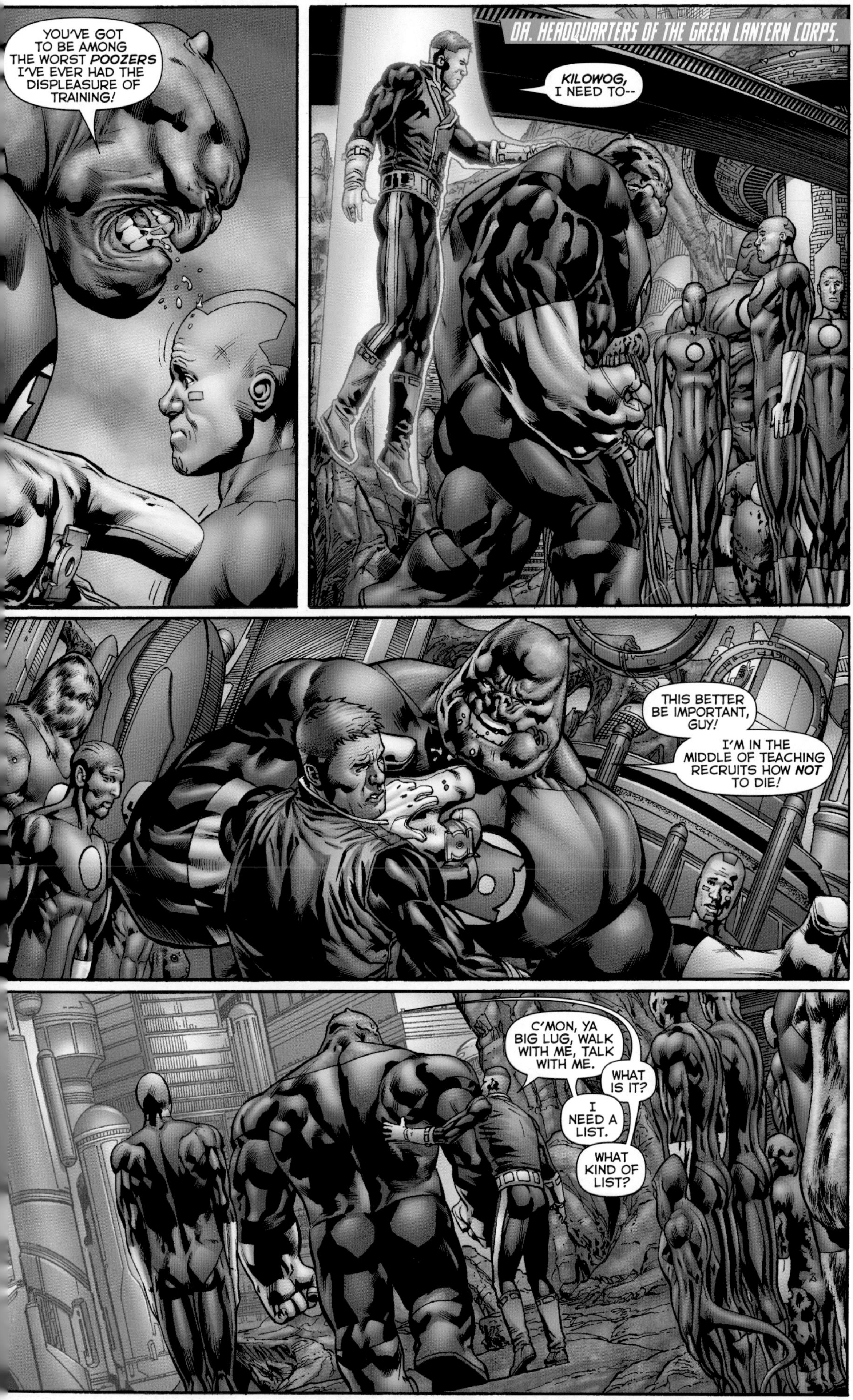
YOU'VE GOT TO BE AMONG THE WORST POOZERS I'VE EVER HAD THE DISPLEASURE OF TRAINING!
OA. HEADQUARTERS OF THE GREEN LANTERN CORPS.
KILOWOG, I NEED TO--
THIS BETTER BE IMPORTANT, GUY!
I'M IN THE MIDDLE OF TEACHING RECRUITS HOW NOT TO DIE!
C'MON, YA BIG LUG, WALK WITH ME, TALK WITH ME.
WHAT IS IT?
I NEED A LIST.
WHAT KIND OF LIST?

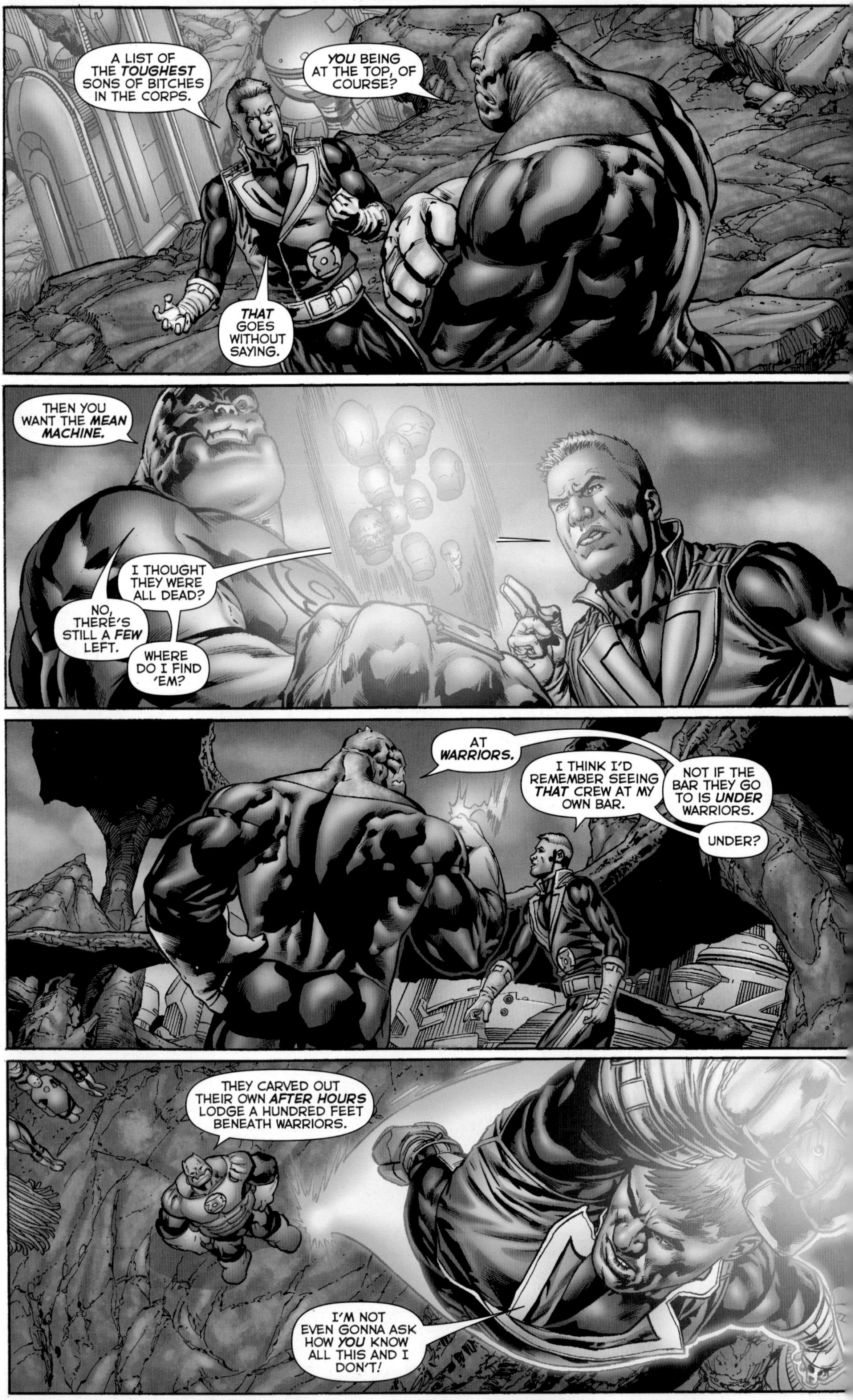
A LIST OF THE TOUGHEST SONS OF BITCHES IN THE CORPS.
YOU BEING AT THE TOP, OF COURSE?
THAT GOES WITHOUT SAYING.
THEN YOU WANT THE MEAN MACHINE.
I THOUGHT THEY WERE ALL DEAD?
NO, THERE'S STILL A FEW LEFT.
WHERE DO I FIND 'EM?
AT WARRIORS.
I THINK I'D REMEMBER SEEING THAT CREW AT MY OWN BAR.
NOT IF THE BAR THEY GO TO IS UNDER WARRIORS.
UNDER?
THEY CARVED OUT THEIR OWN AFTER HOURS LODGE A HUNDRED FEET BENEATH WARRIORS.
I'M NOT EVEN GONNA ASK HOW YOU KNOW ALL THIS AND I DON'T!

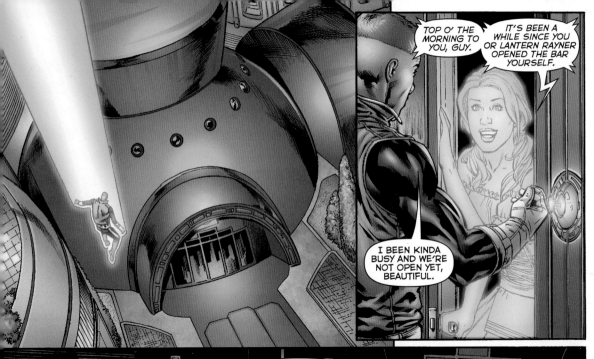

TOP O' THE MORNING TO YOU, GUY.

IT'S BEEN A WHILE SINCE YOU OR LANTERN RAYNER OPENED THE BAR YOURSELF.

I BEEN KINDA BUSY AND WE'RE NOT OPEN YET, BEAUTIFUL.

WOULD YOU LIKE ME TO GO OVER THE ACCOUNTS RECEIVABLE INVOICES WITH YOU INSTEAD OF THE MANAGER?

NO PAPER PUSHING FOR ME, I'M HERE ON OTHER BUSINESS.

RING, SCAN AREA AND COMPARE IT TO STEWART'S ORIGINAL ARCHITECTURAL PLANS.

SHOW ANY STRUCTURAL DEVIATION THAT'D--

WELL WHADDAYA KNOW...

...I GOT ME SOME GROUNDHOG PROBLEMS.

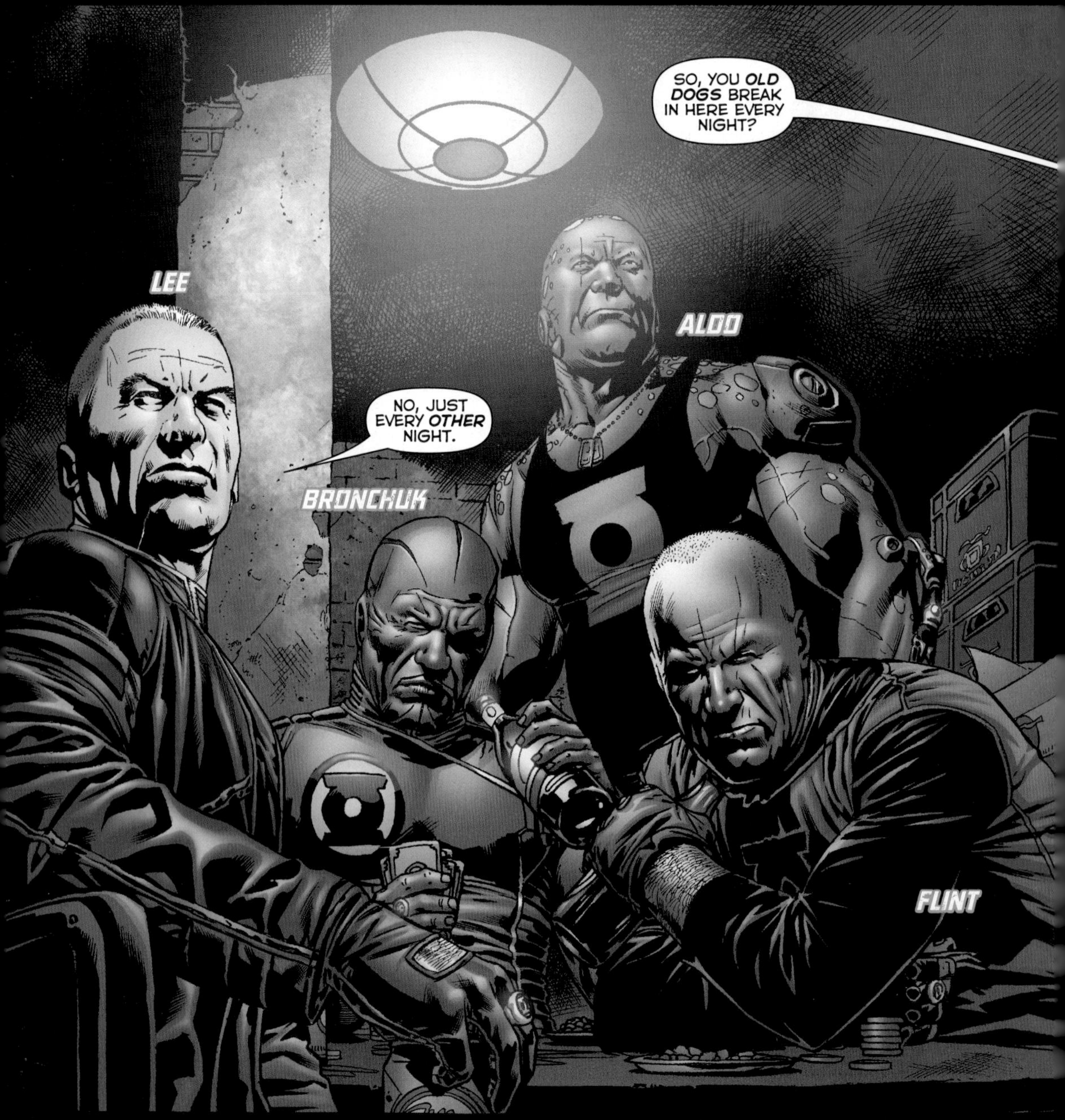
SO, YOU OLD DOGS BREAK IN HERE EVERY NIGHT?
NO, JUST EVERY OTHER NIGHT.
LEE
ALDO
BRONCHUK
FLINT

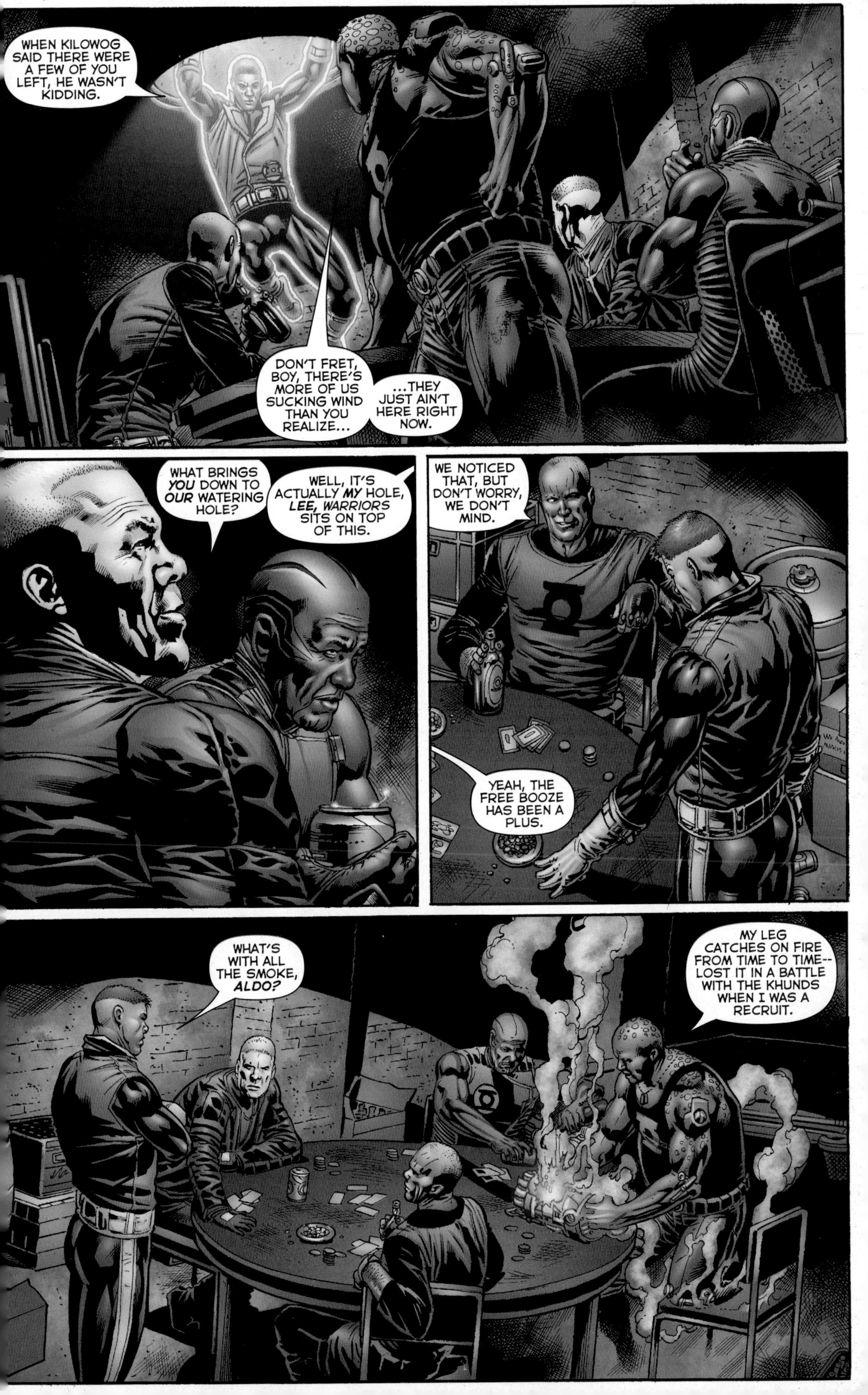

WHEN KILOWOG SAID THERE WERE A FEW OF YOU LEFT, HE WASN'T KIDDING.
DON'T FRET, BOY, THERE'S MORE OF US SUCKING WIND THAN YOU REALIZE...
...THEY JUST AIN'T HERE RIGHT NOW.
WHAT BRINGS *YOU* DOWN TO *OUR* WATERING HOLE?
WELL, IT'S ACTUALLY *MY* HOLE, *LEE, WARRIORS* SITS ON TOP OF THIS.
WE NOTICED THAT, BUT DON'T WORRY, WE DON'T MIND.
YEAH, THE FREE BOOZE HAS BEEN A PLUS.
WHAT'S WITH ALL THE SMOKE, *ALDO?*
MY LEG CATCHES ON FIRE FROM TIME TO TIME--LOST IT IN A BATTLE WITH THE KHUNDS WHEN I WAS A RECRUIT.

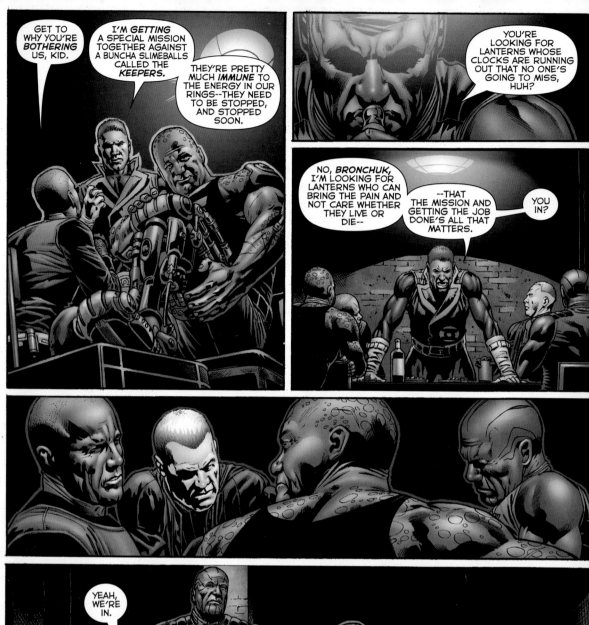

GET TO WHY YOU'RE *BOTHERING* US, KID.

I'M *GETTING* A SPECIAL MISSION TOGETHER AGAINST A BUNCHA SLIMEBALLS CALLED THE *KEEPERS.*

THEY'RE PRETTY MUCH *IMMUNE* TO THE ENERGY IN OUR RINGS--THEY NEED TO BE STOPPED, AND STOPPED SOON.

YOU'RE LOOKING FOR LANTERNS WHOSE CLOCKS ARE RUNNING OUT THAT NO ONE'S GOING TO MISS, HUH?

NO, *BRONCHUK,* I'M LOOKING FOR LANTERNS WHO CAN BRING THE PAIN AND NOT CARE WHETHER THEY LIVE OR DIE--

--THAT THE MISSION AND GETTING THE JOB DONE'S ALL THAT MATTERS.

YOU IN?

YEAH, WE'RE IN.

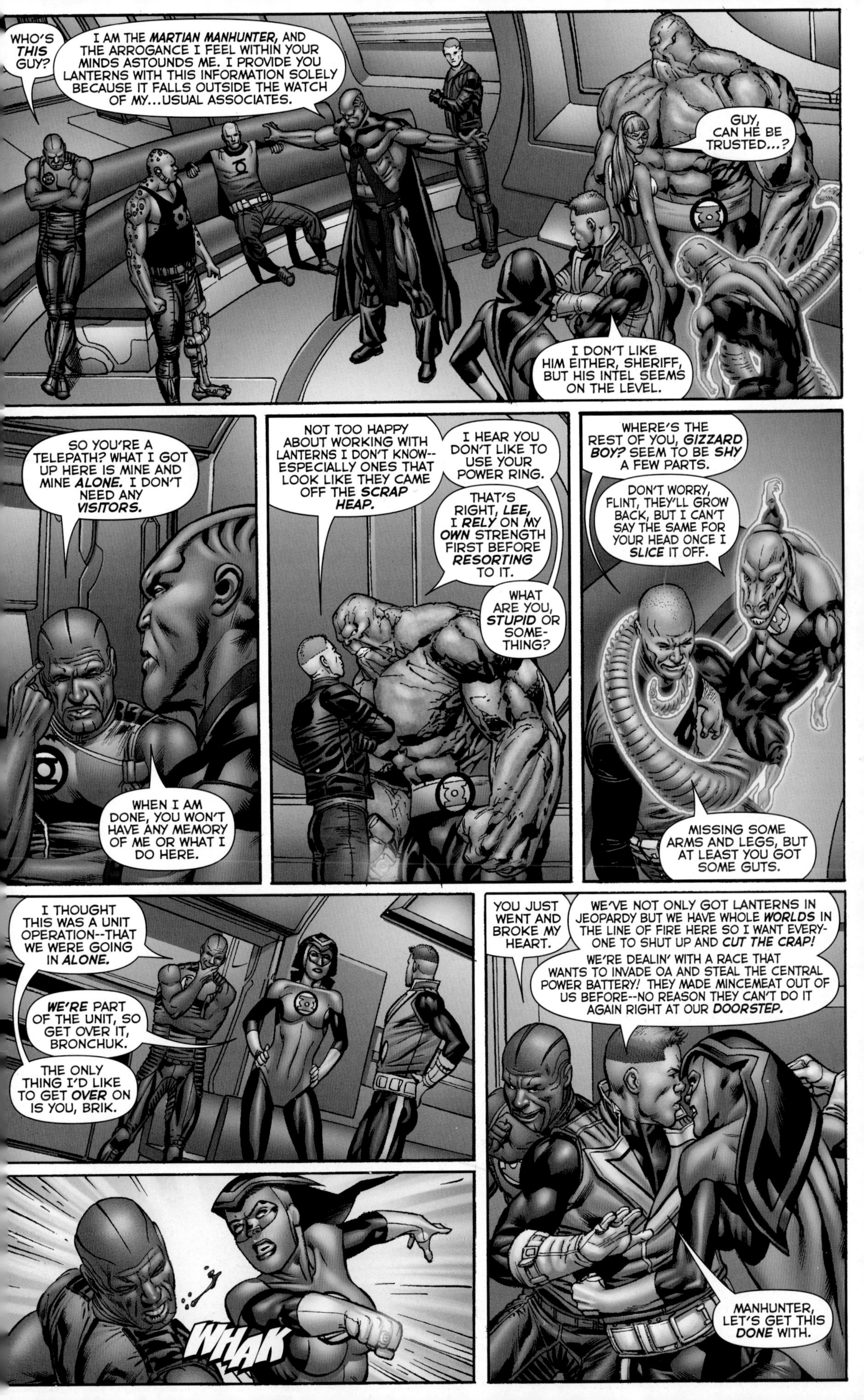
WHO'S *THIS* GUY?
I AM THE *MARTIAN MANHUNTER,* AND THE ARROGANCE I FEEL WITHIN YOUR MINDS ASTOUNDS ME. I PROVIDE YOU LANTERNS WITH THIS INFORMATION SOLELY BECAUSE IT FALLS OUTSIDE THE WATCH OF MY...USUAL ASSOCIATES.
GUY, CAN HE BE TRUSTED...?
I DON'T LIKE HIM EITHER, SHERIFF, BUT HIS INTEL SEEMS ON THE LEVEL.
SO YOU'RE A TELEPATH? WHAT I GOT UP HERE IS MINE AND MINE *ALONE.* I DON'T NEED ANY *VISITORS.*
WHEN I AM DONE, YOU WON'T HAVE ANY MEMORY OF ME OR WHAT I DO HERE.
NOT TOO HAPPY ABOUT WORKING WITH LANTERNS I DON'T KNOW--ESPECIALLY ONES THAT LOOK LIKE THEY CAME OFF THE *SCRAP HEAP.*
I HEAR YOU DON'T LIKE TO USE YOUR POWER RING.
THAT'S RIGHT, *LEE,* I *RELY* ON MY *OWN* STRENGTH FIRST BEFORE *RESORTING* TO IT.
WHAT ARE YOU, *STUPID* OR SOME-THING?
WHERE'S THE REST OF YOU, *GIZZARD BOY?* SEEM TO BE *SHY* A FEW PARTS.
DON'T WORRY, FLINT, THEY'LL GROW BACK, BUT I CAN'T SAY THE SAME FOR YOUR HEAD ONCE I *SLICE* IT OFF.
MISSING SOME ARMS AND LEGS, BUT AT LEAST YOU GOT SOME GUTS.
I THOUGHT THIS WAS A UNIT OPERATION--THAT WE WERE GOING IN *ALONE.*
WE'RE PART OF THE UNIT, SO GET OVER IT, BRONCHUK.
THE ONLY THING I'D LIKE TO GET *OVER* ON IS YOU, BRIK.
WHAK
YOU JUST WENT AND BROKE MY HEART.
WE'VE NOT ONLY GOT LANTERNS IN JEOPARDY BUT WE HAVE WHOLE *WORLDS* IN THE LINE OF FIRE HERE SO I WANT EVERY-ONE TO SHUT UP AND *CUT THE CRAP!*
WE'RE DEALIN' WITH A RACE THAT WANTS TO INVADE OA AND STEAL THE CENTRAL POWER BATTERY! THEY MADE MINCEMEAT OUT OF US BEFORE--NO REASON THEY CAN'T DO IT AGAIN RIGHT AT OUR *DOORSTEP.*
MANHUNTER, LET'S GET THIS *DONE* WITH.

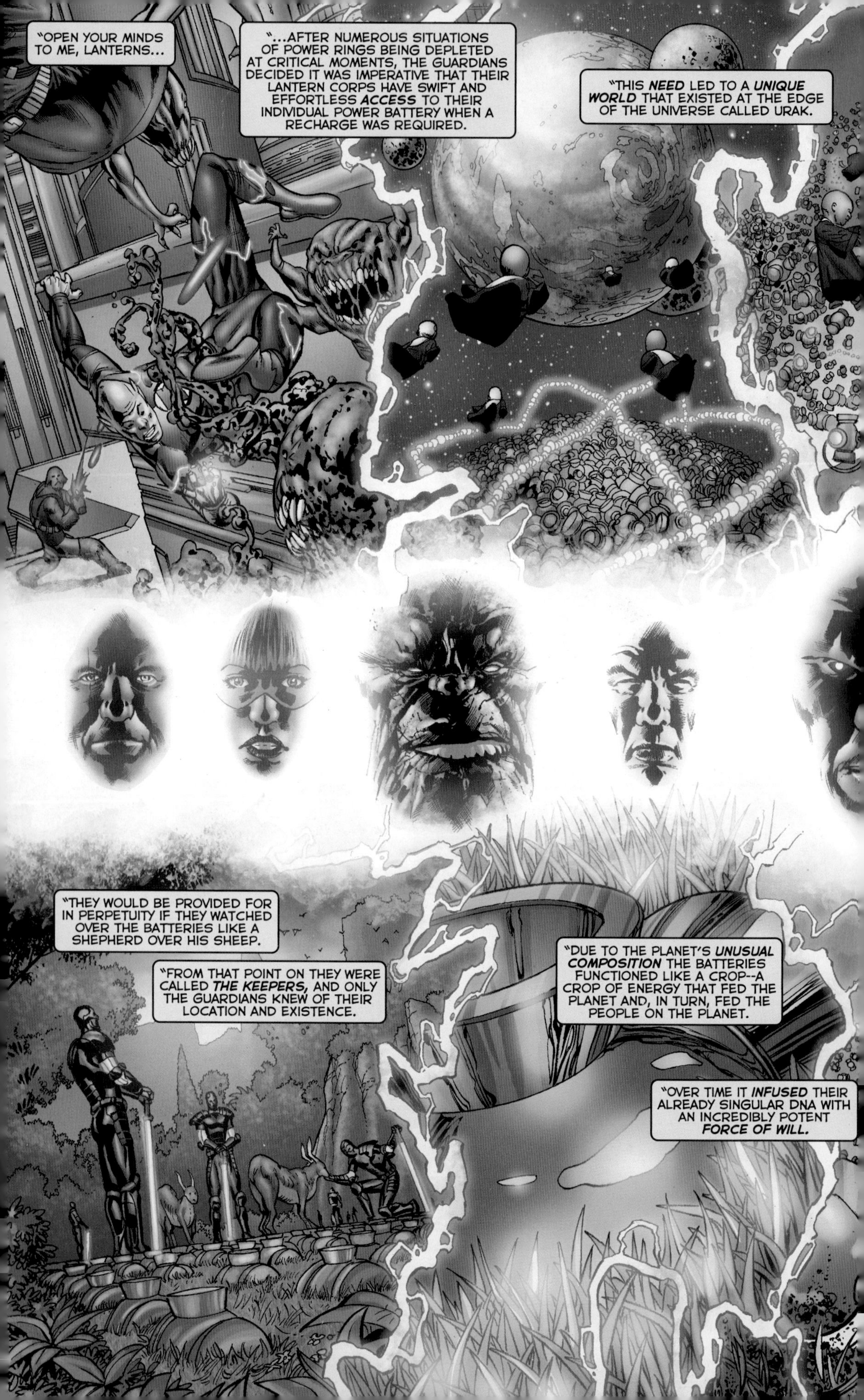
"OPEN YOUR MINDS TO ME, LANTERNS...
"...AFTER NUMEROUS SITUATIONS OF POWER RINGS BEING DEPLETED AT CRITICAL MOMENTS, THE GUARDIANS DECIDED IT WAS IMPERATIVE THAT THEIR LANTERN CORPS HAVE SWIFT AND EFFORTLESS ACCESS TO THEIR INDIVIDUAL POWER BATTERY WHEN A RECHARGE WAS REQUIRED.
"THIS NEED LED TO A UNIQUE WORLD THAT EXISTED AT THE EDGE OF THE UNIVERSE CALLED URAK.
"THEY WOULD BE PROVIDED FOR IN PERPETUITY IF THEY WATCHED OVER THE BATTERIES LIKE A SHEPHERD OVER HIS SHEEP.
"FROM THAT POINT ON THEY WERE CALLED THE KEEPERS, AND ONLY THE GUARDIANS KNEW OF THEIR LOCATION AND EXISTENCE.
"DUE TO THE PLANET'S UNUSUAL COMPOSITION THE BATTERIES FUNCTIONED LIKE A CROP--A CROP OF ENERGY THAT FED THE PLANET AND, IN TURN, FED THE PEOPLE ON THE PLANET.
"OVER TIME IT INFUSED THEIR ALREADY SINGULAR DNA WITH AN INCREDIBLY POTENT FORCE OF WILL.

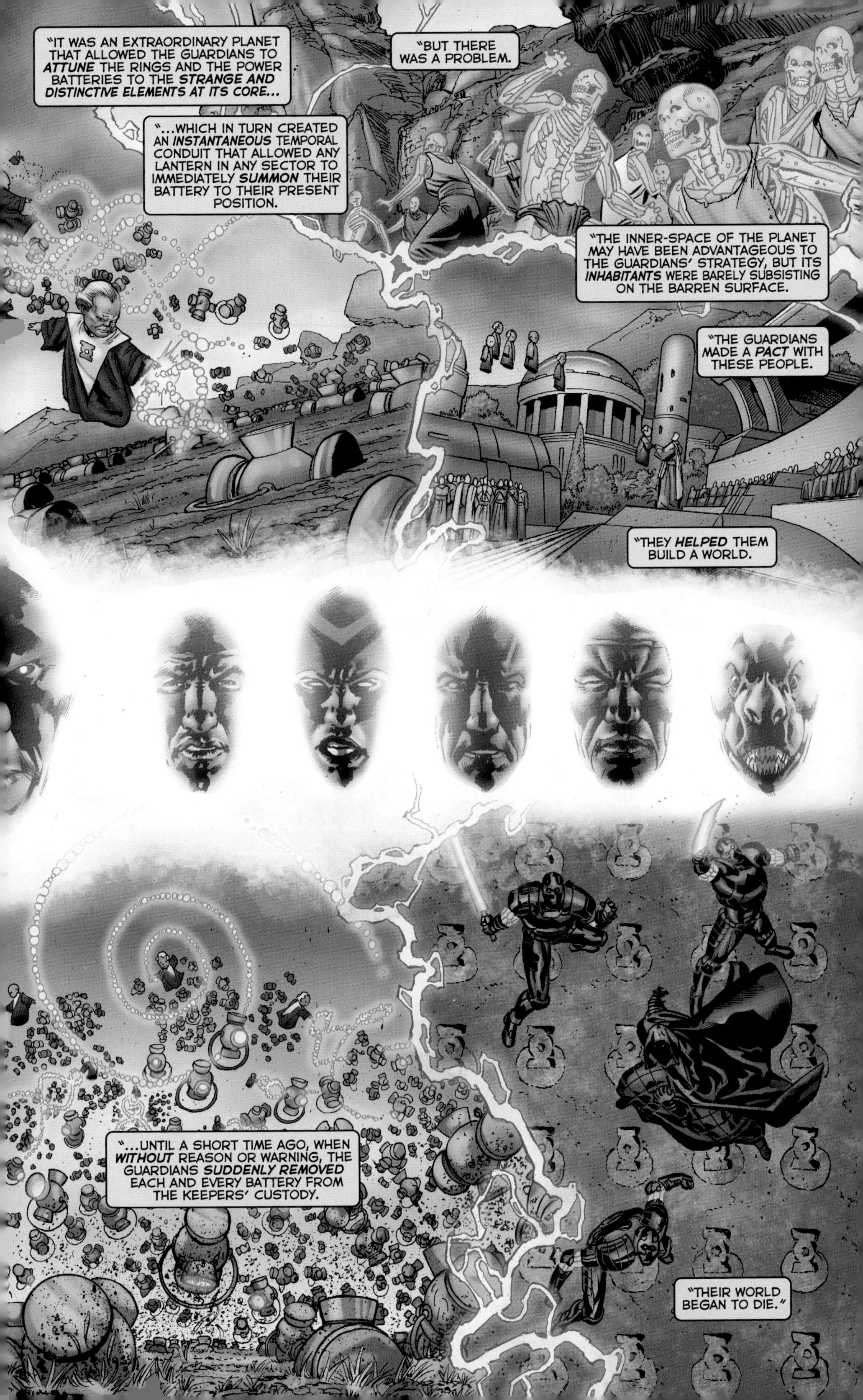
"IT WAS AN EXTRAORDINARY PLANET THAT ALLOWED THE GUARDIANS TO *ATTUNE* THE RINGS AND THE POWER BATTERIES TO THE *STRANGE AND DISTINCTIVE ELEMENTS AT ITS CORE...*
"...WHICH IN TURN CREATED AN *INSTANTANEOUS* TEMPORAL CONDUIT THAT ALLOWED ANY LANTERN IN ANY SECTOR TO IMMEDIATELY *SUMMON* THEIR BATTERY TO THEIR PRESENT POSITION.
"BUT THERE WAS A PROBLEM.
"THE INNER-SPACE OF THE PLANET MAY HAVE BEEN ADVANTAGEOUS TO THE GUARDIANS' STRATEGY, BUT ITS *INHABITANTS* WERE BARELY SUBSISTING ON THE BARREN SURFACE.
"THE GUARDIANS MADE A *PACT* WITH THESE PEOPLE.
"THEY *HELPED* THEM BUILD A WORLD.
"...UNTIL A SHORT TIME AGO, WHEN *WITHOUT* REASON OR WARNING, THE GUARDIANS *SUDDENLY REMOVED* EACH AND EVERY BATTERY FROM THE KEEPERS' CUSTODY.
"THEIR WORLD BEGAN TO DIE."

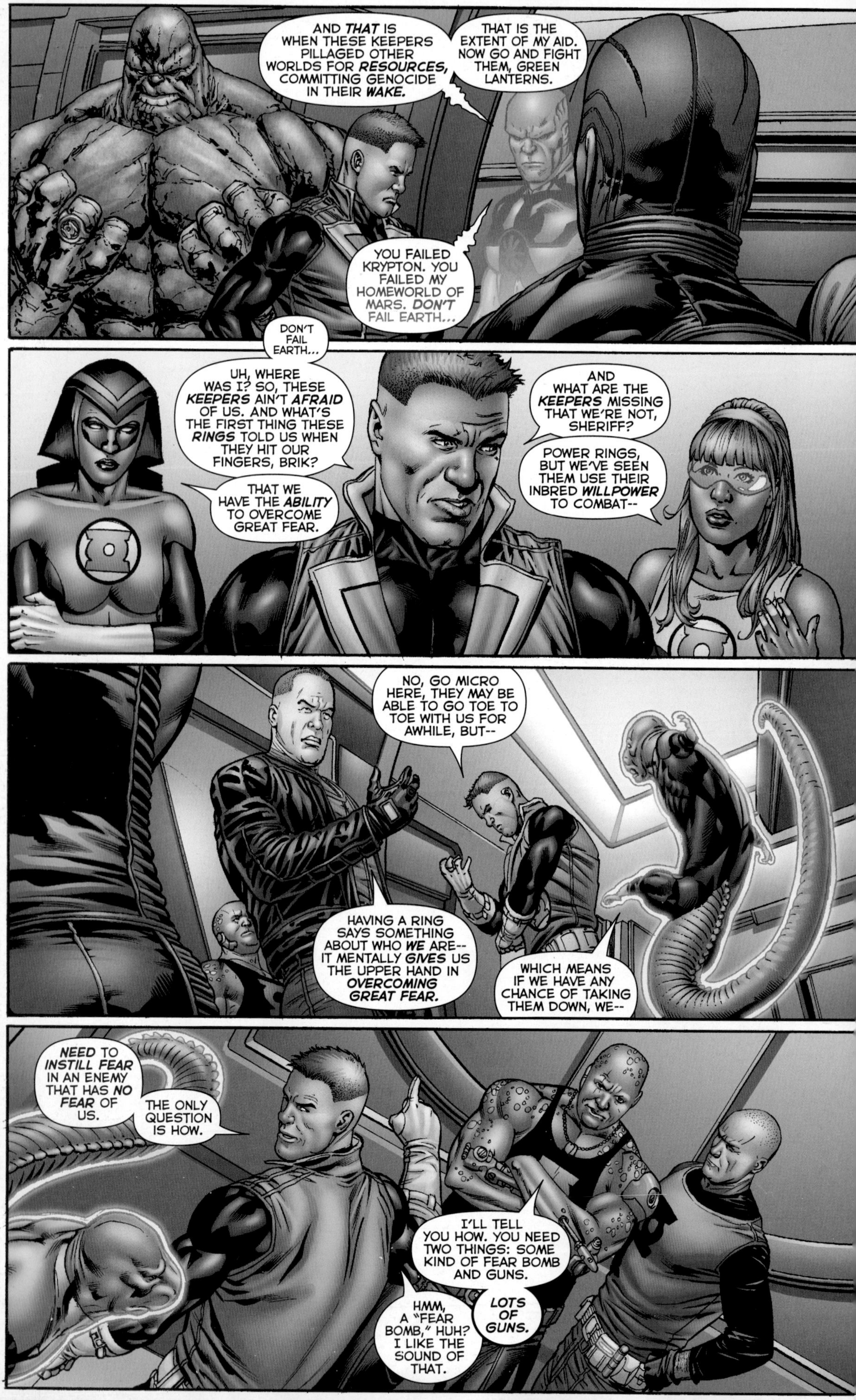
AND THAT IS WHEN THESE KEEPERS PILLAGED OTHER WORLDS FOR RESOURCES, COMMITTING GENOCIDE IN THEIR WAKE.
THAT IS THE EXTENT OF MY AID. NOW GO AND FIGHT THEM, GREEN LANTERNS.
YOU FAILED KRYPTON. YOU FAILED MY HOMEWORLD OF MARS. DON'T FAIL EARTH...
DON'T FAIL EARTH...
UH, WHERE WAS I? SO, THESE KEEPERS AIN'T AFRAID OF US. AND WHAT'S THE FIRST THING THESE RINGS TOLD US WHEN THEY HIT OUR FINGERS, BRIK?
THAT WE HAVE THE ABILITY TO OVERCOME GREAT FEAR.
AND WHAT ARE THE KEEPERS MISSING THAT WE'RE NOT, SHERIFF?
POWER RINGS, BUT WE'VE SEEN THEM USE THEIR INBRED WILLPOWER TO COMBAT--
NO, GO MICRO HERE, THEY MAY BE ABLE TO GO TOE TO TOE WITH US FOR AWHILE, BUT--
HAVING A RING SAYS SOMETHING ABOUT WHO WE ARE-- IT MENTALLY GIVES US THE UPPER HAND IN OVERCOMING GREAT FEAR.
WHICH MEANS IF WE HAVE ANY CHANCE OF TAKING THEM DOWN, WE--
NEED TO INSTILL FEAR IN AN ENEMY THAT HAS NO FEAR OF US.
THE ONLY QUESTION IS HOW.
I'LL TELL YOU HOW. YOU NEED TWO THINGS: SOME KIND OF FEAR BOMB AND GUNS.
LOTS OF GUNS.
HMM, A "FEAR BOMB," HUH? I LIKE THE SOUND OF THAT.

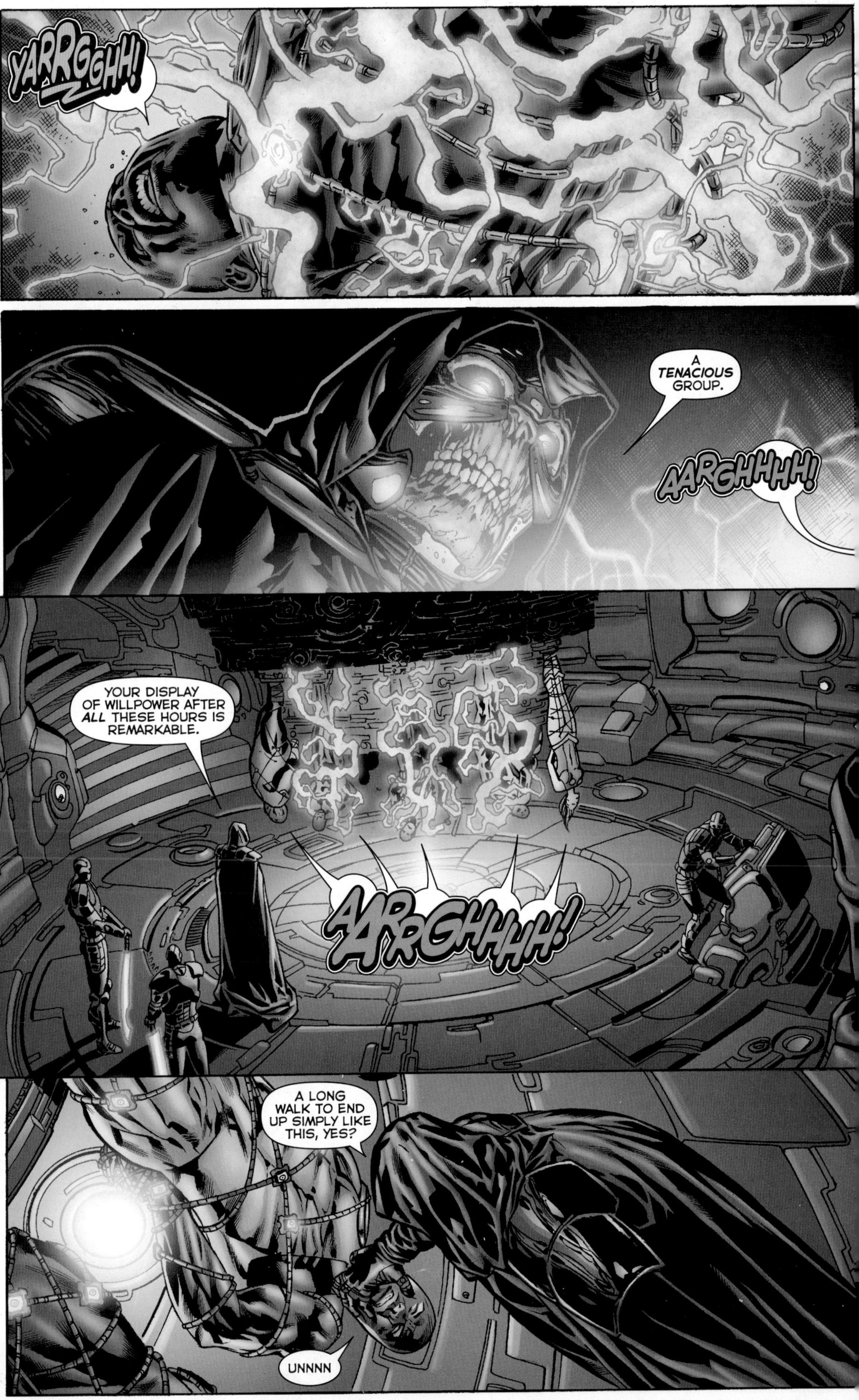
YARRGGHH!
A TENACIOUS GROUP.
AARGHHHH!
YOUR DISPLAY OF WILLPOWER AFTER ALL THESE HOURS IS REMARKABLE.
AARRGHHHH!
A LONG WALK TO END UP SIMPLY LIKE THIS, YES?
UNNNN

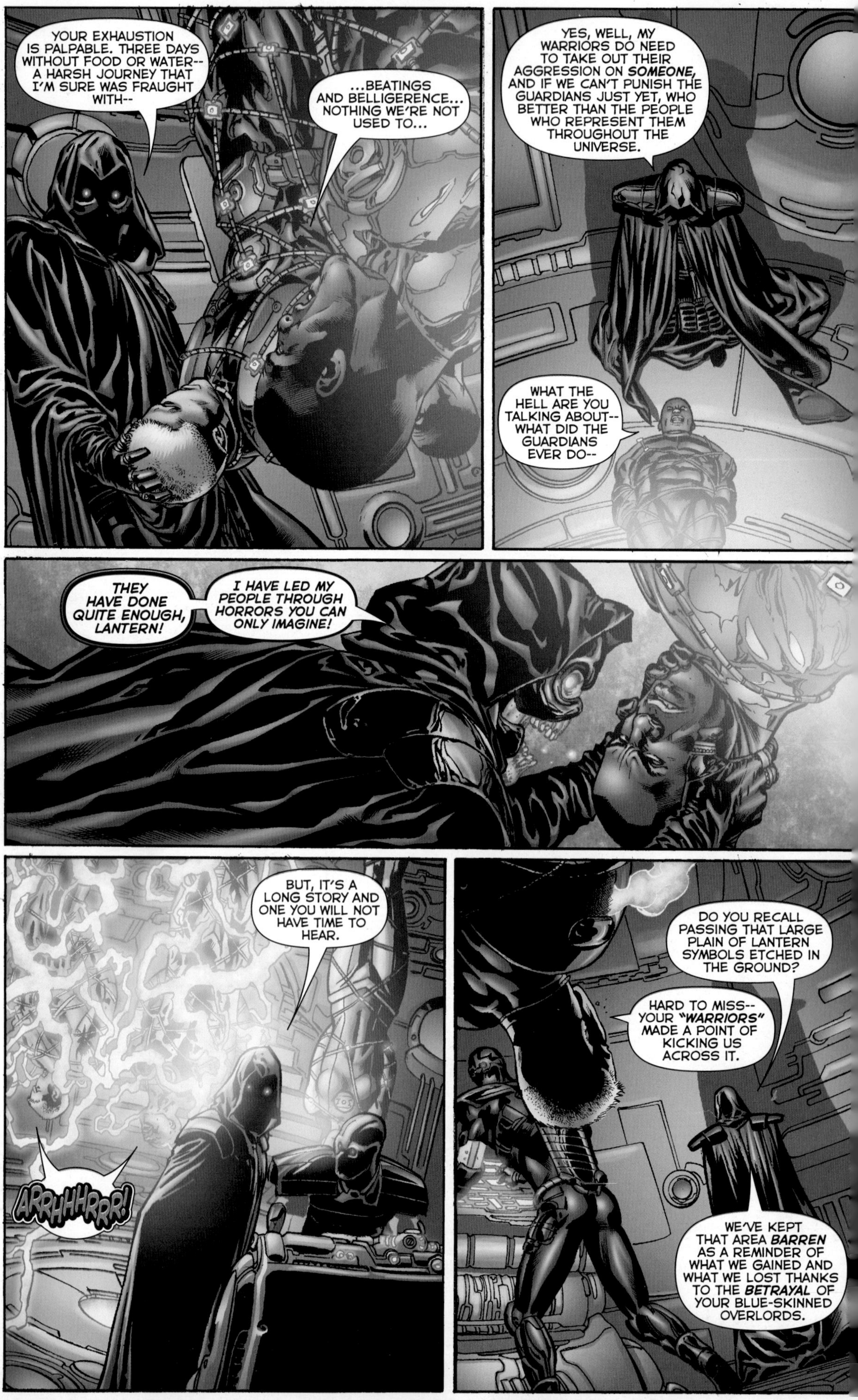
YOUR EXHAUSTION IS PALPABLE. THREE DAYS WITHOUT FOOD OR WATER-- A HARSH JOURNEY THAT I'M SURE WAS FRAUGHT WITH--
...BEATINGS AND BELLIGERENCE... NOTHING WE'RE NOT USED TO...
YES, WELL, MY WARRIORS DO NEED TO TAKE OUT THEIR AGGRESSION ON *SOMEONE*, AND IF WE CAN'T PUNISH THE GUARDIANS JUST YET, WHO BETTER THAN THE PEOPLE WHO REPRESENT THEM THROUGHOUT THE UNIVERSE.
WHAT THE HELL ARE YOU TALKING ABOUT-- WHAT DID THE GUARDIANS EVER DO--
THEY HAVE DONE QUITE ENOUGH, LANTERN!
I HAVE LED MY PEOPLE THROUGH HORRORS YOU CAN ONLY IMAGINE!
BUT, IT'S A LONG STORY AND ONE YOU WILL NOT HAVE TIME TO HEAR.
ARRHHHRRR!
DO YOU RECALL PASSING THAT LARGE PLAIN OF LANTERN SYMBOLS ETCHED IN THE GROUND?
HARD TO MISS-- YOUR *"WARRIORS"* MADE A POINT OF KICKING US ACROSS IT.
WE'VE KEPT THAT AREA *BARREN* AS A REMINDER OF WHAT WE GAINED AND WHAT WE LOST THANKS TO THE *BETRAYAL* OF YOUR BLUE-SKINNED OVERLORDS.

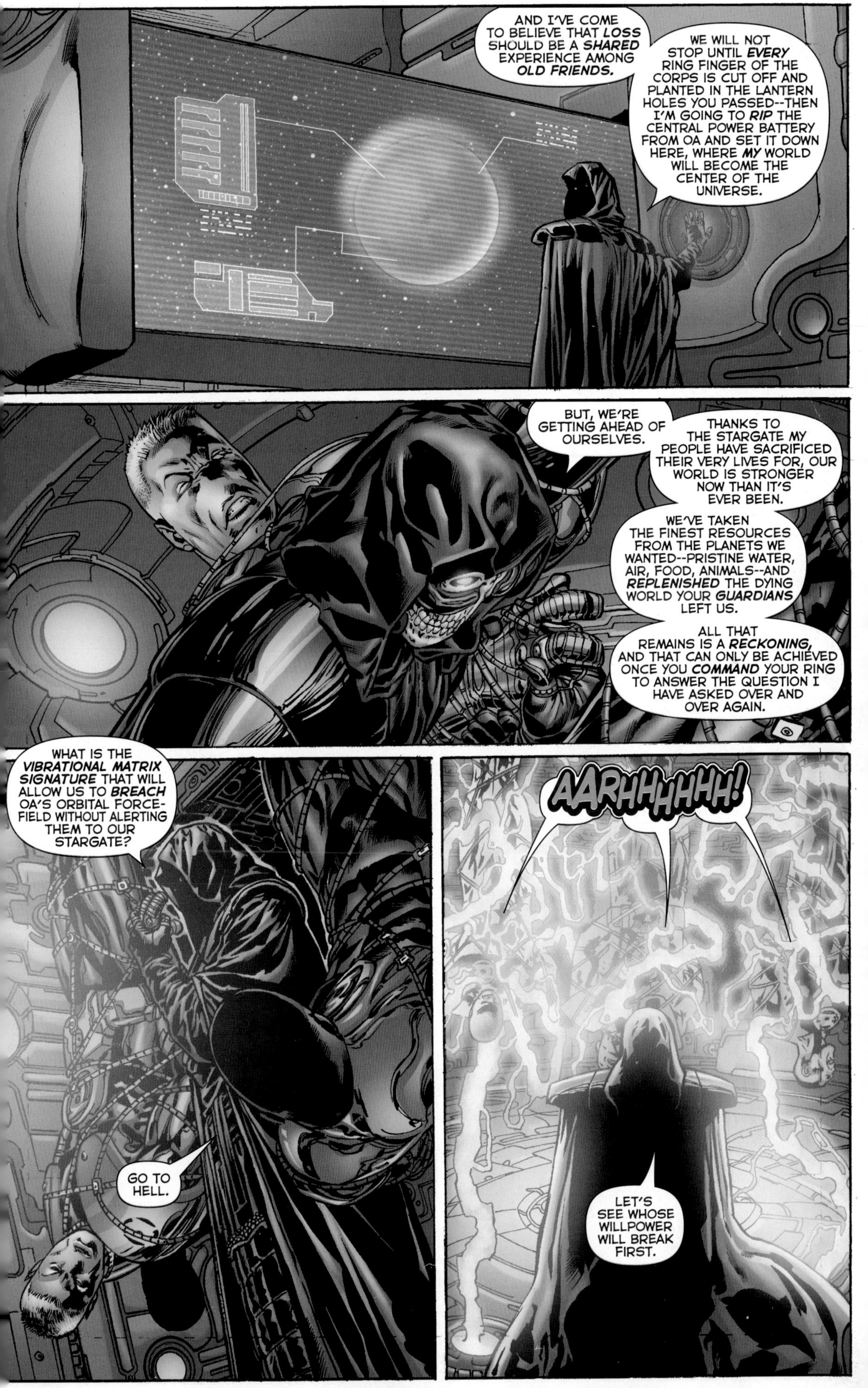
AND I'VE COME TO BELIEVE THAT LOSS SHOULD BE A SHARED EXPERIENCE AMONG OLD FRIENDS.
WE WILL NOT STOP UNTIL EVERY RING FINGER OF THE CORPS IS CUT OFF AND PLANTED IN THE LANTERN HOLES YOU PASSED--THEN I'M GOING TO RIP THE CENTRAL POWER BATTERY FROM OA AND SET IT DOWN HERE, WHERE MY WORLD WILL BECOME THE CENTER OF THE UNIVERSE.
BUT, WE'RE GETTING AHEAD OF OURSELVES.
THANKS TO THE STARGATE MY PEOPLE HAVE SACRIFICED THEIR VERY LIVES FOR, OUR WORLD IS STRONGER NOW THAN IT'S EVER BEEN.
WE'VE TAKEN THE FINEST RESOURCES FROM THE PLANETS WE WANTED--PRISTINE WATER, AIR, FOOD, ANIMALS--AND REPLENISHED THE DYING WORLD YOUR GUARDIANS LEFT US.
ALL THAT REMAINS IS A RECKONING, AND THAT CAN ONLY BE ACHIEVED ONCE YOU COMMAND YOUR RING TO ANSWER THE QUESTION I HAVE ASKED OVER AND OVER AGAIN.
WHAT IS THE VIBRATIONAL MATRIX SIGNATURE THAT WILL ALLOW US TO BREACH OA'S ORBITAL FORCE-FIELD WITHOUT ALERTING THEM TO OUR STARGATE?
GO TO HELL.
AARHHHHHH!
LET'S SEE WHOSE WILLPOWER WILL BREAK FIRST.

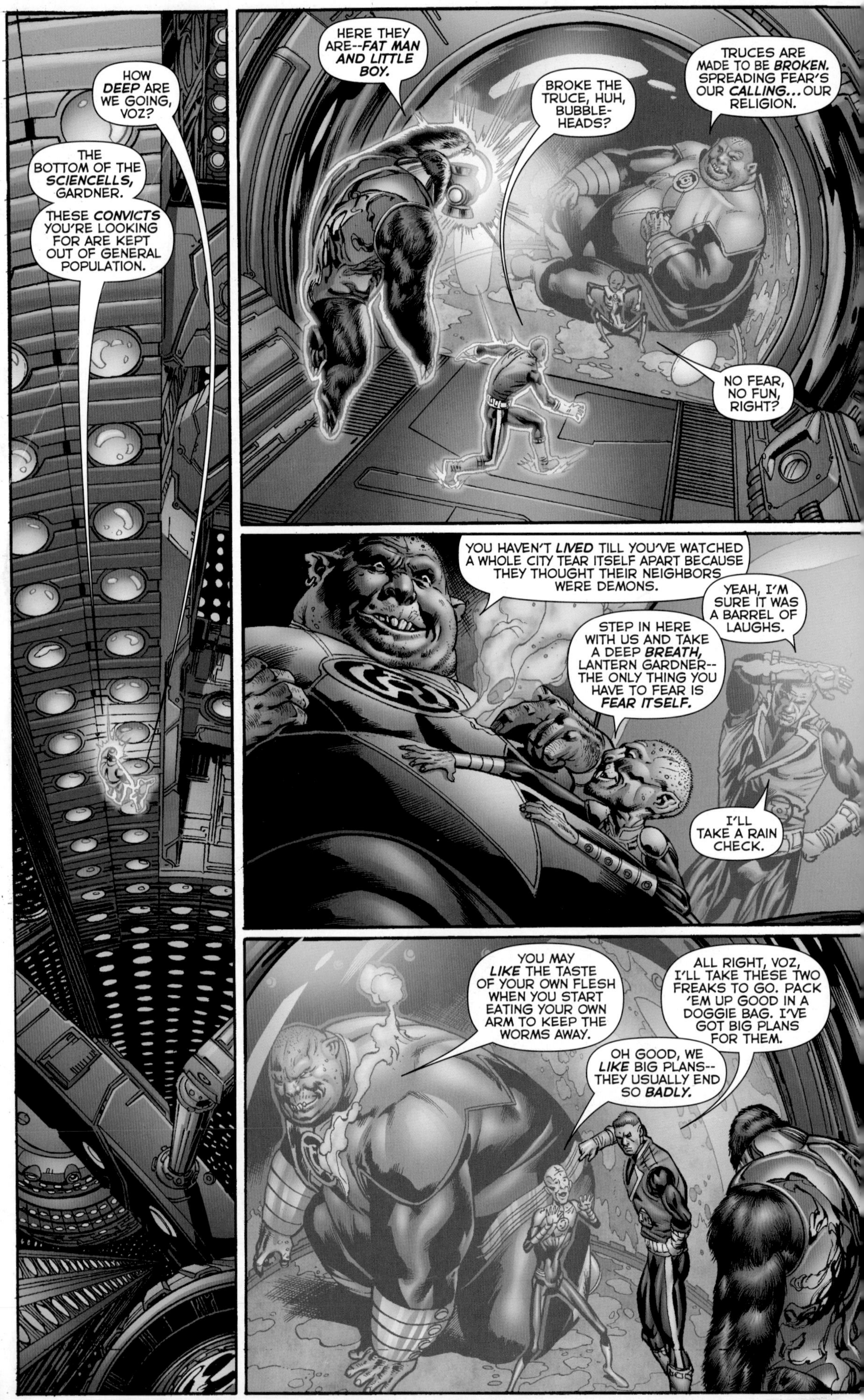

HOW DEEP ARE WE GOING, VOZ?
THE BOTTOM OF THE SCIENCELLS, GARDNER.
THESE CONVICTS YOU'RE LOOKING FOR ARE KEPT OUT OF GENERAL POPULATION.
HERE THEY ARE--FAT MAN AND LITTLE BOY.
BROKE THE TRUCE, HUH, BUBBLE-HEADS?
TRUCES ARE MADE TO BE BROKEN. SPREADING FEAR'S OUR CALLING... OUR RELIGION.
NO FEAR, NO FUN, RIGHT?
YOU HAVEN'T LIVED TILL YOU'VE WATCHED A WHOLE CITY TEAR ITSELF APART BECAUSE THEY THOUGHT THEIR NEIGHBORS WERE DEMONS.
YEAH, I'M SURE IT WAS A BARREL OF LAUGHS.
STEP IN HERE WITH US AND TAKE A DEEP BREATH, LANTERN GARDNER-- THE ONLY THING YOU HAVE TO FEAR IS FEAR ITSELF.
I'LL TAKE A RAIN CHECK.
YOU MAY LIKE THE TASTE OF YOUR OWN FLESH WHEN YOU START EATING YOUR OWN ARM TO KEEP THE WORMS AWAY.
ALL RIGHT, VOZ, I'LL TAKE THESE TWO FREAKS TO GO. PACK 'EM UP GOOD IN A DOGGIE BAG. I'VE GOT BIG PLANS FOR THEM.
OH GOOD, WE LIKE BIG PLANS-- THEY USUALLY END SO BADLY.

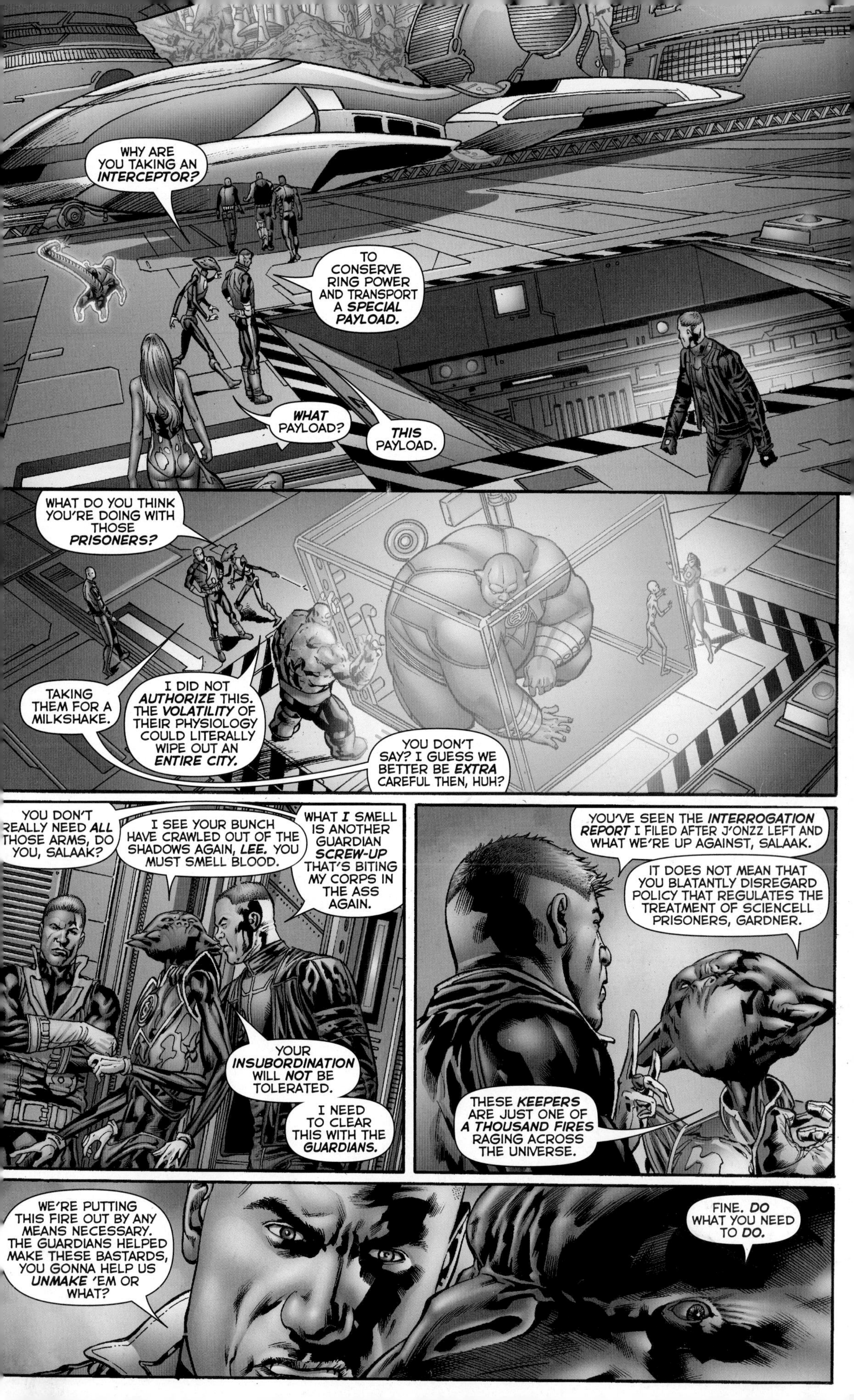

WHY ARE YOU TAKING AN *INTERCEPTOR?*
TO CONSERVE RING POWER AND TRANSPORT A *SPECIAL PAYLOAD.*
WHAT PAYLOAD?
THIS PAYLOAD.
WHAT DO YOU THINK YOU'RE DOING WITH THOSE *PRISONERS?*
TAKING THEM FOR A MILKSHAKE.
I DID NOT *AUTHORIZE* THIS. THE *VOLATILITY* OF THEIR PHYSIOLOGY COULD LITERALLY WIPE OUT AN *ENTIRE CITY.*
YOU DON'T SAY? I GUESS WE BETTER BE *EXTRA* CAREFUL THEN, HUH?
YOU DON'T REALLY NEED *ALL* THOSE ARMS, DO YOU, SALAAK?
I SEE YOUR BUNCH HAVE CRAWLED OUT OF THE SHADOWS AGAIN, *LEE.* YOU MUST SMELL BLOOD.
WHAT *I* SMELL IS ANOTHER GUARDIAN *SCREW-UP* THAT'S BITING MY CORPS IN THE ASS AGAIN.
YOUR *INSUBORDINATION* WILL *NOT* BE TOLERATED.
I NEED TO CLEAR THIS WITH THE *GUARDIANS.*
YOU'VE SEEN THE *INTERROGATION REPORT* I FILED AFTER J'ONZZ LEFT AND WHAT WE'RE UP AGAINST, SALAAK.
IT DOES NOT MEAN THAT YOU BLATANTLY DISREGARD POLICY THAT REGULATES THE TREATMENT OF SCIENCELL PRISONERS, GARDNER.
THESE *KEEPERS* ARE JUST ONE OF *A THOUSAND FIRES* RAGING ACROSS THE UNIVERSE.
WE'RE PUTTING THIS FIRE OUT BY ANY MEANS NECESSARY. THE GUARDIANS HELPED MAKE THESE BASTARDS, YOU GONNA HELP US *UNMAKE* 'EM OR WHAT?
FINE. *DO* WHAT YOU NEED TO *DO.*

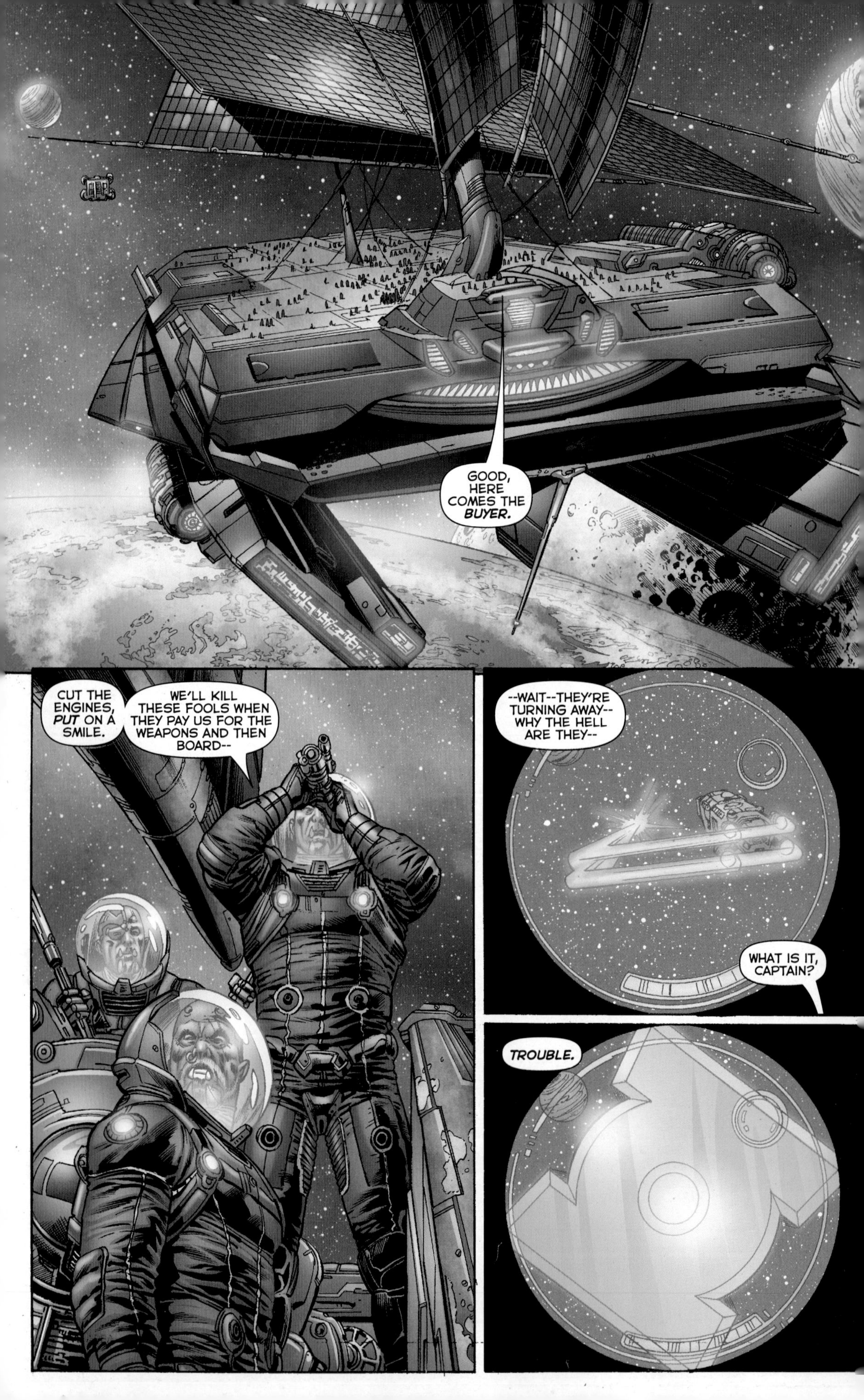
GOOD, HERE COMES THE BUYER.
CUT THE ENGINES, PUT ON A SMILE.
WE'LL KILL THESE FOOLS WHEN THEY PAY US FOR THE WEAPONS AND THEN BOARD--
--WAIT--THEY'RE TURNING AWAY--WHY THE HELL ARE THEY--
WHAT IS IT, CAPTAIN?
TROUBLE.

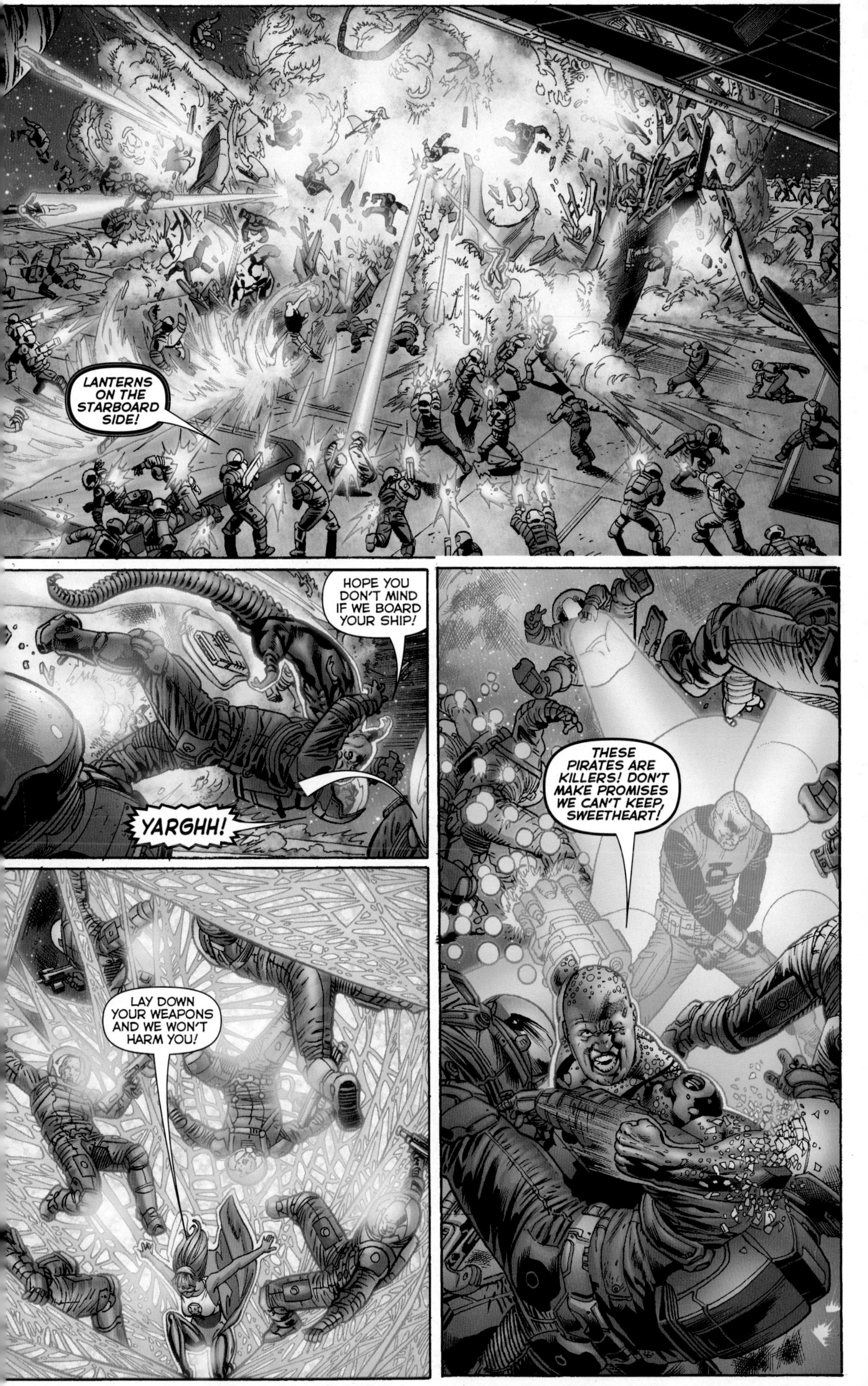
LANTERNS ON THE STARBOARD SIDE!
HOPE YOU DON'T MIND IF WE BOARD YOUR SHIP!
YARGHH!
THESE PIRATES ARE KILLERS! DON'T MAKE PROMISES WE CAN'T KEEP, SWEETHEART!
LAY DOWN YOUR WEAPONS AND WE WON'T HARM YOU!

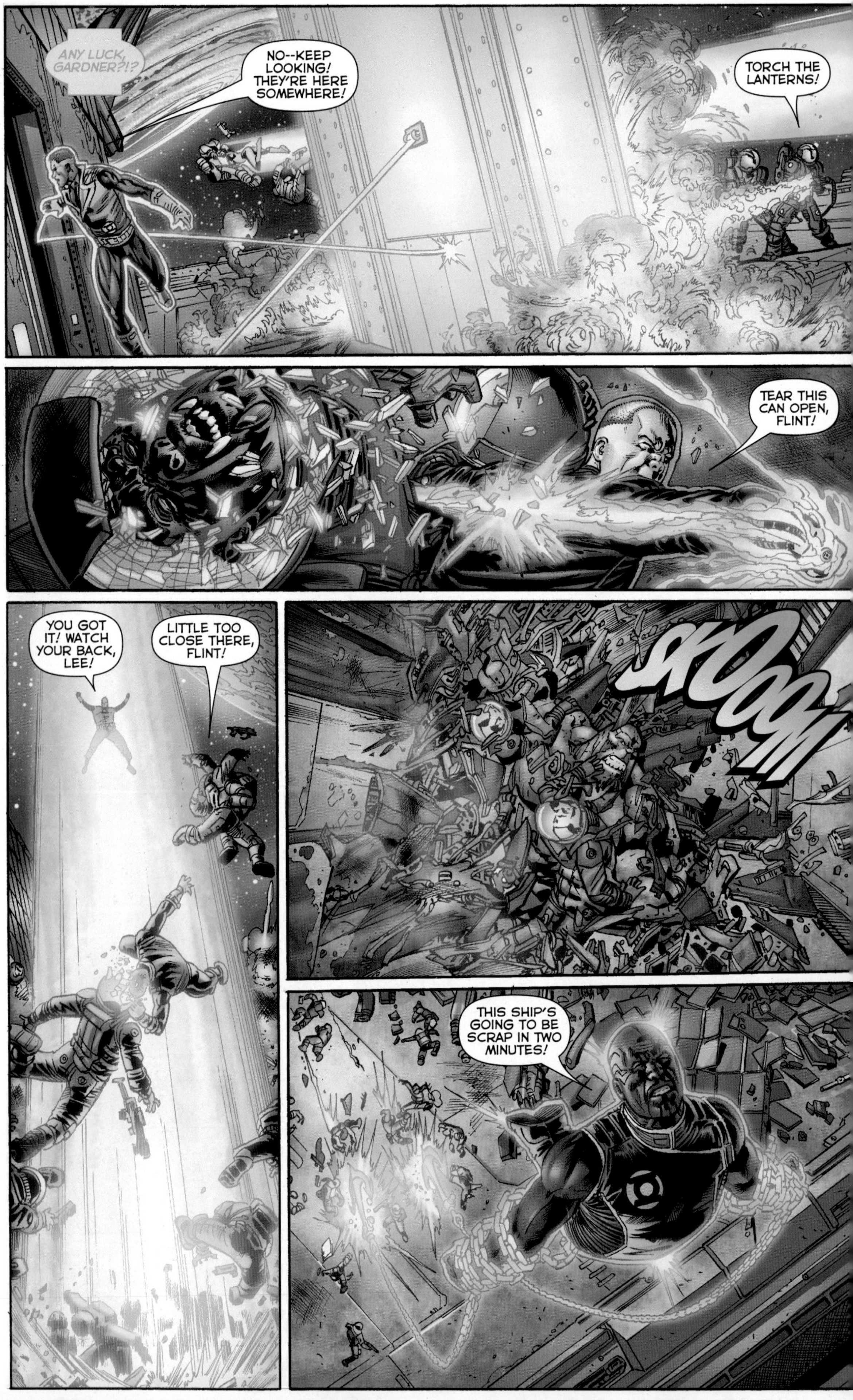
ANY LUCK, GARDNER?!?
NO--KEEP LOOKING! THEY'RE HERE SOMEWHERE!
TORCH THE LANTERNS!
TEAR THIS CAN OPEN, FLINT!
YOU GOT IT! WATCH YOUR BACK, LEE!
LITTLE TOO CLOSE THERE, FLINT!
SKOOM
THIS SHIP'S GOING TO BE SCRAP IN TWO MINUTES!

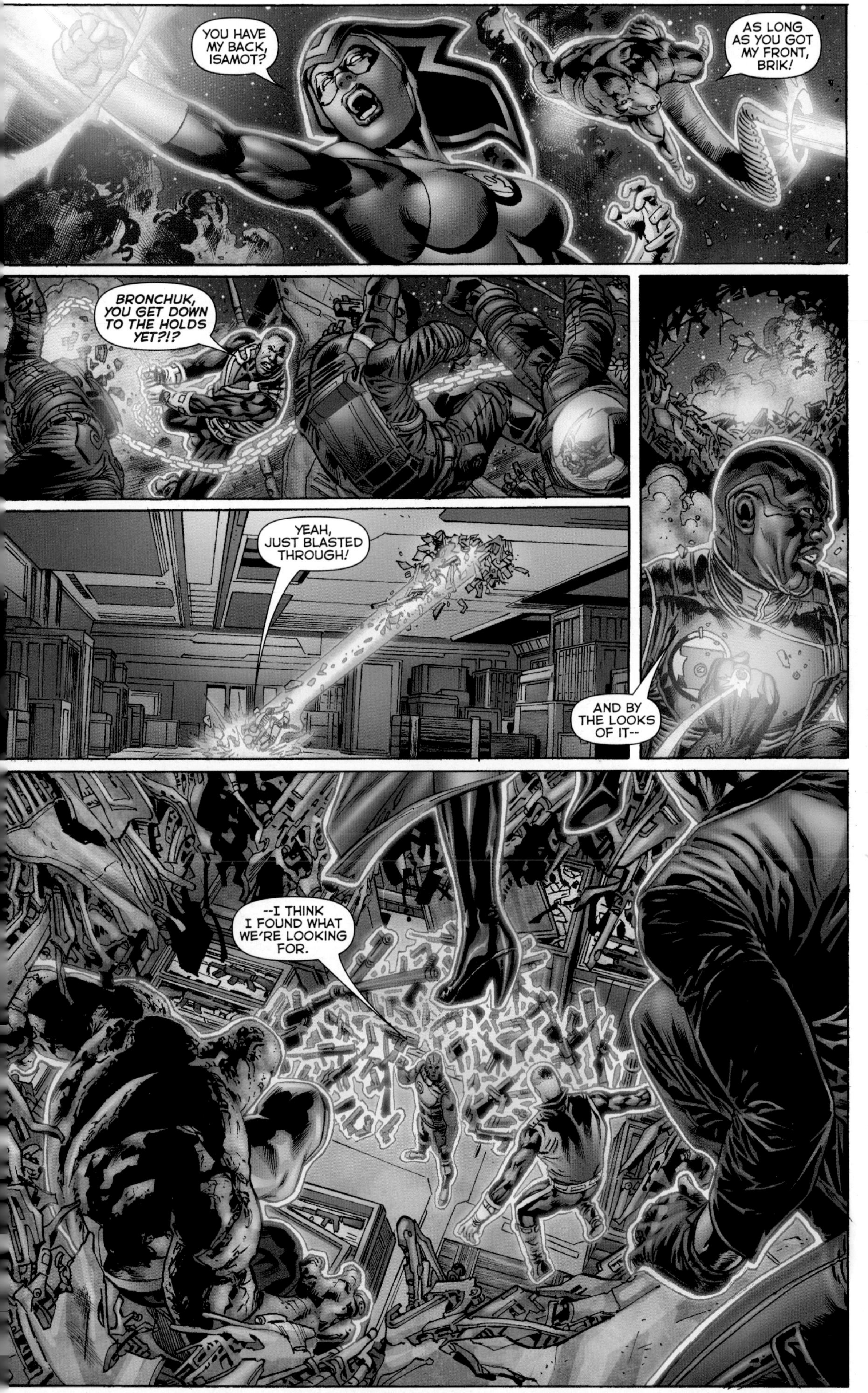

YOU HAVE MY BACK, ISAMOT?
AS LONG AS YOU GOT MY FRONT, BRIK!
BRONCHUK, YOU GET DOWN TO THE HOLDS YET?!?
YEAH, JUST BLASTED THROUGH!
AND BY THE LOOKS OF IT--
--I THINK I FOUND WHAT WE'RE LOOKING FOR.

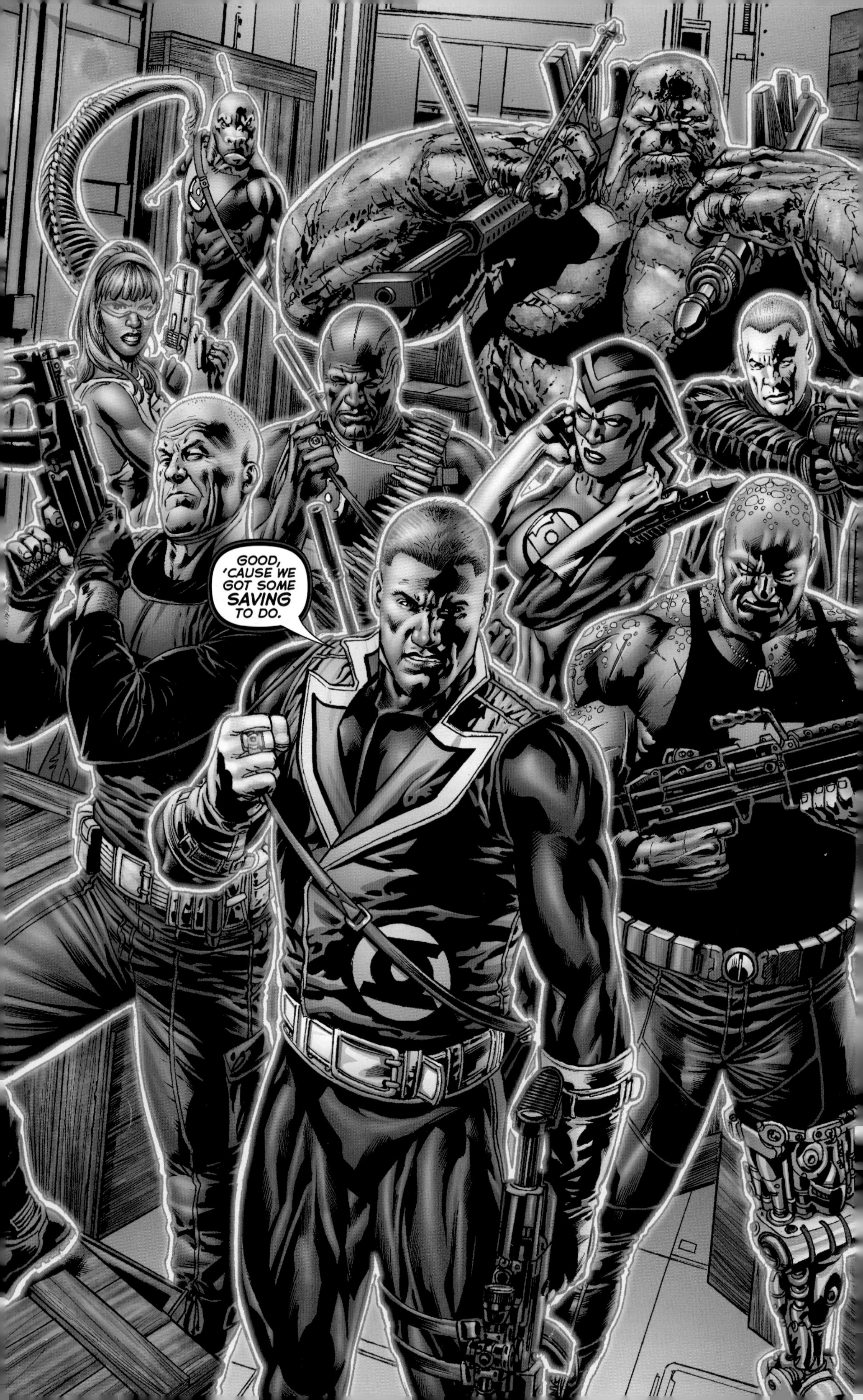
GOOD, 'CAUSE WE GOT SOME SAVING TO DO.

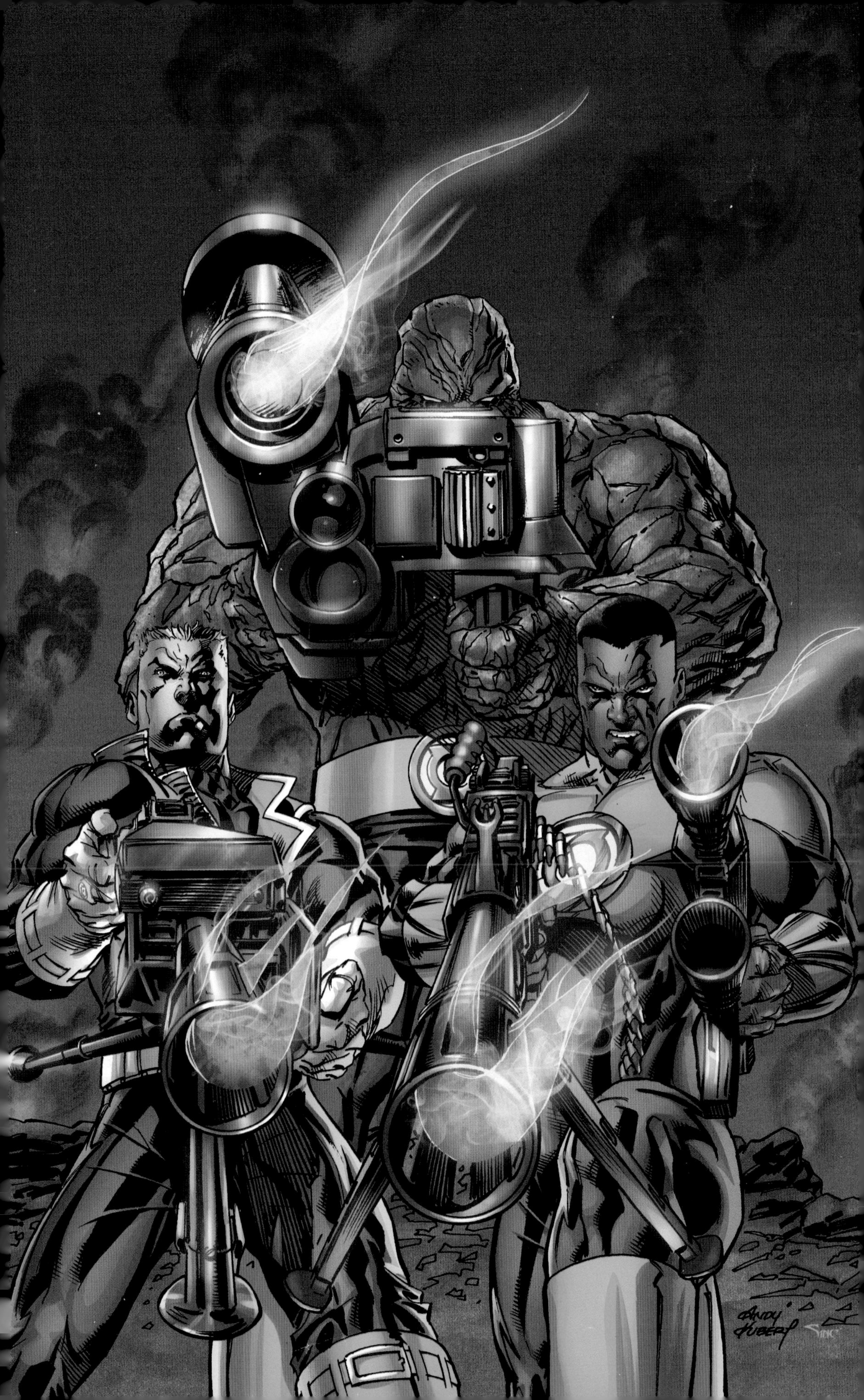
ANDY KUBERT
SINC

FEARSOME

PETER J. TOMASI writer **FERNANDO PASARIN** penciller **SCOTT HANNA** inker cover by **ANDY KUBERT** with **ALEX SINCLAIR**

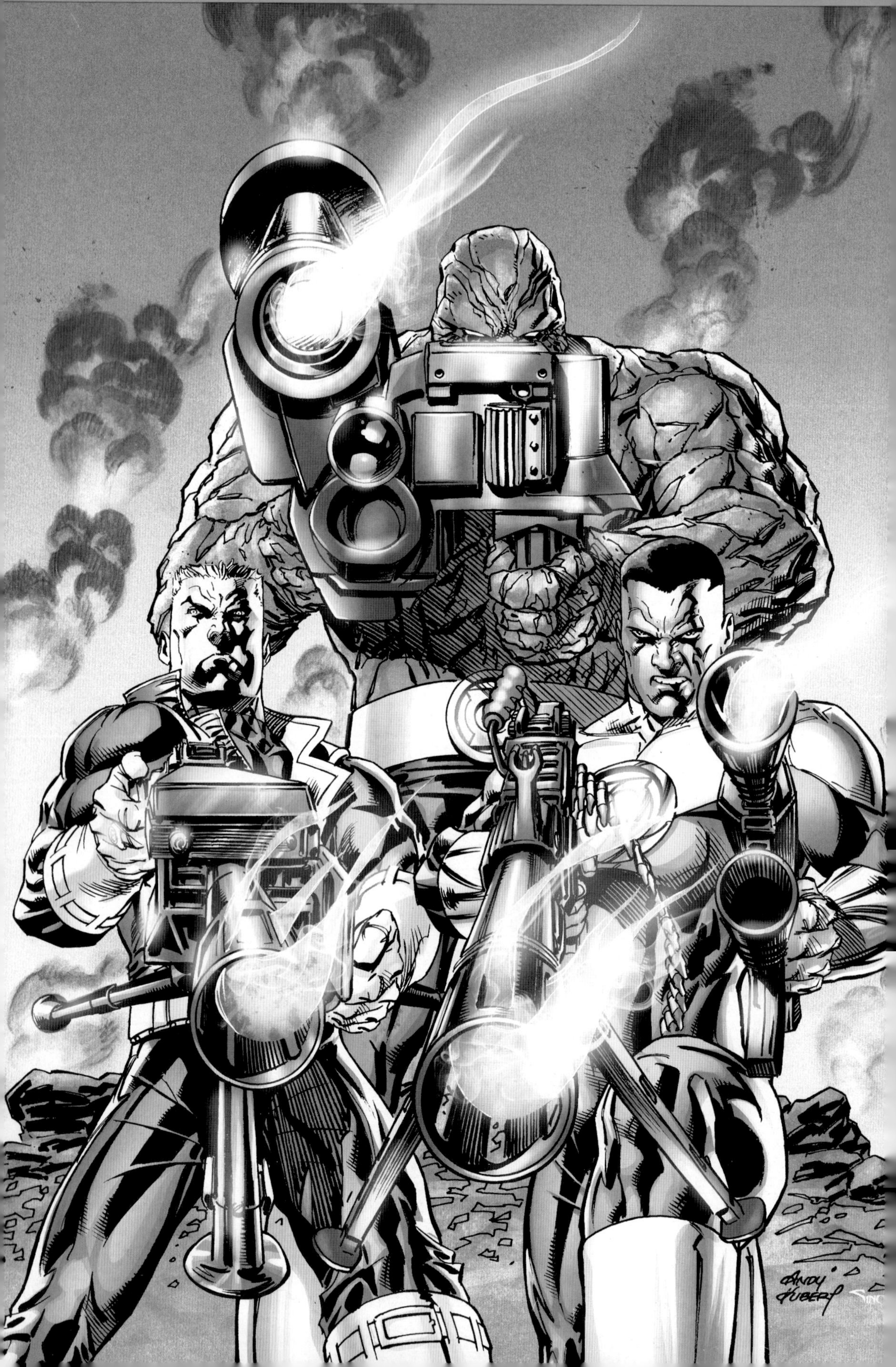

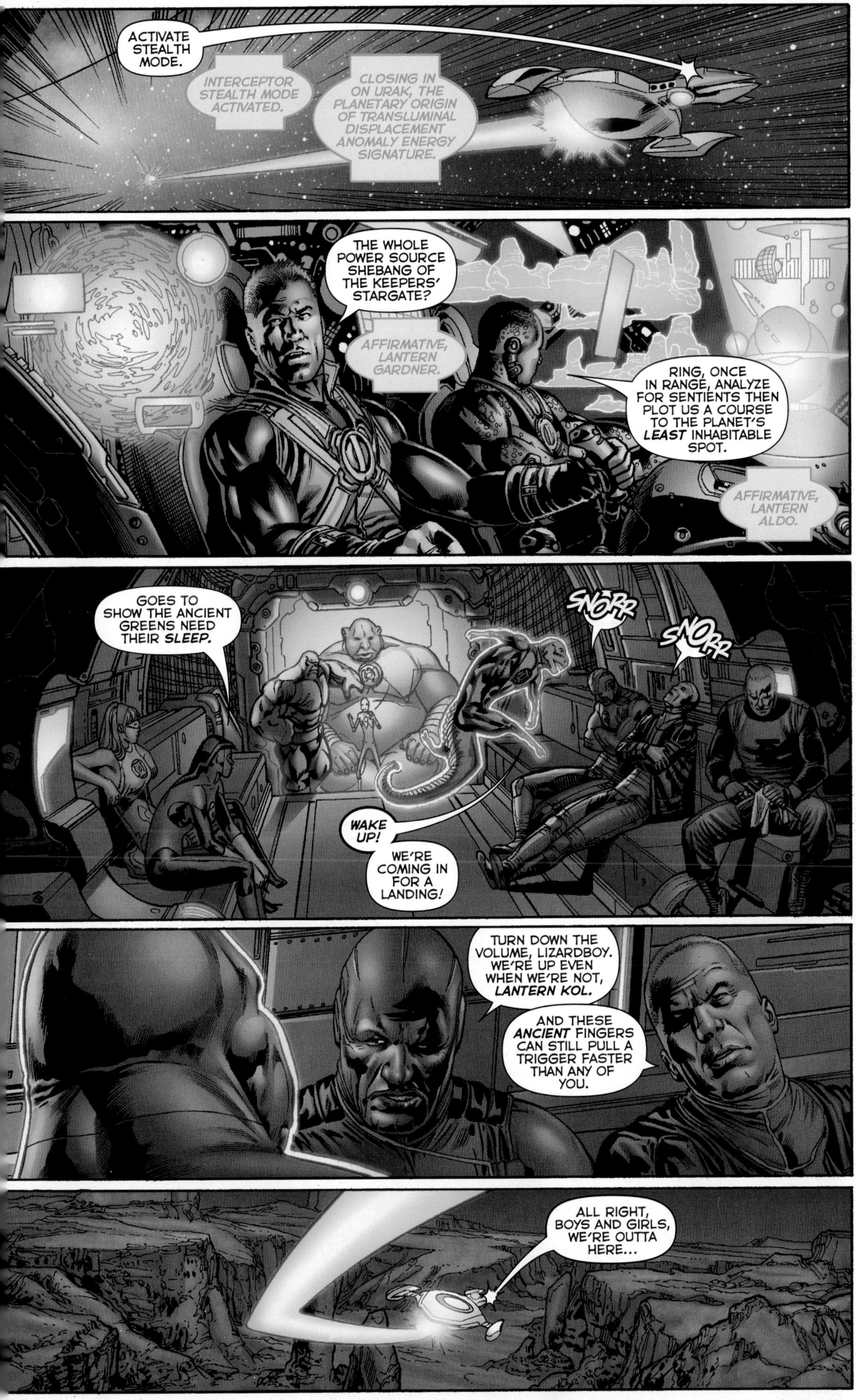
ACTIVATE STEALTH MODE.
INTERCEPTOR STEALTH MODE ACTIVATED.
CLOSING IN ON URAK, THE PLANETARY ORIGIN OF TRANSLUMINAL DISPLACEMENT ANOMALY ENERGY SIGNATURE.
THE WHOLE POWER SOURCE SHEBANG OF THE KEEPERS' STARGATE?
AFFIRMATIVE, LANTERN GARDNER.
RING, ONCE IN RANGE, ANALYZE FOR SENTIENTS THEN PLOT US A COURSE TO THE PLANET'S *LEAST* INHABITABLE SPOT.
AFFIRMATIVE, LANTERN ALDO.
GOES TO SHOW THE ANCIENT GREENS NEED THEIR *SLEEP.*
SNORR
SNORR
WAKE UP!
WE'RE COMING IN FOR A LANDING!
TURN DOWN THE VOLUME, LIZARDBOY. WE'RE UP EVEN WHEN WE'RE NOT, *LANTERN KOL.*
AND THESE *ANCIENT* FINGERS CAN STILL PULL A TRIGGER FASTER THAN ANY OF YOU.
ALL RIGHT, BOYS AND GIRLS, WE'RE OUTTA HERE...

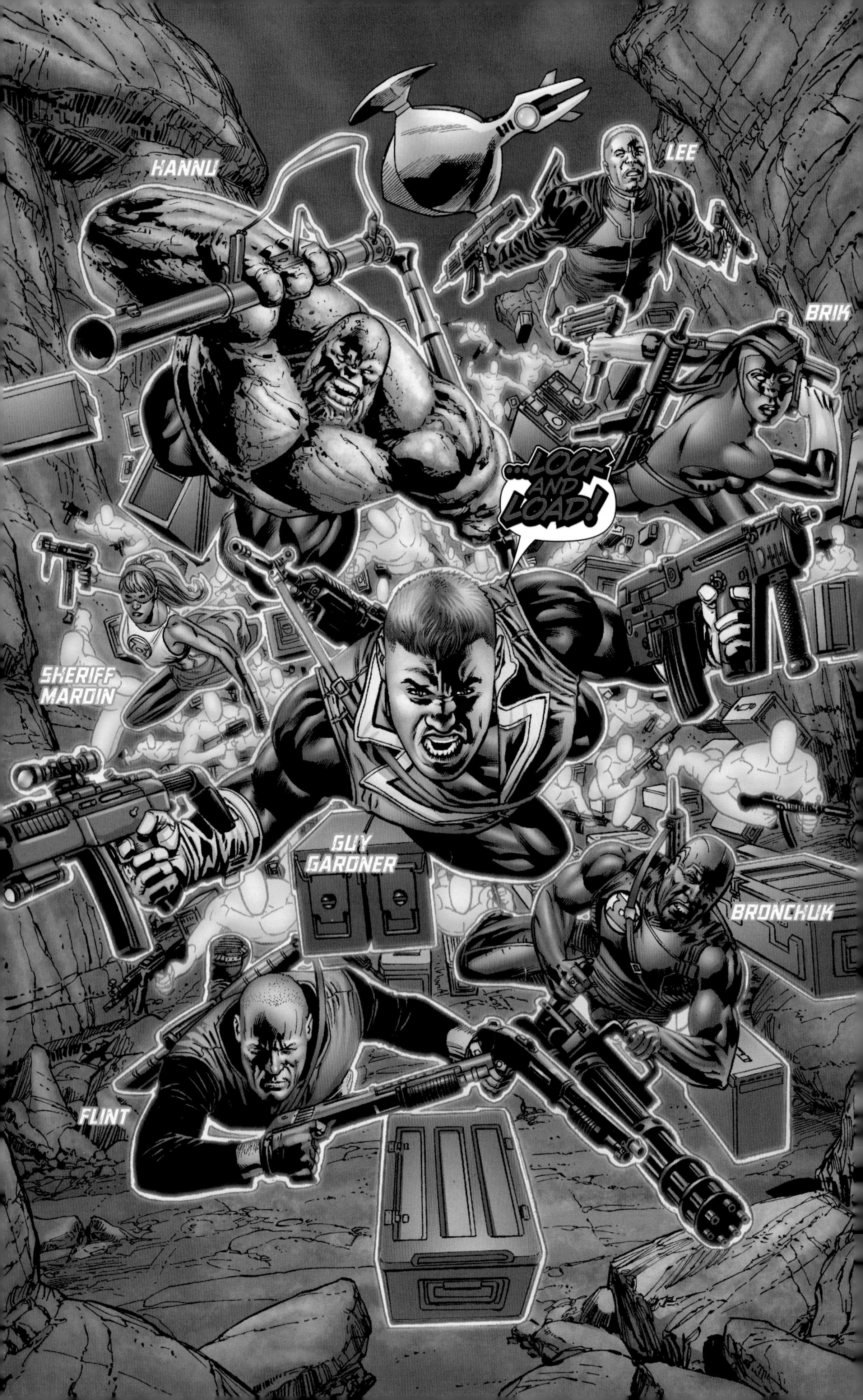

HANNU
LEE
BRIK
...LOCK AND LOAD!
SHERIFF MARDIN
GUY GARDNER
BRONCHUK
FLINT

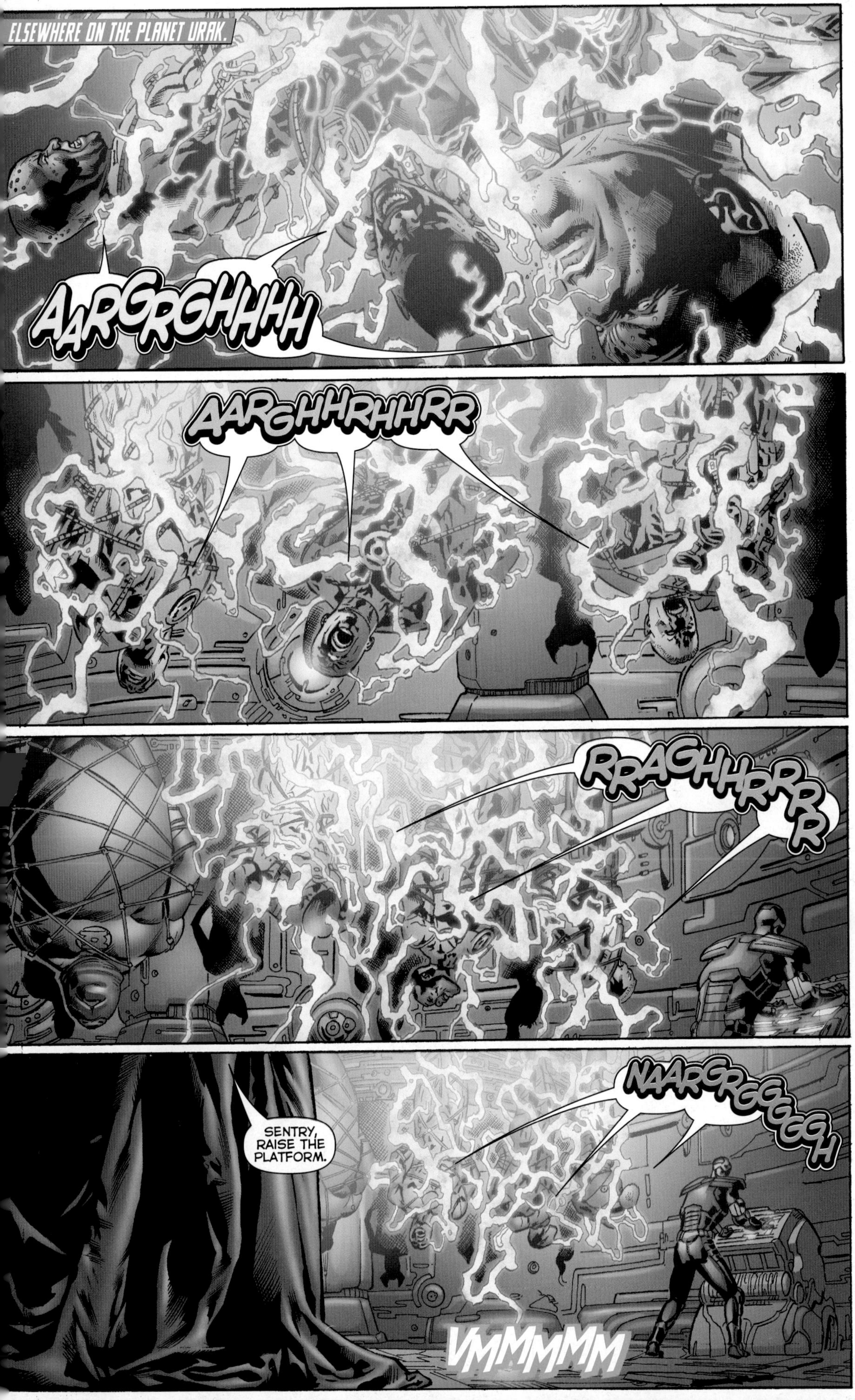
ELSEWHERE ON THE PLANET URAK.
AARGRGHHHH
AARGHHRHHRR
RRAGHHRRRR
SENTRY, RAISE THE PLATFORM.
NAARGRGGGGH
VMMMMM

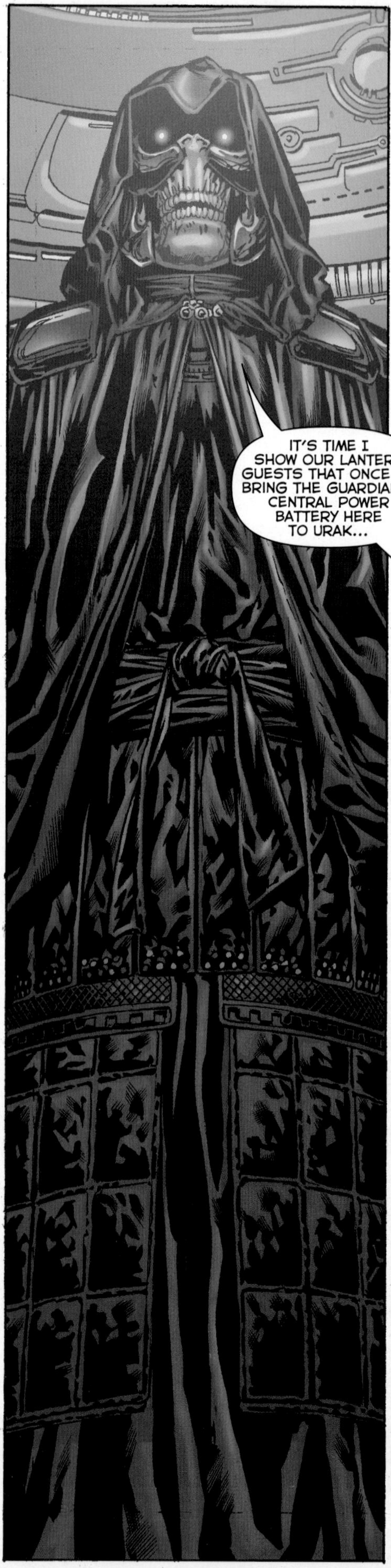
IT'S TIME I SHOW OUR LANTERN GUESTS THAT ONCE WE BRING THE GUARDIANS' CENTRAL POWER BATTERY HERE TO URAK...

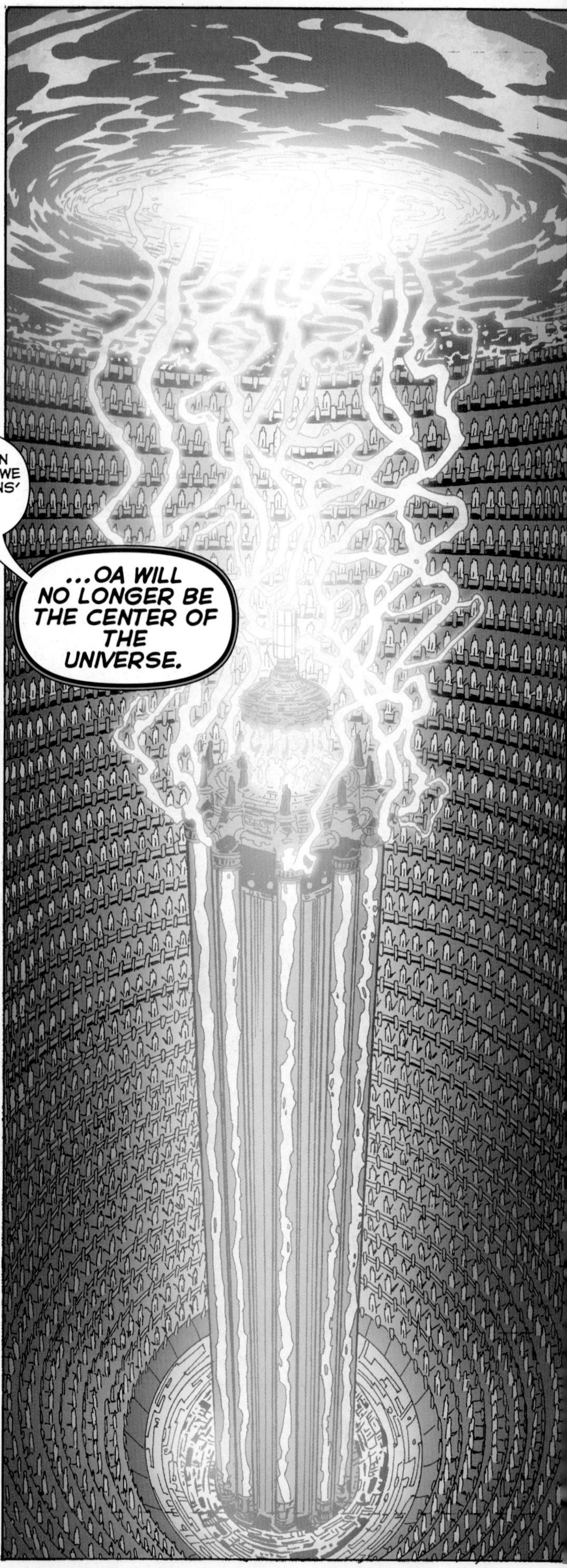
...OA WILL NO LONGER BE THE CENTER OF THE UNIVERSE.

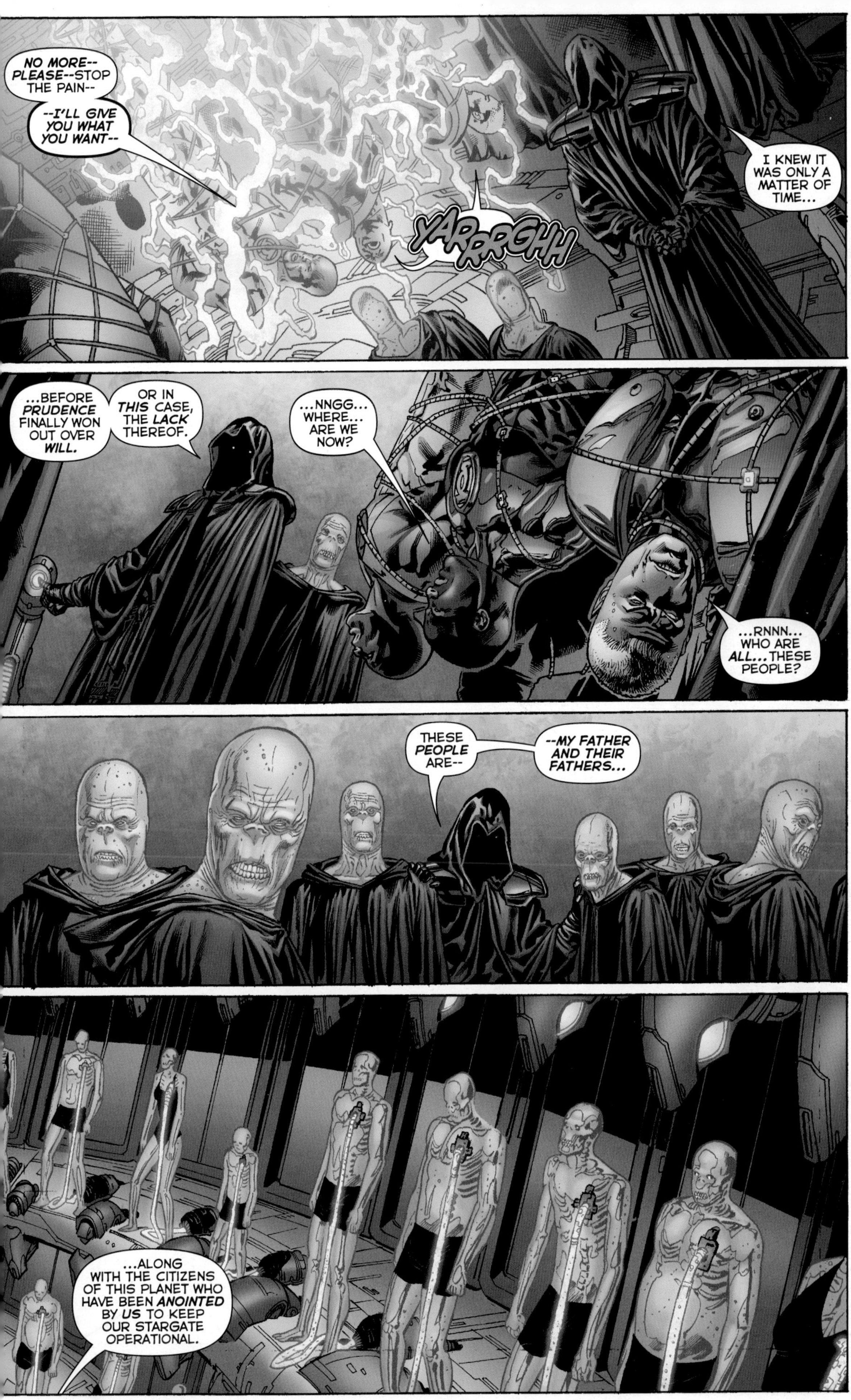
NO MORE--
PLEASE--STOP THE PAIN--
--I'LL GIVE YOU WHAT YOU WANT--
YARRRGHH
I KNEW IT WAS ONLY A MATTER OF TIME...
...BEFORE PRUDENCE FINALLY WON OUT OVER WILL.
OR IN THIS CASE, THE LACK THEREOF.
...NNGG... WHERE... ARE WE NOW?
...RNNN... WHO ARE ALL...THESE PEOPLE?
THESE PEOPLE ARE--
--MY FATHER AND THEIR FATHERS...
...ALONG WITH THE CITIZENS OF THIS PLANET WHO HAVE BEEN ANOINTED BY US TO KEEP OUR STARGATE OPERATIONAL.

WE ARE A LEGACY OF WILLPOWER... ...A LEGACY OF MONARCHS.

MORE LIKE A *LEGACY OF TYRANTS* BY THE LOOKS OF ALL THIS!

THOSE POOR PEOPLE AREN'T JUST KEEPING THE STARGATE RUNNING, THEY'RE *KEEPING YOU AND YOUR FATHERS RUNNING TOO,* AREN'T THEY?!?

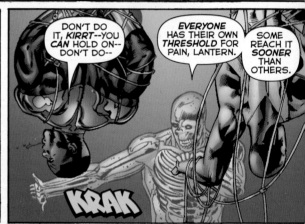

TO SERVE OUR PEOPLE, WE HAVE TO SERVE OURSELVES, LANTERN JOHN STEWART.

IT'S A SIMPLE CONCEPT THAT THE GUARDIANS NEVER GRASPED. THEY CALLED US UNDESERVING LEECHES AS THEY RIPPED AWAY THE POWER BATTERIES THEY ONCE STORED HERE--DESTROYING THE SUSTENANCE *THEY* CREATED--THROWING OUR ECOSYSTEM INTO CHAOS.

THIS STARGATE WE DEVELOPED IS POWERED *BY* THE PEOPLE AND *FOR* THE PEOPLE.

OUR FUTURE, AND THAT OF THE UNIVERSE, WILL BE IN *OUR* HANDS. WE WILL NO LONGER BE AT THE MERCY OF OTHERS. THEY WILL BE AT THE MERCY OF US.

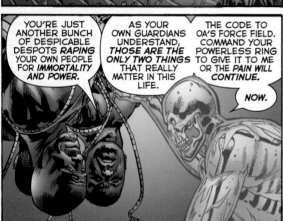

YOU'RE JUST ANOTHER BUNCH OF DESPICABLE DESPOTS *RAPING* YOUR OWN PEOPLE FOR *IMMORTALITY AND POWER.*

AS YOUR OWN GUARDIANS UNDERSTAND, *THOSE ARE THE ONLY TWO THINGS* THAT REALLY MATTER IN THIS LIFE.

THE CODE TO OA'S FORCE FIELD. COMMAND YOUR POWERLESS RING TO GIVE IT TO ME OR THE *PAIN WILL CONTINUE.*

NOW.

DON'T DO IT, *KIRRT*--YOU *CAN* HOLD ON--DON'T DO--

EVERYONE HAS THEIR OWN *THRESHOLD* FOR PAIN, LANTERN.

SOME REACH IT *SOONER* THAN OTHERS.

KRAK

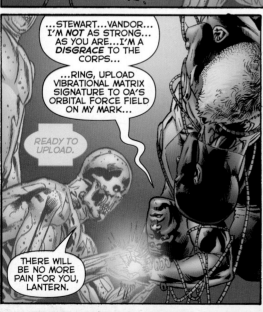

...STEWART...VANDOR... I'M *NOT* AS STRONG... AS YOU ARE...I'M A *DISGRACE* TO THE CORPS...

...RING, UPLOAD VIBRATIONAL MATRIX SIGNATURE TO OA'S ORBITAL FORCE FIELD ON MY MARK...

READY TO UPLOAD.

THERE WILL BE NO MORE PAIN FOR YOU, LANTERN.

YOU'RE GIVING THEM THE DAMN *KEY* TO OPENING OA'S *FRONT DOOR,* KIRRT!

WHAT ARE--

...I'M SORRY, JOHN...

GOD HELP ME, KIRRT--

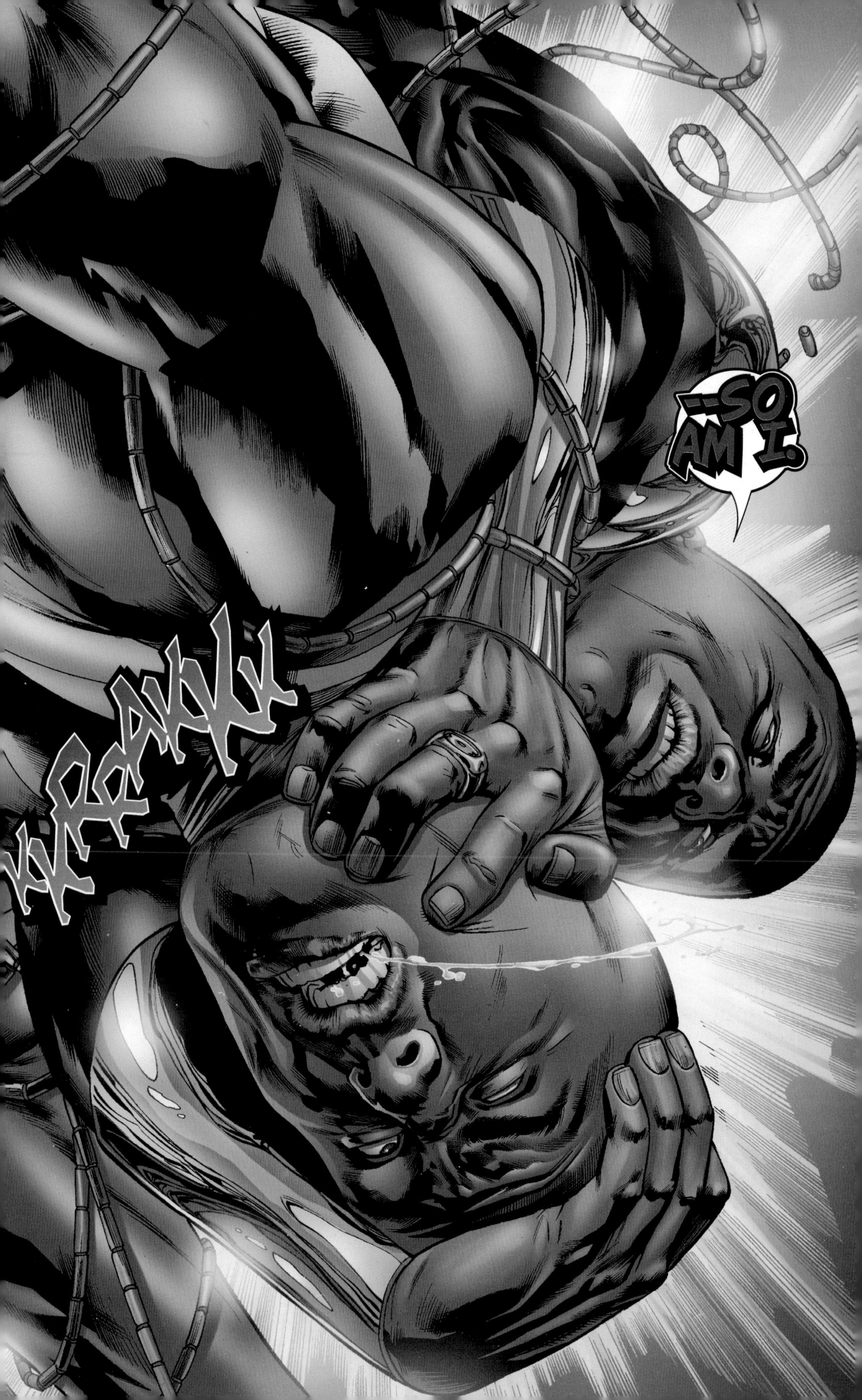
--SO AM I.
KRRAKK

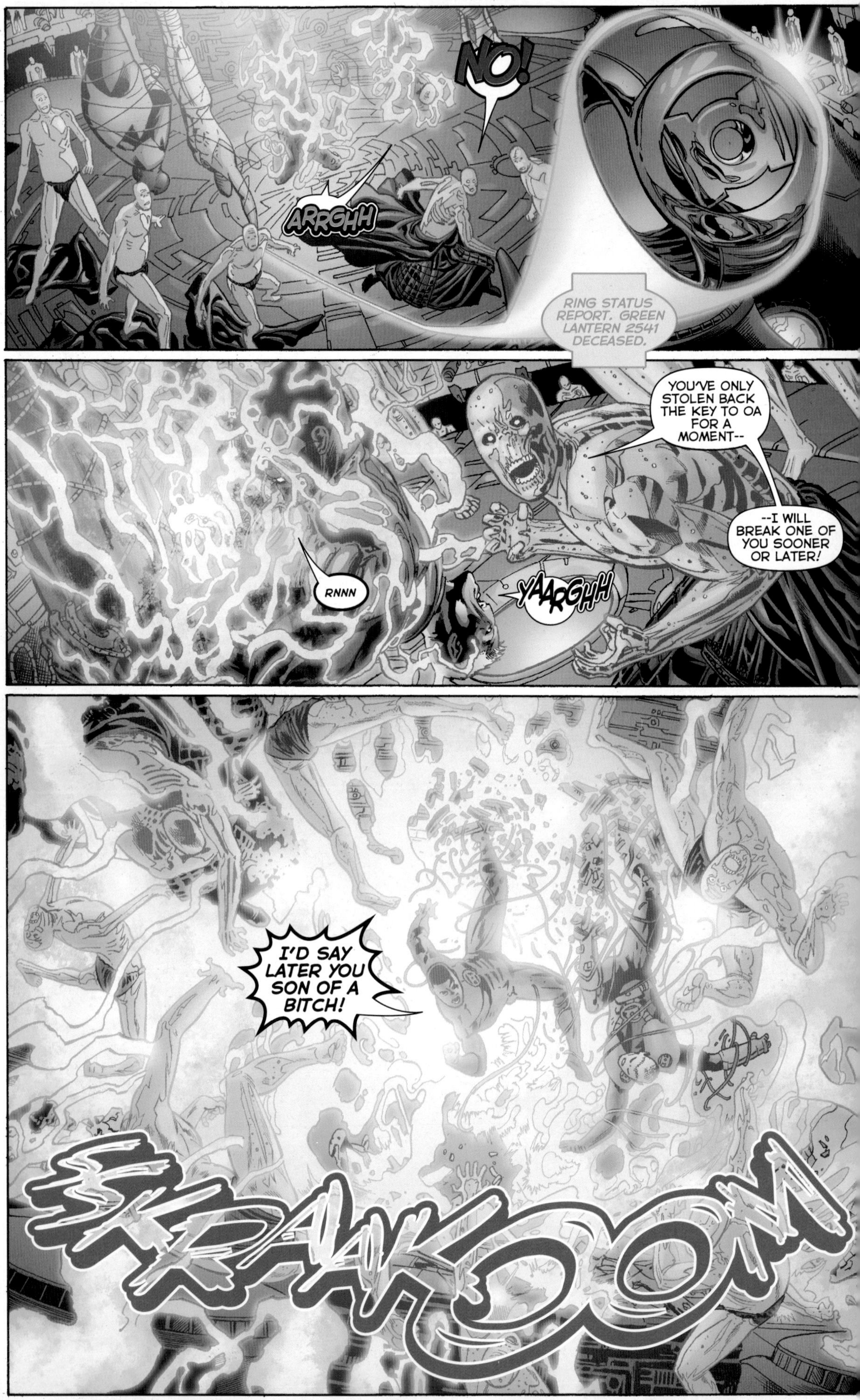
NO!
ARRGHH
RING STATUS REPORT. GREEN LANTERN 2541 DECEASED.
YOU'VE ONLY STOLEN BACK THE KEY TO OA FOR A MOMENT--
--I WILL BREAK ONE OF YOU SOONER OR LATER!
RNNN
YAARGHH
I'D SAY LATER YOU SON OF A BITCH!
SKRAAKOOM

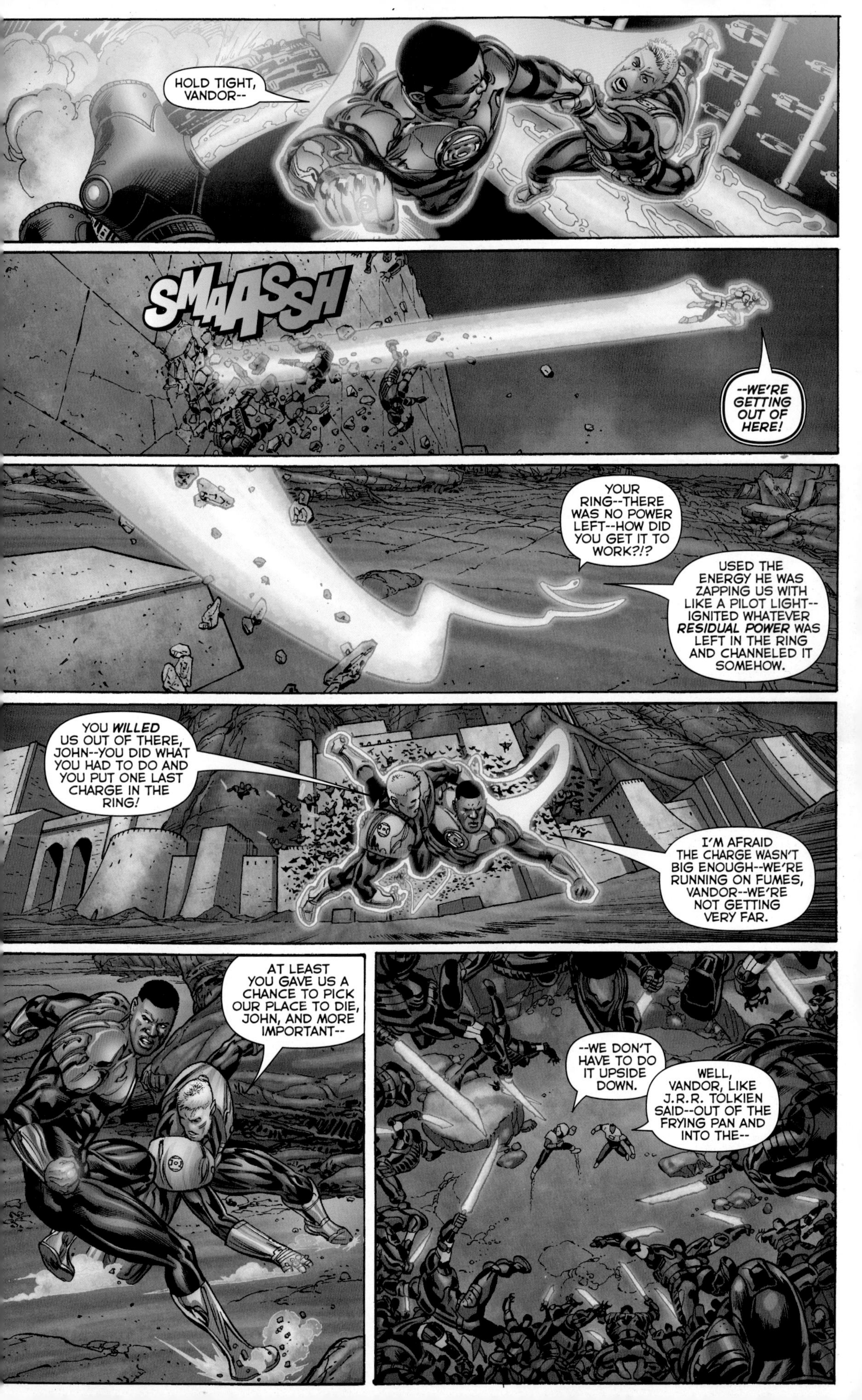
HOLD TIGHT, VANDOR--
SMAASSH
--WE'RE GETTING OUT OF HERE!
YOUR RING--THERE WAS NO POWER LEFT--HOW DID YOU GET IT TO WORK?!?
USED THE ENERGY HE WAS ZAPPING US WITH LIKE A PILOT LIGHT--IGNITED WHATEVER RESIDUAL POWER WAS LEFT IN THE RING AND CHANNELED IT SOMEHOW.
YOU WILLED US OUT OF THERE, JOHN--YOU DID WHAT YOU HAD TO DO AND YOU PUT ONE LAST CHARGE IN THE RING!
I'M AFRAID THE CHARGE WASN'T BIG ENOUGH--WE'RE RUNNING ON FUMES, VANDOR--WE'RE NOT GETTING VERY FAR.
AT LEAST YOU GAVE US A CHANCE TO PICK OUR PLACE TO DIE, JOHN, AND MORE IMPORTANT--
--WE DON'T HAVE TO DO IT UPSIDE DOWN.
WELL, VANDOR, LIKE J.R.R. TOLKIEN SAID--OUT OF THE FRYING PAN AND INTO THE--

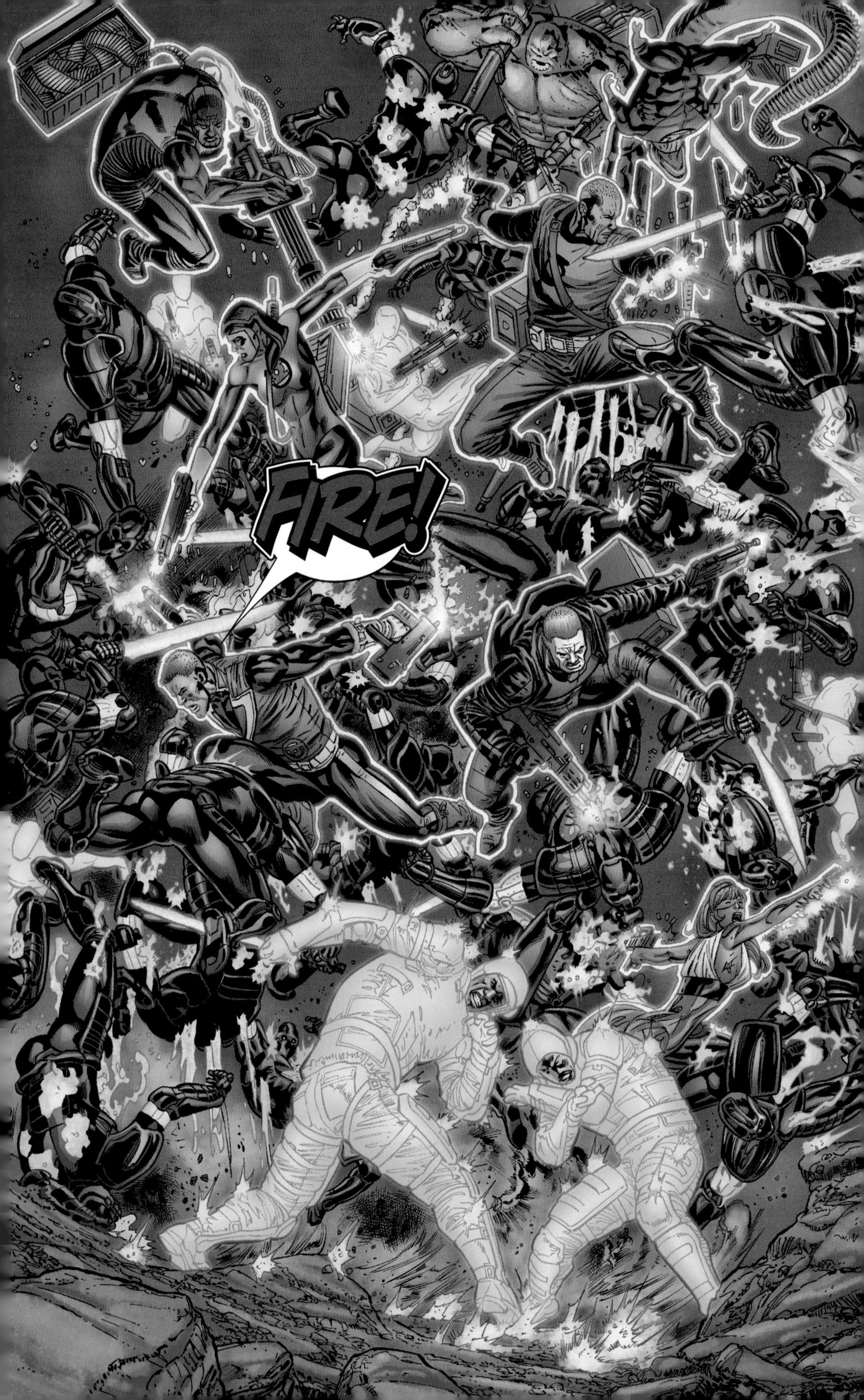
FIRE!

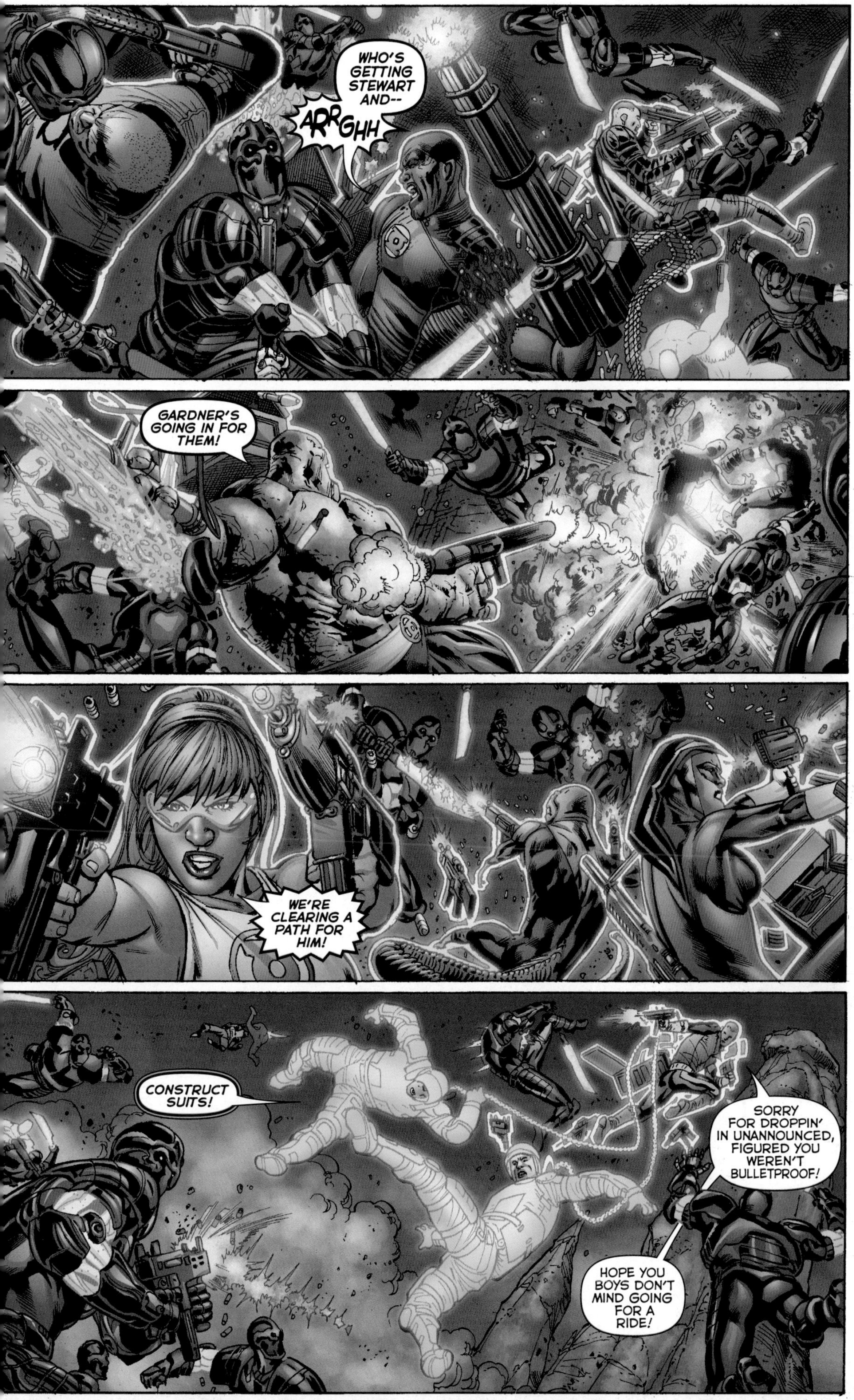
WHO'S GETTING STEWART AND--
ARRGHH
GARDNER'S GOING IN FOR THEM!
WE'RE CLEARING A PATH FOR HIM!
CONSTRUCT SUITS!
SORRY FOR DROPPIN' IN UNANNOUNCED, FIGURED YOU WEREN'T BULLETPROOF!
HOPE YOU BOYS DON'T MIND GOING FOR A RIDE!

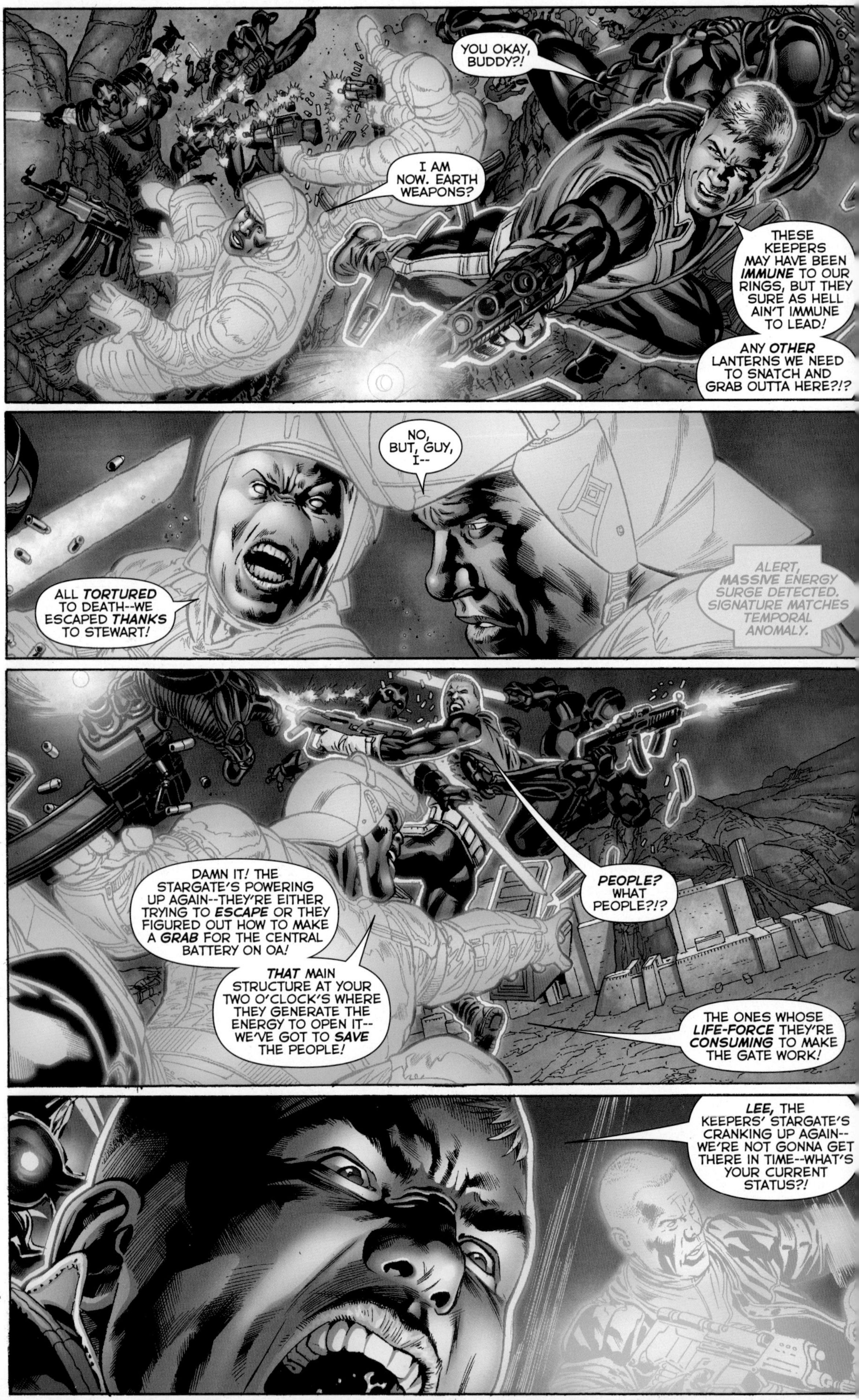

YOU OKAY, BUDDY?!
I AM NOW. EARTH WEAPONS?
THESE KEEPERS MAY HAVE BEEN IMMUNE TO OUR RINGS, BUT THEY SURE AS HELL AIN'T IMMUNE TO LEAD!
ANY OTHER LANTERNS WE NEED TO SNATCH AND GRAB OUTTA HERE?!?
NO, BUT, GUY, I--
ALL TORTURED TO DEATH--WE ESCAPED THANKS TO STEWART!
ALERT, MASSIVE ENERGY SURGE DETECTED. SIGNATURE MATCHES TEMPORAL ANOMALY.
DAMN IT! THE STARGATE'S POWERING UP AGAIN--THEY'RE EITHER TRYING TO ESCAPE OR THEY FIGURED OUT HOW TO MAKE A GRAB FOR THE CENTRAL BATTERY ON OA!
THAT MAIN STRUCTURE AT YOUR TWO O'CLOCK'S WHERE THEY GENERATE THE ENERGY TO OPEN IT--WE'VE GOT TO SAVE THE PEOPLE!
PEOPLE? WHAT PEOPLE?!?
THE ONES WHOSE LIFE-FORCE THEY'RE CONSUMING TO MAKE THE GATE WORK!
LEE, THE KEEPERS' STARGATE'S CRANKING UP AGAIN--WE'RE NOT GONNA GET THERE IN TIME--WHAT'S YOUR CURRENT STATUS?!

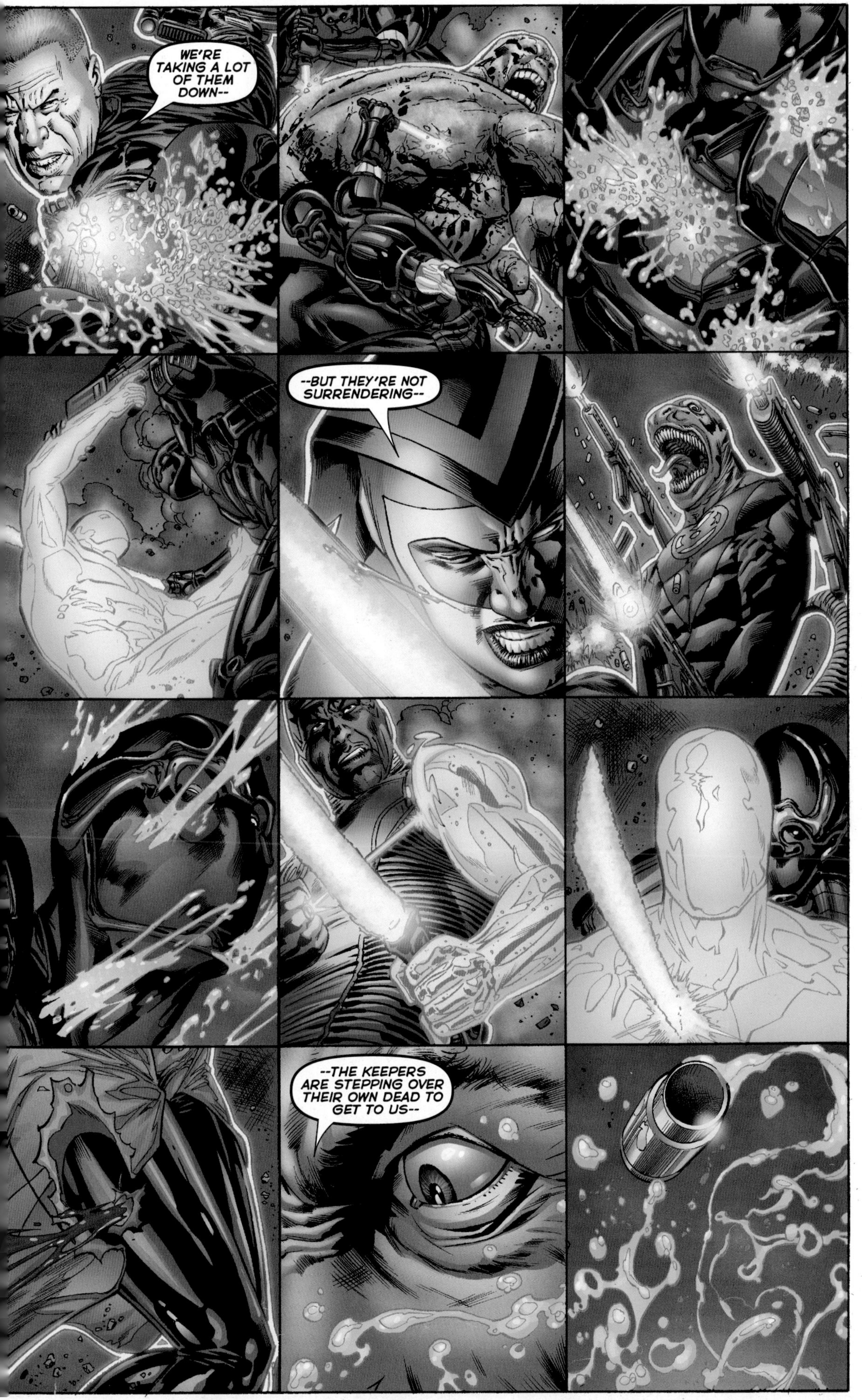
WE'RE TAKING A LOT OF THEM DOWN--
--BUT THEY'RE NOT SURRENDERING--
--THE KEEPERS ARE STEPPING OVER THEIR OWN DEAD TO GET TO US--

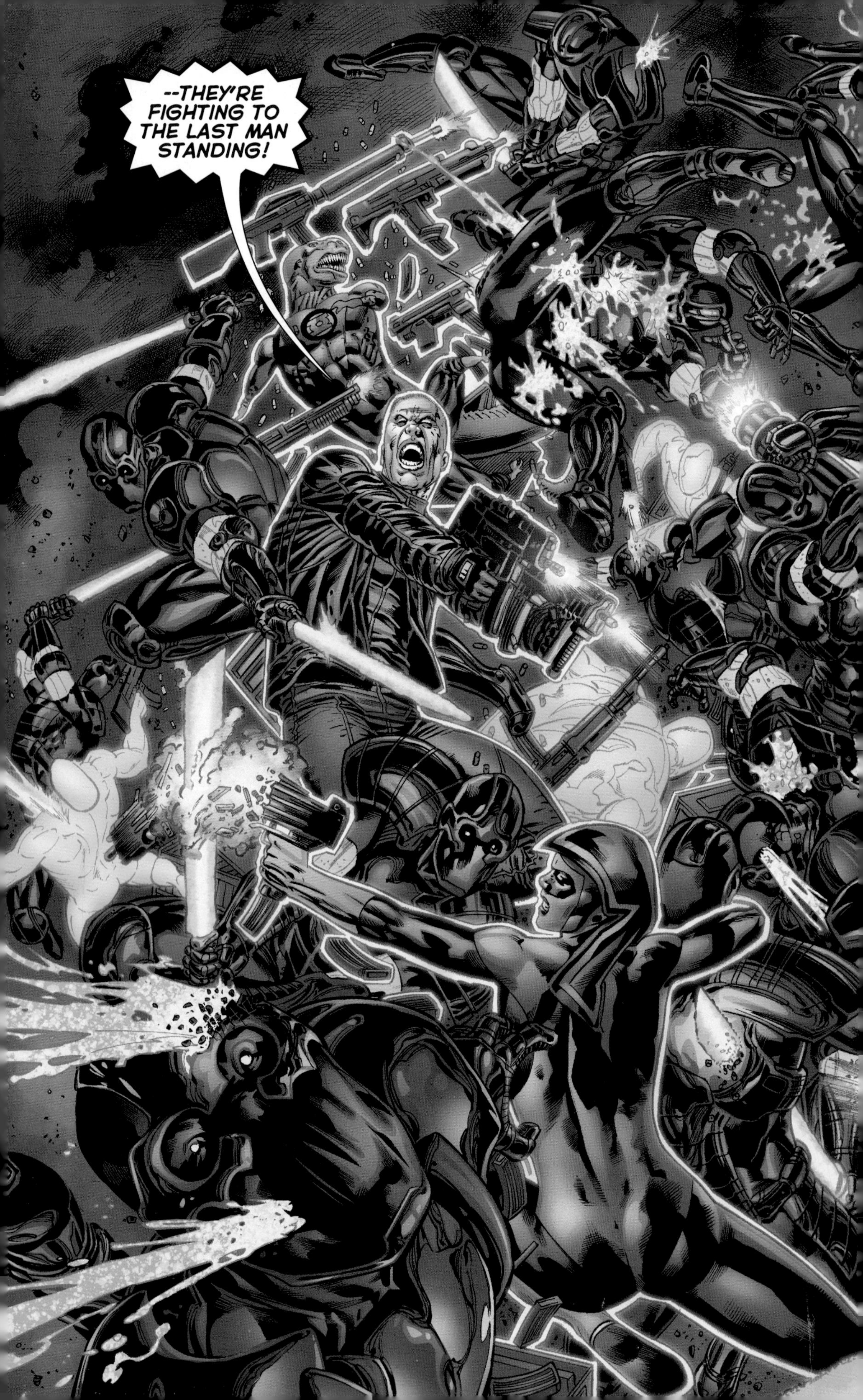
--THEY'RE FIGHTING TO THE LAST MAN STANDING!

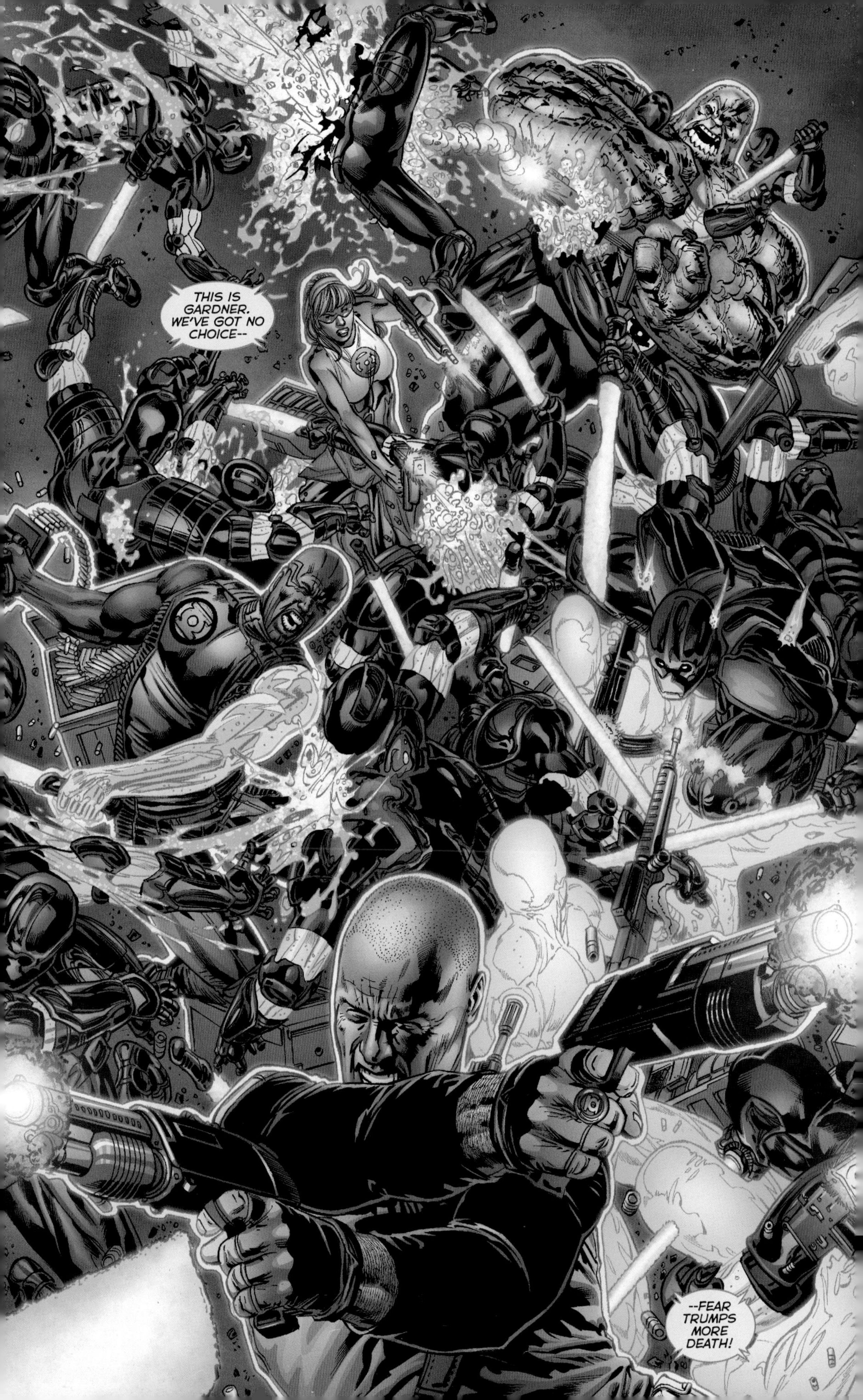
THIS IS GARDNER. WE'VE GOT NO CHOICE--
--FEAR TRUMPS MORE DEATH!

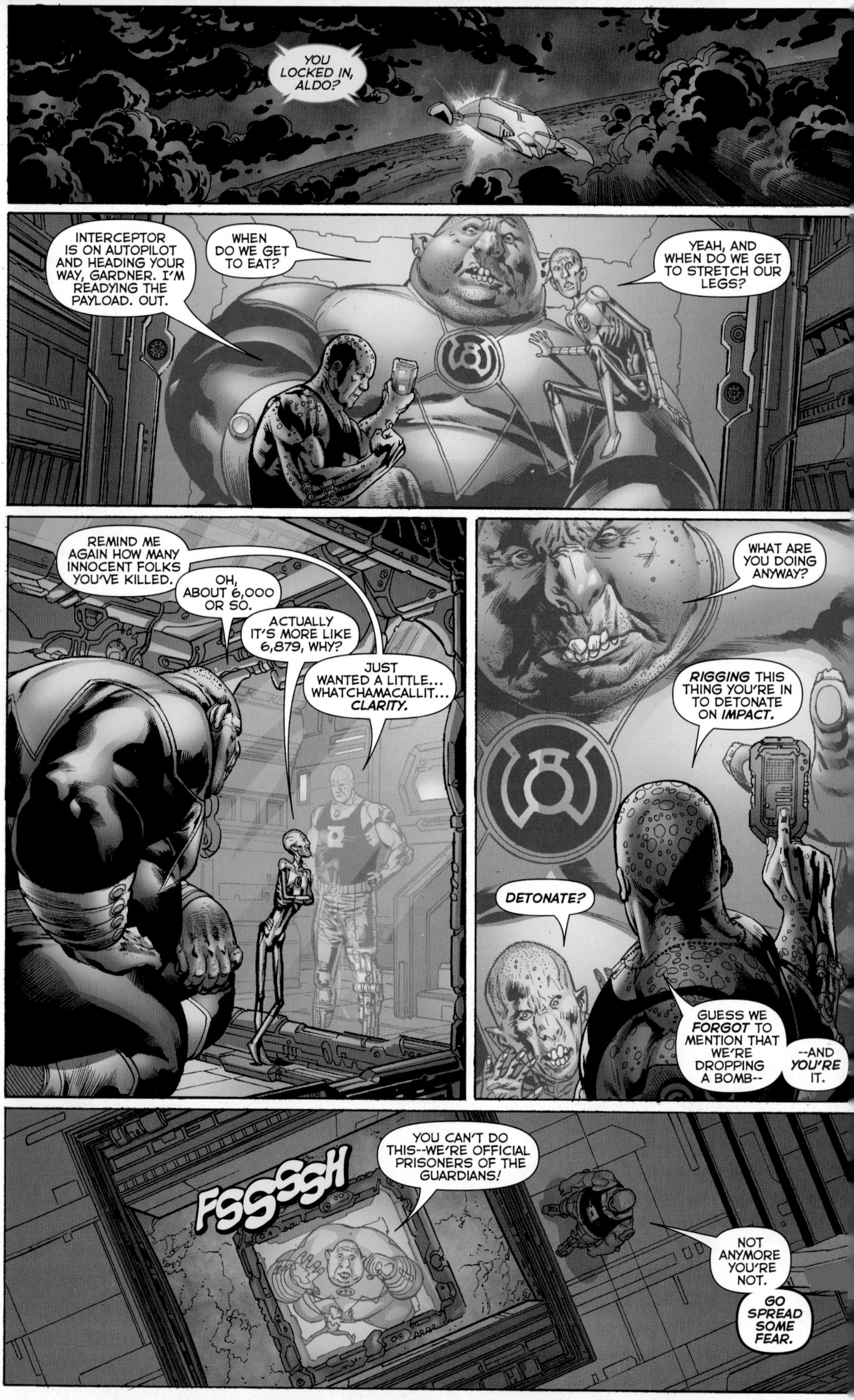
YOU LOCKED IN, ALDO?
INTERCEPTOR IS ON AUTOPILOT AND HEADING YOUR WAY, GARDNER. I'M READYING THE PAYLOAD. OUT.
WHEN DO WE GET TO EAT?
YEAH, AND WHEN DO WE GET TO STRETCH OUR LEGS?
REMIND ME AGAIN HOW MANY INNOCENT FOLKS YOU'VE KILLED.
OH, ABOUT 6,000 OR SO.
ACTUALLY IT'S MORE LIKE 6,879, WHY?
JUST WANTED A LITTLE... WHATCHAMACALLIT... CLARITY.
WHAT ARE YOU DOING ANYWAY?
RIGGING THIS THING YOU'RE IN TO DETONATE ON IMPACT.
DETONATE?
GUESS WE FORGOT TO MENTION THAT WE'RE DROPPING A BOMB--
--AND YOU'RE IT.
FSSSSH
YOU CAN'T DO THIS--WE'RE OFFICIAL PRISONERS OF THE GUARDIANS!
NOT ANYMORE YOU'RE NOT.
GO SPREAD SOME FEAR.

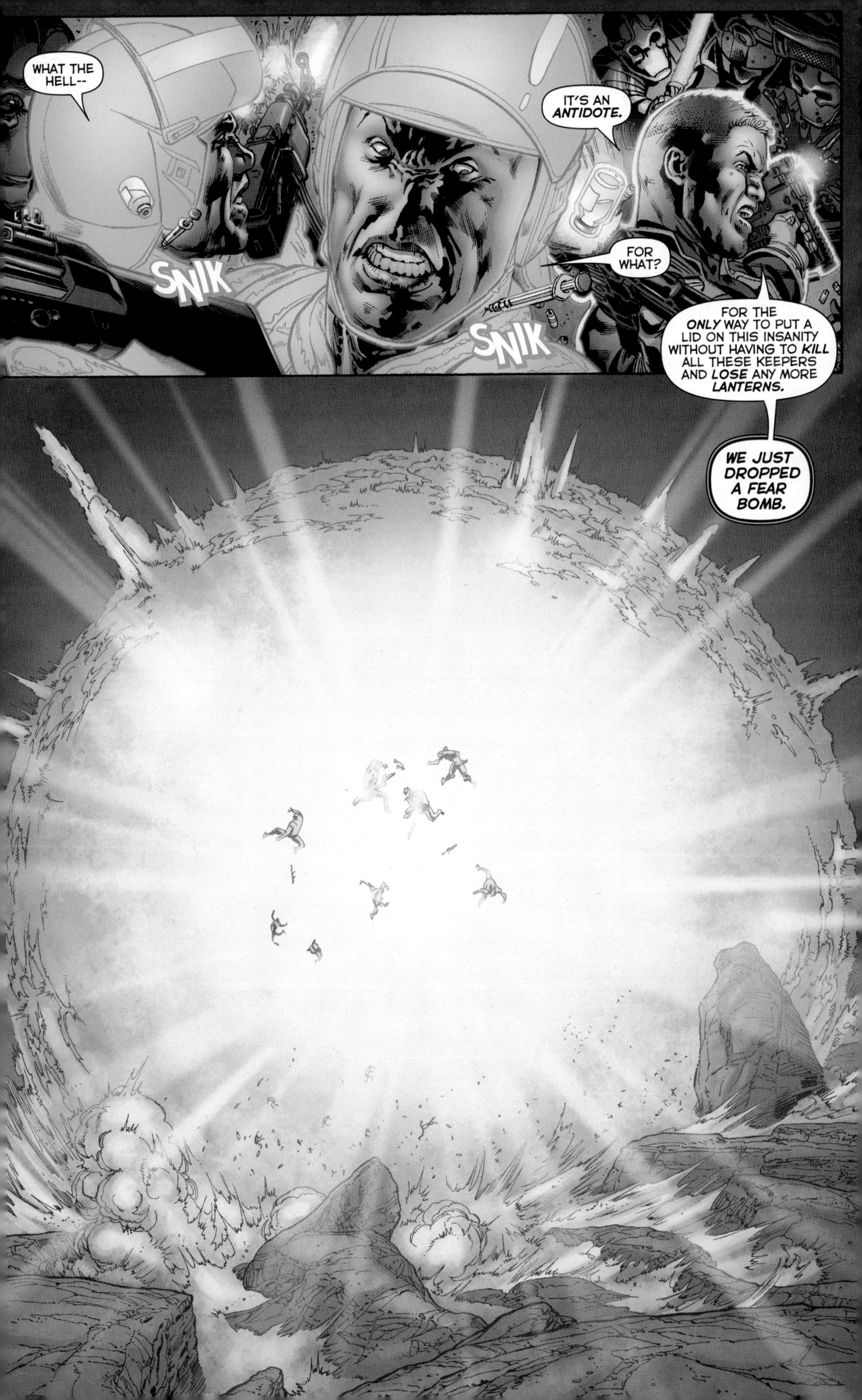
WHAT THE HELL--
IT'S AN ANTIDOTE.
SNIK
FOR WHAT?
SNIK
FOR THE ONLY WAY TO PUT A LID ON THIS INSANITY WITHOUT HAVING TO KILL ALL THESE KEEPERS AND LOSE ANY MORE LANTERNS.
WE JUST DROPPED A FEAR BOMB.

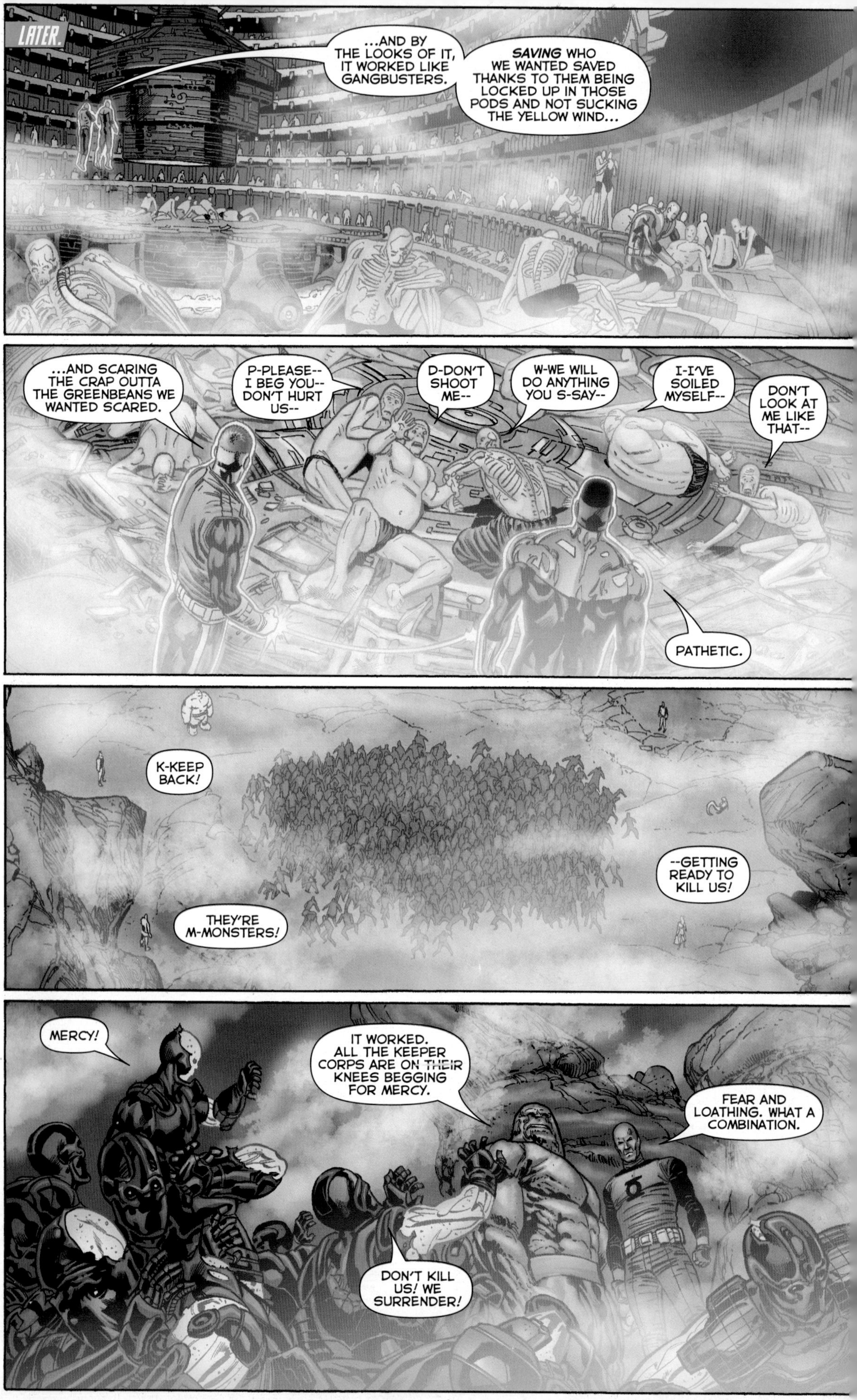
LATER.
...AND BY THE LOOKS OF IT, IT WORKED LIKE GANGBUSTERS.
SAVING WHO WE WANTED SAVED THANKS TO THEM BEING LOCKED UP IN THOSE PODS AND NOT SUCKING THE YELLOW WIND...
...AND SCARING THE CRAP OUTTA THE GREENBEANS WE WANTED SCARED.
P-PLEASE-- I BEG YOU-- DON'T HURT US--
D-DON'T SHOOT ME--
W-WE WILL DO ANYTHING YOU S-SAY--
I-I'VE SOILED MYSELF--
DON'T LOOK AT ME LIKE THAT--
PATHETIC.
K-KEEP BACK!
THEY'RE M-MONSTERS!
--GETTING READY TO KILL US!
MERCY!
IT WORKED. ALL THE KEEPER CORPS ARE ON THEIR KNEES BEGGING FOR MERCY.
FEAR AND LOATHING. WHAT A COMBINATION.
DON'T KILL US! WE SURRENDER!

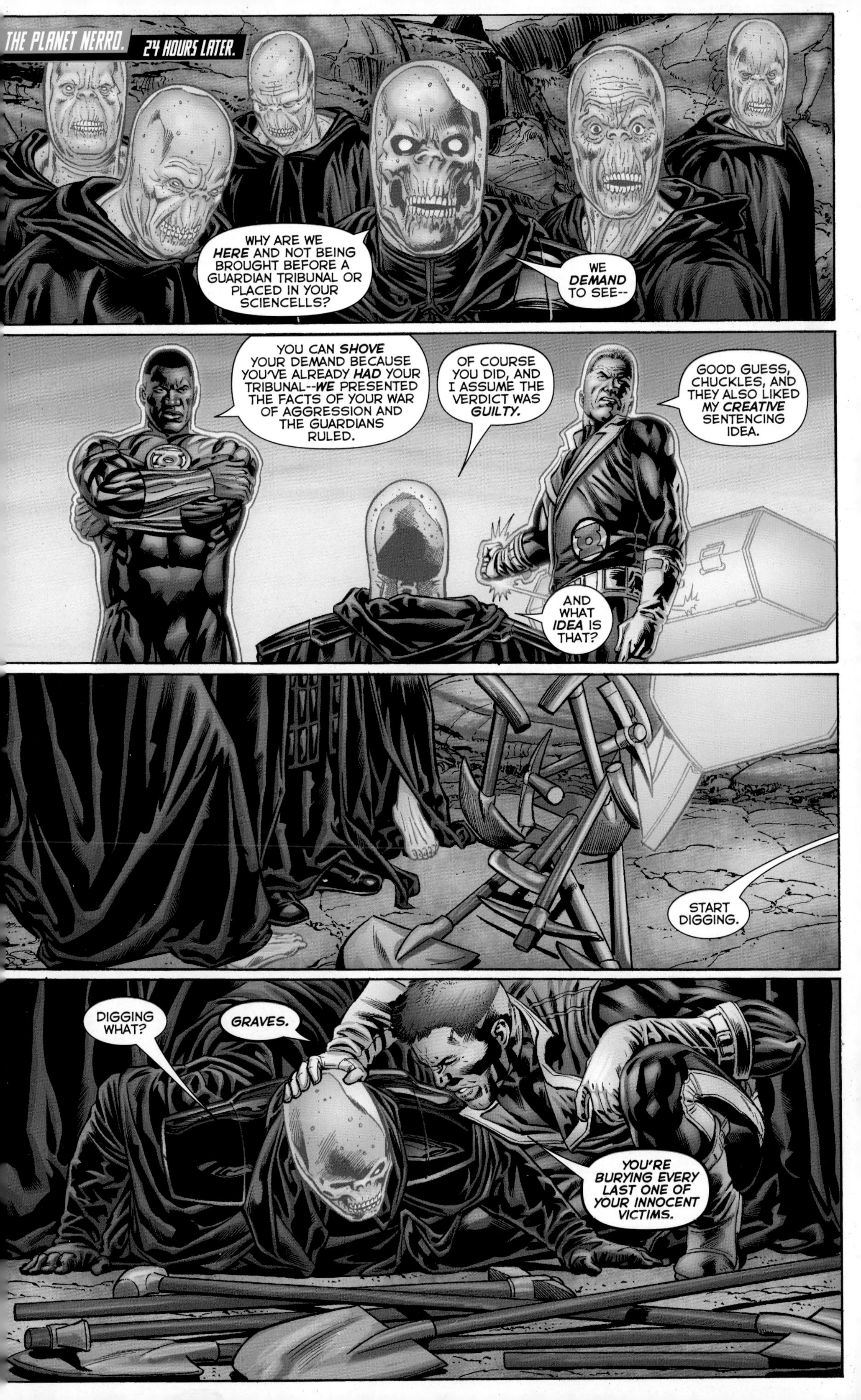
THE PLANET NERRO.
24 HOURS LATER.
WHY ARE WE HERE AND NOT BEING BROUGHT BEFORE A GUARDIAN TRIBUNAL OR PLACED IN YOUR SCIENCELLS?
WE DEMAND TO SEE--
YOU CAN SHOVE YOUR DEMAND BECAUSE YOU'VE ALREADY HAD YOUR TRIBUNAL--WE PRESENTED THE FACTS OF YOUR WAR OF AGGRESSION AND THE GUARDIANS RULED.
OF COURSE YOU DID, AND I ASSUME THE VERDICT WAS GUILTY.
GOOD GUESS, CHUCKLES, AND THEY ALSO LIKED MY CREATIVE SENTENCING IDEA.
AND WHAT IDEA IS THAT?
START DIGGING.
DIGGING WHAT?
GRAVES.
YOU'RE BURYING EVERY LAST ONE OF YOUR INNOCENT VICTIMS.

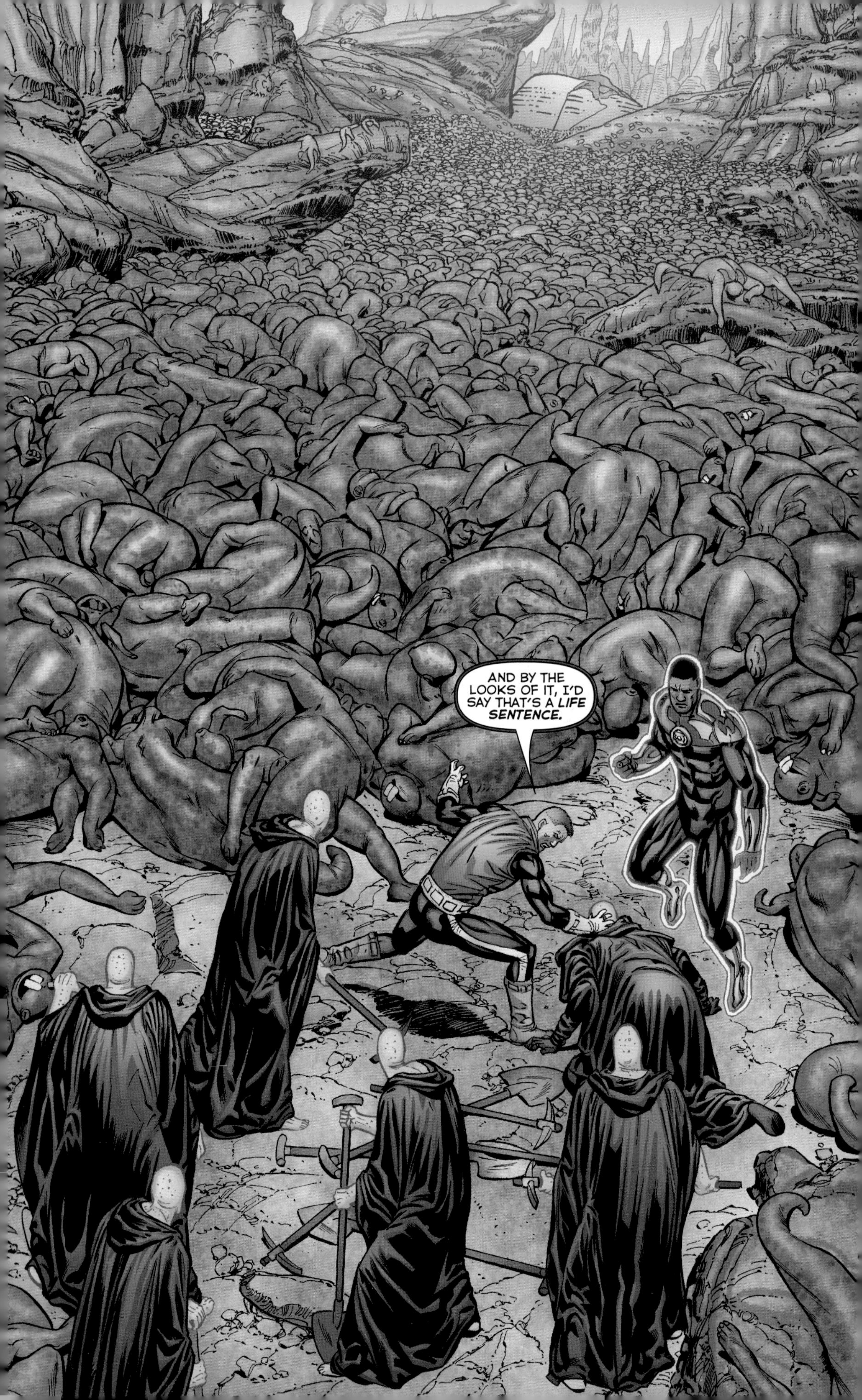
AND BY THE LOOKS OF IT, I'D SAY THAT'S A *LIFE SENTENCE.*

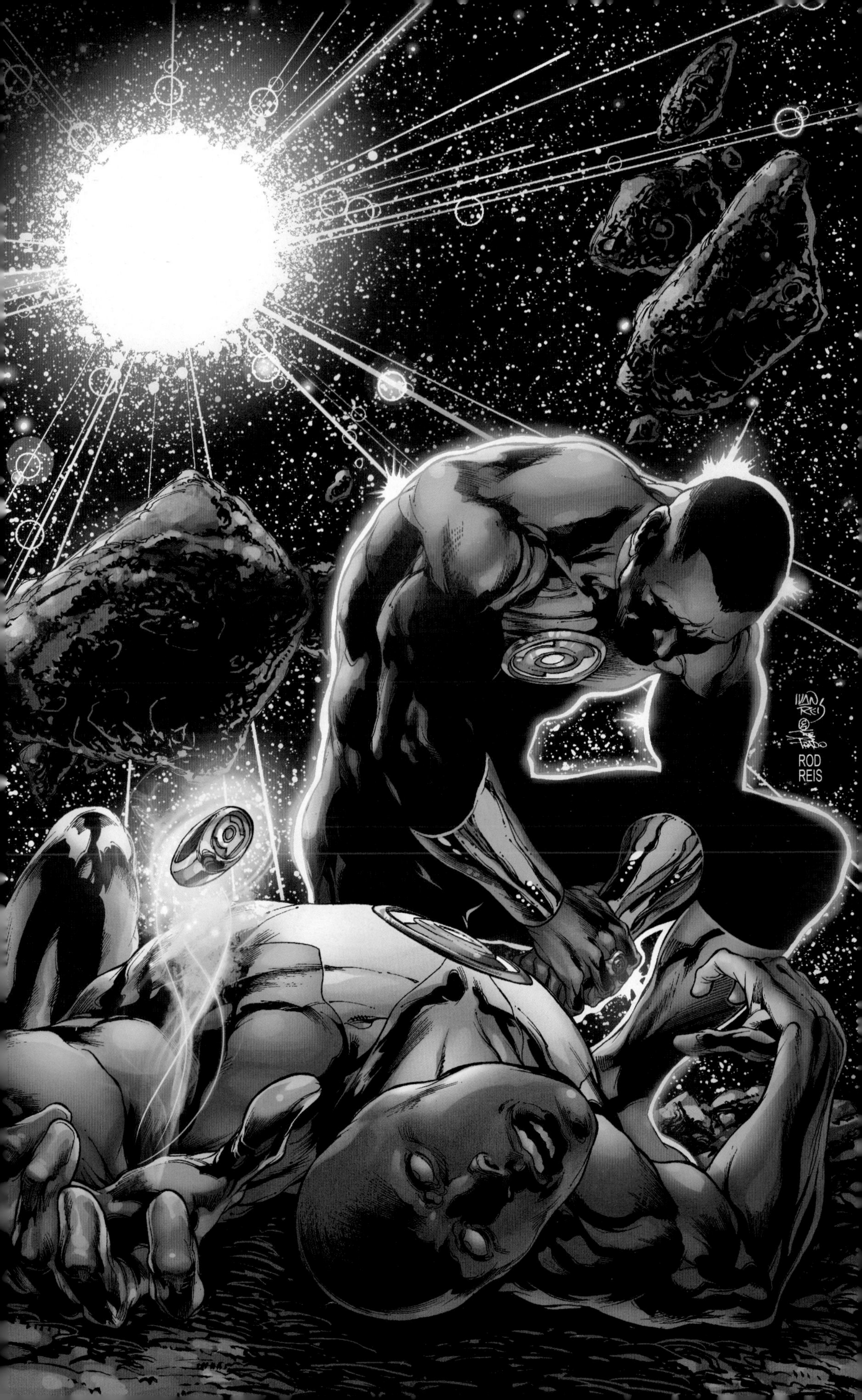
ROD
REIS

RENDERING HONOR

PETER J. TOMASI writer **CLAUDE ST. AUBIN** penciller **SCOTT HANNA** inker cover by **IVAN REIS, JOE PRADO & ROD REIS**

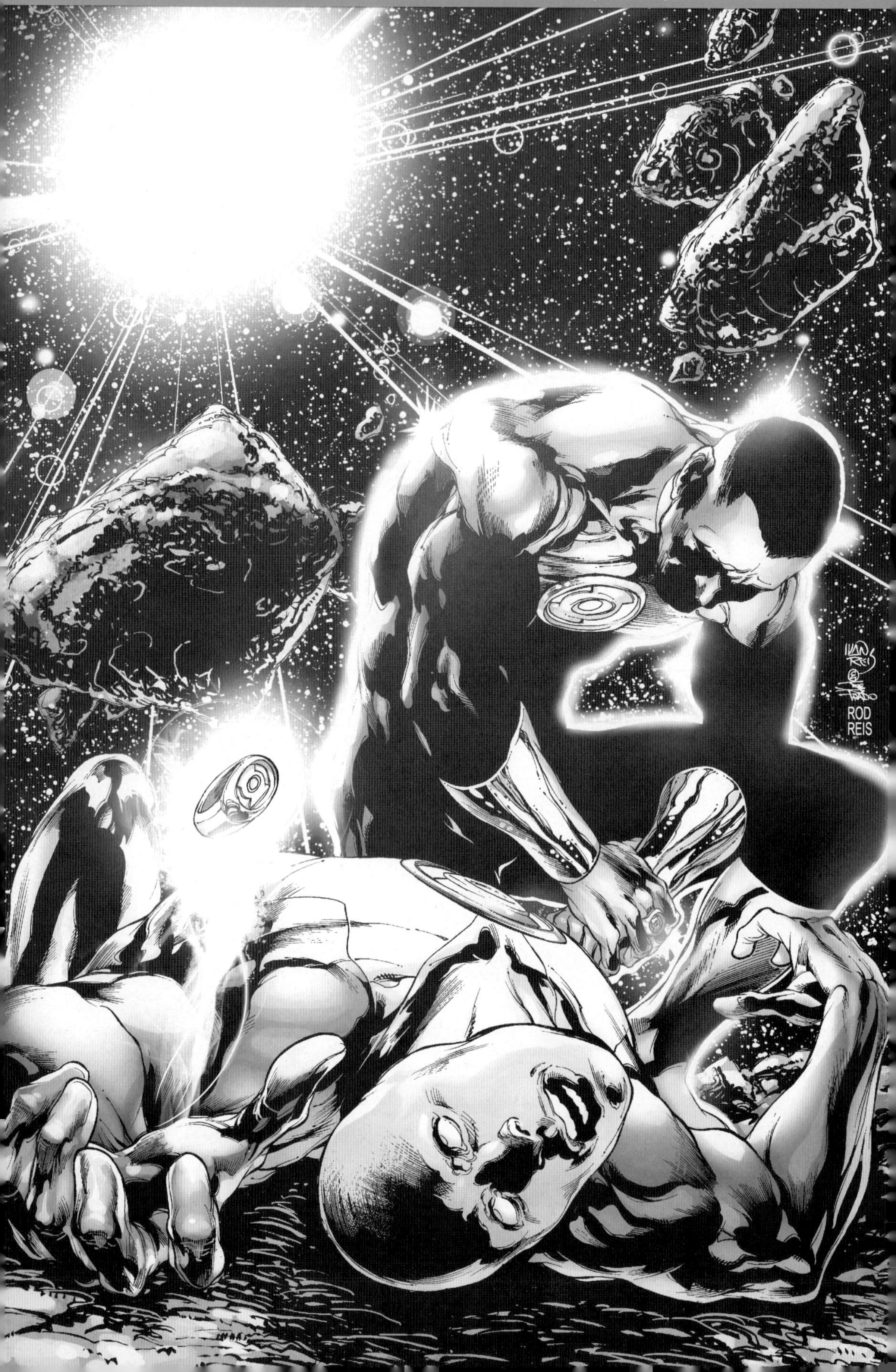

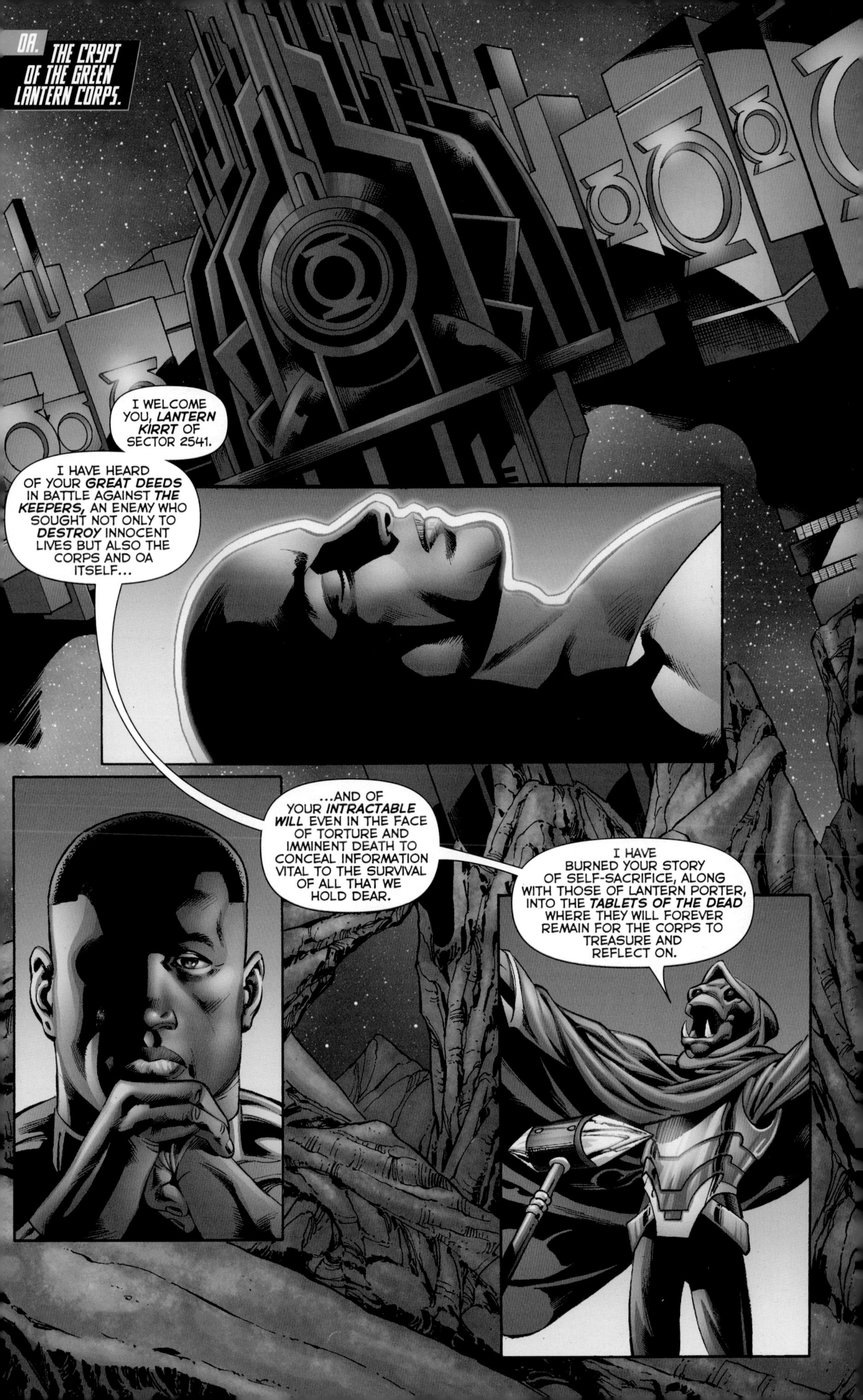
OA. THE CRYPT OF THE GREEN LANTERN CORPS.
I WELCOME YOU, LANTERN KIRRT OF SECTOR 2541.
I HAVE HEARD OF YOUR GREAT DEEDS IN BATTLE AGAINST THE KEEPERS, AN ENEMY WHO SOUGHT NOT ONLY TO DESTROY INNOCENT LIVES BUT ALSO THE CORPS AND OA ITSELF...
...AND OF YOUR INTRACTABLE WILL EVEN IN THE FACE OF TORTURE AND IMMINENT DEATH TO CONCEAL INFORMATION VITAL TO THE SURVIVAL OF ALL THAT WE HOLD DEAR.
I HAVE BURNED YOUR STORY OF SELF-SACRIFICE, ALONG WITH THOSE OF LANTERN PORTER, INTO THE TABLETS OF THE DEAD WHERE THEY WILL FOREVER REMAIN FOR THE CORPS TO TREASURE AND REFLECT ON.

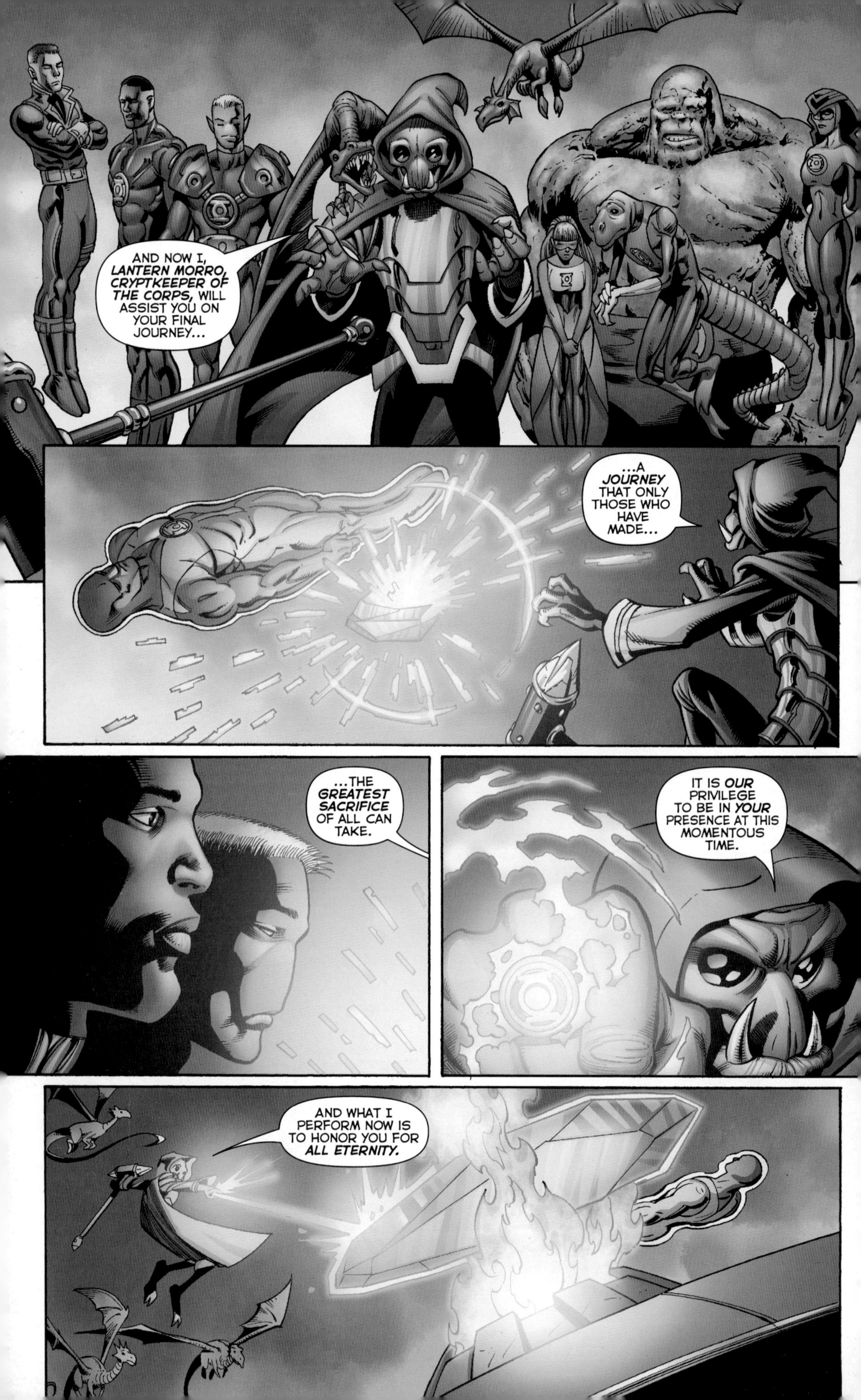
AND NOW I, *LANTERN MORRO, CRYPTKEEPER OF THE CORPS,* WILL ASSIST YOU ON YOUR FINAL JOURNEY...
...A *JOURNEY* THAT ONLY THOSE WHO HAVE MADE...
...THE *GREATEST SACRIFICE* OF ALL CAN TAKE.
IT IS *OUR* PRIVILEGE TO BE IN *YOUR* PRESENCE AT THIS MOMENTOUS TIME.
AND WHAT I PERFORM NOW IS TO HONOR YOU FOR *ALL ETERNITY.*

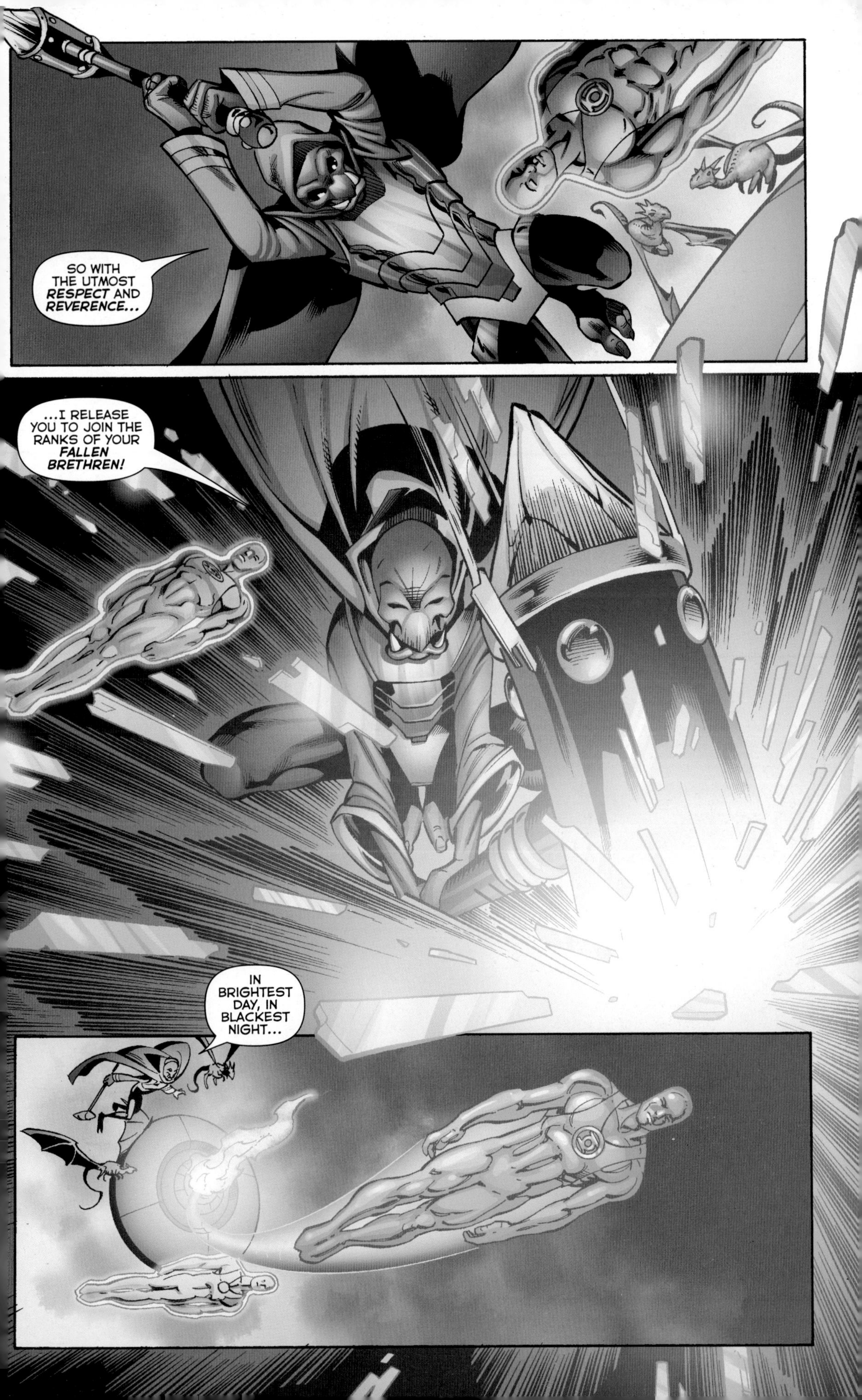
SO WITH THE UTMOST *RESPECT* AND *REVERENCE*...
...I RELEASE YOU TO JOIN THE RANKS OF YOUR *FALLEN BRETHREN!*
IN BRIGHTEST DAY, IN BLACKEST NIGHT...

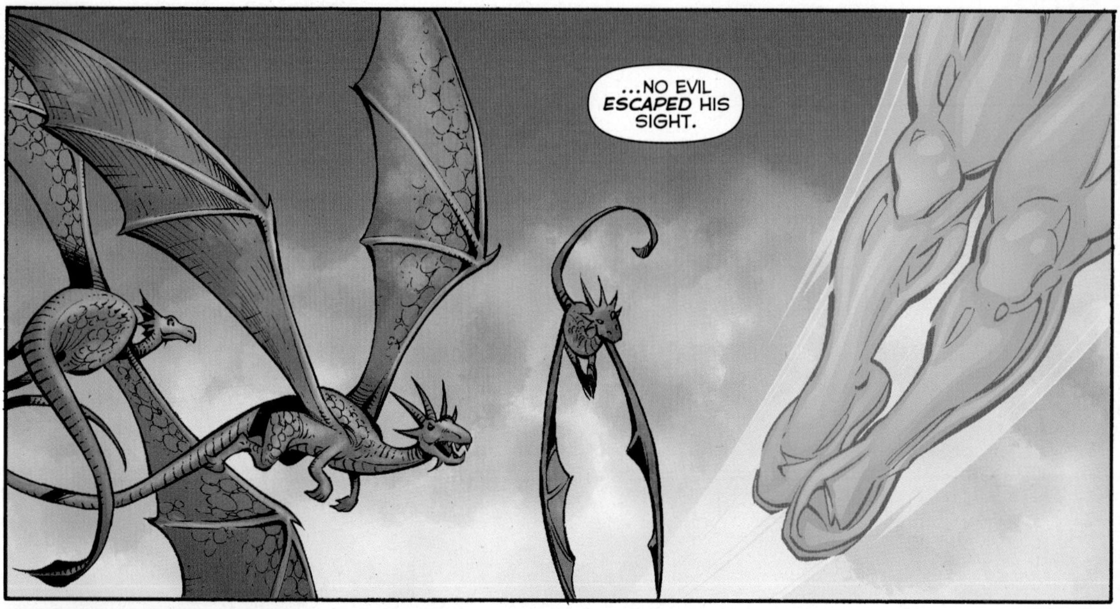
...NO EVIL ESCAPED HIS SIGHT.

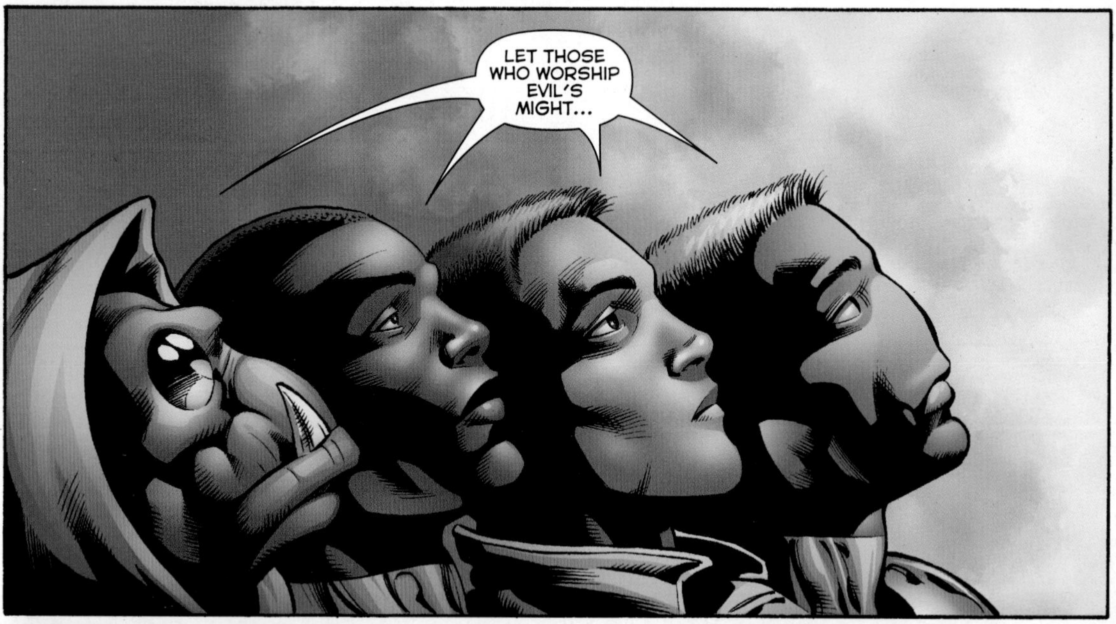
LET THOSE WHO WORSHIP EVIL'S MIGHT...

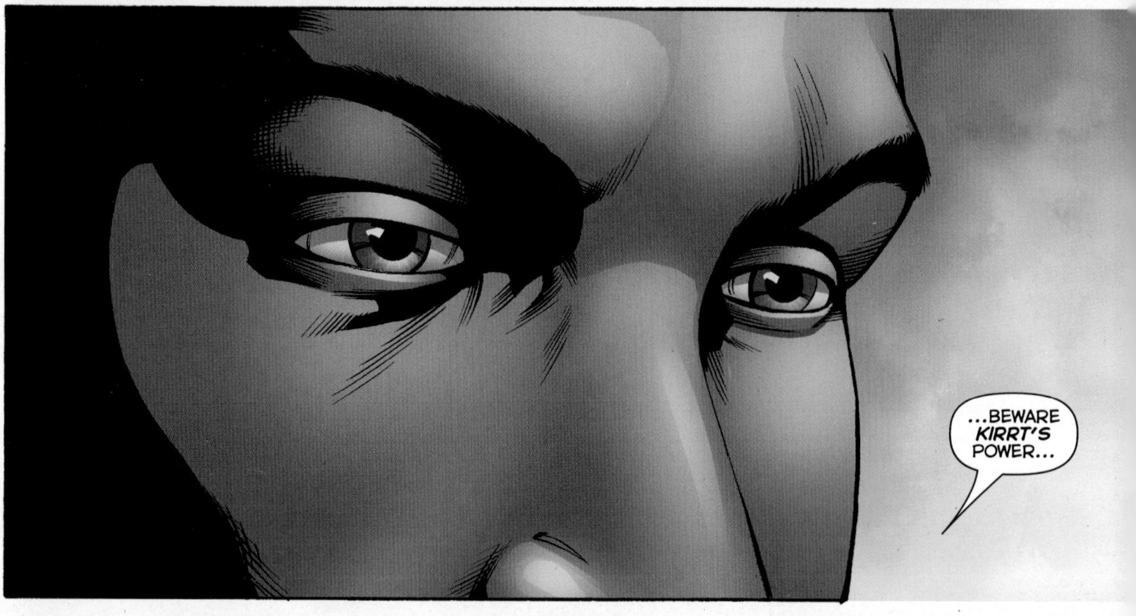
...BEWARE KIRRT'S POWER...

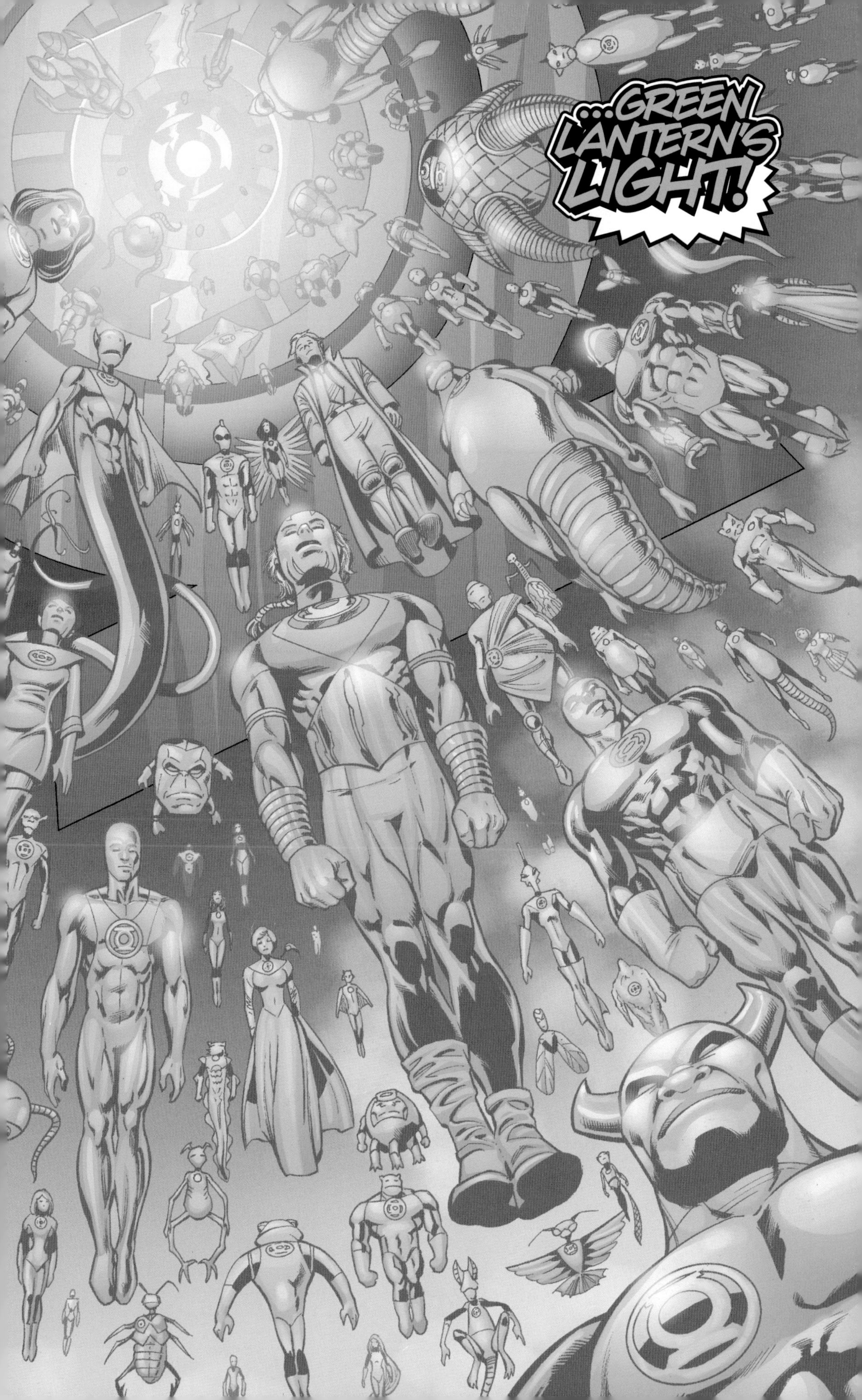
...GREEN LANTERN'S LIGHT!

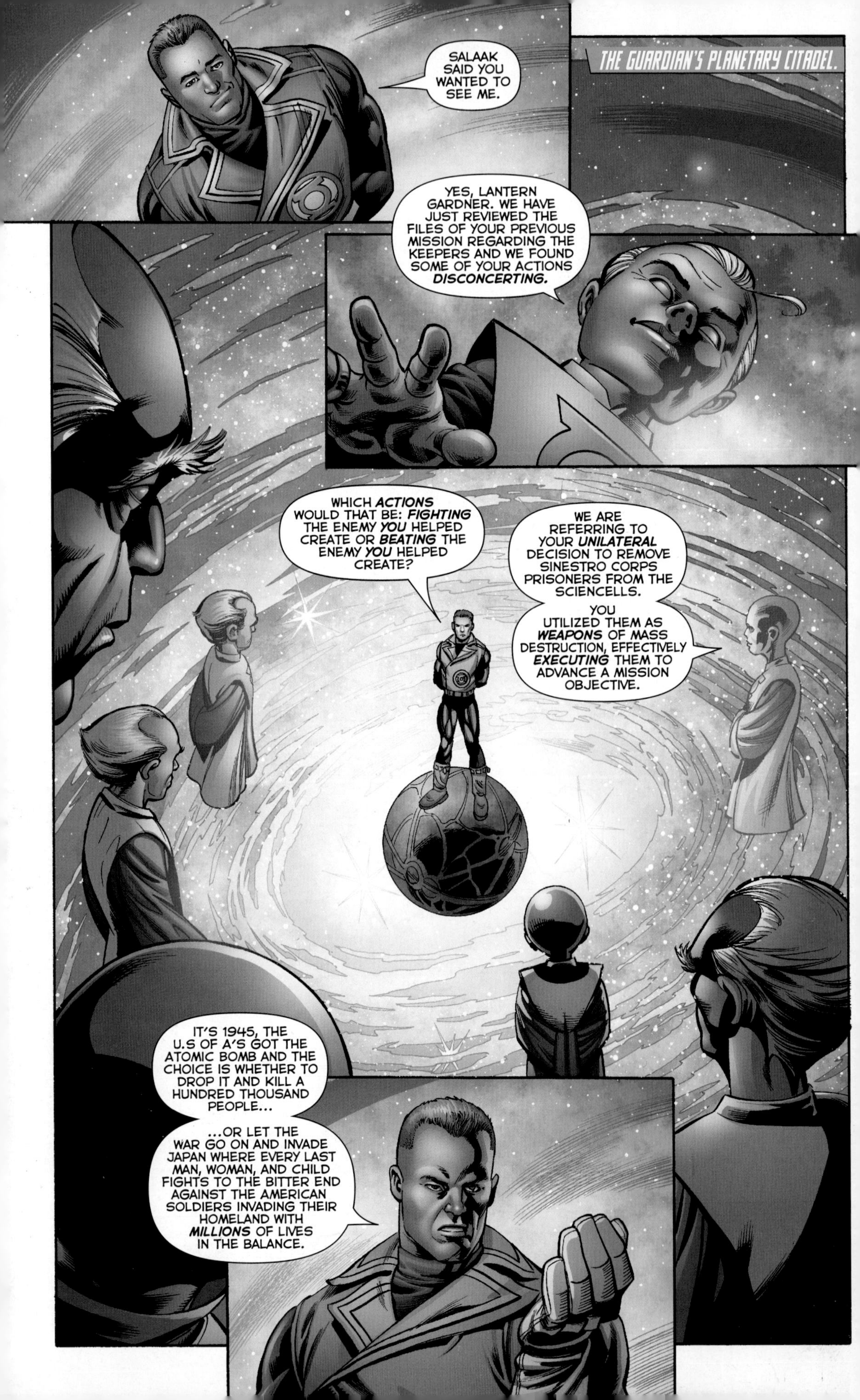
SALAAK SAID YOU WANTED TO SEE ME.
THE GUARDIAN'S PLANETARY CITADEL.
YES, LANTERN GARDNER. WE HAVE JUST REVIEWED THE FILES OF YOUR PREVIOUS MISSION REGARDING THE KEEPERS AND WE FOUND SOME OF YOUR ACTIONS DISCONCERTING.
WHICH ACTIONS WOULD THAT BE: FIGHTING THE ENEMY YOU HELPED CREATE OR BEATING THE ENEMY YOU HELPED CREATE?
WE ARE REFERRING TO YOUR UNILATERAL DECISION TO REMOVE SINESTRO CORPS PRISONERS FROM THE SCIENCELLS.
YOU UTILIZED THEM AS WEAPONS OF MASS DESTRUCTION, EFFECTIVELY EXECUTING THEM TO ADVANCE A MISSION OBJECTIVE.
IT'S 1945, THE U.S OF A'S GOT THE ATOMIC BOMB AND THE CHOICE IS WHETHER TO DROP IT AND KILL A HUNDRED THOUSAND PEOPLE...
...OR LET THE WAR GO ON AND INVADE JAPAN WHERE EVERY LAST MAN, WOMAN, AND CHILD FIGHTS TO THE BITTER END AGAINST THE AMERICAN SOLDIERS INVADING THEIR HOMELAND WITH MILLIONS OF LIVES IN THE BALANCE.

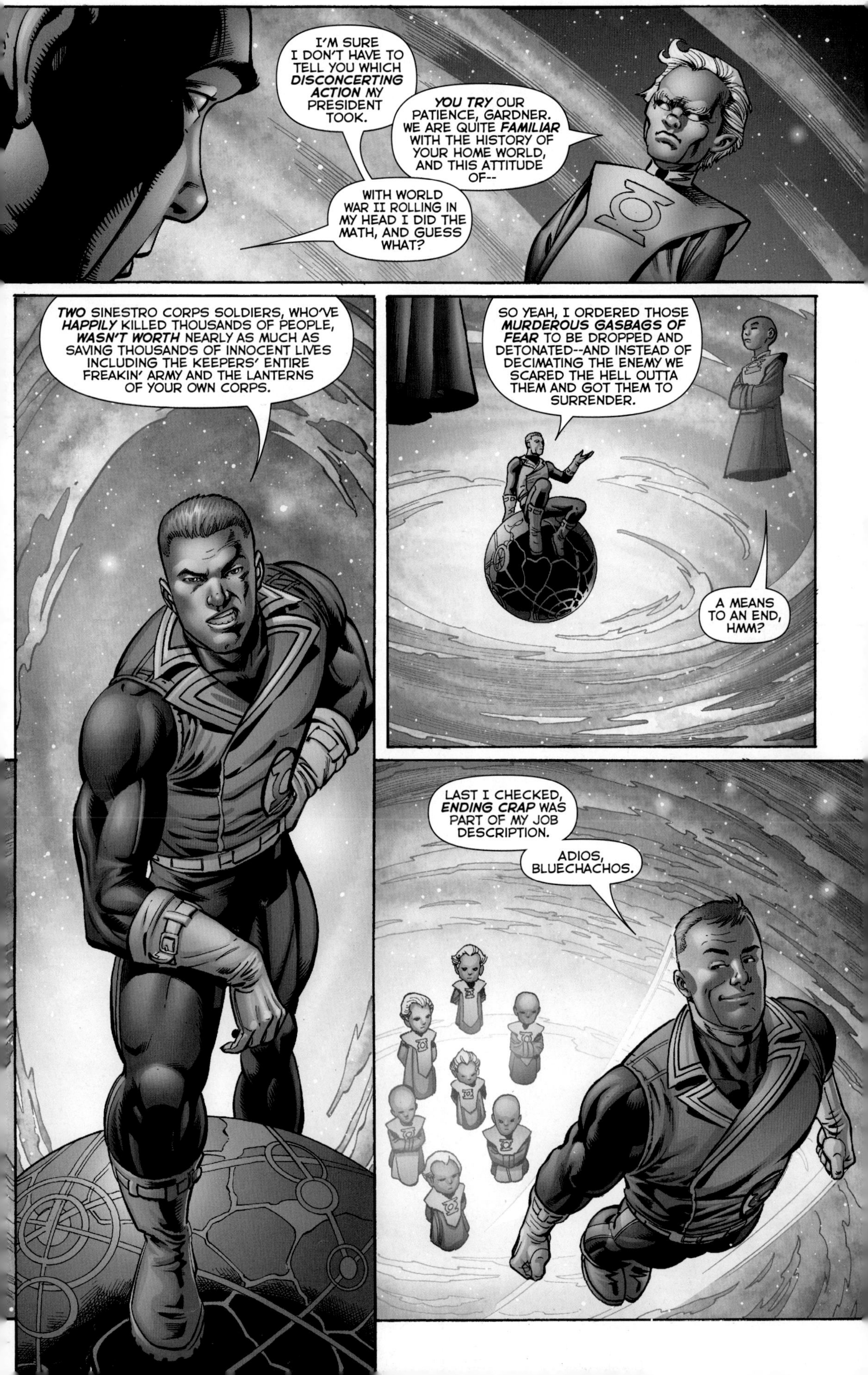

I'M SURE I DON'T HAVE TO TELL YOU WHICH DISCONCERTING ACTION MY PRESIDENT TOOK.
YOU TRY OUR PATIENCE, GARDNER. WE ARE QUITE FAMILIAR WITH THE HISTORY OF YOUR HOME WORLD, AND THIS ATTITUDE OF--
WITH WORLD WAR II ROLLING IN MY HEAD I DID THE MATH, AND GUESS WHAT?
TWO SINESTRO CORPS SOLDIERS, WHO'VE HAPPILY KILLED THOUSANDS OF PEOPLE, WASN'T WORTH NEARLY AS MUCH AS SAVING THOUSANDS OF INNOCENT LIVES INCLUDING THE KEEPERS' ENTIRE FREAKIN' ARMY AND THE LANTERNS OF YOUR OWN CORPS.
SO YEAH, I ORDERED THOSE MURDEROUS GASBAGS OF FEAR TO BE DROPPED AND DETONATED--AND INSTEAD OF DECIMATING THE ENEMY WE SCARED THE HELL OUTTA THEM AND GOT THEM TO SURRENDER.
A MEANS TO AN END, HMM?
LAST I CHECKED, ENDING CRAP WAS PART OF MY JOB DESCRIPTION.
ADIOS, BLUECHACHOS.

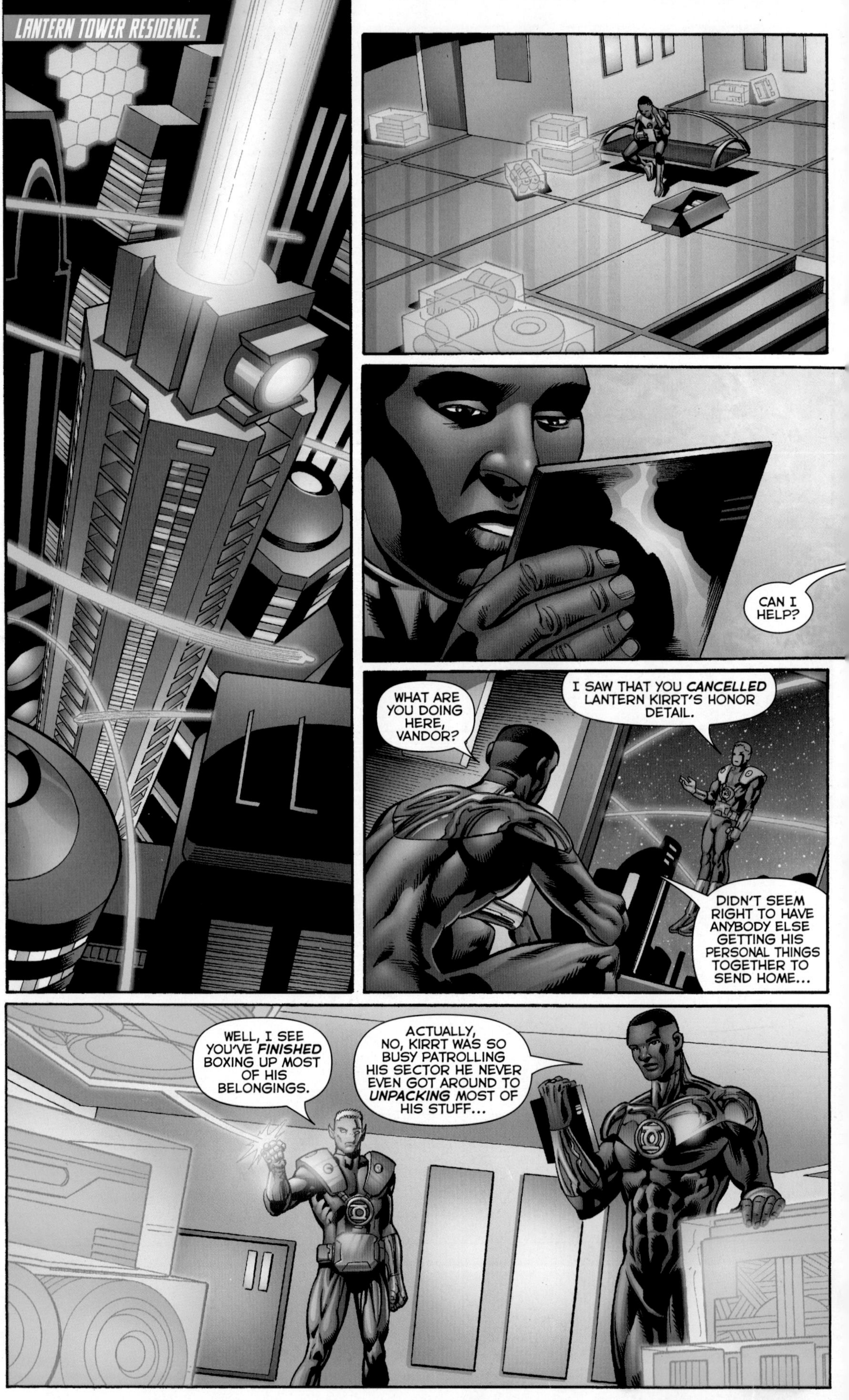
LANTERN TOWER RESIDENCE.
CAN I HELP?
WHAT ARE YOU DOING HERE, VANDOR?
I SAW THAT YOU CANCELLED LANTERN KIRRT'S HONOR DETAIL.
DIDN'T SEEM RIGHT TO HAVE ANYBODY ELSE GETTING HIS PERSONAL THINGS TOGETHER TO SEND HOME...
WELL, I SEE YOU'VE FINISHED BOXING UP MOST OF HIS BELONGINGS.
ACTUALLY, NO, KIRRT WAS SO BUSY PATROLLING HIS SECTOR HE NEVER EVEN GOT AROUND TO UNPACKING MOST OF HIS STUFF...

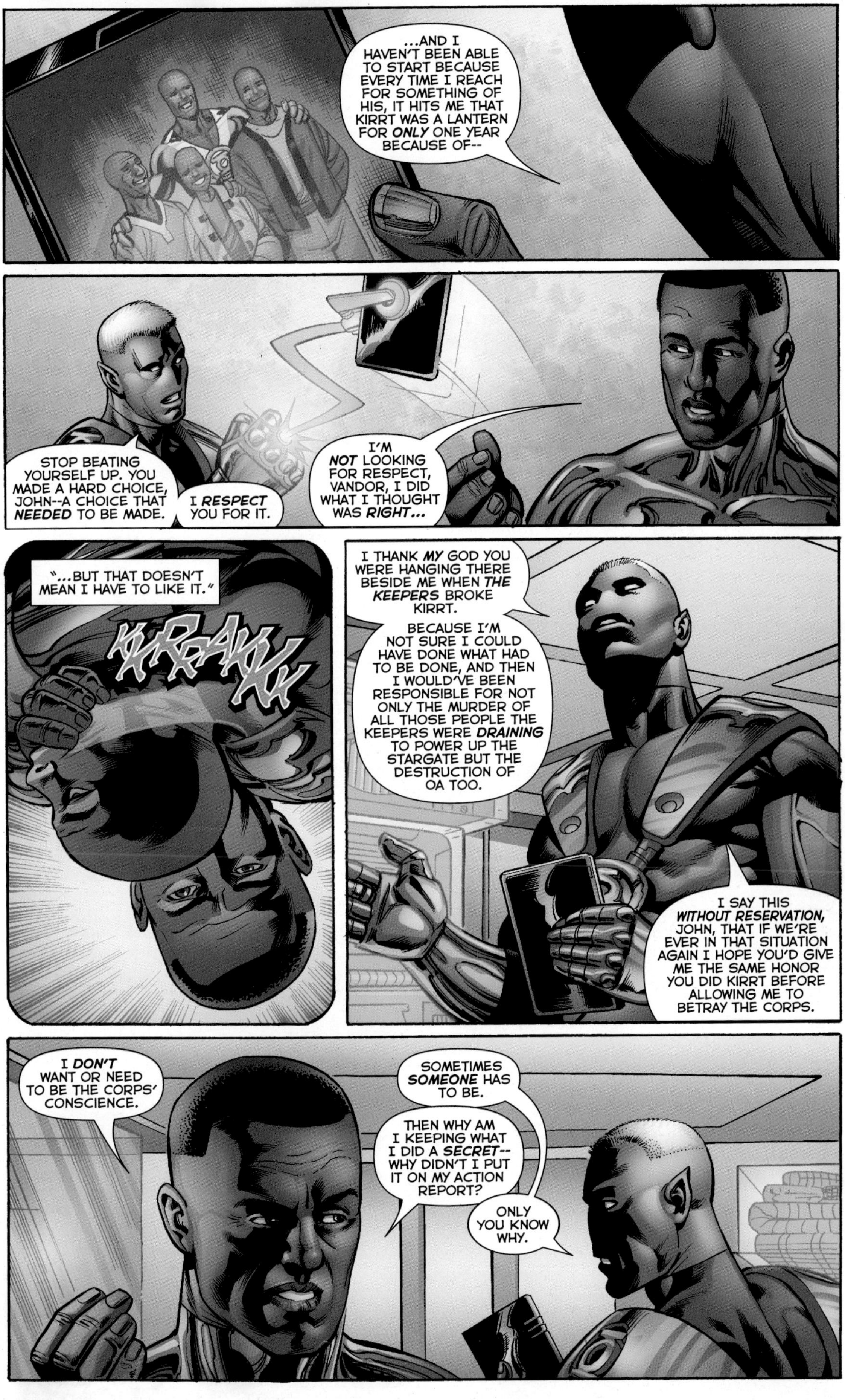

...AND I HAVEN'T BEEN ABLE TO START BECAUSE EVERY TIME I REACH FOR SOMETHING OF HIS, IT HITS ME THAT KIRRT WAS A LANTERN FOR ONLY ONE YEAR BECAUSE OF--
STOP BEATING YOURSELF UP. YOU MADE A HARD CHOICE, JOHN--A CHOICE THAT NEEDED TO BE MADE.
I RESPECT YOU FOR IT.
I'M NOT LOOKING FOR RESPECT, VANDOR, I DID WHAT I THOUGHT WAS RIGHT...
"...BUT THAT DOESN'T MEAN I HAVE TO LIKE IT."
KKRRAKKK
I THANK MY GOD YOU WERE HANGING THERE BESIDE ME WHEN THE KEEPERS BROKE KIRRT.
BECAUSE I'M NOT SURE I COULD HAVE DONE WHAT HAD TO BE DONE, AND THEN I WOULD'VE BEEN RESPONSIBLE FOR NOT ONLY THE MURDER OF ALL THOSE PEOPLE THE KEEPERS WERE DRAINING TO POWER UP THE STARGATE BUT THE DESTRUCTION OF OA TOO.
I SAY THIS WITHOUT RESERVATION, JOHN, THAT IF WE'RE EVER IN THAT SITUATION AGAIN I HOPE YOU'D GIVE ME THE SAME HONOR YOU DID KIRRT BEFORE ALLOWING ME TO BETRAY THE CORPS.
I DON'T WANT OR NEED TO BE THE CORPS' CONSCIENCE.
SOMETIMES SOMEONE HAS TO BE.
THEN WHY AM I KEEPING WHAT I DID A SECRET--WHY DIDN'T I PUT IT ON MY ACTION REPORT?
ONLY YOU KNOW WHY.

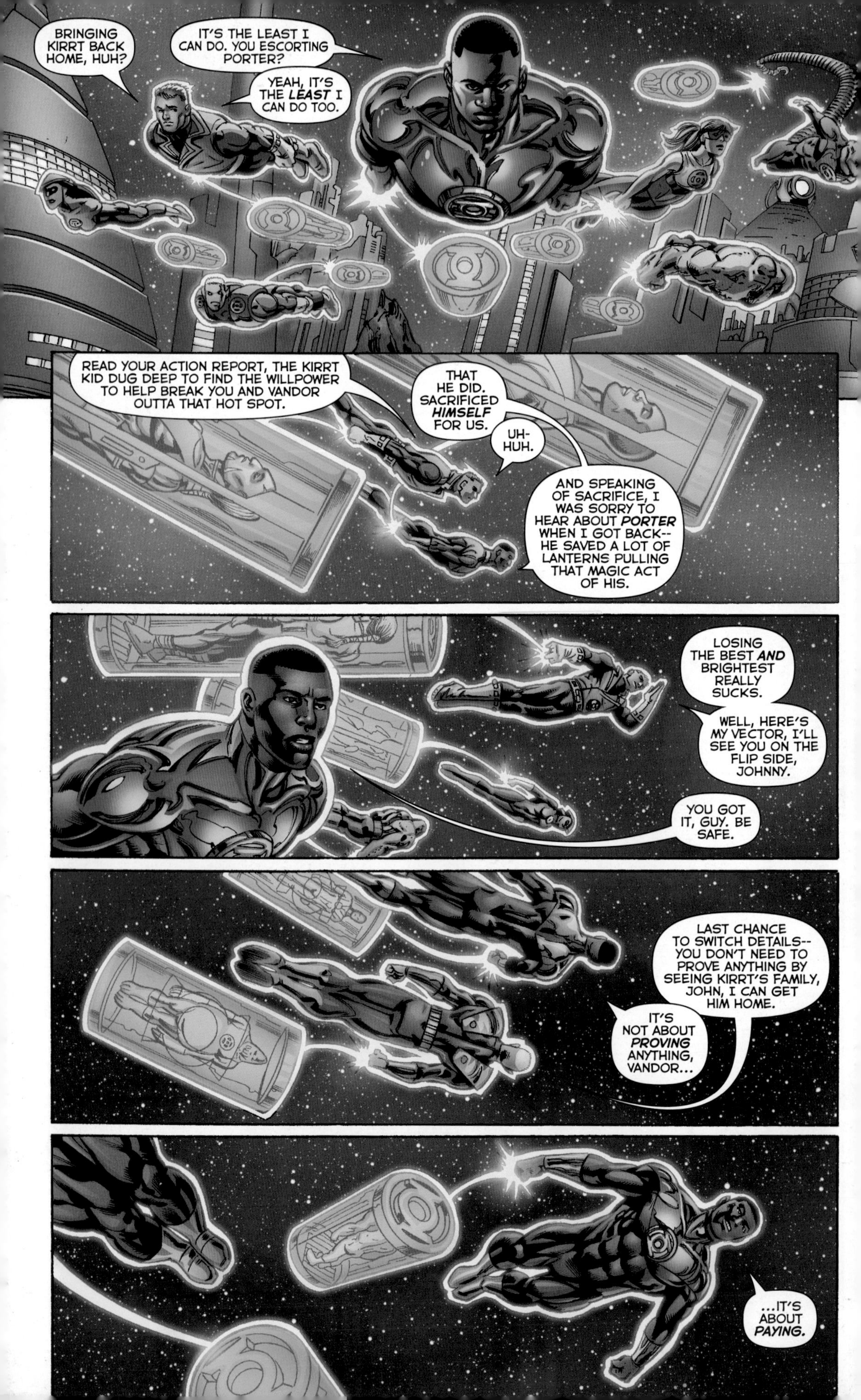
BRINGING KIRRT BACK HOME, HUH?
IT'S THE LEAST I CAN DO. YOU ESCORTING PORTER?
YEAH, IT'S THE *LEAST* I CAN DO TOO.
READ YOUR ACTION REPORT, THE KIRRT KID DUG DEEP TO FIND THE WILLPOWER TO HELP BREAK YOU AND VANDOR OUTTA THAT HOT SPOT.
THAT HE DID. SACRIFICED *HIMSELF* FOR US.
UH-HUH.
AND SPEAKING OF SACRIFICE, I WAS SORRY TO HEAR ABOUT *PORTER* WHEN I GOT BACK-- HE SAVED A LOT OF LANTERNS PULLING THAT MAGIC ACT OF HIS.
LOSING THE BEST *AND* BRIGHTEST REALLY SUCKS.
WELL, HERE'S MY VECTOR, I'LL SEE YOU ON THE FLIP SIDE, JOHNNY.
YOU GOT IT, GUY. BE SAFE.
LAST CHANCE TO SWITCH DETAILS-- YOU DON'T NEED TO PROVE ANYTHING BY SEEING KIRRT'S FAMILY, JOHN, I CAN GET HIM HOME.
IT'S NOT ABOUT *PROVING* ANYTHING, VANDOR...
...IT'S ABOUT *PAYING.*

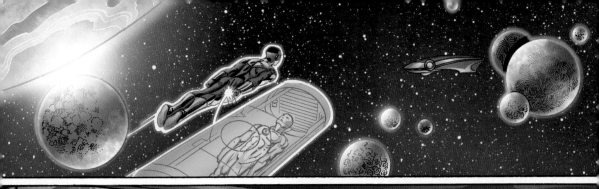

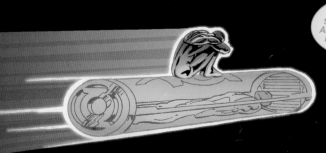

NOW DEPARTING SECTOR 1345 AND CROSSING INTO SECTOR 1346.

SEVEN HOURS UNTIL ARRIVAL AT PLANET LORROR.

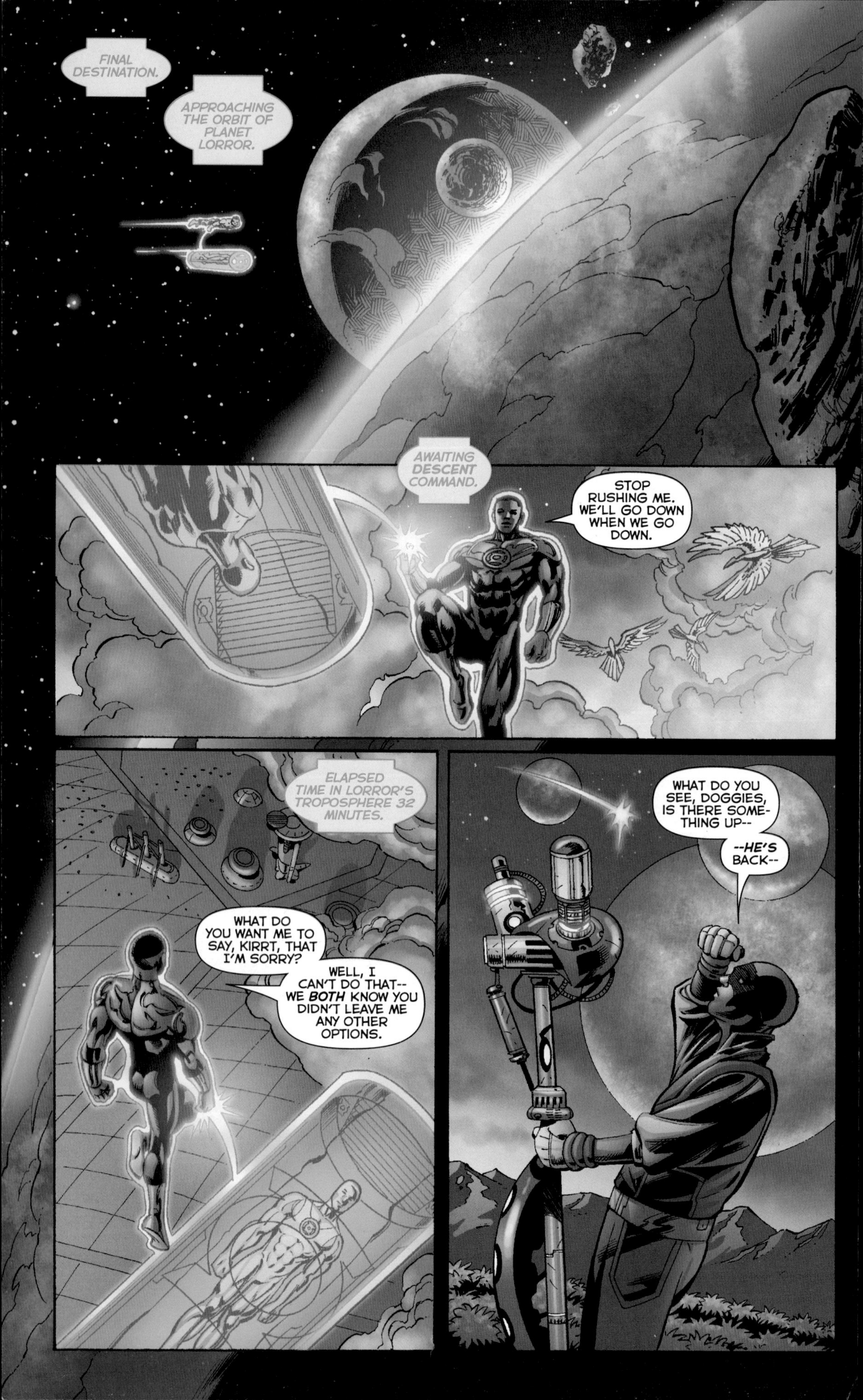
FINAL DESTINATION.
APPROACHING THE ORBIT OF PLANET LORROR.
AWAITING DESCENT COMMAND.
STOP RUSHING ME. WE'LL GO DOWN WHEN WE GO DOWN.
ELAPSED TIME IN LORROR'S TROPOSPHERE 32 MINUTES.
WHAT DO YOU WANT ME TO SAY, KIRRT, THAT I'M SORRY?
WELL, I CAN'T DO THAT-- WE *BOTH* KNOW YOU DIDN'T LEAVE ME ANY OTHER OPTIONS.
WHAT DO YOU SEE, DOGGIES, IS THERE SOME-THING UP--
--*HE'S* BACK--

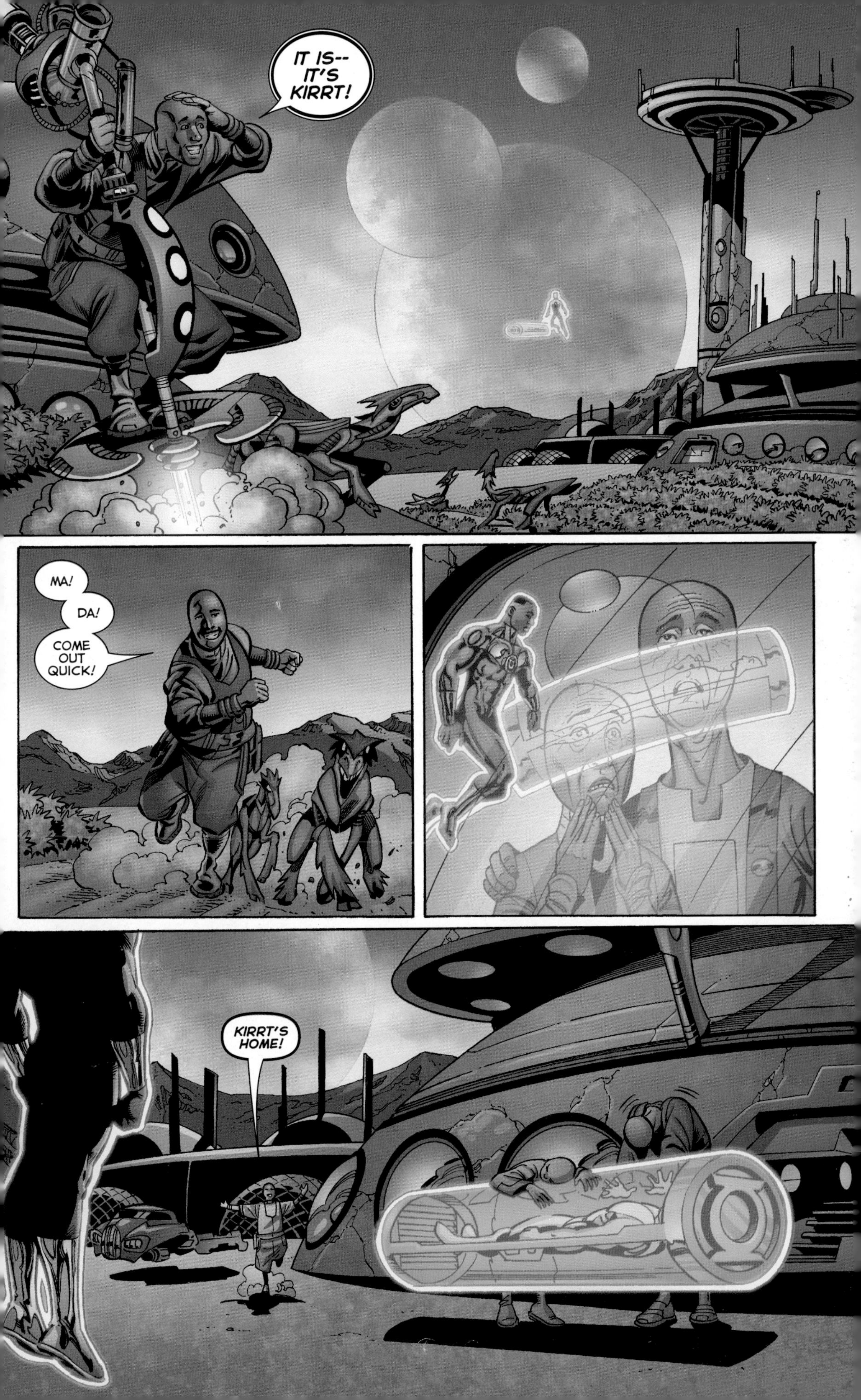
IT IS--
IT'S
KIRRT!
MA!
DA!
COME
OUT
QUICK!
KIRRT'S
HOME!

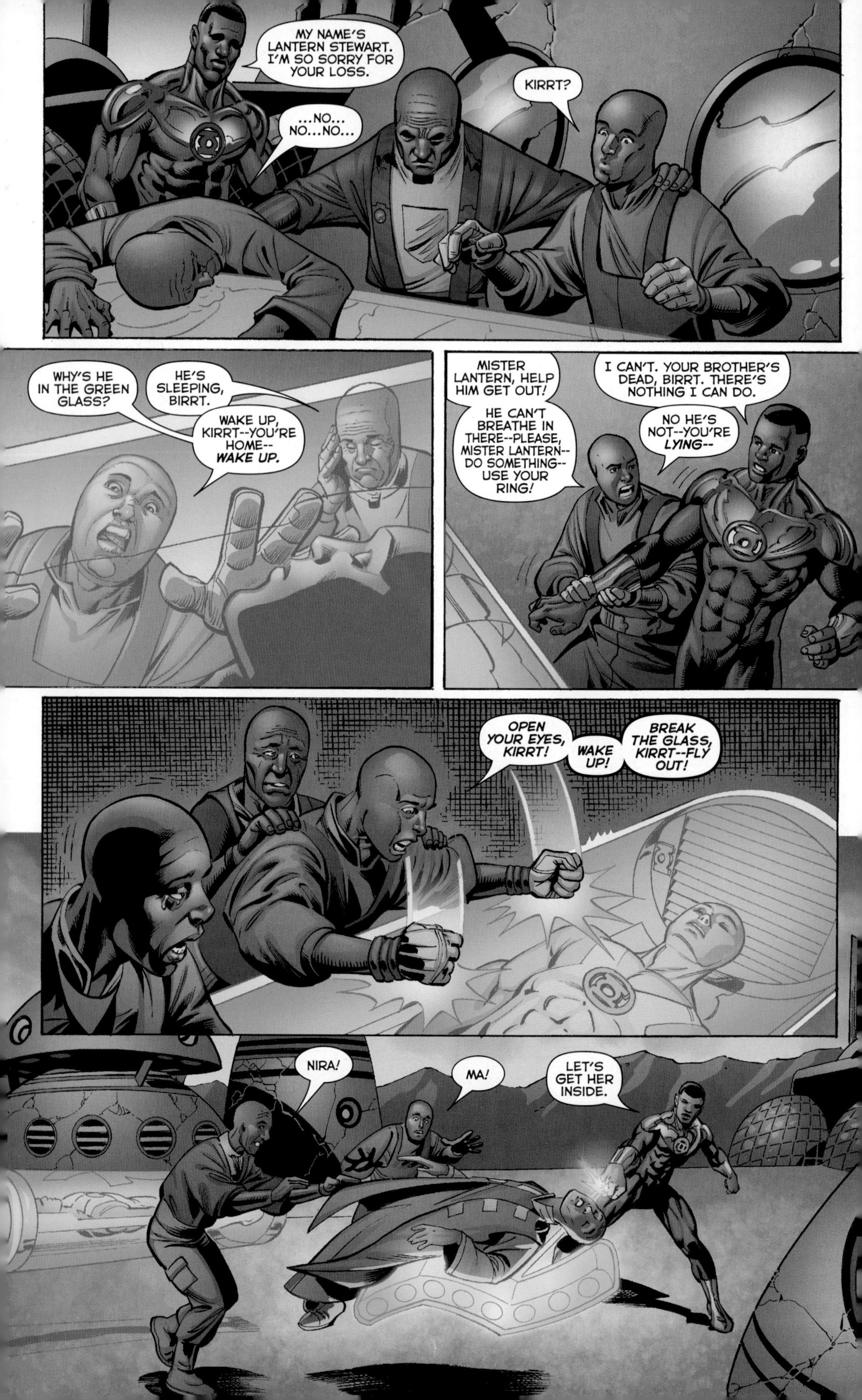
MY NAME'S LANTERN STEWART. I'M SO SORRY FOR YOUR LOSS.
...NO... NO...NO...
KIRRT?
WHY'S HE IN THE GREEN GLASS?
HE'S SLEEPING, BIRRT.
WAKE UP, KIRRT--YOU'RE HOME-- WAKE UP.
MISTER LANTERN, HELP HIM GET OUT!
HE CAN'T BREATHE IN THERE--PLEASE, MISTER LANTERN--DO SOMETHING--USE YOUR RING!
I CAN'T. YOUR BROTHER'S DEAD, BIRRT. THERE'S NOTHING I CAN DO.
NO HE'S NOT--YOU'RE LYING--
OPEN YOUR EYES, KIRRT!
WAKE UP!
BREAK THE GLASS, KIRRT--FLY OUT!
NIRA!
MA!
LET'S GET HER INSIDE.

MY BOY ALWAYS TRIED TO BE FEARLESS, JUST LIKE ALL OF YOU IN THE CORPS ARE...

PLEASE, DON'T TAKE THIS THE WRONG WAY, SIR, BUT THAT'S A COMMON MISUNDERSTANDING.

WE'RE NOT CHOSEN BECAUSE WE'RE FEARLESS. WE'RE CHOSEN BECAUSE OF OUR ABILITY TO *OVERCOME* GREAT FEAR--TO PUSH PAST IT IN MOMENTS OF LIFE AND DEATH AND TRY TO DO OUR DUTY.

SOMETIMES WE CAN...AND SOMETIMES WE CAN'T.

IF THERE'S ONE THING I'VE LEARNED OVER THE YEARS, IT'S THAT *ONLY* THE DEAD ARE FEARLESS, SIR.

I THINK A SMALL PART OF KIRRT ALWAYS WORRIED HE DIDN'T HAVE WHAT IT TAKES TO BE A LANTERN...

THE MOMENT KIRRT GOT A POWER RING *PROVED* HE HAD WHAT IT TAKES TO BE IN THE CORPS, SIR.

I'M SURE KIRRT WOULD BE HAPPY TO KNOW A VETERAN WHO SPEAKS SO HIGHLY OF HIM IS THE ONE THAT BROUGHT HIM HOME TO US.

I-IT WAS MY HONOR, SIR.

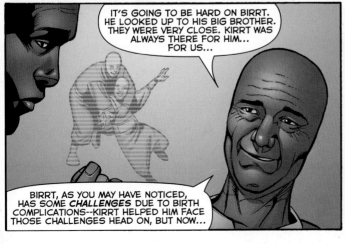

IT'S GOING TO BE HARD ON BIRRT. HE LOOKED UP TO HIS BIG BROTHER. THEY WERE VERY CLOSE. KIRRT WAS ALWAYS THERE FOR HIM... FOR US...

BIRRT, AS YOU MAY HAVE NOTICED, HAS SOME *CHALLENGES* DUE TO BIRTH COMPLICATIONS--KIRRT HELPED HIM FACE THOSE CHALLENGES HEAD ON, BUT NOW...

BIRRT? WHERE ARE YOU?

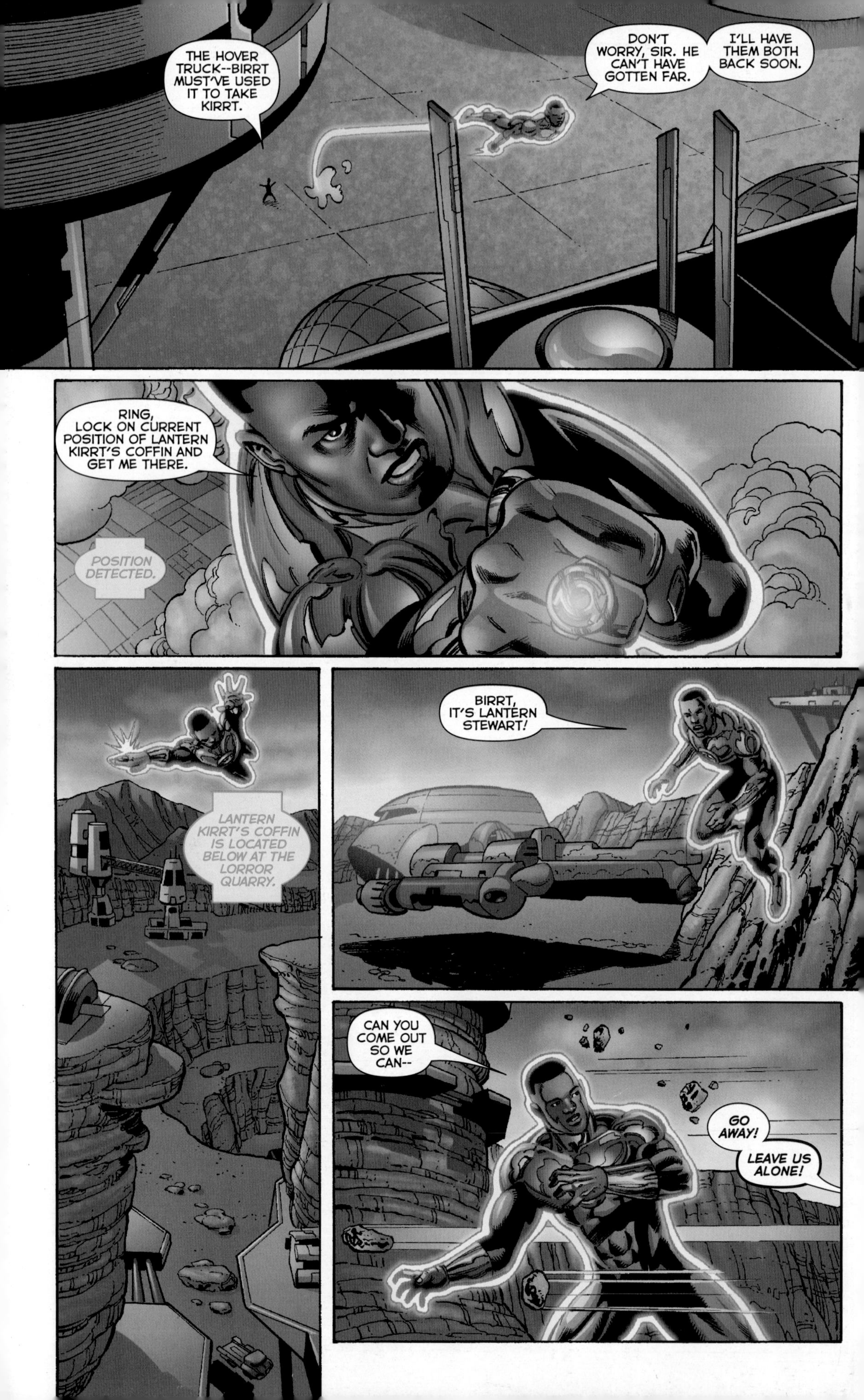
THE HOVER TRUCK--BIRRT MUST'VE USED IT TO TAKE KIRRT.
DON'T WORRY, SIR. HE CAN'T HAVE GOTTEN FAR.
I'LL HAVE THEM BOTH BACK SOON.
RING, LOCK ON CURRENT POSITION OF LANTERN KIRRT'S COFFIN AND GET ME THERE.
POSITION DETECTED.
LANTERN KIRRT'S COFFIN IS LOCATED BELOW AT THE LORROR QUARRY.
BIRRT, IT'S LANTERN STEWART!
CAN YOU COME OUT SO WE CAN--
GO AWAY!
LEAVE US ALONE!

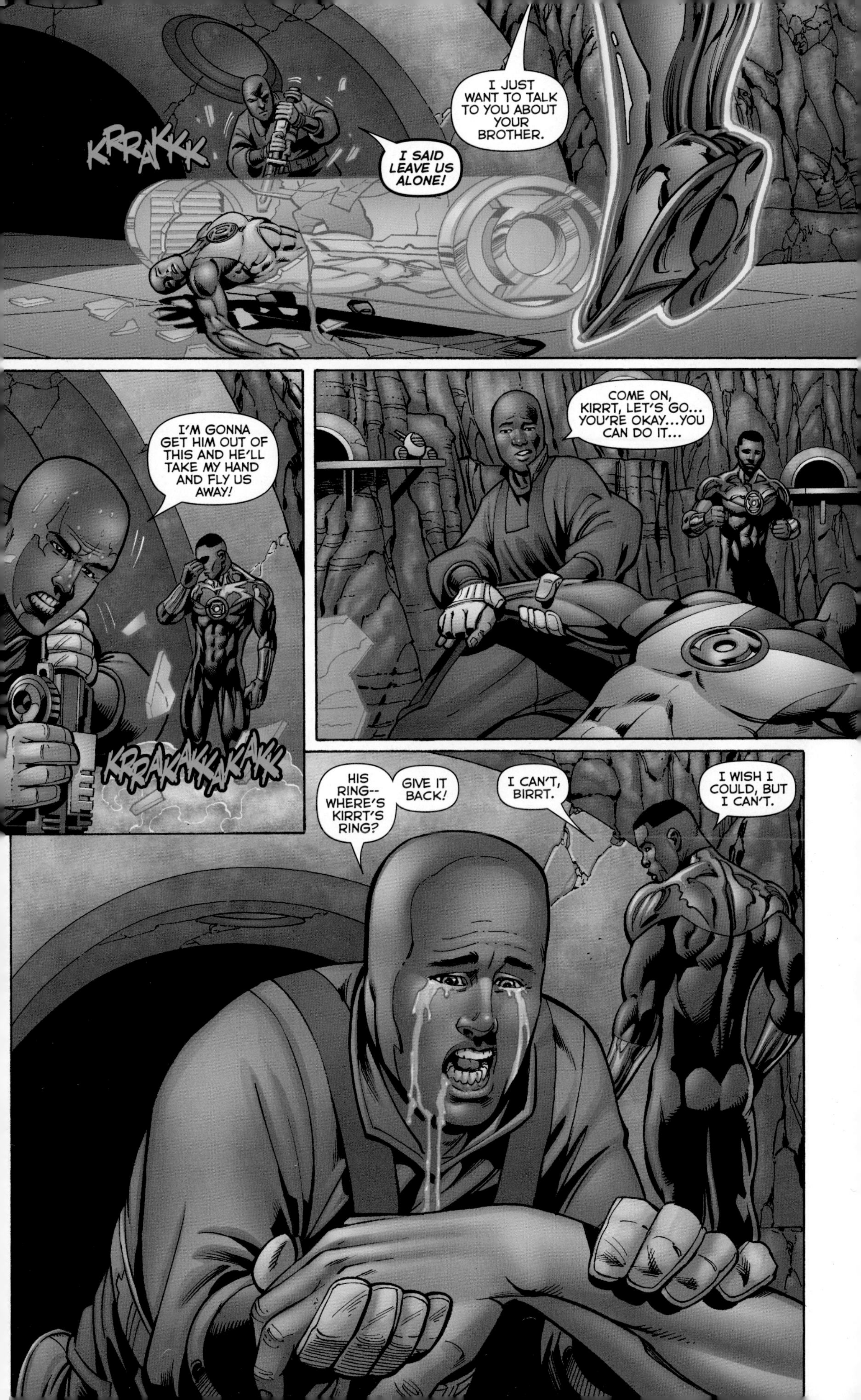
KRRAKKK
I JUST WANT TO TALK TO YOU ABOUT YOUR BROTHER.
I SAID LEAVE US ALONE!
I'M GONNA GET HIM OUT OF THIS AND HE'LL TAKE MY HAND AND FLY US AWAY!
KRRAKKAKKAKK
COME ON, KIRRT, LET'S GO... YOU'RE OKAY...YOU CAN DO IT...
HIS RING-- WHERE'S KIRRT'S RING?
GIVE IT BACK!
I CAN'T, BIRRT.
I WISH I COULD, BUT I CAN'T.

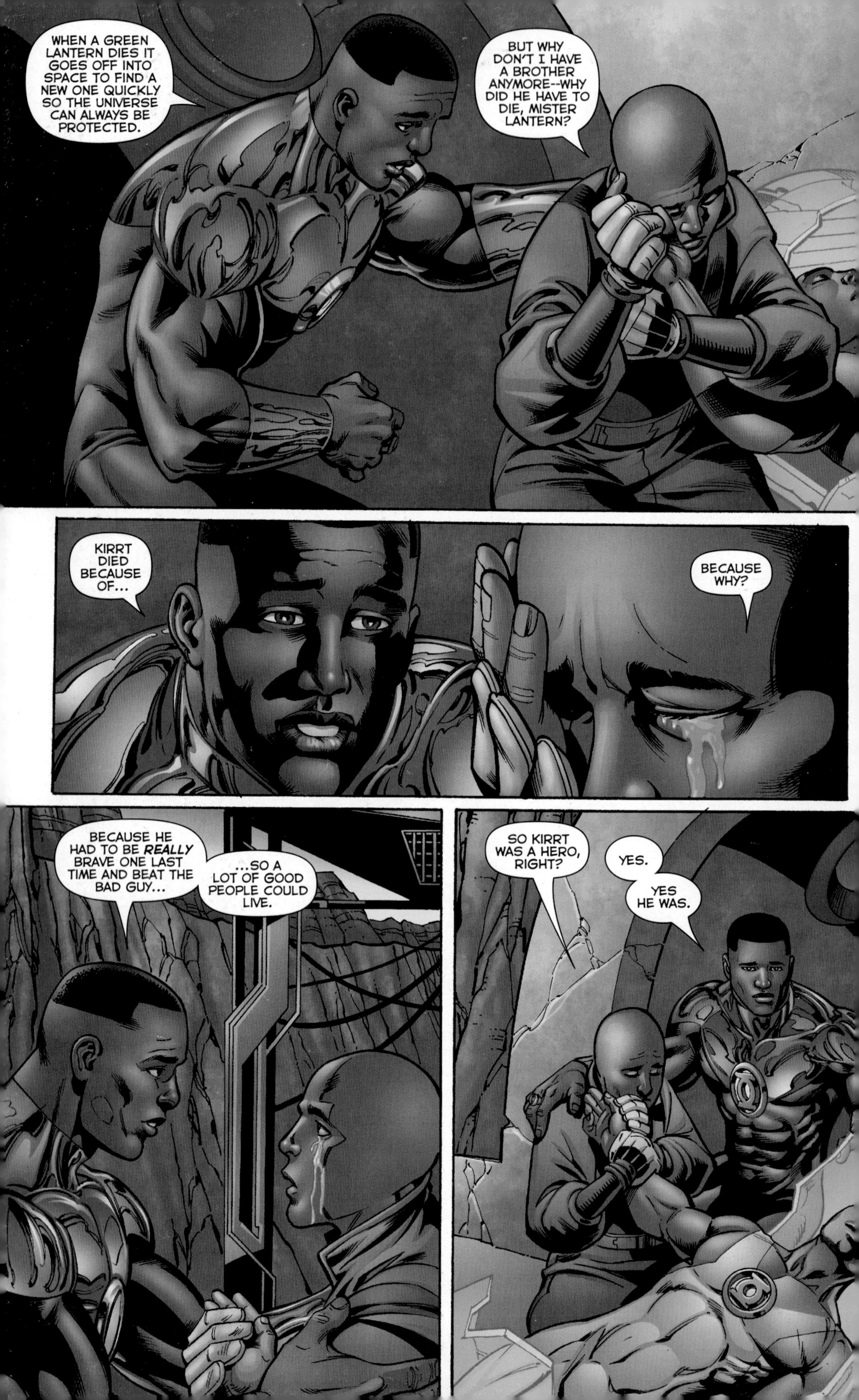
WHEN A GREEN LANTERN DIES IT GOES OFF INTO SPACE TO FIND A NEW ONE QUICKLY SO THE UNIVERSE CAN ALWAYS BE PROTECTED.
BUT WHY DON'T I HAVE A BROTHER ANYMORE--WHY DID HE HAVE TO DIE, MISTER LANTERN?
KIRRT DIED BECAUSE OF...
BECAUSE WHY?
BECAUSE HE HAD TO BE *REALLY* BRAVE ONE LAST TIME AND BEAT THE BAD GUY...
...SO A LOT OF GOOD PEOPLE COULD LIVE.
SO KIRRT WAS A HERO, RIGHT?
YES.
YES HE WAS.

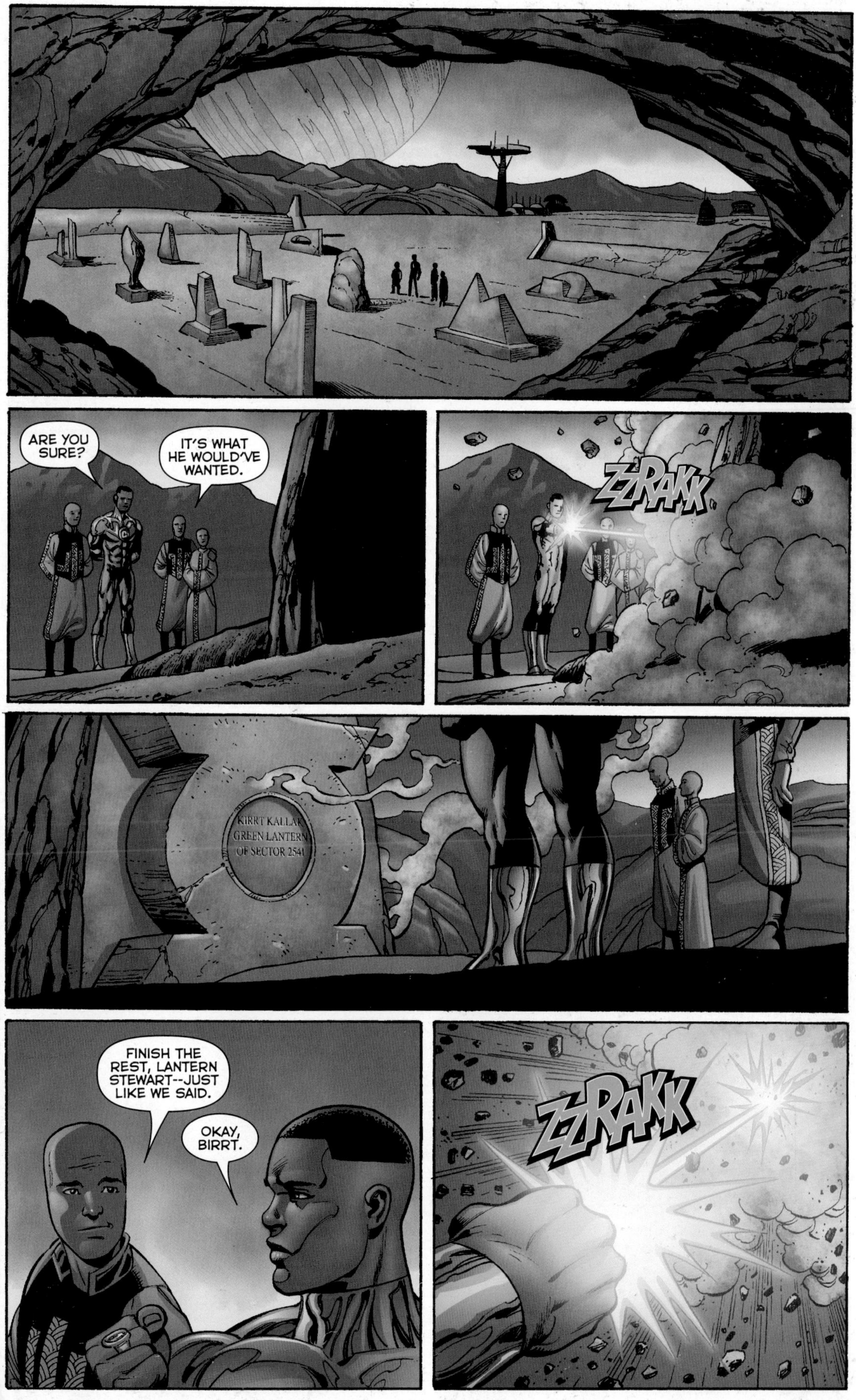
ARE YOU SURE?
IT'S WHAT HE WOULD'VE WANTED.
ZZRAKK
KIRRT KALLAK
GREEN LANTERN
OF SECTOR 2541
FINISH THE REST, LANTERN STEWART--JUST LIKE WE SAID.
OKAY, BIRRT.
ZZRAKK

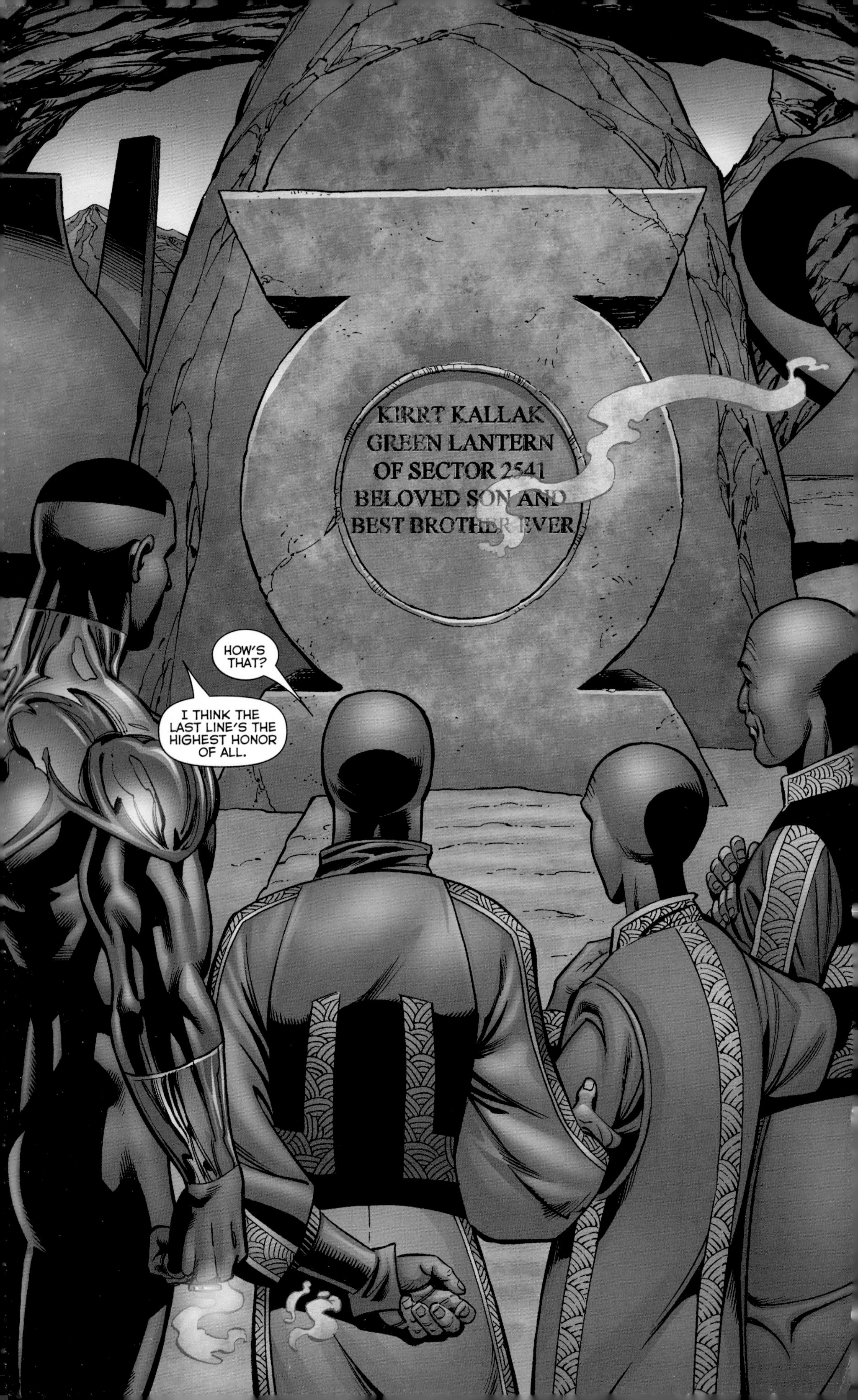
KIRRT KALLAK
GREEN LANTERN
OF SECTOR 2541
BELOVED SON AND
BEST BROTHER EVER
HOW'S THAT?
I THINK THE LAST LINE'S THE HIGHEST HONOR OF ALL.